THE
CALL-UP

THE
CALL-UP

A History of National Service

Tom Hickman

headline

First published in 2004
by HEADLINE BOOK PUBLISHING

10 9 8 7 6 5

ISBN 0 7553 1240 6

Front cover: 'The HQ nutters' of Royal Artillery Battery, Düsseldorf
(self-captioned by Glyn Jones, top right). Inside flap: the main gate guard
at Düsseldorf – 'the best official skive ever'.

Back cover: Returned from operations in the Indian Ocean, Pilot Officer
Ian Wormald (with tankard) and colleagues drink a toast in Malta; Duke
of Wellington private, Reuben Holroyd, waits for dusk and the order to
attack during the Korean War; HMS *Defiance* at Devonport, a naval
training school where Lawrence Bell became an electrical artificer,
was in fact three old sailing and steam ships dating back to the Chinese
opium wars of the nineteenth century; King's Own Scottish Borderers'
Second Lieutenant Willie Purves (left), the only national serviceman
to win a DSO, in an engagement in Korea in which his batman,
Smyttan Common, won the MM.

Cataloguing in Publication Data is available from the British Library

Typeset in Minion by Avon DataSet Ltd,
Bidford-on-Avon, Warwickshire

Printed and bound in Great Britain by
Mackays of Chatham plc, Chatham, Kent

Headline's policy is to use papers that are natural, renewable and
recyclable products and made from wood grown in sustainable forests.
The logging and manufacturing processes are expected to conform to the
environmental regulations of the country of origin.

HEADLINE BOOK PUBLISHING
A division of Hodder Headline
338 Euston Road, London NW1 3BH

Every effort has been made to fulfil requirements with regard to
reproducing copyright material. The author and publisher will be glad to
rectify any omissions at the earliest opportunity.

www.headline.co.uk
www.hodderheadline.com

Contents

Acknowledgements

It goes without saying that I'd like to thank all the men I've interviewed for this book. In particular I'm grateful to Phil Wilkinson and Gordon Williams, who suggested other lines worth following up, provided me with contacts, and put up with my coming back again and again with more questions; Adrian Walker, who read the manuscript and put me straight on a number of details; and, above all, David Prest of Whistledown Productions, without whose generosity in giving me access to the database of his own research my job would have been considerably harder.

Permission to quote from published works has been given by: Constable & Robinson Limited (*Brasso, Blanco & Bull* by Tony Thorne); Hodder and Stoughton Limited (*Life in the Jungle* by Michael Heseltine); John Blake Publishing Limited (*Johnny Briggs: My Autobiography* by Johnny Briggs); PFD on behalf of the Estate of Auberon Waugh (*Will This Do?* by Auberon Waugh); The Random House Group Limited (*What's It All About?* by Michael Caine, *Skip All That: Memoirs* by Robert Robinson, *Chips With Everything* by Arnold Wesker); Scott Ferris Associates (*The Best Years of Their Lives* by Trevor Royle).

INTRODUCTION

For king (and queen) and country

The ink was barely dry on Germany's surrender in 1945 when the British people voted Winston Churchill out of 10 Downing Street. Churchill's lion's roar had sustained them during the years of war. But public opinion had taken a leftward shift; Britain, people felt, could be a fairer place under Labour. Labour won the election in a landslide. And the new Prime Minister, Clement Attlee, began to implement the vision of the welfare state – a free national health service, family allowances, social security and full employment – while committing his government to nationalising gas, electricity, steel and the railways.

Attlee would soon also have to implement a policy that had not been widely foreseen – the introduction of compulsory military service for the first time in British history.

Conscription had been favoured in continental Europe for 150 years before it was first seen in Britain halfway through the First World War, when the flood of volunteers reduced to a trickle and 'laggards' could not be shamed into joining up. Conscription had again been introduced in 1939 at the start of the Second World War. But obligatory service in the armed forces in peacetime (even if the word would soon require inverted commas) was without precedent, and there were impassioned arguments, not just on political and strategic grounds, but on economic ones; the war had brought Britain to its knees, industry was shattered, there was a chronic shortage of housing, and many doubted that the country should be deprived of any manpower.

Attlee was reluctant to make a decision – he, with his party, had opposed conscription in 1939 and he was well aware that many of his parliamentary colleagues still held to the pacifist tradition that went back to the 19th-century champion of working-class socialism, Keir Hardie. But one of his election promises had been to speedily bring home and release the 5 million men who had fought the war and who remained scattered across the globe from Jamaica to Japan – and the 'khaki vote' had been a big factor in his win. What Attlee had to balance against this, however, was that Britain was obligated to do its share in getting the occupied countries back on their feet – an undertaking that would last for some years – and British imperial will needed to be re-established in the colonies and dependencies if the country's trading might was to be regained. This was all the more important now that the loss of India, the jewel in Britain's imperial crown, was imminent – India had been promised independence for its help during the Second World War.

The Japanese surrender did not take place until three weeks after Labour took office, and bitter bits and pieces of fighting stemmed from it, as they had following victory in Europe – wars do not end neatly. In Europe, British forces were still involved in clashes with partisans in Italy trying to lay claim to the Adriatic port of Trieste on behalf of the Yugoslav communist government; and in Greece, where they found themselves fighting the resistance movement that had grown up during the German occupation and now wanted a socialist state instead of the return of the monarchy (Britain would not be able to withdraw until 1948). In the East, a power vacuum was created in Indochina and the Dutch East Indies, under Japanese occupation during the war. British troops from Burma had quickly reclaimed Malaya, Singapore and Hong Kong on Britain's behalf; but the French and Dutch did not immediately have the forces to do the same in their colonial territories, and Britain committed units on their behalf. In Indochina the Vietnamese nationalist communist leader Ho Chi Minh had begun the armed struggle that a decade later would escalate into the Vietnam War; in the Dutch East Indies, where the nationals were as keen to see the back of the Dutch as the Vietnamese were to see the back of the French, an Indonesian government was already in place, reinforced by military units.

More fundamentally, Britain had to resolve big issues on its own behalf that had simmered before the war began: the future of India, where Hindu–Muslim hatred was moving out of control, and the future of Palestine, where Arab–Jewish hatred was making the country as ungovernable as India.

Britain had taken Palestine from the Turks near the end of the first world conflict, subsequently being granted a League of Nations' mandate to administer the territory – and had soon found itself in an untenable position of its own making, on one hand promising independence to the Arabs but on the other supporting the setting up of a Jewish national homeland, in anticipation of which, in 1935, 60,000 Jews arrived. The struggle for Palestine led to Arab attacks on Jewish settlements up to the outbreak of war, abated during it, and broke out again after it, with loss of life on both sides. Some 100,000 Jewish survivors of Nazi atrocity in Europe wanted to come to Palestine, but Britain was forced to restrict the flow of refugees to 1,500 a year, turning back illegal ships and rounding up immigrants who got ashore. In local Jewish newspapers, British troops were compared to the SS.

By the end of 1945, with the intention of forcing the creation of a Jewish state, the underground Haganah army were organising disturbances and acts of sabotage, while the extremist Irgun organisation and a splinter group known as the Stern Gang were mounting a terror campaign that included shootings, bombings and the destruction of aircraft on RAF bases. Two British NCOs were kidnapped and hanged, and their bodies booby-trapped. In July 1946 a group of Jews dressed as Arabs entered the King David Hotel in Jerusalem (which housed the Secretariat of the Government of Palestine and the headquarters of the British forces) and planted 500 lb of explosives hidden in milk churns in the basement. The explosion brought down one wing of the building; 91 bodies were recovered.

Despairing of a resolution, Britain relinquished its mandate in February 1947 and withdrew from Palestine three months later, by when 338 troops had been killed, passing the problem over to the United Nations, which, postwar, had replaced the League of Nations. The state of Israel was proclaimed; hundreds of thousands of Palestinians fled; and at once the first of the Arab–Israeli wars broke out.

Throughout 1946 and 1947 India was in a state of civil strife caused by religious and political frictions that had always been there but which the prospect of independence gave full rein. Hindus and Muslims carried out hideous massacres of each other, the British army struggled to maintain any semblance of order, and by June 1947, despite all efforts to avoid partition, it was evident that India would have to become two states, mainly Hindu India and mainly Muslim Pakistan. Britain still aimed at achieving a phased transition of power but as Earl Mountbatten, viceroy and then briefly governor-general, said, India was 'like a ship on fire in mid-ocean, with a hold full of ammunition'. In July 1948 the British left more quickly than they had intended, terminating two centuries of colonial rule. Over 200,000 people died in Hindu–Muslim fighting; over 10 million people migrated either side of the India–Pakistan divide.

While these matters were being played out, more in hope than expectation that there seemed some chance of a return to world sanity, Attlee continued with the call-up under the 1939 legislation.

Attlee had doubts about the need for peacetime conscription right from the beginning of his premiership. Churchill scathingly dismissed him as 'a modest man with much to be modest about', but unhampered by Churchill's imperialistic mentality, Attlee's view was that the impending loss of the subcontinent made it unnecessary to keep open the Mediterranean route to it – indeed he doubted Britain's ability to keep it open – or to continue financing a large military presence in the Middle East. Britain, he believed, could afford to do neither, anyway. He was critical of the size of the forces that the armed services were demanding – in one estimate 425,000 men (including 150,000 conscripts) for all three services of army, air force and navy, in another an army alone of 847,000.

In February 1946 he raised the matter of conscription in Cabinet. Opinion was divided. Attlee's deputy, Herbert Morrison, was not in favour; Manny Shinwell – Minister of Fuel and Power but later Secretary of State for War and then Minister of Defence – was strongly against, instead supporting a well-paid professional army. The main opponent was Sir

Stafford Cripps, President of the Board of Trade and Minister of Economic Affairs, the man with the difficult job of economic reconstruction, who was against any move that would take anyone away from industry.

There was, however, staunch support from Ernest Bevin, the veteran trade union leader who had been in charge of conscription as Minister of Labour and National Service in Churchill's wartime coalition and was now Attlee's Foreign Secretary. When he was General Secretary of the Transport and General Workers Union, Bevin supported the view that compulsory recruitment was 'industrial conscription' – something that later could be used to quash protests like the General Strike of 1926. Subsequently he changed his mind and in the postwar Cabinet was an ardent advocate, calling a secret meeting of key sections of the Labour movement and speaking passionately for the extension of conscription as part and parcel of the move to peace. He and other Labour leaders sold conscription to the unions and a doubtful party rank and file; one of his arguments was that conscription would help 'democratise' the country.

Attlee's hope of quickly releasing the veterans of the war was altruistic – and unrealistic. The exigencies of restoring world order took precedence; and though regulars whose time had expired between 1939 and 1945 were gradually discharged and wartime conscripts came out under the age-and-length-of-service scheme,[1] there were considerable delays, which caused unrest in the ranks, particularly in the Far East. Indiscipline was rife; there were mutinies in Egypt and Malaya. The worst involved young men of the Parachute Regiment who had taken part on D-Day and fought their way across the Ardennes and the Rhine, only to find themselves posted to a camp near Kuala Lumpur in Malaya where living and sanitary conditions were atrocious. Here, ten months after the Japanese surrender, they refused to return to their lines, around 250 of them were arrested and court-martialled, with a dozen sentenced to between two and eight years with hard labour (sentences that were later quashed).

Whatever the split in Cabinet and his own personal feelings, Attlee had little choice: peacetime national service was inescapable; regular recruitment was going badly, insufficient to make good the huge loss of skilled men coming out of the forces, and, without the Indian regiments that had previously carried out duties in the Far East and Arabia, the army, already stretched too thin, had no hope of meeting the demands being made on it.

The White Paper brought forward in May 1946 was, however, a holding operation that did not look beyond 1948. It set national service at two years for 1947 and on a sliding scale for the following year, which, by the December, assuming no unforeseen circumstances, would reduce the requirement to 18 months. Men called up between the end of the war and January 1947, like those who had fought in the war, went in 'for the duration', an open-ended commitment that in practice meant a minimum of two years, nearer three years for many and over three for some. The government now intended, for the first time, to implement a fixed period of service.

As part of its plans the government promised that all men already in uniform would be released by the end of 1948, before the new breed of conscripts began to go into uniform.

The White Paper was tentative, and brief, but it was intended to show that Britain meant business, both as international policeman and imperial power; that the burden of national defence would be imposed across all society, not just on public-spirited public schoolboys; and, mindful of the sorry state of preparedness in 1939, that a pillar of the policy was to fashion a strategic reserve of trained men that could be mobilised on outbreak of a major war. Britain did not want to be caught out as it had been in 1939.

Behind the scenes there was intense debate, mainly connected with the length of service (which was to remain a bone of contention throughout the period of national service, with Labour factions constantly calling for a reduction). Cripps and Morrison advocated a year, Cripps because he thought that that was all the economy could stand, Morrison because, as he saw it, there was 'little to gain from maintaining large armed forces if the result is that in the economic field we become a second-class power'. On the other hand, the armed forces' Chiefs of Staff called for three years (the RAF wanted four for aircrew). Even that was not good enough for the Chief of the Imperial General Staff, Lord Montgomery. He demanded a longer-term commitment to create what he called his 'New Model Army'. He accepted the government's suggestion of 18 months' full-time service, but demanded that this should be followed by five and a half years' part-time service with the reserve, to which the government agreed.

The future of Egypt brought the government and the Chiefs of Staff into headlong collision.

Egypt was neither colony nor protectorate: the British were there under a prewar treaty connected with the Suez Canal, but had made the country its main Mediterranean base – and the populace was growing increasingly hostile to their presence. Bevin wanted to move the base to Mombasa in Kenya. The COS dug in their heels, arguing that a British withdrawal from Egypt would create yet another power vacuum, this time in the Middle East. The row went on throughout 1946, out of public view. Finally Montgomery threatened the collective resignation of the COS, and the government caved in – a decision they came to regret.

Humiliated by the military chiefs Attlee may have been, but he was not prepared to give in to another Montgomery demand and enshrine national service permanently in British legislation – something that the staunch Bevin believed should happen and eventually would (although he had told the Labour movement that national service was only a short-term expedient). Attlee thought that to make conscription permanent was a strategy of despair; he was convinced, too, that the coming atomic age would validate the view that many tenets of conventional warfare were outmoded. Ever a realist, he also knew that a permanent system would cause uproar among his own backbenchers and that the Opposition, although vocal supporters of conscription, would table an amendment, which almost certainly would carry the House. The formulated legislation established conscription for five years only – from January 1949, when the Act would come into force, until January 1954 – after which it could be extended only by yearly Order in Council.

Having passed its first reading in March 1947 with little dissent, the National Service Bill was expected to sail through its second. But a shock was in store. In April, 72 Labour MPs rallied around Hugh Crossman, defied the Labour whip and voted against it (along with the Liberals, 85 MPs in all), with over 70 others abstaining. The Bill was passed but the government was shaken by the size of the revolt – and three days later reduced the length of national service from 18 months to 12. Churchill was apoplectic, calling the move sheer panic in the face of pressure from a minority, an out-and-out political decision. He also branded the ringleaders 'degenerate intellectuals' and issued a statement from Chartwell saying that his party considered the original proposal the minimum defence arrangement. The service chiefs piled in, pointing out that a twelve-month commitment would tie up as many regulars in training as 18 months but without the concomitant return in manpower, and such a short length of service would mean that conscripts could not be sent further than Germany and the nearer Mediterranean garrisons.

Amid unabated acrimony the Act became law in May 1947.

Under the Act, all men normally residing in Great Britain were liable for national service from the age of eighteen, other than clergymen, the blind, the mentally and physically unfit, and those serving in government positions overseas. Indefinite exemption was given to underground miners, seagoing fishermen, merchant seamen and some agricultural workers, as long as they stayed in their employment. Deferment of liability was permitted for those completing apprenticeships or professional qualifications or taking a degree at university. When the war in Europe ended, the upper age of call-up had been reduced from forty-one to thirty. The Act reduced the limit further, to twenty-six. Full-time service was to be followed by six years part-time, with a further period on the non-active reserve.

Northern Ireland was excluded from the legislation as it had been in the Second World War because of worries of dissent in the Catholic community; Northern Ireland MPs publicly declared a wish for inclusion and the government added a clause allowing young men from the Six Counties to volunteer for national service, which, hardly surprisingly, few did. An interesting sidelight on national service was that the Channel Islands and the Isle of Man, crown dependencies that were not (and are not) part of the United Kingdom, took opposing views. The Isle of Man government (the Tynwald) voted for inclusion under the Act. The legislative assemblies of Jersey and Guernsey voted against.

Occupied by the Germans from June 1940 until May 1945 as the Channel Islands had been, their decision was understandable; Jersey, in fact, was so sickened by its wartime experience that it even disbanded its

Royal Militia (whose 11 officers and 193 other ranks had sailed for England on a potato ship ahead of the German arrival, and formed the nucleus of the 11th Battalion of the Hampshire Regiment). Both decisions upset many of the islands' older generation and were to be debated time and again. In April 1954 Jersey changed its mind on the national service issue ('We should be ashamed of being the only country in the British Commonwealth not to have national service,' said Senator Collas, president of the island's defence committee), and passed the National Service (Jersey) Bill by 26 votes to 25. In the five remaining years of conscription, about 1,000 Jerseymen served in the British armed forces. Guernsey stuck to its decision, although in June 1954 it passed the National Service (Guernsey) Law that was only to be put into operation in a declared state of emergency.

How matters might have unfolded over the length of national service is difficult to tell – the situation was overtaken by events. In June 1948 Soviet forces closed entry to Berlin in an attempt to prevent the other co-occupiers, America, France and Britain, from unifying the western part of Germany. Overnight, the wartime alliance with the USSR was shattered; and for 15 months the British and Americans were forced to make 2,700 flights to bring supplies to the beleaguered city. Now the military presence in Germany was seen as the bulwark against communist aggression amid fears that the Red Army might overrun the whole of western Europe – a fear that was to increase in August 1949 when the Soviets exploded the A-bomb, four or five years ahead of what the West thought possible. The free world also experienced anxiety that outside Europe, countries one by one could fall to communist control – the domino effect. In response to communist insurgency in Malaya, Britain sent more troops, and bulked up the garrison in Hong Kong against the possibility of invasion from communist China.

In December 1948 – a month before men were to be called up under the twelve-month legislation – the National Service Amendment Act came into being, reinstating 18 months as the term of service, with the reserve commitment down to four years.

A. V. Alexander, Minister of War, tried to put a brave face on the volte-face, speaking of flexibility as 'a specifically British virtue' and the need to unite the country behind the national service issue. 'If we had only to consider the building up of army reserves, I would still say that a twelve-month period of service would be sound and defensible,' he told the House without much conviction – before going on to list the 'buts'. A total of 41 MPs voted against the Act at the second reading, but with the Iron Curtain down and the Cold War up and running, rebellion was muted.

The government was grateful that Montgomery had moved on. Following the Berlin crisis he had pushed to increase national service, not to 18 months but to two years. Indeed he had again used threats, as he had done earlier so successfully: if he did not get his way, he said, the military members of the Army Council would resign. Fortunately the state of affairs was defused a few days later when Montgomery stepped down as CIGS to become chairman of the military committee of the Western European Union.

Events forced another change to the length of national service in June 1950, 17 months after the postwar legislation went 'live': the Korean War broke out and conscription was raised to the two years that Montgomery had called for (with part-time service again lowered, to three and a half years), at which it was to remain until the end. The communist North invaded the South, the Americans came to the aid of the South, the Chinese came to the aid of the North (with Soviet backing) and Britain, with many other countries, was sucked into the conflict under the flag of the United Nations.

Korea finally turned the British people against conscription. They had already had their fill of sacrifice – austerity measures including higher taxation, even stricter rationing than during the Second World War, the diversion of domestic production to exports – but, by and large, conditioned by six years of war and worries that the world was on the way to self-destruction, they had accepted conscription's necessity. But after the loss of hundreds of British lives in three years of Korean fighting, they had had enough.

Yet it took the catalyst of the Suez débâcle in 1956 – when Britain mounted military action against Egypt, after President Nasser nationalised the Suez Canal, and humiliatingly had to abort under American pressure – for the government, Conservative from 1951, to accept that the need for national service was done. By then, despite flashpoints, there was a thaw in the West's relationship with the Soviet Union (to a considerable degree due to Churchill's last prime ministerial crusade, made possible by the death of Stalin), which signalled a more hopeful international future; and Harold Macmillan, who after Suez had succeeded Churchill's luckless successor, Anthony Eden, accepted that tactical nuclear weapons were not only a greater deterrent than massed forces on the ground but, in the event of conflict, made such forces largely irrelevant – as Attlee, and others, had predicted. Macmillan had also learnt one of the lessons of Suez: that the burdens of empire were no longer worth the bearing; Britain could no longer hold dominion over peoples who wanted it to be gone.

How long national service lasted is open to interpretation. Many sources count it from the implementation of the 1947 Act in January 1949, making it a little over 13 years from first man in to last man out; others argue that, even if their service was under wartime legislation, men called up from the end of the Second World War were no less peacetime conscripts, and therefore calculate national service at a little over 17 years; yet others take a halfway position from the introduction of fixed-term service in January 1947. Depending on how the years were calculated, national service put as many as 2.3 million young men, almost all of them in their late teens and early twenties, into uniform to serve king (and then queen) and country for what basically was little more than pocket money – all that the nation could afford; the 1947 Act had to remove the hopes of paying national servicemen a gratuity, which had been floated in the White Paper, and dispensed with the demob suit, which, until then, had been the entitlement of every serviceman returning to civilian life. However measured, national service was a military and social phenomenon, and it shaped the way generations thought.

In the first years of national service, conscripts got 28 shillings a week (which, taking 1951 as an example, compared with an average wage of £8 8s 6d); in the final full year of 1962, 38s 6d (compared with an average wage of £15 7s). For that they were sent all over the globe to occupy, to impose British rule, to police and, where necessary, to fight and even die.

In a preamble to a review of a book about a regiment's experiences in Malaya, *The Times* in 1953 noted that the newspapers had recently been commenting on 'the Queen's hard bargains – those National Servicemen of bad character or poor physique whom the Services must accept', and suggested it was a pity that more was not heard about the majority, 'seen at [their] best on the hills of Korea, the deserts of Egypt, or the plains of Germany'. The review was headed 'The Queen's Good Bargains'.

1

For gawd's sake don't take me

They didn't need to come looking for you – you gave yourself up. BBC radio and the newspapers prominently carried information about when an age group was due to register for national service – there were no individual letters.

> The authorities pretended it was up to you to register, to let them know
> that you were ready and willing. But they knew all along you were there.
> They'd known from the minute you were born. By registering you simply
> let them know that you both knew what they already knew. And that
> made it official.[1]

It was a simple process for everybody: name, address, occupation, preference for navy, air force or army, all solemnly recorded in the military service register. Well, not simple for Arnold Wesker, son of East End first generation Jews, then dreaming about being an actor, not a playwright:

Sergeant:	Name of father?
Me:	Joseph
Sergeant:	Profession?
Me:	Tailor's machinist
Sergeant:	Where was your father born?
Me:	Russia

Sergeant:	Russia?
Me:	Yes, Russia
Sergeant:	Whereabouts in Russia?
Me:	Ukraine. Dnepropetrovsk
Sergeant:	[Less jaunty] Name of mother?
Me:	Leah
Sergeant:	Profession?
Me:	Sometimes tailor's machinist, sometimes cook
Sergeant:	[Slightly nervous] Where was *she* born?
Me:	Transylvania
	[He thinks I'm taking the piss, there's no such place]
	Honest, Sergeant. Transylvania
Sergeant:	[Really nervous now] Whereabouts in Transylvania?
Me:	Gyergoszentmiklos
Sergeant:	Look, would you take this form home with you, fill it up and send it back? Next![2]

At registration, anyone off to university or completing professional articles or an apprenticeship made this known. Deferment for the period involved was automatically granted (just as a second failure in a professional exam meant it was automatically withdrawn). The armed forces preferred men who had been deferred: at twenty or twenty-one they were more mature than the average intake of eighteen- and nineteen-year-olds, and many brought skills that could be put to good use. In fact, the majority of those with a university place chose to do national service before taking it up; if they were down for Oxford or Cambridge, they had no choice: Oxbridge had tacitly agreed to take men only after their service and while the agreement was not always adhered to,[3] most places were allocated, so to speak, in a forward-booking system.

It was two weeks after registration that a notice arrived, asking a man to report for a medical examination (it did ask, but it was mandatory: failure to report without good cause could bring a fine up to £100 and up to two years in jail – and the notice was addressed to you individually). In large conurbations, examinations took place at the Labour Exchange (it was the Ministry of Labour and National Service in those days) on a Saturday, when it closed for other business. But in small towns and semi-rural areas, examinations were often conducted wherever premises could be found – church halls, drill halls, schools during holidays. In London and big garrison towns, army establishments were frequently used.

The medical, in almost all cases conducted by a civilian panel of five GPs, was only one element at the examining board: there was also a basic written intelligence test and a brief chat with an interviewing officer.

What was it to be then: navy, air force or army?[4] A lot of men fancied being a Jolly Jack Tar coming back home to mum with a parrot in a cage; even more fancied streaking across the wide blue yonder – the Battle of Britain lived on in the imagination of the wartime generation. Many, less romantically inclined, still thought the RAF was the one to go for: discipline was known to be more relaxed than in the army (after basic training you wore shoes!), living conditions were better, certainly on operational bases, it was rare for the RAF to have to sleep under canvas – and, all things considered, you were less likely to be shot at.

Interviewing officers, invariably avuncular retired service chaps, often gave the impression that the choice of service requested at registration was taken into account. For the mass of men it was not. Unless they had a good education or specific trade skills, they were almost certainly heading for the army – the army took 72 men in every 100 (with four in ten going to the 'teeth' arms of infantry, Royal Artillery and Armoured Corps), the RAF 26 (precious few of whom would get anywhere near an aircraft) and the navy only two.[5]

There were ways of increasing your chances of getting into the air force or navy. One was by belonging to an appropriate cadet corps. Another was by training with the RAFVR or RNVR (the reserves, in both cases) before national service liability. While most men who took this route worked hard to get their grounding, a few found token membership enough to swing it. Malcolm Stoakes, a diesel engineering apprentice in Gillingham, Kent, recalled:

> I had a trade and I could sail quite well. But at the yacht club where I went two guys told me the chances of getting into the navy were next to nothing

3

if I didn't belong to the RNVR. So I joined, just for a couple of weeks before I went in and it did the trick. Mind, I arrived in Plymouth for basic training as a stoker on HMS *Raleigh* in my uniform, got off the train, and discovered I was the only one out of 400 blokes. They put me in charge – and I didn't have a bloody clue.

Hopkin Maddock, in London 'from my valley in mid-Glamorgan' and just qualified as a pharmacist, was another who joined the naval reserve and turned up only half a dozen times and also made it into bell bottoms. 'I don't think they read these things carefully,' he says. He did not tell the interviewing officer that he was a pharmacist, only that he had a BSc, 'otherwise they'd have given me the exalted rank of sick-berth attendant – and I wanted to experience the real navy'.

Doctors and dentists were the only national servicemen certain to go into the military equivalent of their civilian occupation. But all three services were on the lookout for skilled men who had served their time in electrical, mechanical (and for the navy, shipwright) trades. The army needed wireless operators, cipher clerks, telegraphers (a high proportion of Post Office apprentices found themselves in the Signals Corps); the RAF needed men in ground-to-air communications; the navy had short-ages in the engine rooms. Lawrence Bell from Middlesbrough, his instru-ment apprenticeship with ICI completed, was filling out forms for the army at his examining board 'when this navy chap came round asking if there were any engineers. There were about half a dozen of us. He said, "Tear those up and fill in these" – and I was in the navy.'

Given in particular the army's need for bodies, the mass of conscripts outside the technical trades were unlikely to find a niche for their civilian experience. But those coming in from certain occupations had a better chance than most of something directly or indirectly comparable: press photographers often went to aerial reconnaissance; musicians to regi-mental bands (*Bond* film soundtrack composer John Barry signed on for three years to make sure and played trumpet in the band of the 2nd Battalion, Green Howards, in Egypt and Cyprus); anyone with knowledge of nursing to the Royal Army Medical Corps (the actor Oliver Reed found himself in it because among his many jobs he had been a hospital porter).

Roy Booth from New Malden in Surrey, a drayman in the City of London, found himself in the Medical Corps, but not because he had any medical experience:

> So far as I was concerned the army was the army, it was all one to me. I hadn't been in the cadets at school because my mum and dad couldn't afford the gear – they had a hell of a job finding the money for my first school uniform. But when I was interviewed I said I objected to fighting. It was a joke really, a casual remark, I didn't feel strongly about it. But that's how I wound up in the medics, I think. The interviewing officer said, 'We'll find you something else to do.'

From 1950, signing on for three years was a way of ensuring entry to the air force or to a particular branch of the army (the navy never offered the option: seven years was its lowest term). Hugh Grant, from the Scottish village of Beauly, north of Inverness, where he worked on a dairy farm, signed on when he went for his medical, purely on impulse. A poster on the wall caught his eye, proffering to regulars only an opportunity that enticed him:

> It declaimed 'IT'S A MAN'S LIFE IN THE GLIDER PILOT REGIMENT' and down below in smaller print, 'And the Parachute Regiment'. But I was not into reading small print. Glider pilot! – what a perfect solution to my problem – to do my National Service and at the same time gain valuable flying experience to boot.[6]

Some weeks later Grant was informed by letter that the Glider Pilot Regiment had disbanded and the Army Air Corps that would replace it had not yet been formed, 'so I was headed for better or worse into the open arms of the Parachute Regiment . . .'

In the interests of overall fairness within the services themselves, all branches were at least theoretically obliged to take national servicemen, but units like the Paras and the Royal Marines, which had always prided themselves on being entirely volunteer outfits, disliked the dilution and did so reluctantly. 'It's only an educated guess on my part,' says Grant, 'but in a battalion of 800 or 900 men there were no more than a score at best of pukka national servicemen.'

The whole examination process was supposed to take about two hours, but it depended on how many men belonged to an age group and where they lived; some places could find themselves with scores if not hundreds of men at one time. And the hours they waited before the medical, never mind the intelligence test and interview, could stretch into the afternoon, which meant that many went down the pub. Wherever boards were held, large posters warned: *Do not pass water as you will be required to give a sample*. If you had been to the pub the warning was difficult to heed; it was difficult to heed even if you were just sitting there and were driven by necessity or plain nervousness. In Exeter, broadcaster Ned Sherrin, then a sixth-former with a place waiting for him at Oxford, simply could not wait and when called upon to perform his first small duty for his country 'had to run the taps for what seemed like hours' in search of stimulus. Summonsed from his home in Holyhead in north Wales, Malcolm Higgins, fresh from A levels, found himself in the same predicament in Wrexham. A chap who had been out for a few pints offered to fill his specimen jar for him 'and I let him, but he could have been riddled with diseases or pregnant for all I knew'. Hugh Grant turned up at the Meeting Rooms in Inverness, ten miles from home, took himself off for several pints of lager in the lunch break and, on his return, not only found the specimen jar inadequate but realised to his consternation that there were no plumbing facilities. There happened to be, however, an empty milk bottle and he 'ended up with a full specimen flask in one hand and a three quarters full milk bottle in the other'.[7] Down in London, there was no milk bottle to rescue Tony Thorne, another ex sixth-former. Having returned to the Wandsworth primary school where his medical was being conducted, he sat cross-legged for hours, rose when he was bidden, his knees pinned together 'like a girl in a tight skirt', and to his astonished discomfort was gestured behind a curtain by an attractive young woman where, again, the specimen jar awaited but no contingency for any overflow. He was mopping up, under the young woman's disdainful eye, when a sergeant in the RAMC came in and told him: 'You can't piss your way out of the Army'.[8]

'Fill the specimen jar, please.' At his medical in Acton the inventor Trevor

Baylis, until then studying to be a soil engineer, could not resist the old reply: 'What, from here?' At least buckets were provided to take the surplus. 'I'll never forget the ping of the pee on the metal, all those lads, the sighs of relief . . .' Baylis found the occasion

> a comic ritual. There were these people in white coats looking like they were off the bacon counter at Sainsbury's and us in a line bollock-naked. This chap stuck a spatula in my mouth and asked, 'You don't suffer from piles?', then lifted my testicles with the same spatula and asked, 'Any mental problems?' And then he looked up my backside and asked, 'Suffering from headaches?' Extraordinary.

Baylis might have been less the jaunty 'beatnik and scallywag' he admits to having been if the doctor examining his private parts had been female. Such a thing did occur, if not all that often. It happened to Stanley Colk, a junior clerk in a Sheffield brewery, whose medical took place 'in some rooms above a garage', who remembers 'the awful moment, drop your trousers and say "ah". It was a lady of about fifty who did it to me, a naïve little eighteen-year-old, who'd held a girl's hand and that was about all. Exposing myself to this large lady – for me it was horrific.' Grammar school boy Glyn Jones, from the Welsh mining village of Pontygwaith, suffered the same experience. 'I was shy with her, but everyone was in the same boat. I was mortified, but I was so confused I didn't have time to dwell on it.' Roy Booth went to a local territorial army centre and found himself being given the once-over by a Queen Alexandra's Royal Army Nursing Corps officer – who was accompanied by a number of QARANC nurses.

> She was a bit butch, brogue shoes, woollen stockings, and she was Hattie Jacques' double. And she had a thin stick, like a conductor's baton, which she waved at the nurses who were ticking things on clipboards. We were all stripped and most of the lads were using whatever papers they were carrying as figleaves. One or two were brazenly showing off their tackle but Hattie Jacques put a stop to that with a deft flick of her baton. When she said 'cough', I coughed – choked actually.

Like national servicemen almost without exception, Booth had no idea that the coughing routine was to diagnose hernias: 'I thought she did it to cop a feel.' 'I knew a fellow who had a woman doctor at his medical,' adds Baylis. 'He got an erection and she whacked it with something, I forget what, but he said she nearly took the top off.'

Until 1951 a man's physical fitness for service was assessed under a relatively crude system introduced during the First World War. In 1951 the RAF tried out the more sophisticated Canadian Pulheems method,[8] which was then adopted for all three services. Broadly speaking, for most of the national service years, four grades existed: one passed a man fit for frontline duty if necessary; two and three[9] relegated him to 'lines of communication only'; and four rejected him outright. Few, if any, national servicemen knew what the distinction between grades two and three was or, indeed, what 'lines of communication only' meant. By and large such a distinction did not trouble the RAF and navy, who took the pick of those they wanted; in most men's opinion it did not trouble the army, who took everybody else, either. But that was because they believed the army ignored such niceties – once you were in, you were in and the army did with you as they liked.

A song sung by the first conscript army in the Great War and which kept some popularity in the conflict that followed it, trickled through to the national service generation:

> Send for the boys of the Old
> Brigade
> To keep old England free!
> Send for me father and me
> Mother and me brother,
> But for gawd's sake don't send me!

Or, at least, the last line of this stanza did, slightly amended: 'For gawd's sake don't take me' was a known, mock-despairing cry. Most men would not have chosen to be taken, but they accepted national service as a fact of life and were prepared to think of it as an adventure, a breathing space to consider their options for the future, a chance (perhaps) to travel. Some of this wartime breed, following in the footsteps of their fathers and their older brothers, went further, wanting, like Glyn Jones, to experience war, 'to find out what it was like to be shot, to find out how I would react to danger – a need to be tested is at the back of many men's minds' or, like Mike Hollingworth from Leeds, who, as a merchant navy engineering officer had indefinite exemption but came ashore between his second engineer's and his chief's certificates because national service was something he felt he had to do: 'As someone who'd grown up in the war, I'd spent six years of my life rehearsing for it.' Norman Kenyon had a personal reason for choosing to give up his deferment as an apprentice engineer in a Manchester company that made steam turbines for power stations – he did it for the sake of his twin brother: 'John was a cost accountant in the same firm and he didn't have deferral. He was completely different to me. Me, I was rough and ready, I belonged to the boxing club, I could look after myself. John was very shy and awkward, I knew he wouldn't cope without me. So I went in with him, to look after him.' Kenyon knew that the forces always kept twins together.

Some men were so keen they could not wait, seeking the call-up at seventeen and a half, the earliest the law allowed. One was Mike Faunce-Brown, who had left his public school at sixteen because the family money ran out and, after nearly two years on his father's farm in Wales, had found that 'mucking out the cows and the pigs wasn't my cup of tea. So I got on to the War Office and said, "Have me as soon as you'll take me." '[10] Another was Bruce Kent, not yet Monsignor Bruce Kent the driving force behind the Campaign for Nuclear Disarmament (CND) but a public schoolboy at Stonyhurst who, concerned that his father's Canadian citizenship might make him ineligible, got in touch with the War Office to confirm the situation. Derek Brearley, a machine-tool apprentice from Halifax, was keen to go at eighteen for the very practical reason that he had decided 'I would lose a lot less money at eighteen than I would when I was twenty-one and qualified.'

There are instances of men disguising physical conditions to ensure they were not turned down:

When I went for the medical my own family doctor was on the examination panel. I had been suffering quite a lot from asthma and it would have been no problem to get declared unfit. However, I told him that it was under control and that I would be all right. The other point about the medical which remains particularly clear in my memory is going to have my hearing tested. On entering the room I stood at the end of a line of men, the doctor said, 'Can you hear my watch ticking?' I replied that I could and he told me not to be so stupid because he was talking to the person at the other end of the line.[11]

The comedian Ronnie Corbett, a clerk in the Ministry of Agriculture at the time, was concerned about something he could not disguise: that he stood only five feet one inch tall. 'My great fear was being turned down because of my height. I would have hated that, to have come home and people say, "Well, you're too small for the air force", you know, like the fish they throw back in the sea.' In fact, Corbett had always suffered from sinusitis and catarrh and was told he was being turned down on medical grounds. He started to go away, turned back and successfully pleaded: 'Please, if you can bend the rules. I don't want to be not allowed to do it.'[12]

There were other men determined to evade national service who thought that failing the medical was their best chance of doing so. When the chips (or the trousers) were down, perhaps fewer men than claimed otherwise tried it on: there are no estimates on record of how many did. Plenty of suggestions circulated on how the fiddle might be achieved. Claiming flat feet or defective eyesight were popularly believed to have the best chance, but there were numerous half-baked notions: swallowing soap to foam at the mouth; eating cordite (where did you get cordite?) to induce sweating and increase the heart rate, or nutmeg, which allegedly produced the same symptoms (the photographer David Bailey, then a window dresser who had already been a debt collector, carpet salesman and Fleet Street copyboy, failed at this one and went with the RAF to Malaya); eating a dozen or two eggs so that albumin would be found in your urine (that did not work either and nor for some days did your bowels). At his medical in Sheffield, the actor Brian Blessed met a fellow who 'informed me that he had spent hours pouring tealeaves down his throat in the firm conviction that it would show on the X-ray machine as TB'.[13] Throwing a fit might work, it was said, though this was unlikely without a medical record of epilepsy and, presumably, carrying it off required considerable thespian talent. Brian Blessed himself, a plasterer desperate to take up a drama school scholarship, tried, with some stoic wincing, to show that a slightly deformed anklebone made him unsuitable – but as the local newspapers had featured him as the Yorkshire schoolboy boxing champion he had no chance of convincing the panel who did, however, compliment him on his acting (they knew about the scholarship too). Perhaps acting did work for those drama students that Peter O'Toole (who himself did national service in the navy, at sea as a signalman) claimed to have taught how to get rejected: too much alcohol, too little food and sleep, and a suitable degree of twitching. More extreme suggestions were jumping repeatedly from a height to induce flat feet or sticking a knitting needle into your ear to perforate an eardrum.

No area of national service has been subject to more exaggeration and the biographer Michael Holroyd (who became liable for conscription after two years as a solicitors' clerk showed he was unsuited to the law) had his tongue firmly in his cheek when he wrote:

> With a pair of violet-tinted spectacles and an Irish walking-stick I advanced upon Reading where I was to be examined medically. I had been up late the previous night recalling past illnesses and had mustered an impressive garrison of them. Water-on-the-knee and in the eye, bow-legs, an allergy to elastoplast: I revealed all, I sang. The result was a disaster. After a gruelling day I was graded 3, ensuring for myself not exemption but the choice of two years either as an Army caterer or in the Pioneer Corps, digging field latrines. Throwing away my stick and spectacles I appealed, and admitting nothing beyond Church of England, was re-graded 1.[14]

A different school of thought recommended failing the intelligence test rather than the medical, a route that the playwright Alan Ayckbourn took in Scarborough, where he was appearing in rep. Despite having two A levels – which his documentation showed – he chose to answer all the questions wrongly. 'I'm sure Haileybury wouldn't be very proud of you,' the interviewing officer told him.[15] The broadcaster Russell Harty, according to what he said in a radio discussion about national service in 1986, failed his written test – at the time he was at Oxford University. Yet what he described bears no relation to the test devised for national service entry, which consisted of simple progressions ('what is the next number in the sequence 2-5-8'), word sequences and symbols:

> I had to go one morning and I sat at a desk. 'If your cylinder head is back-divided with your sump, what lesions adhere to the first forward roll' – those were the kind of questions. And I sat looking at these while all round me the Oxford yobs were busy scratching away on paper. At the end of this I'd failed and they'd sailed through. It was a humiliating process.[16]

That Harty did not do national service can be confirmed: why he was rejected is another matter – his on-air explanation owes more to comic effect than accuracy.

Dr John Blair, honorary reader in History of Medicine at the University of St Andrews and the author of the centenary history of the Army Medical Corps, points out:

> Some curious things did happen at medical boards and men were turned down for many reasons and perhaps for none. It all came down to which doctor saw a man on the day and many things are a matter of interpretation. Some people have flat feet and walk perfectly well, others can't and it was very difficult for a doctor with very little time to tell one from the other. If a man pretended to be deaf, again, that required interpretation that could be wrong. You don't see much of duodenal ulcers nowadays but you did a lot in the fifties. Some men consulted their GP complaining of non-existent or dubious symptoms and would arrive with their X-rays under their arm, which in those days were often of poor quality and therefore difficult to decide what they showed. It was known for medical students particularly to swallow animal blood, present themselves with a history of peptic ulcers and offer a stool sample. The doctor could not know how the blood came to be in the stool and might accept the story. In a few cases there was collusion. I'm afraid it's known that a few GPs connived to help a family friend stay out of national service – someone with minimal asthma, say, would be given a phoney certificate. I have no idea how many men tried to pull the wool but the number who succeeded was extremely small. Nevertheless I would

say that medical boards could be a bit of a lottery. Two chums of mine shared a room in students' residence. At their medical one was found to have primary tuberculosis, was rejected and spent four months in hospital. The other was taken. Years later the second chap, who had become a consultant, had his chest X-rayed and there was scarring at the top of one lung – which indicated that he too had had tuberculosis and should not have been called up.

A lottery? The satirist Peter Cook failed his medical because of hay fever, he claimed ('But I wrote to them,' he said in a newspaper interview, 'saying, you will call me up if there's an emergency, won't you?'). There are some recorded cases of men getting rejected by claiming to be homosexual – not a winning strategy, generally, as in most medical and psychiatric opinion of the period, homosexuality (a criminal offence until 1967 and in the armed forces until 2000) was not just a perversion but a weakness of character that would respond to a bit of military discipline. There is even a case of a man with a broken leg who, instead of sending a doctor's certificate as would have been expected, and being allocated a later date, hobbled into his medical board on crutches on the half-chance that he might be turned down – and was. But the lottery could work the other way, as Malcolm Higgins attests:

My medical was most peculiar in that we went in to everything in twos: hearing, balance, eye test. I was with a guy with bottleglass spectacles who without them tried to read the chart off a blank wall. When he was pointed at the chart he couldn't read even the biggest letter. Yet when I was serving in Germany I met him again and he was a tank driver. I couldn't believe it.

2

Am I hurting you?

Six weeks or so after the medical, an envelope dropped through the letterbox, 'squat, nasty, khaki',[1] stamped OHMS. 'Oh, help me, Saviour,' men said it stood for. Inside was a third-class rail warrant to a named destination – the first definite indication of a man's fate. At the examining board the interviewing officer might have remarked to, say, a baker fresh out of college that the army needed bakers, and the soon-to-be conscript had left thinking an army baker he was to be. The reality was that as all the colleges where bakery was taught were despatching their finished students at the same time, there was a limit to how many bakers the army could accommodate, and a baker who could not be a baker had to be something else. A junior reporter from Woodford in Essex named Leslie Thomas, who would later make his reputation with *The Virgin Soldiers*, the most popular novel about national service, discovered he was in the Pay Corps: 'The daft thing is, I could do 120-130 words a minute shorthand, and I could type, and I could write reasonable English. And they put me adding up figures, which I really can't do.'[2] There was also a postal order in the envelope – the conscript's first day's pay. Four shillings is the sum so often quoted that virtually all national servicemen believe that is what they got, but it was five shillings from September 1950 and sixpence more from April 1956.

There were tears: mothers at home too upset to go to the station, girlfriends and fiancées on the platform. Glyn Jones, on his way to the

Artillery in Oswestry, remembers 'mother stood at the top of the twenty-four steps of our miner's cottage, father already gone down the pit, crying her eyes out, and I walked away carrying my cardboard suitcase.' Some dads took time off from work to accompany their sons. 'We talked on the tram,' remembers Stanley Colk, off to the RAF. 'When my train pulled in my father, who wasn't very tactile – men weren't – suddenly hugged me and cried. And I sat on the train thinking, "My father loves me!" I never saw my father cry ever again.'

Year in year out, twice a month and once in December because of Christmas, an average of 6,000 young men (over 10,000 at the peak of the Korean War) said their goodbyes and delivered themselves up, almost always on a Thursday in the army and air force, a Monday in the navy. Journeys by steam train in the forties and fifties were slow and connections tortuous. Many men were convinced that the War Office cynically sent them as far as possible from their homes and it could seem that way. Arthur Main found himself travelling from Aberdeen to the Green Jackets at Winchester, having been denied the Gordon Highlanders in his home city – although he had been with the regiment in the cadets and in Aberdeen University Senior Training Corps. The military historian Adrian Walker, with the Somerset Light Infantry on his doorstep in Taunton, was despatched to the Ox and Bucks Light Infantry in Oxford. Men of Irish extraction 'ordinarily resident'[3] on the mainland (which made them liable for national service) may not have been surprised to be taking the overnight ferry to Belfast, on their way to one of Northern Ireland's army training depots – but the almost equal numbers of Cockneys heading in the same direction were.

In the first chaotic years of national service the army sent almost everybody to primary training camps, and sorted out which regiments or corps they would go to afterwards. Later, most training was done at brigade[4] and individual corps depots. Until an upgrading programme began in 1955, accommodation was dilapidated, not to say primitive, even in Aldershot and Catterick, the largest garrisons in the south and north of England. Some camps were stone or brick and had once housed the soldiers of the 18th and 19th centuries, most were the leftovers of the two world wars – the wooden 'spiders' of four huts fanned around communal washrooms and latrines ubiquitous – and all were freezing in winter, with heating dependent on potbellied stoves for which there was never enough fuel.[5] The RAF's reception centre at Padgate near Warrington, then in Lancashire, where all recruits initially went for kitting out and some rudimentary licking into shape before basic training proper elsewhere, was as bad as anything in the army, and Cardington in Bedfordshire, which replaced it from 1953, was only marginally better. The navy's training bases – Portsmouth, Chatham, Devonport, Plymouth (all shore establishments but, in the navy's way of doing things, prefaced HMS, as if they were seagoing) – were regarded as adequate, even comfortable by the standards of the time.

Conscripts arriving at the army's smaller training units frequently found a humane welcome – the Kenyon twins, who turned up on their own at the Royal Engineers depot in Honiton, Devon, after travelling overnight from Manchester, were invited into the guardroom and given a cup of tea. Norman remembers 'sitting there drinking it, looking out the window at the lads marching on the square and this officer explaining what we'd be doing – he was really considerate'. But most, especially those bound for the big corps depots like the RASC in Aldershot, the Royal Signals or Armoured Corps in Catterick, or whichever was the RAF's operating intake centre, experienced such shock and awe that they felt as if they had arrived in prison or, worse, hell. Shouted in and out of the back of three-tonners, conscripts were harried through kitting out, harried in and out of the barber's chair, and harried in and out of the cookhouse where they ate using their just-issued cutlery, always known as eating irons.

Most men found the kitting out a small pantomime as they passed down a long counter and were piled with articles for which they had to sign. Here they encountered the services' curious penchant for backward description: drawers, cellular, green; socks, pairs, two; overalls, denim; blouse, battledress . . . The air force and navy normally had a tailor on hand to make alterations to uniforms, but that rarely happened in the army, though most men later paid to have these done themselves. 'If it fits you must be deformed,' the quartermaster routinely bellowed. It caused never-ending glee among the storemen when conscripts asked for a half-size in boots – there were no half-sizes. Again the air force and navy usually let men try on a pair or two; in the army you almost always got what was lobbed to you.

The haircut had been anticipated, but not the extremity of it. Many men had taken the precaution of getting cropped, including Michael Heseltine, who, having been to Oxford and become liable for national service on failing his accountancy exams, was on his way to the Guards at Caterham in Surrey:

> I was also concerned that my relatively long hair was not going to provide a bumper harvest for some demon Army barber. After lunch on that bleak January Friday, I set off for the Washington Hotel for my last rendezvous with the man who had been cutting my hair ever since I came to London. 'Take it off,' I said. 'Take it off like an Army barber would take it off. They're not going to make a fool of me.' Almost with tears in his eyes, he faithfully carried out my instruction.[6]

There were tears in other eyes. Malcolm Higgins, in the Artillery at Oswestry, remembers a Teddy Boy in his intake, 'all scars, talking out of the side of his mouth, a hard Cockney with padded shoulders in his drapes – and this immaculate Tony Curtis, quiff and duck's arse. And as this beautiful hair fell to the floor – he cried.' Roy Booth, with the RAMC at Church Crookham in Hampshire, 'had got my Teddyboy off' but refused point-blank to let the barber touch his crewcut. 'I just wasn't prepared to let them bugger around with it. But they marched me to the guardroom, a corporal held me down and they took the lot off.' The Southampton and England Under-23 left winger, John Sydenham, called into the Ordnance Corps at Middle Wallop, 'had had a good trim and got rid of the long sideburns, which I thought would satisfy them, but they ran the clippers almost up to my forehead. I've always been a sun worshipper and I tan almost black, so I had this black face that was white all round the edge and I looked like a clown.' The broadcaster Michael Parkinson, then a Yorkshire newspaper reporter, was another who had been crewcutted before arriving at the Royal Army Pay Corps in Devizes

> and already looked a bit like Yul Brynner. I really didn't need a haircut but I was sat in the chair like everybody else and the barber looked at the NCO, a national serviceman called Fotheringham, smirking behind me, who

18

winked – I watched him in the mirror – and on the nod the barber ran the shears right over the top of my head so I really was bald. Fotheringham was a Somerset boy with ruddy cheeks, I'll never forget him, and I thought, 'One day I'll get you, you bastard.' And I did. I went back to Devizes after I was commissioned and when I was duty officer I inspected his billet. He was a smart soldier, but I managed to find a single hair under his bed. I doubled him round the square, and I charged him. I'm not a vindictive person. It's the only time in my life I've consciously sought revenge on anybody and I'm still ashamed of what I did.

Complaints about forces' haircuts were frequently raised in the House of Commons[7] where it was suggested that barbers 'were more fitted to practise as carpenters or metal shearers'. What added insult to injury was that conscripts had to pay for what was done to them (ninepence or a shilling the going rate) and it was done to them every week they were in basic training.

The evening of the first day found huddles of shorn young men sorting out their bedding[8] and trying to make sense of their clothing and equipment – and each other. Scouse and Geordie, Jock and Mancunian, Cockney and Brummie: in an age when almost no one had been anywhere outside his home town or village it could be hard to understand what others were saying. With the Royal Engineers at Honiton, Derby man Roy Battelle, a turner from a company making diesel engines, was not only nonplussed but thought 'my broad Derbyshire sounded like a BBC announcer compared with some of them'.

Not all who had arrived were always still there at lights out. 'By 1830 hours some 1,250 recruits had reported in and a few had already absconded,' John Lyon-Maris, with the RASC in Aldershot, observed in notes he kept at the time. Between them, the military and civil police soon rounded up such miscreants.

It was an odd experience for the majority of men to sleep away from home for the first time, never mind in a room of strangers. Others were accustomed to it: public schoolboys, and orphans like Leslie Thomas, a Barnardo's boy, familiar with dormitories; those who had moved away from home to do their apprenticeships; those like bricklayer Cliff Holland (called to the Manchester Regiment training depot at Chester) who had gone into lodgings when his family broke up.

Some men cried in the dark. 'My mind went back to when I was six and went to boarding school,' says the broadcaster John Dunn, arrived at RAF Padgate having spent a year after leaving King's College in Canterbury travelling on the continent. Malcolm Higgins heard no one cry 'but I did hear the grinding of teeth in sleep and someone went sleepwalking.' Yet the novelist Gordon Williams, a reporter on a group of local newspapers in Renfrewshire, settling down at Padgate, was happy to have a bed of his own for the first time: 'We were fairly middle-class Scots, but over the years I'd slept with my brother, I'd slept with my aunts, uncles, grand-father . . . The first two or three nights in the RAF I really felt like a virgin bride.'

However men felt, morning came too soon. Reveille in the services is at 6.15 but training NCOs appeared from 5 o'clock onwards, as the fancy took them. 'Hands off cocks and on socks' – men were startled awake by a bellow that echoed in barrack rooms across the land, accompanied by the clatter of pace stick on metal fire buckets, lockers, bedends. They bolted to the ablutions where there were too few basins and latrines, where the basins had no plugs (men used twists of newspaper, or later bought plugs of their own) and the latrines sometimes had no seats or even doors. More often than not, men shaved in cold water; those who had never shaved in their lives would soon discover that the services did not tolerate bum-fluff. The playwright Alan Bennett, who did his training with the Yorks and Lancs Regiment in Pontefract, was later to write, 'it was touch and go which I got to first – puberty or the call-up';[9] he was not alone.

The first few days were a bewildering blur. Men bundled up their civilian clothes in brown paper and string (in the early years they were instructed to bring their own) and sent them home: a psychological umbilical cord cut. They paraded for the issue of their service number – eight digits in the army, seven in the air force,[10] six in the navy – which they stamped, stencilled or inked on everything they now owned. They had their photograph taken for the 12-50 ID card that was to be carried at all times and received their AB64 paybook, part one of which would record their service, part two their credits and debits. They got their tetanus and typhoid inoculation, invariably, before throwaway syringes existed, administered with a blunt needle and which, invariably, made one or two faint and put one or two in the infirmary. And they were introduced to the alien world of service life, its pecking order and its nomenclature, its parade ground rituals, its obsession with cleaning and polishing, its readiness to exact punishment for supposed infringement of its rules.

*   *   *

Within their first 14 days, recruits took a second intelligence test and an aptitude test, and were seen by the unit medical officer, to ensure that they were free from infection and, up to the early fifties in the army, to judge whether they should go to a command physical training centre for some beefing up before undertaking basic training; the general standard of health and nutrition had risen during the war but, paradoxically, a proportion of men from London and the big industrial towns were of poor physique. More importantly, the MO had to satisfy himself that recruits should even have been called up.

Throughout the fifties the newspapers carried stories about men with disabilities being passed by medical boards and then having to be discharged by the services or, in extreme instances, of men dying while in uniform.[11] 'The problem was that many examining board doctors were retired, over seventy, and they found the Pulheems grading system hard to get hold of – and sometimes they came widely adrift,' comments Dr John Blair. And there was a second problem: the 95 boards around the country were so intent on not allowing lead-swingers to escape the net that they were inclined to pass genuinely unsuitable men that the forces had to reject later.

In July 1953, after considerable criticism – and an admission in the House that out of 300,000 examinations 20 men 'almost deaf and almost blind' had been passed as medically fit for service and that an undisclosed number rejected as unfit had been called up 'through clerical errors' – the Minister of Labour and National Service introduced some safeguarding measures. These included subjecting board members to yearly reviews, not appointing anyone over sixty-five and preferably only those with service experience, and introducing the right for men to appeal if they felt their grading was wrong. It's uncertain that things improved:[12] a govern-

21

ment report in 1956 commented that boards seemed almost as keen as ever in catching those deliberately trying to fail their medical and continued to push men through.

The buck stopped with the depot medical officers – almost all, in army and air force, national servicemen themselves.[13] They carried a heavy workload (in his time at Padgate one estimated he had given 25,000 injections alone) and an even heavier responsibility. While men might be discharged at any time in their service, the bulk of those who went out did so during basic training. The armed forces rejected over 1% of national servicemen passed by medical boards – some 25,000–30,000 in 13 years.[14] Over half were because of psychiatric problems. MOs had been given some psychiatric training in the forces and they could refer cases to a command psychiatrist; nonetheless, recruits showing signs of mental or emotional instability caused them great anxiety. The culture MOs worked in was frequently reluctant to acknowledge such problems; and, too, they were wary of being taken for a ride: a few men continued to try to work their ticket. The most widely publicised discharge from the army on psychiatric grounds was that of rock and roll singer Terry Dene (real name Williams), who entered the Green Jackets at Winchester in July 1959, collapsed two days later, and after two weeks in army and civilian hospitals was released, suffering from 'emotional strain'. But problems less than such complete disintegration were difficult to diagnose. Was a man who wet the bed traumatised by his service or seeking a way out? In most such cases an NCO would already have had the man woken every hour of the night and escorted to the latrines – which, it has to be said, often effected a cure. Bruce Kent remembers a fellow recruit at Hounslow 22 Training Camp who followed orders to blanco his kit and did – everything including his underwear and uniform. Graham Williams, like his brother Gordon a local paper reporter but at the Armoured Corps general training camp in Carlisle, remembers 'a beautiful opera singer who sat on his bed filing his feet bloody and got whipped off to hospital'. Both men were discharged. Kent and Williams believe that they did take the army for a ride, and perhaps they did. But an MO having to make a judgement was very aware of what might happen if a discharge was not recommended.

*   *   *

Basic training – six weeks in the army corps, air force and navy, up to three months in the infantry and the RAF Regiment (responsible for the defence of airfields), four months in the Guards – revolved around the parade ground. The army and air force stamped around it, the navy simply closed up the heel – 'which probably stems from the days when they were scared of stamping down on rotten decks of old ships,' says the journalist Neal Ascherson. In his training at Lympstone in Devon with the Royal Marines – who drilled in the naval tradition but as arduously as anything in the army – he discovered that 'banging boots was extremely distasteful to the Marines. They said the army did it to damage the spinal column and dull the brain.' The Guards on the other hand stamped ferociously and at the depot in Caterham, Mike Hollingworth enjoyed every moment: 'Drilling and marching look easy but they aren't. The individual doesn't know how they're done. You see a group of recruits and they can't get their limbs into the proper shape. NCOs move with a spring in their heels, their arms seem lubricated. Recruits – they flail. Then suddenly there's a click in their heads and they start looking like soldiers. Drilling is a skill, like abseiling.' Or dancing in the chorus line: the Grenadiers took Hollingworth's intake to London's Victoria Palace Theatre, where the Crazy Gang were performing, specifically to watch the movement and coordination of the chorus line.

But the chorus line did not wear regulation-issue boots embedded with 13 metal studs, and recruits did. Most had never worn boots, hours on the parade ground gave almost all of them blisters and some had the skin torn off their feet. The pressures of the situation and men's pride meant very few were willing to go sick to get treatment: it was grin and bear it. In any event the MO could do little except prescribe antiseptic cream. A man could be excused boots but his condition had to be extreme during training: he could not go on the parade ground or do a guard duty in shoes. But some did get dispensation. One was the actor Johnny Briggs, at Catterick with the Royal Armoured Corps, whose ankles swelled so badly in boots that he

> was issued with a much prized little chitty which I carried everywhere in case I was challenged for always wearing comfortable shoes . . . That was

magic because, as a result, I didn't have to go on parades and was excused
the much hated guard duty... I ended up wearing women's shoes. Not
high heels, of course, but the flat, lace-up shoes that were issued to the
Women's Royal Army Corps. They were wonderful and I was the envy of
most of the guys in the barracks ...[15]

The majority of men broke in their boots before they were broken by
them and many came to regard them as the most satisfying of footwear. 'I
loved my boots,' says Trevor Baylis, who trained with the Sussex Regiment
at Shorncliffe. 'When I came back to the regiment after qualifying as a PTI
[physical training instructor] I loved running in them.'

Yet boots were more than footwear in the army and RAF Regiment. The
rest of the air force and the navy got one pair: the RAF Regiment and the
army got two, and they were totemic. Men who had never even cleaned a
pair of shoes ('That's what happens when you have a granny living with
you,' comments Stanley Colk) now spent hours heating spoons to erase
the pimples from the leather and circling spit and polish into it. Toecaps
and heels sufficed for everyday boots: best boots had to shine with the
same lustre on their side surfaces. Taking only a size four, Malcolm Higgins
had to be issued with a pair of officer's brown boots made of smooth
leather, which were easy enough to polish black and which, under Higgins'
circling duster, came up like glass: 'No one else's ever came close. My boots
were things of beauty.'

Some men hated the activity, but many found it hypnotic, almost
measuring their military progress by the fetishistic quality of their boots,
best. 'Sometimes I thought I was a moron, but I loved sitting on my bed
and bulling my boots until they were immaculate,' says Cliff Holland.
Many got satisfaction out of blancoing their packs and webbing, buffing
brasses, cap badges and buttons,[16] and in learning how to shrink their
berets, which when issued were universally acknowledged to look like
cowpats. (It was only when basic training was behind them that some
would shrink them further, to the size of rakish yarmulkes.) A battledress
scrubbed or shaved of its fuzz, its creases sharpened by soap ironed inside
them, made even the unmilitary feel they began to approach the impec-
cable smartness of the NCOs. In the immediate postwar years when there

were no electric irons – which, when there were, men had to supply themselves – the battledress was slept on, although later national service-men thought this was an old soldier's tale. 'You damped the seams and stretched the BD out on top of the mattress and under the blankets, after it had dried fairly crisp,' explains John Lyon-Maris. 'There were ripple-like creases, but they fell out as soon as you put it on. How effective was it? Well, more than not doing it at all.'

The Guards took bulling – service-speak for cleaning and polishing derived, unsurprisingly, from bullshit – like drill, to their own heights (bulling was even called a 'shining parade') and Mike Hollingworth revelled in it:

> You sat bolt upright astride your bed with sleeves rolled up and your braces down off the shoulders, a mark of respect, presumably, don't ask me why. And you had to learn the curious rituals of the whole brigade – how, for example, are the buttons grouped on the Welsh Guards' tunic – but your regiment in particular. And while you worked, your trained soldier[17] or squad NCO or occasionally your officer would come along and ask you questions.

There were no detailed regulations as to what bull should consist of: it was a commanding officer's responsibility. Everywhere men cleaned their billets, washrooms and latrines and polished the floor with 'bumpers' (blocks of weighted wood attached to broom handles); in the RAF when wearing boots men skated around the floor on squares of old blankets and anyone who neglected to do so quickly heard the chorus, 'Pads!' It was common practice to blacken and polish the billet stove, but at various times in different units men were made to polish the top coal in the fuel bin, prise dirt from between floorboards with a matchstick, buff up nailheads, scrape urinals with razor blades, and much else. Such manic chores could extend to a man's kit. It was known for recruits to scrape and polish the eyelets of their boots, polish the studs, blacken the soles, polish spare bootlaces and make them up into tiny wheels tied off with black cotton, blacken brown plimsolls (which when used turned their feet black), and buff their mess tins (even though they had to eat out of them on exercises). Every morning men made a square of their blankets and sheets in alternate layers and stood by their beds for their NCOs' inspection. Once a week, when an officer carried out inspection, men also laid out everything they owned in a prescribed manner so demanding that it could involve lining up every item on every bed by stretching a thread the length of the billet. Up to the early 1950s – when, again, so much criticism got into the papers that the practice stopped – men used cardboard to stiffen not just their ammo pouches and large and small packs, but even every item of clothing.

For the main weekly inspection some men stayed up half the night getting ready. Others chose to put their mattresses on the floor, laid out like primitive altars, and sleep on the wire mesh of their beds. Others gave up their beds to their layouts and slept on the floor. When he arrived at the Service Corps in Aldershot, Derrick Johns, from Evesham in Worcester-shire, who had suspended his solicitor's articles to get his national service out of the way, remembers a Teddy Boy climbing out of a three-tonner, carrying a guitar: '"What's that for?" an NCO asked. "For something to do in the evening," he said. No wonder the NCO laughed.'

✻   ✻   ✻

If haircuts, medical boards and other matters constantly concerned the Commons and the newspapers, so did the kind of food that recruits were getting.

Up to 1954 the services had problems feeding their recruits, especially during 1950 when 18 months' national service suddenly became two years, men were held in while more came, and food budgets ran out. Food, in fact, was scarcer in Britain after the war than during it because America had stopped its lease-lend, and the country had little cash to buy it. Until 1952 sugar, tea, butter, cheese, eggs, margarine, cooking fat, bacon and meat were all rationed, with bacon and meat staying on ration for another two years, and men handed over their ration books on arrival at the depots and were issued with a card on which each day's three meals were marked off at the cookhouse by the orderly NCO – usually with the bent tine of a fork.[18]

Yet the assumption that food was poor in the early years and improved later is not always borne out by men's experience. Norman Kenyon at

Honiton in 1949 thought the food plentiful and more varied than at home: 'A lot of fish – fish was cheap in those days. I remember being sent to the cookhouse by the RSM [Regimental Sergeant-Major] to collect fish scraps for the workshop cat. When I brought them back he said, "That's too good for the damn cat" and ate them. But I was on the boxing team and I got special rations – bacon and eggs, luxuries then.' At Padgate in 1946 from a factory job in Nottingham and a family background of hand-me-downs, the novelist Alan Sillitoe found 'Few moaned about the food at camp, because the diet was good, and we were easy to satisfy after six years of rationing.'[19] Four years later the first meal that Ray Selfe, a cinema projectionist from Croydon, had at Padgate 'consisted of two sausages, burnt on the outside, raw in the middle, a greasy mount of yellowing onions and a large amount of watery reconstituted powdered potato'. There was dry bread, shrivelled apples and urns of tea and cocoa – 'though those who tried both said there was no difference' – with nothing to sweeten them. His first breakfast was unsweetened porridge, reconstituted egg on bread and more tea and cocoa. The following year at the same reception centre, Colin Clark found 'compared to Eton, the food wasn't bad at all'[20] but, three years on, another factory worker, Joe Ashton, considered 'The food was ten times worse than any gaol I've visited as an MP (including Strangeways the day after the riots) and not much of it either.'[21]

'The quality varied enormously and it all depended on the cook-sergeant,' says Dr John Blair. 'In some places the food was really excellent.[22] As a generalisation I would say what was served was stodgy but adequate.' At Oswestry in 1955 Malcolm Higgins was less concerned about the food – 'which was OK' – than about 'the entire Welsh population of sparrows in the roof girders of the dining hall. You had to keep one eye on them and one on your plate. If you weren't alert you got some unwanted seasoning.'

Many men's memory of the food in basic training was of grease swimming in puddles of tomato juice and some could not eat any of it. The actor Gabriel Woolf survived the RAF entirely on bread and jam and thereafter, having a UK posting and never more than three weeks away from home at a time, 'I used to stoke up on week-ends . . . and cross the intervening desert like a camel.'[23] Derrick Johns lived on twice-weekly food parcels from his girlfriend, which she sent in square biscuit tins.

'There were always men who complained about everything and just ate chips in the NAAFI,'[24] says John Keenan, a butcher from Blackpool who became a Catering Corps officers' mess cook in Germany. Dave Garyford from Wickford in Essex (who had a City and Guilds Catering diploma before becoming an army cook and serving in Egypt) adds: 'Any army cookhouse is as good or bad as the people running it, as can be said of any catering establishment. Some training depots were undoubtedly good. The best that can be said for most is that meals were regular, three times a day.'

It was possible to complain about the food to the duty officer on his round of the dining hall, although an indignant cook-sergeant could see to it that you ended up with a spot of potato peeling for your temerity. The humorist Willie Rushton, with the Armoured Corps at Catterick, one day did complain, if hardly seriously:

> I realised that I had found this leaf – we were having some sort of stew, I don't know what dead animal it was, but something obviously the army had bought en bloc. 'Sergeant-major, there's a leaf in my stew.' The officer said, 'That's definitely a leaf.' So we paraded off, bringing the stew to the kitchens where there was a sergeant cook, head chef or whatever, standing there. 'What's this? A leaf. We can't have leaves in the stew.' The man then pulled out this huge military manual of army cooking and turned to page 308 where it said: Stew, other ranks, for the use of, and there was something like 500 tons of beef, 4,000 tons of potato and onions – and one bay leaf.[25]

Dave Garyford is full of praise for the Aldershot Catering Corps kitchens 'where I learned to cook to hotel standards'. But he adds: 'The pity of it is so few of us got to use such knowledge.'

A single joke about food reverberated down the national service years: *Who called the cook a cunt?*, with the rejoinder: *Who called the cunt a cook?*

*   *   *

There was more to basic training than drill and bull: physical training, weapons instruction to varying degrees of intensity (airmen got on to a rifle range only once or twice, sailors not at all), fieldcraft, map reading, lectures on men's particular armed service. Whatever conscripts thought of the food, most put on weight, even as they were made fit by their visits to the assault course and gym, their route marches, their runs through the countryside or nearby parks or surrounding streets. In the infantry, a man had to complete a timed five miles (the Royal Fusiliers, based in the Tower of London, did this around the moat – 12 circuits). 'We couldn't not be fit,' says Mike Hollingworth. 'We marched, we climbed nets, we swung on ropes, we marched and we marched again. Stressed executives today pay good money for what I was doing for free. I loved every minute of it including the "milling"[26] – even though a corporal in the Irish Guards broke my nose.' Says Glyn Jones: 'I got so fit I could deliberately let a bus go by and catch it.'

Later in training, recruits began to get rostered for guard duty, the most detested of all duties and one that followed men throughout their service. Between 6.15 when the guard was mounted in the evening and the 12 hours until it was dismounted, men did two two-hour 'stags' or camp patrols, with four hours off between them when they could attempt to sleep in the guardroom, fully clothed, under naked bulbs, on mattressless beds. Most units offered the small incentive of the 'stick man': parading seven men instead of the six required, the duty officer allowing the best turned out to stand down, but even this was considered to have an ulterior motive. 'A transparent way of getting everyone to bull like mad,' says Rodney Dale who, his A levels done, had come from the Fenland village of Haddenham to the Suffolk Regiment at Bury St Edmunds. If not necessarily for the right reason, he was always stick man:

> Could I, on whose report a school teacher had once written: 'Tries to excel without effort' be so smart so consistently? Perhaps the answer lay in . . . my possessing a car . . . The permanent guard corporal had a girlfriend in the town, and when I was stick man he would immediately seek my co-operation in driving him down to see the wench. As some sort of palliative he would bring me a large helping of fish and chips from the shop in which she served.[27]

Usually the guard was mounted with loaded rifles, but unlike when serving in the world's trouble spots, the ammunition was then taken away and locked in a box under the guard commander's bed, except at nervous times when the IRA made a mockery of the army by raids on regimental armouries.[28]

The short straw on guard duty meant the main gate, where a man stood with his rifle and challenged those going in and out, but where he could be scrutinised by any passing officer. The rest in their turn prowled the camp, armed with pick helves. On stag or in the guardroom, time passed with excruciating slowness. Supper came over in the middle of the evening – bad luck on those on stag whose food was cold and congealed when they got it. The one good thing about guard duty, recruits thought, was that, authorised as they were to move stealthily around the camp, they were sometimes able to steal fuel for the billet.

*　＊　＊*

It was difficult for young men from so many different backgrounds to be cooped up together unable, in the first four weeks, even to go out of camp because the services thought they were still a disgrace to the uniform. And they had almost no money to spend in the NAAFI canteen – after stoppages (including the much-resented 'barrack-room damages' for damages that had not occurred) there was about 23 shillings left from their original 28 (about 30 from 38s 6d), a slice of which went on dusters and cleaning materials. Married men, who made up 6–7% of recruits, were worst off: to qualify for the married man's allowance that went to their wives (the maximum was £3 – nothing for children), they had to send home a minimum of ten shillings and sixpence.

Things would get at least marginally better for many once out of training, with additional money for passing trade examinations or for add-ons such as marksmanship or qualifying as parachutists; and very much better for everyone in their last six months when they went on to regulars' pay. For some, promotions would bring additional financial reward. In the meantime, men who did not smoke or drink got by more easily than those who did and those who sent money home. But some remained badly off throughout their service and bulled other people's boots or did their guards to raise a bit of cash. The going rates were usually 2s 6d and ten shillings respectively.[29]

Lads from urban areas were at first more unsettled than those from the countryside: rural lads were self-sufficient, townies missed the entertainment. Those who coped least well were those from working-class backgrounds in the towns and cities who had not been subjected to any discipline, who were used to having cash in their pockets, and going on the rampage on a Saturday night to let off steam.

Inevitably there was some bullying. The art critic Brian Sewell, at Aldershot with the Service Corps, knew 'a rather religious fellow who was badgered so unmercifully for kneeling to say his prayers, that he fled to Brompton Oratory for sanctuary'. As a rule men drew on their inner resources to resolve their problem – or someone sorted it out on their behalf. Willie Purves (later Sir William Purves, head of the Hong Kong and Shanghai Banking Corporation), a junior bank clerk from a village near Kelso, was given a bad time when he found himself badged into the Black Watch at Fort George in Inverness.

From my part of the Borders, everyone went into the King's Own Scottish Borderers [KOSB, pronounced Kosbe] training barracks in Edinburgh. I suppose the Black Watch were one man short so I got taken in. These guys were all streetwise, and most knew each other. I looked about sixteen. And for the first two or three weeks my life was hell. They wouldn't let me sleep in my bed. I was tossed out every night, I'd get back in and they'd toss me out again. I just stuck to it. Then I was accepted. That was a great growing-up experience for a little boy from the country whose widowed mother was the village teacher and had somewhat protected him.

Trevor Baylis went to the aid of 'a natural victim' who did not have Purves' resolve. Baylis got off his bed, walked over to the tormentor 'and nutted him. He went down, poleaxed, disappearing into the space between two beds. When he stood up there was so much blood pouring from his nose it looked like I'd hit him with a shovel.'[30]

'It was important not to have airs and graces,' comments Brian Sewell, who had the good sense not to heed his mother and bring his violin, which at the time he practised four hours a day. 'Such people did get bullied, as did those who did not cooperate in the shared duties of the barrack room or who refused to make a serious effort that got the platoon into trouble. But later there was an exchange of skills, the sewing on of buttons for ironing or cleaning brasses as people came to support each other.' Some, he observes, found the 'girly domestic skills required by the army beyond the gender barrier – a sort of self-emasculation.'

Some – those only marginally over the army's intelligence threshold but unequal to army life – had no skills to exchange, but fellow recruits usually rallied round, bulling items of their kit or helping them over the assault course. Eric Brown, a Cardiff plumber, remembers a farm labourer with him at Wrexham in the Welsh Fusiliers 'who was one of those poor sods who swung his right arm with his right foot[31] and was bogging awful at everything. One day going on parade he was in such a tizzwozz he grabbed someone's electric iron and ironed the sleeve of his uniform with his arm still in it. The day after his arm was one enormous blister.' Cliff Holland remembers 'a lad called Patterson who was always being shouted at – he couldn't get up in the morning so he tried to save time by going to bed fully dressed, which got him into more trouble. One weekend when he went home he took his rifle – which was obviously illegal – and painted it. He couldn't understand why no one was pleased.'

It was interesting how barrack-room camaraderie could bring opposites together; men who could not read or write or who did so with difficulty, turned to the better educated to help them. Malcolm Higgins remembers being told: 'You're a clever bloke, Taffy, read that.'

> It was on green paper, in biro, what he'd done to her the last time they were together, what she was going to do to him next time. It was filth as far as I was concerned at that period of my life. When I looked up he said: 'Writes a lovely letter, doesn't she?' And he dictated something similar to her and I faithfully wrote it down. It was a humbling experience. For the first time really, I realised there were different kinds of people.

Letters from and to girlfriends during basic training took on an almost obsessional significance and men waited anxiously for the post corporal's delivery after lunch, incoming envelopes regularly inscribed with SWALK (sealed with a loving kiss) and sometimes a lipsticked imprint. Derrick Johns' girlfriend wrote every day, 'and for five or ten minutes it was like holding hands'. He wrote every day, too, 'but I didn't always have the money for the postage'. Many outgoing envelopes were also SWALKED; a few were inscribed NORWICH ((K)nickers off ready when I come home).

There was considerable horseplay in barrack-room life: the blacking of private parts with polish or soot happened often. And practical joking: men coming in at night when others were asleep would wake them up to ask them if they wanted to buy a battleship or have a pee, and heavy sleepers would have their bed carried out and deposited in the middle of the square. Filling rolled-up socks with jam was a favourite jape, or sewing up the arms or legs of someone's denims. The novelist Tom Sharpe, arrived at the Marines depot in Lympstone from Lancing College, recalls:

> There were a good number of Glaswegians in our squad . . . One of their favourite pranks was to fill a condom with urine and put it down the top bunk of a bootneck [marine] who'd 'gone on the piss' in Exeter. The thing would burst when he climbed in, dripping on the fellow below, who would go out of his mind with rage.[32]

Coping in the barrack room was a matter of temperament. For the very shy (some men got undressed behind their locker door or showered in bathing trunks), for the aesthetic or bookish who could not accept the rough and tumble, it could be an uncomfortable experience. 'At first, two or three out of 20 men were reading comics, which I thought was extremely childish,' says Ron Batchelor, a Londoner who had done three years as a craftsman on building sites on his way to becoming a structural engineer before going into the air force. 'At the end of six weeks almost all of us were reading comics – we'd gravitated to the lowest denominator.' As Glyn Jones says:

> Everyone farted loudly. At the beginning, I thought that was awful, it was something I never did before I went in the army. But within a few weeks I was doing it. It was great fun in a group of men to lift up your leg and let rip. I was also brought up not to swear – the first time I heard my father swear was when he took me for a pint on leave. But after a while I couldn't put a sentence together without half a dozen swear-words.

✶   ✶   ✶

The lexicon of profanity volleyed across the parade ground as NCOs drilled their squads (not in the Marines – they frowned on it as much as boot-banging), but there was really only one swear-word. Many men half a century ago blinked at its use; the middle and respectable working classes did not tolerate it at home and many had heard very little of it anywhere. But in the services it was used as adjective, noun, verb and exclamation mark. Trevor Baylis once heard his platoon corporal tell the sergeant-major about a jammed rifle and say: 'The fucking fuckwit fucking fucked the fucker,' and it still makes him laugh.

> The use of the F word took getting used to. I mean, it wasn't like we hadn't heard it before but it took some getting used to, used all the time. Most people didn't take offence – the prissy-prissy types did – but most of us were at it in no time. The swearing, I think, was part of the camaraderie. Surprising how, when you came out of the army, you cleaned up your act.[33]

The theatre director Sir Peter Hall, during basic training at RAF West Kirby, looked around his fellow recruits, 'who were fucking and blinding at me as I tried to read [and] I felt that my luck had run out'. He had 'no moral objection to others having no other descriptive adjective in their vocabulary ... it just made conversation monotonous.'[34]

Those physically different from the norm were most often the butt of the parade ground's rough humour: the very tall ('I didn't know they stacked shit that high'); the red-haired ('that man who's had his head up a jam-ragged tart'); those of an unfortunate build or gait ('the man who's marching like a pregnant duck/a constipated fairy/a vulture that's shit itself/the one with piles'). Bruce Kent was truly shaken when his sergeant came up to him on parade and said: '"What do you think you are? A pregnant nun?" For me, a Roman Catholic, very orthodox, I was really mortified, shocked, at someone talking about nuns in that way.'[35]

Over the jolt of such verbal assaults, most men took it in their stride. 'You had to see the screaming, the jumping up and down for what it was, shrug, what a bugger, see the funny side,' says Roger Horton, who went into the air force from a City of London insurance office. Many came to regard drill as a kind of theatre in which the NCOs gave a performance of cleverly paced rage, much of it funny as well as coarse. 'Am I hurting you? I should be, I'm standing on your hair.' 'Swing your arm or I'll tear it off, stick it up your arse and have you for a lollypop.' 'You weren't born, you were pissed up a wall and the sun hatched you out.' But it was less funny when you were the target and men thoroughly disliked being made to repeat an insult, however mild. For Glyn Jones

That was hard to take, especially when it was said for something unfair. 'You're a dozy, sloppy gunner, what are you?', and you had to shout, 'I'm a dozy, sloppy gunner, Sergeant.' You had to clench your fists and your buttocks. What made me laugh was that the roughest lads found being insulted the hardest to take, they wanted to lash out. The posher boys, it just rolled off their backs.

Retained at work because he was engaged on a contract for the Iraqi oilfields which the government considered essential, Roy Battelle was twenty-three 'and felt grown up compared with the eighteen-year-olds – and to be told my rifle was dirty after I'd pulled it through 20 times, and be called a manky soldier, which I never was, never, and have to say it – it was belittling.' Trevor Baylis refused to play by the army's rules, and got charged (put on a fizzer, under the catch-all 'anything contrary to good order and discipline' section 50 of King's or Queen's Regulations). In response to the appended 'What are you?' he replied: 'Insulted, Sergeant.' 'And I was,' he says. 'The nearest I'd come to being insulted before was my mother saying to me, "Trevor, if you're not up in a minute I'll bring your breakfast up to you." '

Transgressions brought punishment. A misdemeanour on the square might get a man doubled round it, his rifle held above his head (sometimes a Bren – which weighed 23 lb) or given a spell of spud-bashing (while, very likely, a machine for the job lay idle nearby), scrubbing crusted pots and pans or climbing into the grease trap out the back of the cookhouse to ladle out the scum. A spot of blanco on a belt brass or a speck of dust down a rifle barrel or a piece of kit deemed on inspection not up to standard – which might also have been swept from the bed, trampled on or thrown out the window – could bring the same retribution. Roy Battelle was told his shaving brush and toothbrush were dirty, saw them dropped in a bucket and flung outside the billet, and was sent to sweep out the massive bad-weather drill shed with his toothbrush: 'That was a favourite – you did about a yard in an hour.' A recruit who got charged was double-marched into the commanding officer without belt and headdress and received a number of days CB (confined to barracks), often referred to as jankers (under punishment to muster in the navy). Jankers meant a miserable time. After his day's work, a man paraded behind the guard in best dress and full kit to be inspected like the guard when it mounted, turned up again when it dismounted, and spent his evening doing anything the guard commander could think of. As often as not that meant back to the cookhouse, but it could also mean cleaning windows or shovelling coal or, if there was nothing more useful, painting coal heaps white,[36] digging weeds with a knife and fork or cutting grass with scissors.

The cookhouse was the usual destination for those on their first Sunday church parade who declared themselves to be atheists or agnostics. The following Sunday most men had a religion.[37]

By and large, NCOs acted by the values of the culture. A few abused their position – including some national servicemen who became instructors – and it could happen from the moment men walked in the gates: when Graham Williams waited for his army haircut at the Armoured Corps in Carlisle, 'a wee corporal came down the line telling us we'd get the treatment if we didn't pay him two bob. We did. It didn't make any difference.' Ray Selfe discovered that his corporal at Padgate enjoyed letting his flight queue in the NAAFI and then, as the first man reached the counter, order everyone outside. 'Some of us were only caught twice on this and sat at the tables smoking cigarettes, watching the expectations of those in the queue about to be frustrated.' At Canterbury with the West Surreys, Tony Thorne found that the corporals inspected men's china mugs before meals and smashed any they considered 'shitty':

This ritual was repeated three times a day, every day, and the corporals never tired of it. Often the corridor looked like a snowstorm. Twice I bought a brand new mug and had it smashed the same day. On one occasion the whole of No 3 Squad had their mugs smashed. Mug-smashing was a perk of Corporaldom and they loved it.[38]

But the majority of men, on balance, did not think they were bullied. 'Of course I disliked the absurd rituals and the ignorant ranting of the NCOs, but overall it didn't worry me and I certainly wasn't bullied,' says the broadcaster John Dunn, who at RAF Cardington stood out in a way that NCOs could not have ignored: at six feet seven and broad built, there was no uniform big enough for him, 'so I went on parade wearing a green sports jacket, grey flannel trousers, an RAF shirt and black tie, and boots, with webbing holding the lot together – I was a bizarre sight.' He adds: 'My own view is that basic training was not as brutal as some say.'

At first, most thought it was brutal, though many army platoons and airforce flights grew to like their NCOs so much that, before their passing-out, they bought them lighters or cigarettes. 'I didn't enjoy taking orders, especially from people I thought lesser than me,' says Arnold Wesker (who famously refused to bayonet a dummy during his RAF basic – a central issue in his play *Chips With Everything*) 'but eventually I had a great deal of affection for our corporal. He turned out to be a softie. He had to bully. It was bullying, or what we construed as bullying, that made us into a squad.' By the end of his six weeks at Honiton, Roy Battelle was another who had changed his mind: 'I respected them, yes, respected them. In the beginning I wanted to murder them, I really mean that. By the end I realised everything they'd done turned me into a soldier.' Don Bullock from Mexborough, who did his basic at Strensall, the training depot of the six Yorkshire regiments, had perhaps more reason for gratitude. He had got so fed up with his sergeant yelling in his face 'that I threw my rifle at him. I said, "I'm f-ing going home, I didn't want to f-ing come here." ' I was frogmarched into the barrack room and given a good talking to. I can only reflect back and say that had I been a soldier and not a new recruit I would have spent my two years in a military prison.' What most men came to understand was that the armed forces had little time to turn out recruits and if the way they did it was crude, it was effective. It commanded unquestioning obedience, as Hugh Grant demonstrated in a Pavlovian way when he went to see his unit's PSO (personnel selection officer).

Before moving on for trade training (basic training *was* trade training for the infantry), all recruits saw their PSO, to discuss their future service. A week before his passing-out, Grant – one of only 14 recruits from an intake of 48 to make it through Para training at Aldershot and who, had he failed, as a three-year regular with a national service obligation would have been posted out to another regiment – went for his interview.

> As I was leaving the room, the elderly major suddenly asked, 'Grant – will you jump?' A strange request I thought, but maybe he wanted to test my reflexes. Nine weeks of following orders blindly kicked in. I turned towards the Major, put my feet together and executed a small leap in the air. As I landed with a clatter I saw a look of sheer disbelief on his face. 'No-no!' he said wearily. 'I meant will you parachute?'[39]

'If you want to turn ordinary men rapidly into good soldiers, you must first strip them of their ordinary manhood – and regular bullying and humiliation do this faster and more efficiently than other means,' says Nicholas Harman, later a journalist on *The Economist* and *Panorama*, who was another who came through Caterham with the Guards. 'It was a blunt way of getting absolute obedience, but I don't see anything wrong with that,' says Brian Sewell. At a national service exhibition at the Imperial War Museum almost exactly 40 years after he had reported for duty, Monsignor Bruce Kent commented: 'Thank God they didn't ask me to kill anyone, because I'd have done it without question.'[40] Cliff Holland adds: 'If you're under fire you can't hold a meeting about it. If someone says duck, move, go, you will – and in Malaya it saved my life.'

It surprised even many who hated basic training, or thought they remained aloof from it, how hard they tried at their passing-out parade – which family and girlfriends were invited to attend – not just for themselves but for their platoon sergeant, on whom their performance reflected. A very few whose lack of coordination had been despaired of were denied the privilege of passing off the square. One was Norman Kenyon's twin, John. His military career had gone much as his brother, who passed out as best recruit, had feared: 'Last on parade, not dressed properly, gaiters on the wrong feet – he spent a lot of time in the cookhouse.' At the very last moment John Kenyon was marched off the parade ground. 'His rifle was waving around like a boy scout waves a pole,' says Norman. 'I didn't know what they'd done with him, but it was all right. They'd sat him in the guardhouse to book everyone out on their first leave.'

The airman in his best blues, the soldier in kilt or trews or (the majority) in bog-standard BD, went on that leave and walked about feeling ten feet tall, 'probably looking very poncy,' as Sir William Purves puts it. But milkmen and posties everywhere had a regular putdown, shouting across the road: 'Good job we've got a navy!'

3

A class act

Most old Etonians facing national service assumed that they would become officers. Eton, after all, bred leaders (18 prime ministers). Much the same assumption was made at other public schools such as Winchester, Harrow, Shrewsbury, and Stonyhurst, the Catholic public school in Lancashire, 'a very military school with seven VCs, more than any other school', according to Monsignor Bruce Kent. Many public schoolboys sought the Guards (there were lots of lords and honourables in the Guards, though religion played a big part where the Grenadiers were concerned – a regiment formed by the Catholic aristocracy in the name of Charles II). Others coveted the superior end of the Armoured Corps – especially the Cavalry – or the Rifle Brigade. 'The Cavalry was a family tradition,' says Mike Faunce-Brown. 'An uncle was a brigadier in the 13th/18th and another a colonel in the same regiment. There were various generals in the ancestor line going back several hundred years.'[1] Some chose elsewhere for personal reasons. 'My father was a regular soldier who had commanded a battalion of the Royal Hampshires and he wanted me to get a commission in his old regiment,' says the one-time *Panorama* reporter Richard Lindley. 'He would have been very disappointed if I hadn't – he wouldn't have been able to talk to his friends.'

Some candidates who went forward as potential officers were sponsored by schools with close links to particular regiments and corps, which gave them an entrée, but nothing worked as well as the old school

41

tie. Bruce Kent's personnel selection officer at Hounslow when he interviewed him said: '"Oh, I went to Stonyhurst. Tell me where you want to go and I'll fix it for you." I wanted the Armoured Corps and that's what I got.'[2] 'Most of us had fathers who were absolutely set on putting us into one regiment or other,' wrote the journalist-novelist Tom Stacey, who became a subaltern in the Scots Guards. 'They wrote to the Commanding Officers or saw them in their clubs.'[3] John Lyon-Maris, Blundell's and JTC cadet training behind him, was not enamoured of finding himself in the RASC and, while wanting a commission, certainly did not want it in the corps. As he lived in Sussex he wrote to the colonel of the Sussex Regiment through his father, 'and shamelessly worked it'. When Michael Heseltine found himself national service-bound he worked it shamelessly too. He was 'determined that, if I had to do it, I wanted to serve in one of the foremost regiments of the British Army.'[4] His father, a TA colonel in the Royal Engineers who, after the liberation of Belgium in the Second World War went there to rebuild the country's roads and bridges, pulled strings, his son had a chat with the colonel of the Welsh Guards, and Heseltine walked into the brigade's potential officer squad at Caterham.

Influence could come in unexpected guises, as Colin Clark, who wanted to be an RAF pilot but sensed at the end of his assessment that his chances were touch and go, found out:

> [The examiner] stood at the window, deep in thought.
>
> 'Look at that bloody sports car!' he suddenly yelled. I had parked the Allard in front of the building.
>
> 'It's mine,' I said.
>
> 'Crikey! Well, if you can drive that, you can certainly fly a plane,' he said, and he passed me right away.[5]

In the late forties the army called almost exclusively on the public schools for its national service officers, from which the regular officer class was drawn, like, after all, wanting to attract like. But as Britain's global problems piled up from 1950 onwards and the army swelled (reaching a postwar peak of 440,000), sheer necessity made them lower their sights and turn to the grammar schools. Nonetheless, the old school tie continued to prevail at the pukka end of the spectrum. For their part, the air force and navy were less interested in a man's family background than his education and whether he had cadet or reserve experience – the products of the public schools, of course, continued to meet the criteria.

Fewer graduates than might have been expected became officers, largely of their own choosing. The army and the air force desperately sought graduates particularly in maths and physics (in the army as specialists in gunnery and radar) but, as the RAF in the mid-1950s publicly stated, 'Graduates make a poor showing at officer selection boards'. When a representative of the chemical industry toured the universities in 1955 to interview honours science grads, he found that of the 15% who had done national service, hardly any had been commissioned and many had turned down the opportunity even to try. He also found that the majority of those who had not yet done their time were trying to get jobs in perm-anently deferred occupations. The British Association for Commercial and Industrial Education at its conference the previous year had been highly critical of graduates' attitudes; the educated had 'a clear lack of enthusiasm and duty,' it said. The association also wondered why those who had done national service preferred to be HQ clerical staff than officers, and concluded it was because they 'did not want responsibilty; and a fear of failure'.

To have a chance at RAF aircrew, cadet or reserve experience was a virtual necessity. The navy demanded reserve experience and, more than the other two services, sought maturity; almost all the few national service-men it elevated were graduates. One was Lord Lawson, the former Chancellor Nigel Lawson, who was possibly the only national serviceman the navy commissioned who had *not* been in the RNVR. Having gone from Westminster public school to Oxford where he took a first in philosophy, politics and economics, he arrived at HMS *Victoria* in Portsmouth, aged twenty-two, with no naval training at all. 'What happened was something of a freak,' he says. 'The navy rather bent its own rules – I didn't push it. I rather think they noticed me because I was blessed with a strong pair of lungs, which were an asset on the huge parade ground.' Lawson's exceptional national service continued: after serving on the frigate HMS *Relentless*, based in Londonderry, and then as first lieutenant on a former German E-boat,[6] he got his own command. *The Gay Charger*, a motor torpedo boat based at Gosport, was used to sea-trial new electronic and telecommunications equipment – 'the smallest vessel in the Royal Navy but even in 1955 costing a quarter of a million'. The ex E-boat ran on diesel, the British boat on aviation gasoline that was highly inflammable. 'It would not', says Lawson, 'have been a good idea to run it into the harbour wall.'

Unlike the army and navy, which waited to see how a man shaped up in basic training, the air force picked most of its national service potential officers even before they were conscripted (including about three-quarters of those who became aircrew). 'It paid to know how the system worked,' says Phil Wilkinson, who was in 'the light blue section' of the cadets at Maidstone Grammar.

Most men seeking a commission in the air force wanted to be aircrew (and most wanted to be pilots). The air force put candidates through a rigorous examination at RAF Hornchurch in Essex that involved written papers, tests of perception and dexterity, eye–hand coordination and acuity of hearing (listening to different frequencies on earphones) – and a medical 'so tough they almost failed you if you needed a filling in your tooth', says David Piercy. He had been in his ATC at Carnoustie and had not been pre-selected, but 'my Scottish education stood me in very good stead'. The failure rate was high: 1,300 men out of the 6,000 selected for aircrew training during the national service years failed to get their wings. Michael Myers was one of only four from 80 on his course chosen for pilot training, 'although some of the others were offered aircrew jobs like navigator and gunner'.[7] The broadcaster John Dunn failed to make aircrew because of his height. He did get a ground commission, 'but at the time I was devastated. I definitely wanted to be aircrew. I thought that if I could be a pilot I could do commercial flying afterwards. In fact, I was prepared to sign on for five or even eight years to get it. But they measured my thighs and they were too long – if I'd had to eject I'd have left my legs behind.'

The failure rate continued to be high during pilot training, mostly because men did not make the grade;[8] 'but some were bounced for indiscipline or flying too low', says Barry Purcell, a student engineer with De

Havilland at Hatfield who was already flying Tiger Moths and Chipmunks before he passed through Hornchurch. In some cases men who had signed on to fly and failed were allowed to reconvert to national service.

In the first few years it was possible for national servicemen to fly and still remain national servicemen. One who did was Michael Myers. A public schoolboy (St Paul's) from Dulwich, he had been in the cadets 'but I asked to be a pilot out of sheer bravado, really – I was scared of heights, even got sick on a roundabout.' The Korean War increased his national service by six months, but he was delighted:

> I had a place at medical school and this was a chance to fly jets – every schoolboy's dream. I rang them up and said, 'I'm not coming yet.' The only thing I have against national service is that I thought being a pilot should be good for pulling the girls but it didn't seem to be. At the time I didn't have a car. In fact I was able to fly a jet before I could drive.

By the mid-1950s it was a matter of signing on for three years or forget about flying: whereas a national service pilot could pass out from an operational flying wing on prop aircraft or the early conventional jets like the Meteor and the Vampire, the increased complexity of the likes of the swept-back-wing Hunter and Javelin took longer – and it was not worth the RAF's while. But for a little longer some national servicemen got to be navigators. One was Mike Watkins 'who grew up on aviation near Heathrow'. At seventeen he had won an RAF flying scholarship and been sent to a civilian flying school, but by the time he was going into uniform the only way he could have got pilot training was by signing on: 'So it was navigator or be an officer in the RAF Regiment. I chose navigator.' After basic training he was one of the last and very few national servicemen chosen to go to Canada to train with NATO. Barry Purcell also went to Canada a year later, as a pilot – but he had signed on.[9] Another national serviceman who became a regular was Ian Wormald, who took a cautious route:

> I'd spent three years studying chemistry but realised I wasn't going to be the nation's leading chemist and left without taking my degree. All my pals in

my part of Suffolk were flying aeroplanes and all that exciting stuff: and I played cricket and rugby, which stands you in good stead in the services. So the life was attractive to me. National service gave me a chance to have a look-see first.

He went in as an 'erk' (aircraftsman), decided the RAF was for him and, having signed on the dotted line, put himself forward for aircrew. It took a year for bureaucracy to work through, and he spent months at a defence radar station near Cromer 'turning up practically every Monday with my hand up, saying, "Please, I want to be a pilot." '[10]

*   *   *

Potential officers (POMs – potential officer material) generally had a torrid time during basic training, whether they did it alongside other recruits, albeit in special squads as happened in the RAF, the army corps and the Guards or, as was usual elsewhere in the infantry, were removed from their individual regiments and brought together at their brigade depots. At RAF Kirkham near Lytham St Annes, David Findlay Clark's POM flight was christened the 'Fucking Professors' and given 'the scruffiest, foulest old hut on the Station . . . the hardest time by the DIs [drill instructors] and our share of ribald and scurrilous comments by the other flights'.[11]

'It was the NCOs' last chance to give you a proper beasting, on the "so you think you're special, do you?" principle,' says Alan Protheroe, a reporter on the *Glamorgan Gazette* badged into the Welch Regiment in Cardiff but moved to the Welsh Brigade depot in Brecon along with POMs from the Welsh Borderers and Fusiliers. Here, in teams of six, POMs carried a telegraph pole everywhere throughout the day at double speed. Finally, they revolted. 'We got back to our Nissen hut one night and just launched the pole straight through the door,' says Protheroe, the Assistant Director-General of the BBC during the eighties and then MD of the Services Sound and Vision Corporation.

It was terribly cold and so we thought 'sod it', and burnt the door in the stove. Then we took the doors off several empty Nissens and burnt those and went on a bit of terrorising – we got on the roof of the sergeants' mess

46

and dropped live point twenty-two ammo down the chimney. We could have been RTU'd [returned to unit] but the CO took a considered view – and after that the regimen was less harsh.

'I think they gave us a pretty rough time,' comments Richard Lindley, removed from the Hampshire Regiment to the Wessex Brigade depot in Exeter. 'Certainly Eaton Hall [one of the army's two NS officer cadet training units] was a doddle after that.' The political commentator Anthony Howard, who had been to Oxford and done his bar finals before call-up to the East Surreys, agrees: Eaton Hall after the Home Counties Brigade POM squad in Canterbury was 'like swapping the YMCA for a posh hotel or a country club'.

Sailors had to satisfy layers of fleet boards that they were worth training as officer cadets (upper yardsmen); soldiers had to convince first their unit selection board and then the War Office Selection Board (the acronym WOSBE pronounced with a 'z' as 'Wozbe'). Those the RAF had pre-selected were already POMs, but airmen who had not gone this route had to make a mark during basic training and then get through the Hornchurch process. Ronnie Corbett was one who did, his height no obstacle, though after commissioning in the Secretarial branch his CO thought

> they might mistake me for a cadet [so] suggested that at all time I ought to wear the full number one dress as it was called – that is the peaked cap, the brass buttons, the works – as much as I had going for me in fact. So I spent the rest of my time at Weeton in a state of splendour.[12]

Wosbe is the most documented of the three services' approach to potential officer selection. In a word, it was about judging whether a POM had officer qualities. The consensus was that these were leadership, ability to discuss topics and express opinions, stamina, enthusiasm and inventiveness – but nothing was ever stated. As a result, men from every corner of the army (the Marines bought into the system, too) came to Barton Stacey near Andover in Hampshire (and very occasionally to alternative camps, all in the south), and tried to impress, like John Bingham, a Sheffield grammar school boy in the RASC, who 'for three days wore a brisk, alert gleam in my eyes, and tried frantically hard to be a clean-limbed young Englishman'.[13]

Over these three days a panel of officers, some of them very senior, set candidates written tests, interviewed them about themselves and their views, watched them in discussions, set them a lecture to give, put them over an assault course, and assessed them in a tactical task entitled 'Situations'. Most men, to some degree, felt they should be judged on their acting ability as well. As Willie Purves points out:

> I enjoyed Wosbe, but it was very phoney. On the first day we had a half-hour debate with three officers sitting there who asked what we were going to talk about. Some guy, public school, polished, suggested euthanasia. I thought I'd been fairly well educated at my local grammar, but the word hadn't crossed my path. I had no idea what the hell we were going to talk about. To cut a long story short, these fellows knew how to debate. I didn't participate at all. That was a negative mark. I was called in and pointedly asked about that. 'Well, Sir, it seemed to me a very artificial debate, people jumping up to say their piece in stilted language. I thought the whole thing very shallow.' But equally I knew that thereafter I had to work a bloody sight harder.

Candidates chose the subject for their five-minute lecture – Michael Parkinson chose butterflies. Received wisdom was that humour was dicey but many employed it successfully. Brian Sewell was unwell when he attended Wosbe – he tottered home afterwards to discover he had mumps – and remembers hardly anything of the three days other than his lecture. 'Other candidates spoke about how to keep a horse or similar subjects. I spoke on the lack of sexual symbolism in Aztec culture. The officer afterwards said, "I don't know whether or not you've been pulling my leg." ' In truth the subject was immaterial: what mattered was the confidence a man showed in talking about it.

'Situations' was rumoured to be the most important element of Wosbe; it was certainly the most surreal, involving men in teams of five, equipped with an assortment of planks, ropes, oil drums and other items in turn having to solve an evolving scenario with the help of the others. Sometimes a team would be presented with a set of circumstances to see who would emerge as the leader. Assessing what was being looked for when this happened to his group, the novelist-playwright Michael Frayn, who was in the Intelligence Corps,

> immediately stepped forward and took command. We had to get from the top of some sentry box across some imaginary ocean with a short plank and a piece of rope. I began to issue a stream of orders, saying 'You climb up on that man's back, then on to the sentry box, pull up the plank, pull up the next man.' And to my amazement, absolutely everyone obeyed this and they all did exactly what I said. The end of it was that they all fell off, and it was only by sheer fluke that they did not break their arms and legs. I then retired quietly into the background, shattered by this experience. I contributed nothing more to the discussion at all. I was so far in the background that I happened to be standing behind the officer who was in charge of the operation. I looked over his shoulder and saw on the clipboard opposite my number the words, 'Has ideas'.[14]

TV and radio programme presenter Robert Robinson also had ideas:

> And it was like a game [which] later became a national pastime under the title 'It's a Knockout'. In my case they gave me a telegraph pole and some rope and you had to work out how your team was going to lay this across an imaginary stream and use it as a bridge. After the log had plunged into the water twice, well short of the opposite bank, I twigged. In the history of this test no one had ever managed it, since the log was about five inches too short. What they were after was intelligent capitulation. 'Lads,' I said, 'let's paddle'. And we waded across. I saw the light of recognition in the eye of the man who was acting as referee. He'd spotted a fellow bullshit artist.[15]

Robinson's fellow radio colleague, Ned Sherrin, also had an inventive approach to a problem. At Wosbe from the Signals, but later commissioned into the West Kents, he cheated on the assault course. 'I got some implement under a line, not over it. The officer had looked away and I slipped it under. I could tell from the look he gave me that he didn't want to ask. I thought I'd shown officer qualities myself.'[16]

The army did not just want to ascertain that a chap could do the job: they wanted to know whether he would fit into the officers' mess. At Wosbe, adjudicators sat in at meals to judge candidates' social skills and conversation and at interview asked what newspaper they read, to which the 'right' answer was *The Times* or *Telegraph*. One man in the Royal Engineers knew he had done well on the practical tests, but in interview said his father took the *News Chronicle* and the *Sunday Despatch*. He was the only one on his course to be RTU'd.[17] Such failure, of course, could have had other reasons but long after the army democraticised officer selection the suspicion remained that the old rules sometimes still applied. Politically, the upper reaches of the army remained high Tory and, as late as 1956, there were newspaper allegations that Wosbe candidates were being asked questions like 'Does your father vote Labour?' and 'Are you a Bevanite?' and failed accordingly. 'I knew nothing of politics, but the brigadier was interested in rough shooting, so we talked about that,' says Mike Faunce-Brown (who went on to a commission in the 13th/18th of family tradition and served in Aqaba, 'keeping the peace between Arabs and Jews in Jordan').[18] Invariably men were asked why they wanted to become officers; a trick question, the young Auberon Waugh decided:

> The answer to this was too obvious to countenance: better food, better pay, the services of a soldier-servant [batman], and the chance to be on top of all the semi-human brutes who had been persecuting me for the past three months. Instead I said that while I would be happy to serve in either capacity, I felt I would make a very bad trooper and could make a better contribution as an officer. This was because I had a burning desire to know the reason for everything, a curiosity not to be encouraged in the other ranks . . .[19]

Passing Wosbe was not a foregone conclusion for anybody. A man might sail through, like the fellow from the Coldstream Guards on Tony Thorne's board who spent three days displaying an attitude of enormous natural superiority. While I rushed around from test to test, he hardly deigned to move himself at all. During one of the discussion panels he asked the examining officer if he might smoke and then lit up a large cigar and talked about Boodles.[20]

In the final analysis, however, it was all-round ability that mattered, not insouciance or even a title. The Lord Willoughby de Eresby, heir to the Earl of Ancaster, fell at the Wosbe hurdle and served his time in Cyprus as a lowly trooper in the armoured section of the Horse Guards, sharing a tent with the journalist Graham Williams ('and he spent all night, nearly every night, playing cards'). Old Etonian Viscount Enfield was sent back to the Green Jackets with a 'deferred watch' (a nearly-but-not-quite assessment that allowed a candidate to return for a second crack six months later), which he considers fair. 'I was keen but I wasn't confident enough,' says Enfield, now the 8th Earl of Strafford. 'Some months in the ranks did me a power of good. I was sent on a lance-corporal's course. I matured.' Other public schoolboys were among the outright failures, including the Salopian *Oldie* editor Richard Ingram (who did his stint as an instructor-sergeant in the Education Corps). Ex-BBC news correspondent and erstwhile MP, Martin Bell, failed (another who went to Cyprus, a corporal in the Suffolk Regiment), as did playwright Alan Bennett (who soon transferred from the Yorks and Lancs to the Intelligence Corps) and the actor Oliver Reed (an old Ewellian – though Ewell Castle was just one of his 15 schools) who, according to his biography, looked every inch the prospective officer at Wosbe and excelled at the physical side, but whose essay on the role of the modern army was 'a scribbled and disjointed muddle: his arguments were sound but his handwriting and vocabulary belonged to a thirteen-year-old. No one, least of all Oliver, had informed the army of his dyslexia.'[21] The dyslexic Reed returned to the Medical Corps and a session with the command psychiatrist.

Wosbe candidates learned their fate after a closing lunch when they were handed little envelopes that contained a slip of paper: Pass, Fail, Deferred Watch. Overall, a quarter did not get through and most were, naturally, upset. Mike Gilman from Burton upon Trent, who had taken a degree in the history of art and architecture at Manchester before going into the Royal Artillery, was unconcerned. 'I was told I didn't have a military personality. My father, who had been a private in the First World War, said that was a compliment.' Gilman went as a clerk to the army Chaplain's Department at Bagshot Park and when 'the Chaplain General came down he used to sit at one end of the table in my office and I'd sit at the other, and we'd put the world to rights. A regular sergeant used to come in and be horrified – a bombardier doesn't usually speak to a major-general.'

∗   ∗   ∗

Officer cadetship was an intermediate stage on the way to commissioning, in army and air force signified by a white disc behind the cap badge, in the navy by three broad white stripes on each shoulder. The army took its embryonic officer to either of its OCTUs (officer cadet training units): Eaton Hall near Chester or Mons at Aldershot. Most air force cadets went to the RAF OCTU at Jurby on the Isle of Man (aircrew trained at various mainland stations, though some of these also went to Jurby for instruction in ground subjects). In the navy, upper yardsmen did their training at sea on carriers, and at bases ashore, finally passing out as probationary midshipmen or sub-lieutenants, depending on age. The Welsh pharmacist, Hopkin Maddock, remembers the two dozen of his 1956 intake – the last national service intake, he thinks – parading at Wetherby in Yorkshire with 1,000 other sailors 'and those stripes made us stand out like nobody's business. We had to be better than everyone at everything'.[22]

OCTUs were first set up in the Second World War when officers had to be commissioned quickly. Eaton Hall, built towards the end of the 19th century as a residence of the Duke of Westminster, was a gothic folly, its profusion of turrets offset by a clock tower like a smaller Big Ben. 'It looked exactly like St Pancras station,' says Anthony Howard. Most cadets were billeted in brick huts in the extensive parkland; the lucky ones lived inside the hall in faded aristocratic splendour. Mons, in contrast, was a typical, sprawling army camp.

The infantry, Marines, Royal Engineers and Military Police spent 16 weeks at Eaton Hall, as did the Ordnance and Intelligence Corps, which in the field were more integrated with the infantry than other corps. The Armoured Corps and Royal Artillery spent 16 weeks at Mons, where the other corps did six, before going their separate ways for specialist training. John Lyon-Maris – headed for the Sussex Regiment but still wearing his Service Corps shoulder flashes – arrived at Eaton Hall to be constantly told: 'You should be at Mons.' 'I was unfortunate enough to be plonked into the middle of a company made up of the Brigade of Guards and the Rifle Brigade, where I was regarded as the lowest of the low and got all the dirty jobs like digging the latrines at battle camp and carrying the cooking hardware. But that was all right.'

In basic training his name had landed him in that group singled out for the NCOs' parade-ground attention, but 'at Eaton Hall a double-barrelled name didn't matter at all, there were chaps there with treble-barrelled names'.

All cadets wore the flashes, lanyards, headgear and cap badges of their parent units; at times the OCTU parade grounds were a sea of berets of colours, various, glengarry bonnets, Marines' peaked hats, the 'bus conductor's' hats of the Guards. What pulled squads of men together were the white discs behind their cap badges and the white tabs (gorgets) on their lapels. Out of camp army officer cadets were instantly recognisable by their riding macs and the fact that they wore hats – hats were de rigueur for officers in mufti and so it was for officer cadets; brown trilbies were most popular but green 'robin hoods' (with feathers) and corduroy flat caps (which some COs frowned on) were popular. Bowlers were obligatory in the Guards; rather fancying one, the biographer Michael Holroyd, who was in the Green Jackets (but eventually commissioned in the Royal Fusiliers) dug an old one of his aunt's out of her garage – once, she had ridden to hounds.

No one in the British army is as powerful by reputation as regimental sergeant-majors[23] and in the national service era the two RSMs who between them presided over almost all the history of Eaton Hall and Mons were the most powerful of them all: Ronald 'Tubby' Brittain of the Coldstream Guards and Desmond Lynch of the Irish Guards. Both were of such physical stature that they dwarfed all around them; Brittain, who went to Mons from Sandhurst, was said to have the loudest voice in the army;[24] Lynch – who trained 80% of all RSMs of his time at Caterham before going to Eaton Hall and then replacing Brittain at Mons – was very little behind him. 'While you are here you will call me Sir and I shall call you Sir,' both told newcomers to their domains. 'The only difference will be that you will mean it.'

NCOs, too, called officer cadets sir (if by name, Mister), but much of the patter was familiar: '*Am I hurting you, Sir? I ought to be, I'm standing on your hair.*' But there was little profanity (discounting moments of exasperation) and no personal insults: the drill instructors were the cream of the army, all Guards warrant officers or other senior NCOs; their authority needed no reinforcement – and they showed those who thought they knew all there was to know about performing on the square otherwise. It was a pleasure to be drilled by Lynch or Brittain. 'I thoroughly enjoyed RSM Lynch, he was so good at his job,' says Richard Lindley. 'At times he had us roaring with laughter, but in an instant could switch us off. Being drilled by him was, I don't know, almost transcendental.' 'The best way to march is to a military band,' says Derrick Johns. 'Well, Brittain was better than a military band.'

At both OCTUs the best recruit in each company became junior under officer, a 'rank' denoted by a scroll-like motif worn on the cuffs, with the pick of them winning the coveted sword of honour as senior under officer. In 1959, when national service was running down, Eaton Hall had closed and its functions absorbed at Mons, Michael Heseltine, then twenty-five, became a JUO – a huge achievement at a time when there were 900 cadets in four huge wings (Armoured Corps, Artillery, Infantry, and Primary for the corps). But he missed out on the privilege of leading the passing-out parade as SUO, 'because it was felt that, at my age, I had an unfair advantage over the rest of the intake'.[25]

Trainee officers in all three armed services were subjected to intense discipline and activity but, like other young men, found time for some high-spirited foolery. At Wetherby, Upper Yardsman Hopkin Maddock was delegated to break the church pennant at the masthead, which he had furled the night before. With the company mustered and on parade, 'the pennant flew from the masthead with one tug of the rope – and showered our captain and officers with confetti. I was the only bloke out of 1,000 on parade who couldn't have been guilty.' At Mons on more than one occasion the adjutant's horse, which followed passing-out parades off the square, was demonstrably groggy because his water bucket had been spiked. At Eaton Hall cadets once famously filled with water the mounted statue of a long-forgotten Duke of Westminster that stood on the corner of the square. They drilled a small hole in the tip of the steed's member, plugging it lightly with wax – which worked loose during the passing-out, in the presence of Princess Margaret. RSM Lynch's favourite escapade also happened at Eaton Hall. The cadets were out at battle camp, dug into trenches, and they were fed up. So they advertised a bring-and-buy sale back at the hall, proceeds to Sir Desmond's Home for Distressed Gentle-folk, 'and 300 spivs from Liverpool turned up with loaded vans, and hundreds and hundreds of other people. Mind you, the commandant had to go down later and apologise to the mayor of Chester.'

*   *   *

Getting to OCTU was not a guarantee of a commission. Very few failed at this stage but it happened.[26] One who came unstuck was the Labour MP for Linlithgow, Tam Dalyell, an old Etonian tenth baronet who was to be commissioned in the Scots Greys – the very regiment that his nine-times great-grandfather had raised in Scotland in 1679, as commander-in-chief of Charles II's forces.

Dalyell had successfully negotiated the Royal Armoured Corps at Catterick and Wosbe, but near the end of his time at Mons, on an exercise over Salisbury Plain when he was acting as troop sergeant, he 'lost' an armoured car:[27]

> The truth is I hadn't got the faintest idea where the thing was – I made a balls of it. They said I panicked and that was true, but my diffi-culty, bluntly, was that a captain who shall be nameless right through training thought I was playing on my name, which I really wasn't, and this was his opportunity. And, bluntly, some of my contemporaries in G Squadron, who shall also be nameless, were shits. One needs a great deal of luck in one's contemporaries in life and it just happens that there I wasn't.

The colonel of the Greys felt that the RTU'd Dalyell should be allowed to try again and, as the regiment was about to embark for Germany, suggested he could fix a transfer to the Queen's Bays. Dalyell chose to stay with the Greys and served his time as a trooper. 'Of course it was potentially a bed of nails, but I am a toughie. And I was quite good tank crew, certainly competent. And I was lucky with the people with me in Germany.'

There was no guarantee that a man would be commissioned back where he started: numbers required in regiments were limited, grand outfits oversubscribed, and poor marks could get someone downgraded, forcing him to seek an opening elsewhere; shortly before passing-out, officer cadets filled in a form, making three choices. Because he needed a second shot at Wosbe, the Green Jackets declined to have the Viscount Enfield back and he transferred to the Royal Sussex. Willie Purves, a JUO at Eaton Hall, had arrived from the Black Watch but hankered for what he considered his regiment – the King's Own Scottish Borderers – which had the added attraction of being about to go to Hong Kong. He made the Kosbe his first choice, the Black Watch his second and was quickly summoned to see an officer – who happened to be Black Watch. 'I marched in and this chap, without looking up, said "Under Officer Purves, I see that you have had the temerity to put the Black Watch as your second choice. We do not accept officers who put us as a second choice. I am erasing it from your application form. Dismiss." '

Nick Harman was not rejected by the Guards – he rejected them. The old Etonian had assumed 'my destiny was to serve with the footguards', but a muddle-up put him, along with another POM called McGuinness from Shrewsbury, in an ordinary squad at Caterham, where they witnessed behaviour they might not have been aware of had they been in the potential officer squad as they were supposed to be.

It was common for NCOs to take dirty or lazy or oddball characters to the bathhouse and scrub them in cold water with big brooms. In some cases the skin came off. I fully accepted the need for discipline and some ritual humiliation, but this was disgusting. It was shaming with what enthusiasm some of my fellows joined in, but that is another matter.

After finishing at Eaton Hall, Harman told the Guards that 'I wanted no part of their undesirable institution. They were horrified. "Don't you realise what an honour this is?" They were particularly horrified because McGuinness turned them down as well and it wasn't a concerted thing.' Instead of the Coldstreams for which he was headed, Harman went to the Royal Fusiliers, 'Cockney blokes, wonderful, funny, many deeply criminal. When they got depressed marching, they'd start to sing: "We are a shower of bastards, bastards are we, we all come from London, the arsehole of the Empire and the universe".'

Some subalterns either volunteered or were simply posted on secondment to armies in the colonies, receiving a culturally enriching as well as a military experience. A single national service officer is on record as serving with the Arab Frontier Force; scores served with the King's African Rifles in East Africa and, on the other side of the continent, with the Royal West Africa Frontier Force in Nigeria, Gold Coast, The Gambia and Sierra Leone. John Lyon-Maris, having got himself out of the RASC and into the Royal Sussex, became the first national service officer to get a secondment to West Africa.[28] The campaigning journalist Paul Foot (badged into the Shropshire Light Infantry) was seconded to the West Indies Regiment in Jamaica, where his father was governor, and remembers the postings officer apologising that 'there are natives in the mess, officers, do you realise, Foot?' – and adding, when Foot expressed enthusiasm – 'We do pay, we pay eight shillings a day extra for this. We call it wog money.'[29]

One group of national servicemen could not fail to become officers: uniquely, doctors entered the armed forces already commissioned. More than a few were distinctly unmilitary and a few, perhaps, had accents that might not have negotiated the usual officer selection process, but the services were in sore need of their skills. The navy badged national service medics into the RNVR as if they were volunteers and in some way did not quite belong to the 'real' senior service. At Lytham St Annes, the RAF's rookie MOs were drilled in seclusion, as were the army's at the Medical Corps depot in Church Crookham in Hampshire. 'They had to learn enough to go on the square without disgracing themselves,' says Dr John Blair.

I think most were acceptable. The navy didn't much go in for marching so NS medical officers weren't exposed; they did cutlass drill at Portsmouth, but where that was normally done at double spacing in the interests of safety, with medical officers it was done at triple spacing. According to friends of mine, in the RAF the medical officers didn't march past anybody and were truly awful.

National service threw together men from all backgrounds and walks of life and assuredly helped to mobilise social change. But that change, often seen as a major side-benefit of national service, was not helped, Anthony Howard thinks, by the way

> The potential officer class, anyone with any pretence of an education, was quickly whisked away as if they might be contaminated by the others. I was at Kingston [the East Surreys' training camp] for a single week before being removed to Canterbury. It was social apartheid from the beginning. Getting a commission was all about having an acceptable accent.[30]

The matter of accents causes Nick Harman some amusement: 'At Caterham, a Scouser in the barrack room said one morning, "You were talking in your sleep, Harman" and I said, "Really, sorry, don't think so" and he said, "Well, it was either you or McGuinness, you both talk funny".' Later, in Korea, Harman's platoon sergeant in the Royal Fusiliers, who during the Second World War had been a temporary captain in an Indian regiment, said he liked the British army because you could tell an officer even in the dark by the way he spoke. 'He was a bright guy and he was joking,' says Harman, 'but he was making a serious point, too.'

*   *   *

In the national service years, the navy commissioned some fifteen hundred conscripts (including Marines and Fleet Air Arm), the air force just over 9,000 and the army 35,000, 26,000 of them at Mons.[31] At the end of their time at OCTU, emergent national service officers, like all national servicemen finishing their training, had their group photo taken and passed proudly off the square. The pleasure of seeing their names gazetted in *The Times* was yet to come but, furnished with a £40 allowance, they had already taken themselves off to one of the services' specialist outfitters to purchase their uniform and accessories (an officer's peaked hat was a fiver, a second-hand Sam Browne belt a pound or two more), in which, understandably, they strutted like peacocks. Robert Robinson

> rushed back from Aldershot in my Second Lieutenant's uniform by the first train and hammered on the front-door. There was no answer. I went round the back and found a key. When I got in my parents were asleep. I had to wake them up to watch me parade round their bedroom in my new uniform. It was the first major anti-climax of my life.[32]

As many would find out if they did not already know, some regular officers at their new postings would be less than welcoming, viewing them, at least until they proved themselves, as transient interlopers. The other ranks they would command were going to be just as likely not to see them as the genuine article and, in addition, national service ORs would always think, in some curious logic of Us and Them, that they had sold out. National service officers had a lot to prove, up and down the chain. For their efforts, the government paid them 13 shillings a day.[33]

4

Now what?

The perversity that seemed to so many to have sent them as far as possible from home for basic training seemed to persist when it came to postings home or abroad. Received wisdom was that you should request the opposite of what you really wanted. The truth was that in days before computer databases armed forces' clerical staff, harassed at all levels of command from the War Office down, jiggled thousands of documents daily, filling gaps in units as necessity demanded. Where a man went was luck of the draw.

Second Lieutenant Brian Sewell, RASC, who had been taken off a draft for Korea to attend Wosbe and still felt guilty about it ('I would have preferred to be a private in Korea than an officer in England'), scrawled across his request form 'Anywhere abroad' – and got Blandford in Dorset. RAMC subaltern David Weatherall (later Sir David Weatherall, professor of medicine at Oxford) asked to serve in Britain because of an innate fear of flying – and got Singapore. Roy Battelle, qualified as a REME fitter-turner, asked for a posting at home because he was married – and got Cyprus: 'Only two of us out of thirty were married and only two of us went abroad – and both to trouble spots. That was a far hope that was.' Some men who were engaged hurried to get married when they knew they were going overseas: a wife qualified for an allowance, up to £3, depending on her husband's rank. Roger Keight from Olton near Birmingham, a lance-corporal after trade training as a REME radio engineer, sought his

CO's permission to marry – as service regulations demanded – and honeymooned in Bournemouth before going to Malta. Eric Brown, a plumber from Cardiff, on his way with the Welsh Fusiliers to Bermuda[1] ('Lucky for me, not so lucky for her') also tied the knot: 'It was a sensible option – we were being separated by the army anyway and being married was worth another thirty-seven and six a week.' He had already had embarkation leave before he and his fiancée made the decision 'but I went to a very fine sergeant-major at Brecon, a very decent man who looked after the national service chaps more than the regulars. I wasn't entitled to any more time, but he agreed – I don't think he even took it to the commanding officer. We were married by special licence and had four days in London.' Trooper Alan Herbert, a finished engineering apprentice from Fairford in Gloucestershire, married his fiancée Zita before going to Germany, and the couple were glad of the extra money: 'We put it into a savings account – Zita still lived with her mum and dad and was working as a typist in a company that manufactured pumps. We had enough to buy some basic furniture when I came back and we set up home.' Herbert would have liked to marry in uniform, 'but I was between regiments – the 3rd Carabiniers and the Hussars – so I didn't belong to anybody'. The date was 23 April, St George's Day, 'and every anniversary I kidded her I got the flags flown on the churches in celebration of it – and she believed me for a bit.'

Unusually, Adrian Walker, who had transferred from the Ox and Bucks to the Intelligence Corps, got to Cyprus by drawing lots. 'There were thirty-odd of us and all but four were headed for Germany. Nobody wanted Germany, we saw it as boring. We all wanted one of the postings to Cyprus whatever the situation there. So our sergeant said we'd draw lots. I've never heard of that happening anywhere else.'

The home or abroad issue was as hit-or-miss in the air force. Having failed only by weeks to make aircrew in late 1956 – the RAF having just called a halt to training national servicemen – Pilot Officer Phil Wilkinson had gone through Jurby and done an intensive course in fighter control but, like other national servicemen with him, was unsure whether his prospects were more exciting in Britain or overseas:

We young tyros had no idea, so we checked with the older members who'd trained with us, who included 'Ginger' Lacy, the Battle of Britain ace. They told us tales of the exotic and richly varied lives we would lead in the Near and Far East stations and underlined the benefits of duty-free existence with the 2nd Tactical Air Force in Germany. Needless to say, they all went overseas. The national service youths were firmly based in the UK.

Aircraftsman Stanley Colk did not even make an application one way or the other – he was on his way to Malta from RAF Rugeley in Staffordshire before he had even finished his six weeks' basic training. 'One day I was suddenly told, "You're going tomorrow." For a moment I thought I was being released. "Where am I going?" "Abroad." "What am I going to do?" "It must be something you wanted to do" – but I hadn't asked anything of anybody. I'm the only airmen I know who never passed out.'

Very few national service sailors got abroad; some made it to the huge bases at Gibraltar, Malta and Singapore, mostly as storemen or writers (clerks),[2] but the majority were employed in the UK in the same jobs. Only a small proportion of the comparatively few conscripts taken by the navy even got to sea. One was Lawrence Bell, whose training as an ICI instrument engineer led to his becoming an electrical artificer, with the rank of petty officer (equivalent to sergeant). He served in the Med on HMS *Vanguard*, a major battleship of the time, one of about 100 national servicemen in a crew of 1,500. 'I considered I'd fallen on my feet,' he says.

In the early years of conscription, one man in two did see service overseas; in the end years it was fewer than one in three. A good proportion served both at home and abroad but, overall, 50% never left Britain and only one man in 12 served in an active theatre of operation.

*   *   *

For a decade of the national service era, the overwhelming majority of the army went overseas by troopship, mostly from Southampton but also from Tilbury in London, and from Liverpool – occasionally augmented by naval aircraft carriers when larger than usual numbers had to be moved quickly – to Korea and, in 1951, to Egypt when violence against the British presence escalated sharply. In 1948 there were 22 troopers, most about 10,000 tons; by 1952 there were 14. Best-known names included the

Dilwara, *Dunera*, *Devonshire* and *Asturias*, which usually went to the Far East; and the Empires *Ken*, *Clyde* and *Cheshire*, which usually covered the Middle East run. The best ships before the purpose-built *Nevasa* and *Oxfordshire* were added in the mid-fifties were the three former German vessels, the Empires *Orwell*, *Halladale* and *Fowey*, the last regarded as the most comfortable of all. Built in Hamburg as the liner *Potsdam*, it was taken as a war prize in 1945, renamed, and given a five-year refit before going into service in 1950.

The Empires *Pride* and *Windrush* had particularly bad reputations. The *Windrush* – famous for bringing the first Jamaican workers to Britain in 1948 – was another former German luxury liner, the *Monte Rosa*, which had plied between Hamburg and Buenos Aires, but it had been used as a trooper and then a hospital ship in the Second World War and was in poor condition when acquired by the British.[3]

Troopships were worlds of their own: anything from 600 up to 2,000 men crammed together below decks in cavernous ill-lit holds, the noise indescribable as boots clumped on the decks and clanged on the companionway ladders, the sustained roar of voices echoing in enclosed spaces, the constant thump of the engines. Accommodation was spartan on the best ships and squalid on the worst. 'I had grown up in the slums, but I had never heard of a ship that had a slum area,'[4] was the considered opinion of Londoner Maurice Micklewhite (not yet Michael Caine), Korea-bound with the Royal Fusiliers, when he saw the *Halladale*; it bemused him that a bunch of men 'born and bred within the sight of London Docks' had to travel to Liverpool to embark. On some ships men slept in iron bunks, on others on three-tiered bunk-beds called 'standees', in yet others in hammocks, almost touching, 'hung from the metal structures like dozens of cocoons waiting for spring to arrive,' Roger Keight thought when he boarded the *Dunera*. Messing arrangements also varied. On some men were detailed daily to the galley several decks up to bring down huge containers of food; others provided canteens.

Despite the conditions, most men found boarding a ship – which sometimes cast off to the strains of martial music from a regimental band on the quay – exciting, the beginning of an adventure. 'Most of us hadn't even been in a car,' says Cliff Holland, who, embarked on the *Halladale* with the Manchester Regiment, thought they were headed for Korea (the war had just started) but found out halfway through the voyage that they were going to Malaya. 'Can you imagine looking out a porthole and seeing an Arab on a camel?' asks Eric Michaels, a painter and decorator transferred out of the Border Regiment into the Manchesters, who followed shortly on the *Dunera*. 'I saw that when we went through the Suez Canal. For a lad who'd never been out of Carlisle, that was a sight I can tell you.' Down the Canal servicemen gathered on the bank to wave and shout out friendly jibes like 'Pinkies!' and 'Get your knees brown!'

Voyages were slow, with stops at various places to unload men and sometimes pick them up; getting to Hong Kong took up to seven weeks. Many men have happy memories of uneventful trips, calm seas, mysterious coastlines, leaping porpoises and hours of sunbathing ('We were told to toughen our skin for Malaya but lads were charged if they got sunburnt bad,' says Eric Michaels. 'You can't damage the army's property'). But sometimes there was trouble, exacerbated by the cramped conditions and extreme heat. A lot of gambling took place to pass the time (mostly the card game crown and anchor) and big losses could result in fistfights, particularly when men from different units were involved. The authorities were aware that, for reasons buried in the past, there could be more than rivalry between some regiments and tried not to assign them to the same passage, but it was not always possible.

The army kept problems to a minimum – and men up to combat scratch – by barrack-room disciplines, regular physical exercise including running round the decks, and gun practice that involved firing at inflated balloons[5] or old oil drums thrown overboard. When ships called into ports such as Valletta on Malta, Aden in the Yemen, Port Said in Egypt and Colombo in Ceylon (Sri Lanka today), the infantry went ashore to slog it out on route marches – which made them glad to get back aboard.

The Mediterranean could be hot but those on their way to the Far East were frequently laid low by what they experienced going through the Canal, the Red Sea and the long stretch of the Indian Ocean. On some ships, depending on the captain, men were able to sleep on the decks (though it meant rising very early when the Lascars hosed them down); but more often than not they were confined to their unventilated quarters below the waterline and, subjected to 100% humidity, large numbers suffered heat exhaustion and rashes. Medical officers, almost all national servicemen, were kept busy with daily sick parades, sometimes of hundreds.

Before entering the Med all ships came through the Bay of Biscay. Storms could hit anywhere, but the Bay was notorious and virtually an entire passenger list could be laid low with seasickness. Men in hammocks – which almost none, naturally enough, had ever slept in – suffered the worst as they swung 30 degrees to one side and then 30 degrees to the other. Ships' crew put large bins in the sleeping quarters, which were in constant use day and night, but, Adrian Walker remembers, 'the floor was a porridge of vomit and equipment'. Acker Bilk, transferred out of the Somerset Light Infantry ('That double marching was a bugger, I was glad to be shot of it') into the Royal Engineers and headed for Egypt, remembers sailor-passengers on his ship going out to join the Mediterranean Fleet 'being sicker than the squaddies. We told them, "You've got another eighteen months of this, mate." '

The *Dunera* hit a Biscay gale while Roger Keight was aboard and, on his way to the canteen, he had to step over prostrate bodies littering the ship. Fewer and fewer appeared in the canteen with the passing days. On one occasion as he tried to eat, Keight watched someone get 'a dollop of this and a dollop of that' in the compartments of his meal tray and attempt to reach a seat.

> He started to walk uphill towards me just as the boat rolled to port. After a few tottering steps the boat rolled to starboard and his plodding uphill suddenly became a rapid downhill gallop. He was still running and holding his tray straight out in front of him when his solar plexus smashed into the end of the table next to me. The collision doubled him up like a penknife, knocked every bit of wind out of him and ejected the tray from his hand. It hit the wall, neatly turned upside-down just as the boat rolled again, travelled rapidly back along the table on which he lay and deposited every bit of his meal all over him.

Bad weather apart, for officers the troopships were an altogether more pleasant experience. They were accommodated in cabins above the waterline with portholes that could let in some air and if, on the older ships, they slept four to a cabin, their circumstances were luxury compared with those endured on the decks below. Their food, too, was better and, on the good ships, excellent. And sometimes, when wives of regular service-men (perhaps with nubile daughters) were travelling to join their husbands, officers enjoyed a more than passable social existence.

Medical Corps Lieutenant David Weatherall was something of an exception. He had left for Singapore on the *Fowey* with a battledress, a threadbare suit and an other ranks' jungle kit. On the first night at sea, when the regular army officers turned out to dine in their immaculate blues, his suit caused comment and the commandant ('he had a hairline moustache and an even thinner sense of humour') ordered him to wear battledress with collar and tie. Later, in the heat of the Red Sea, when the other officers changed into their tropical monkey jackets, Weatherall reverted to his suit – and was ordered to wear jungle kit with collar and tie:

My other ranks' jungle jacket and trousers, provided 'for emergency use' only, were packed in a small ball at the bottom of my luggage. I asked the cabin boy to press them but he was overgenerous with the starch, which precipitated into a series of large white spots, which covered the entire garments from head to foot. My appearance at dinner, in the company of immaculate young Sandhurst products and their elegantly dressed wives, was a nightmare, which drove me to a period of fasting and obtaining all my calories in alcohol.[6]

More typical was RAMC Lieutenant John Donald from Glasgow, posted to Korea and who also travelled on the *Fowey*, in the company of the Royal Scots and an advance party of the Essex Regiment: 'The glittering uniforms at dinner, white jackets, dashing cummerbunds, black ties and silver rank badges and medals, particularly after leaving the Bay of Biscay, were completely beyond my experience.'[7]

Some commissioned national servicemen felt guilty at the disparity between their onboard lives and those of the other ranks, not that they could do anything about it. 'Conditions below were absolutely dreadful,' says Nick Harman, heading for Korea with the Royal Fusiliers on the *Halladale*.

> The overcrowding was amazing – half a dozen blokes sleeping in an area about the same size as a second-class railway sleeper. It was unbelievably hot in the Red Sea in August. Below, all was confusion, heat, noise, the smell of farts and vomit. I went round the ship as orderly officer asking, 'Any complaints, lads?' Something of a joke, really.

The RAF used troopships to move men to parts of the world outside Germany, or occasionally its own air transport, or booked small numbers on to passenger liners to the Med; Stanley Colk, in a party of eight, went on the *Charlton Star* to Malta – where he was to find out he was to be the clerk to his station's senior technical officer ('Can you use a typewriter?' he asked. 'Never mind, you'll learn') – and he was thrilled: 'A passenger ship! Me! It was out of this world!' But for postings to Germany the bulk of airmen, like soldiers, went by troop ferry and train.

The ferries that ploughed back and forth between Harwich and the Hook of Holland – like the *Empire Wansbeck* (a converted Danish mine-layer), the *Empire Parkeston* and the chartered ss *Vienna* – were small, elderly and described by those carried on them as rust buckets and death traps, and men were 'loaded' on to them, according to Karl Miller (later the literary editor of *The Spectator* and *New Statesman* before editing *The Listener*) who went to Germany with the Royal Engineers, 'like a netful of gorillas or a deck of refrigerated whale meat'. The short Channel crossing was frequently rough and when it was there was little chance of any shut-eye on the standees crammed in the airless holds – too many were in the throes of seasickness. Gunner Glyn Jones, on his way to Düsseldorf, was not affected and, as he was nearest the ladder, 'I was made responsible for making sure everyone got out if there was an emergency – which made me think. I do remember how good the sailors were coming round with buckets cleaning up the sick.' His trip continued to be eventful: on one of the trains that took servicemen onwards from Holland his kit was stolen from the rack. 'What I found out too late was that some professional soldiers, the old hands coming through at the same time, were often on the lookout for a good kit and they'd take it, leaving their tatty old stuff behind. It would have been nice to have been warned about such a thing.'

Three trains were colour-coded red, green or blue to make destinations clear: Hamburg, Hanover, and Paderborn and beyond. Accustomed to Britain's decrepit rail system, men were amazed at the size and comfort of the carriages, hauled across Holland by electric locomotives, and by equally immaculate steam engines from the German border. Here papers were checked by German customs and police and men who earlier had thrown cigarettes (purchased with their new-issued BAOR currency[8]) to Dutch rail workers – and even ten years after the Second World War did so feeling like liberators – were suddenly uncomfortable and ill at ease. As Alan Anderson, a Southampton corporation clerk on his way to Paderborn with the Royal Artillery, says: 'We looked at these blokes, grim-faced and officious, and were side-mouthing to each other, jokey but sort of meaning it, "They forgotten who won the war, then, eh?" '

The food provided on the trains made up for such momentary disquiet. Lunch was usually served on the German side of the border, men called in turn to the restaurant car to be served a meal of a quality that was almost unheard of at home until at least the late fifties. 'We [had] learned a very peculiar thing from those returning,' wrote Rodney Dale, transferred from the Suffolk Regiment to the Education Corps at Beaconsfield[9] and with a stint as a sergeant-instructor at a UK unit behind him,

> that on the way out we would think that the food was delicious, and on the way back we would think that the same food was terrible. This, we were told, was because the food in German messes was so good. On the train we ate succulent sausage, and potato fried in several different ways, and it was delicious.[10]

The services moved gradually towards using aircraft as troop transports. By the early fifties Airwork Ltd was operating 20 Handley Page Hermes – introduced in 1948 with a range of 3,500 miles and a cruising speed of 276 mph – for the War Office, cutting the six- or seven-week trip to the Far East (with half a dozen or so stops) to four days. Most of the aircraft were ex-BOAC, [11] commercial aircraft that had flown on the routes to

South Africa, and the interiors were luxurious in their day. In the early years of troop travel other aircraft were less than reliable. Jock Marrs, a cost clerk from Coatbridge in Scotland, posted to Egypt with the RASC in 1952, went on an Avro York from Blackdown, which had to land in Marseille (seven hours to repair an engine), in El Adem (ten hours, ditto), and was then taken out of service in Malta, where the troops waited three days for another plane. 'The York lived up to its reputation as the worst plane in service,' he says. By mid-1955, Airwork and a number of civil charter companies employing an assortment of planes –Yorks, Dakotas, Vikings and Hermes – were responsible for half the army's movements to and from theatres other than BAOR. As a concession to international sensibilities, troops on their way to the Far East wore civilian suits, issued to them at the London Assembly Centre, an unused station on the Underground between Tottenham Court Road and Goodge Street. Here, in tunnels that served as barracks, hundreds of men could be kept overnight, waiting to be moved. In Singapore they handed in their suits, 'civilian, tropical, grey'. In the first few years, troops had to wear their boots with their issue civvies (stowing them overhead during the flight); later the requirement was dropped and they were allowed to wear their own shoes.

Flights to Germany cut the eighteen-hour ship and train journey to 90 minutes (with duty-free beer and cigarettes available), but in the early fifties were taken mostly by service families; by the late fifties, all 200,000 movements a year were by air, a troop air centre having been specially built opposite Düsseldorf civilian air terminal.[12]

By the late fifties, the big troopships were carrying only about a third of all men in transit outside Germany. In 1960, as the last national servicemen were getting their call-up papers, just five troopers were left and one, the forces' favourite, the *Fowey* – which in ten years had made eight trips to and from Korea and altogether had carried over 40,000 men – docked in Southampton for the last time. At the end of 1962 the very last trooper voyage was made by the *Oxfordshire*, which returned the Highland Fusiliers from Singapore to the same dockside.

A few years ago, the national service historian Adrian Walker asked his granddaughter, Rosita, who had flown to Cyprus on holiday with her mother, what the journey had been like. 'She said, "It took an awfully long time" – in fact, four and a half hours. I forbore to tell her that when I went, it took two weeks. But that's how the world's shrunk.'

It is a world whose geography, thanks to package holidays and cheap international travel, and to global television news, is far better known. In the 1950s very few men posted to Cyprus, now such a familiar holiday destination, knew where it was. Cliff Holland had no idea about Malaya: 'You might as well have said Timbuktu. In fact I didn't even know there was a place called Malaya. I was a bricklayer with a very poor secondary education. All I knew was Manchester United, Manchester City, Manchester Ship Canal and a few beers on a Saturday night.' 'Korea? Never heard of the place,' says Albie Hawkins from Gloucester, a Co-op delivery-man ('on the old electrical vehicles') who fetched up fighting there with the Gloucestershire Regiment. Adds Charlie Eadie, an electrical winder from Glasgow who went to Korea with the King's Own Scottish Borderers: 'You could have told me it was on the far side of the moon for all I knew.'

5

'Some bloody police action'

Essentially, the British government saw national service as an insurance policy in the event of future global conflict and did not expect it to stay beyond the resolution of the turmoil and uncertainty left over by the Second World War. The government envisaged national servicemen as a kind of auxiliary that for a few years would flesh out the professional armed forces. It did not envisage anything like the Korean War hitting the fan, or that the armed forces would be so stretched that by the time the fighting was done there nearly three-quarters of the men in the trenches would be conscripts. But that was the way it turned out to be. The only concession the government could make was to stipulate that no conscript under nineteen was to set foot on Korean soil. The situation was so critical, however, that many a near-nineteen-year-old was dropped off in Hong Kong to await his birthday – and then got shipped over.

Men arriving in the Korean summer saw fresh green undergrowth and the round-topped hills filled with colourful azaleas. In the winter, before the snows, those same hills turned brown and barren and, pockmarked by shells and mortars above the abandoned valley paddy-fields, the landscape might just as well have been on the moon.

Korea, the so-called 'land of the morning calm,' 100 miles west of Japan, was a Japanese possession for 40 years until 1945 when it was divided into two countries along the 38th parallel of latitude. The Americans supported the South; the Soviet Union and China supported the communist North. Inevitably there were tensions, which suddenly spilled over at the end of June 1950 when the North invaded the South and quickly captured the capital, Seoul. Korea would have become a wholly communist state had the Americans not immediately sent troops, ships and aircraft, the United Nations then supported its actions – and the Soviet Union failed to use its security council veto. There was no formal declaration of war; the UN described the conflict as 'a police action'.

The first American troops on the ground were sent from occupied Japan. Soft from years of easy living, the 24th Division, 'one of the least impressive forces the US had ever put into battle', were too willing to give ground – and abandon their weapons – and together with the small South Korean army were almost driven into the sea. They were desperately holding a perimeter around the port of Pusan in the toe of the peninsula, when British troops got there[1] from Hong Kong (where, the British government feared, the Chinese might take advantage of the weakened garrison to occupy the colony). Later reinforcements would get some battle training either in Hong Kong or at Hara Mura in Japan. The Middlesex Regiment and the Argyll and Sutherland Highlanders, despatched as 27 Brigade, were pitched straight into the line. Their first impression of Korea was of a pervading smell, which they were to discover came from the barrels of human excrement used to manure the paddy-fields. Pusan quickly became 'Poo-san' or 'Phew-san'. In mid-September the US Marines outflanked the communist forces by carrying out an amphibious assault on Inchon halfway up the west coast and went on to retake Seoul. Their extended supply lines threatened – and under constant attack from naval carrier aircraft[2] – the North Koreans were put into retreat. At the end of the month the Gloucestershire Regiment, together with the Northumberland Fusiliers and the Ulster Rifles, Britain's long-promised 29 Brigade from the UK, arrived.

Had UN Commander-in-Chief Douglas MacArthur stopped at the 38th parallel, the war might have been as good as over but, apparently making a political decision under the UN flag which was to lead to his dismissal by President Truman in April 1951, he pushed on to the Yalu river on the border with Manchuria. Its border threatened, China in December threw the People's Liberation Army into the fight, which once again see-sawed south. Eventually there were an estimated one million Chinese troops in Korea.

As a War Office order prevented eighteen-year-olds from going to Korea – and as over half the Middlesex and a fifth of the Argylls were eighteen-year-old conscripts – both battalions were bolstered by volunteers (in many cases 'volunteers' in the age-old army sense of 'you, you and you'), drawn from other regiments in Hong Kong. Throughout the Korean conflict there were transfers into Korea-bound regiments – and the recall of Second World War reservists who protested bitterly that they had already done their bit.[3] But even if they had volunteered, men resented the loss of their regimental identity. Smyttan Common, a plumber from Coldstream in Scotland, volunteered while he was in Berlin with the Black Watch, but initially disliked having to join the King's Own Scottish Borderers: 'Losing your regimental identity was like losing your own – but at least I stayed Scottish.' Terry Brierley, a gravedigger from Huddersfield – originally in the Duke of Wellington's but who missed the Korean draft when his father was badly injured in a quarry accident – was subsequently transferred into the Northumberland Fusiliers: 'I didn't mind the hackle, but that badge felt alien, a white patch with a ring on it. I called it the frozen asshole, that's what it reminded me of.' Joe Pyper, an Edinburgh joiner, found himself in three different regiments: the Royal Scots Fusiliers on call-up, with whom he went to Germany; then the Argyll and Sutherland Highlanders (oddly, he was sent back to Scotland to join them); and, on arriving in Korea to find the Argylls were just coming out, their stint done, the Kosbes. 'They say you join the army to see the world,' he says. 'I joined the army to see the army.'

The manpower shortage caused reverberations for the British army everywhere and in 1952 there were five national service registrations instead of four, which virtually doubled the intake of the previous year.

To get to Korea, some national servicemen put on their age, like Albie Hawkins of the Gloucestershire Regiment (the Glosters): 'I wasn't the only eighteen-year-old to say I was nineteen and they accepted what we said, turned a blind eye, really – they could have looked at the records. I volunteered because I thought it would be a laugh, over in a month.' He joined his regiment just after 'MacArthur had annoyed the Chinese and dropped us all in the shite, excuse my French. Some bloody police action, eh?'

✳   ✳   ✳

Men arrived at Pusan in a variety of ways: direct by troopships and aircraft carriers, from Japan in all kinds of craft including fishing boats, coal barges, tramp steamers, tank landing ships. Some men flew in from Japan including Albert Tyas, a plumber from Wakefield in the Northumberland Fusiliers, whose Royal Australian Air Force Hastings aborted its first landing attempt because there was 'rifle and Bren gunfire at one end of the runway, clearing the Chinese out – while the Americans erected a marquee at the other without a concern in the world'. As the Ulsters were badly understrength, Tyas joined them.

Commissioned into his home regiment, the King's Own Scottish Borderers, Willie Purves had been posted to Hong Kong as he originally hoped, but after a month spent trying to stop illegal immigrants coming over the closed border with China, the Kosbies were ordered to Korea. He was left with the rear party to clean up the camp and followed on, bringing eight Bren gun carriers (one was lost over the side of the ship unloading). So where were the Kosbies? 'I asked and was told, "Up there somewhere, turn left, go north." We drove, with no idea where we were going, calling in to great American petrol dumps to fill up – just sign a piece of paper. Eventually we came to a little road sign with a bit of tartan diced from a glengarry.' Purves quickly discovered that 'the Chinese were bloody good and they moved fast, rubber shoes, bandoliers of ammunition, a sausage thing around their body with sufficient food for ten days, dried bran, a bag of rice, vegetables. They were far more mobile than we were in our vehicles. If they got behind you, you were in trouble.' The Chinese tactic of attacking in human waves – running straight into withering fire and their own artillery bombardments with total disregard for their lives – was something the UN forces never came to terms with. Troops believed that the cacophony of whistles, drums, klaxon and bugle calls that the Chinese employed as they drove forward was a deliberate ploy to unnerve them, but in fact were their only means of battlefield communication.

As far as the British army's weapons in Korea were concerned, it was the Second World War reloaded: the infantry were armed with the reliable .303 Lee Enfield rifle introduced in 1941. Given the long frontages British units were allocated, many men wanted automatic firepower and acquired American M1 carbines. Platoons also got hold of US Browning medium machine-guns to supplement the trusty British Brens. In the British lines other ranks had an allowance of two bottles of beer a day (as well as a daily tot of rum), and officers and NCOs ranked sergeant and above were able to buy whisky. As the Americans were 'dry', they were willing to trade. As Royal Fusiliers subaltern Nick Harman explains:

> My company had an excellent Browning heavy machine-gun bought for a case of whisky. 'One could acquire a pretty little sub-machine-gun – I forget the make – for a single bottle, better than our antique Stens, which were the poorest weapon ever issued to the British army – they had no stopping power, went off when they felt like it and regularly jammed. A couple of friends and I bought a US jeep for liquor, can't remember how much. We had to abandon it when the rain washed off the paint and showed it had previously belonged to the US Military Police.

For a year the war waged up and down the Korean peninsula before grinding to a halt, more or less straddling the 38th parallel. Here for two years, with occasional big pushes that gained or lost ground at terrible cost, the sides dug in facing each other, reminiscent of the trench warfare of 1914–18. Now the pattern of war was for periods of relative calm punctuated by artillery and mortar barrages of great intensity, frequently the prelude to savage attack and counter-attack.

*   *   *

The weather was also an enemy, capable at times of stunning the Chinese as well as the UN into inability to wage war at all. It could be so cold – commonly minus 20°F but down to minus 40°F in the first winter, the coldest on record – that engines froze solid if not started up at twenty-minute intervals, tanks and wheeled artillery had to be moved backwards and forwards to prevent them sticking to the ground, and men were warned not to breathe through the mouth or they risked frostbite on the lungs. At night, the cold was so intense it was impossible for men standing to in the fighting bunkers, invariably with a fifty-cigarette tin containing a lighted candle for some warmth (and perhaps the straw from the beer crates underfoot), to stay alert for more than two hours and often only managed one; clothes became covered in a layer of ice, icicles formed on the rifle barrels, and rifle bolts and the pins in grenades froze solid unless rubbed with a mix of glycerine and oil. Care had to be taken not to touch metal without gloves or risk removing the skin. In spring the ground thawed, the monsoon rains collapsed bunkers and trenches, roads and bridges were washed away in raging torrents – and insects and rats brought disease. 'It got to you – the weather, the waiting, the constant wondering when the next attack would come, the noise of the guns that all but lifted you off your bloody feet,' says Terry Brierley. 'But it was the rats I hated – they'd be running over you at night. We used to dig a hole maybe twelve feet square and six deep to throw all the rubbish in. When it was full we poured petrol on it and you'd see the rats stream out, hundreds.' The rodents stole milk and sugar to feed their young – and cigarettes to make bedding.

The first two British battalions from Hong Kong came in tropical kit (jungle greens), not because the War Office did not know better, but because there was no time for rekitting; later arrivals continued to think that as Korea was in the Far East, it must be tropical. 'We thought it was going to be red hot, like in Hong Kong,' says Brierley. Even battledress and greatcoat were sliced through by the Siberian wind and some men lost fingers and toes to frostbite. Brierley made friends 'with a chap who was twice as big as me, specifically so that when I was on guard and he was off I could wear his greatcoat over mine'. The British cadged American parkas, hats with flaps, and boots; and puttees popularly replaced gaiters, because they helped keep out the cold (and in the fever season offered protection against the haemorrhagic mite) and, just as importantly, were not liable to scrape together and make a noise on night patrol. By the second winter the British clothing included long johns, windproof combat over-trousers, double-thickness gloves, a new hooded anorak that was better than the American parka and CWW (cold wet weather) boots. Like all troops in Korea, the British had to learn to combat trenchfoot:[4] men were ordered to carry a change of socks and there were daily foot inspections. 'I got to know every man in my platoon by his feet,' says Willie Purves.

The dugouts (nicknamed hoochies) in which men lived were ideally cut into the reverse slope of hills and four feet down to be below the frost line. Protected by sandbags, piled earth, balks of timber, waterproof tarpaper and anything that could be scrounged, these were connected by trenches to the weapon pits on the opposite side, facing the enemy. Dugouts were heated by home-made devices: fireboxes constructed out of ammunition cases, or stoves, called chuffers, made out of shell cases filled with sand into which men dribbled petrol. Unless reasonably ventilated, by morning only the six inches at the bottom of dugouts were breathable – the rest was smoke. Petrol was so dangerous that some units forbade it and ordered men to use diesel, but this was frequently ignored as diesel spoiled the taste of food cooked on the chuffers. An even more dangerous practice was setting fire to plastic explosive sticks that burnt like phosphorus.

Innumerable accidents with exploding burners happened. 'We had so many, men regarded them as a joke,' says John Hollands, a Blundell's public schoolboy from Godstone in Surrey, who was a subaltern in the Duke of Wellington's. In *The Dead, The Dying And The Damned*, the best novel of the Korean War published three years after his national service ended – and which has outsold Leslie Thomas's *The Virgin Soldiers* – Hollands included an incident of a man engulfed in flames, running screaming from a dugout and dying, spread-eagled on the barbed wire. 'In America the publisher used that description in promoting the book and there were calls for it to be banned as being deliberately horrific – but it actually happened.'

Even in the front line the army tried to maintain standards. Men boiled snow for water or shaved in beer or warm tea (made from the icicles that festooned the bunkers), but on occasion they were filthy, not least from the soot thrown off by the chuffers. 'We lived in our clothes for weeks, smothered in lice and crabs,' says Charlie Eadie, in Korea with the Kosbies. 'Then they'd bring us back and delouse us and give us fresh clothes and we'd go back up. Bloody degrading being filthy, but there we are.' In the regular lulls in the fighting any necessary work was done in the middle of the day when it was less cold, 'but of course Johnny Chinaman knew this and he sent over three-inch mortars,' says Willie Purves. 'You'd be doing your ablutions and hear a pop and seek cover. I have a memory of a chap diving into a dugout with his trousers down.'

In the early months of the war British troops grumbled about their grub with justification, consisting as it did of little more than tinned bully beef, steak and kidney or frankfurters, tinned potatoes and hardtack biscuits. Out of the line, someone in each platoon did the cooking; in the line, the food was cooked at a central company point, sometimes in an oven fashioned out of an oil drum, and brought up in hay boxes on the backs of Korean porters. As whatever was cooked in winter froze as it left the frying pans, it could be almost inedible. At least there was never a shortage of tea, sugar and tinned milk – although men often had to hack it, not pour it. Soon the British got a couple of field bakeries up and running and sometimes were able to provide fresh meat and vegetables. In the main, however, the troops again turned to the Americans. Their individual 'C' ration packs contained such items as turkey, pork chops, steak, chicken noodles, pork and beans (almost everyone's favourite) and fruit cocktail – as well as chewing gum, chocolate and cigarettes, and a natty little tin opener. Men cooked their own meals in their mess tins. They did not, of course, stop grumbling, with lugubrious British humour. Edmund Ions, a short-service subaltern in the Border Regiment who volunteered for Korea and was there with the Ulsters observed that:

> Among the new national servicemen I had two cockneys, who were either barrow boys at home, or gave a perfect imitation of being so. They were our resident comics . . . When they settled down to their 'C' rations, sitting close together, they kept up a scornful and inventive patter.
>
> 'Cor, what you got on your menu tonight, Joe? See 'ere, salmon, caviar, steak, pickled onion, tomato sauce, bread 'n butter, loverley.' He held aloft the familiar frankfurter speared on his fork.
>
> Morale was no problem with men like this in the platoon. It was curious to think that at school they might have been the despair of a headmaster.[5]

'I came home with a "tinny" stomach from eating from tins – a lot of food from tins in those days did something to the lining of your stomach,' says Terry Brierley. 'I went to my grandmother's in Aberdovey and ate lots of fresh vegetables and fruit for months before I was right.' Tins, nevertheless, had their uses: 'We made booby traps out of them – hand grenade in, the pin out, the lever jammed against the side, and nailed to a tree with a string to another. I used to put them around my dugout in case they crept up on me at night.'

*   *   *

Why were they in Korea? Most men did not know or even care; they simply got on with it. John Hollands' novel features a visit from a newspaper reporter who could not make out their attitude to the war:

> They seemed to have no interest or concern in it, and when they talked of it, it was either with boastfulness or utter indifference. Few men betrayed any fear but none showed any enthusiasm. On several occasions he had asked men what they were fighting for and every time the answer had been to the same effect. 'How the hell should I know? Better ask the fellows who sent us here.' But strangely there was no bitterness, no demands for the right to voice as well as fight – nothing but calm acceptance.[6]

A very few men were not like that. Some refused to obey orders or deliberately misbehaved to get out of the line, even if it meant going to the glasshouse. Kosbe mortar man Joe Pyper talks of a private in his platoon who would not take his turn on the Bren set up to try to shoot down any enemy plane that came over. 'It was dangerous because you were exposed in the open, and he wouldn't do it. Willie [Purves] had him arrested and he went off to one of those punishment places to be chased up and down hills – field punishment they called that.' Smyttan Common, who was nominally Purves' batman (officers in the field mostly looked after their own boots and personal weapons), talks of an incident 'when things were going badly and a corporal left his position and was refusing to go back. Willie told him, "If you don't, I'll shoot you", and he would have bloody shot him.' In the Royal Fusiliers, Nick Harman 'had this chap who deliberately fired his Bren at night to draw fire. The soldiers knew what he was trying to do – get charged, get sent back to a rear echelon. The NCOs let it be known that they would be out of the platoon area for two hours and he got a thorough beating up.'

Some men purposely shot themselves (almost always in a toe other than the big and little) to get out of the fighting.[7] When Harman was wounded and evacuated there was another of his platoon on the hospital train who he thinks had done that – 'and the train was filled with US army Puerto Ricans who definitely had because they admitted as much'. Adds Terry Brierley: 'I saw a couple of lads shoot themselves in the foot and I didn't blame them. You get to a state where you honestly think you're not coming out.' Some men broke in the conditions. Kosbe infantryman Charlie Eadie went on R and R (rest and recreation) to Japan with a couple of pals and one went to pieces on their return. 'His name was Joe Strangle, a name you don't forget, and he was as right as rain in Tokyo. But when they brought up the truck to bring us back to the front, he refused to get in. He cracked up, a mess he was. But he still got three years in prison.'

Barry Whiting from Purley, who went from his sixth form to the Royal Army Medical Corps, says:

Some men were terrified beyond the point of tolerance. One national servicemen who'd been charged with cowardice came to us to be medically examined. He'd been confronted by Chinese in great numbers and then ordered into caves to flush others out. He simply couldn't do it – he shook like a jelly. He was sent back to the field detention centre in Seoul, a frightening place run by French Canadians who had a brutal reputation. I wish he could have been treated in a more humane way, but I don't know what way. If one man gets away with it others will follow and discipline would quickly break down – thousands of men were terrified, but they stood their ground.

Both sides sought a psychological advantage, firing shell and mortar canisters filled with propaganda leaflets; the UN side also dropped leaflets from aircraft, while the Chinese side frequently left them on the wire entanglements. Almost all the communist messages were aimed at the Americans, telling them it was no disgrace to quit an unjust war and promising safe conduct (with the phonetic forms of 'surrender' printed in both Chinese and Korean), but they came into British hands too. Charlie Eadie used to read them 'and listen to this Chinese woman's voice speaking in English over their loudspeakers telling you what you were doing was wrong, and many a time I thought I'd give in and go over, just creep away in the night'.

Because of the stresses imposed on men, the army rotated its battalions every few weeks: troops were replaced in the front line, those pulled out going into a tented area in reserve, usually about five miles back. The relief was intense for everybody but especially for those whose national service was almost done; superstition, as Charlie Eadie recalls, was 'that was when sod's law said you'd be killed or wounded'. In the Commonwealth Division, the Education Corps section produced *The Crown News*, a Roneoed newsletter that kept men up to date with what was happening in Korea and at home – the full listings inside of the football results were eagerly awaited – and units played in their own scratch football league, weather permitting. Most battalions erected some kind of cinema screen, and British film and radio personalities like Jack Warner, Ted Ray and Frankie Howerd came out to entertain the troops. Perhaps the most popular arrival was singer Carole Carr from the BBC radio variety show *Calling All Forces*, who was the only female in the Commonwealth sector, discounting the nurses in the Norwegian mobile army surgical hospital, when she came out in 1952:

> One of my most vivid memories is the show I did for the Welch Regiment in a rainstorm. They were getting soaked, so I asked them if they wanted me to carry on. They yelled YES, but they had the last laugh. Suddenly the canvas roof over the stage caved in and I was drenched . . . to a wave of cheers and whistles.[8]

At a concert for the Royal Inniskilling Dragoon Guards Carr asked for requests, in reply to which a voice shouted back: 'Don't sing, just stand there!'

Most men served about a year in Korea. Others did more (Terry Brierley served 14 months, transferring from the Northumberlands when they left to the Leicestershire Regiment), but were not asked to endure more than one winter period. In addition to time in reserve, most got a few days' break at the rest centre in Inchon and five days to sample the oriental delights of Tokyo or Kure in Japan. Some men could not afford to go, including Smyttan Common. 'I came from a big family and I left my mother ten and six a week. I drew fifteen shillings. The Australian and Canadians were well paid. We used to say the worst paid men in Korea were the Chinese and ourselves. When it came time for my Tokyo leave I couldn't go because I didn't have enough money to go.' Reuben Holroyd, a printer from Halifax who served with the Duke of Wellington's, only made it because his parents sent him some money. It was little enough. 'We were unable to go back at the end of our five days because of monsoons or typhoons or something, anyway, no planes were flying. So we stayed another five days flat broke and sat in the park looking at the birds.'

When he got to Inchon, Barry Whiting was overwhelmed by the numbers of children, many orphaned or missing limbs, living on the street:

> The kids who were lucky enough to be in an American orphanage came in organised groups to sing for us at the rest camp – and I felt I should be here, doing something. I was glad to be a medic in Korea; I wasn't killing people, I was trying to help. A rough infantryman who was pretty badly injured said to me, 'You know, I used to think you medics were namby-pamby cissies, but now, thank God you're here.' That was rewarding. But I felt I wanted to be in Inchon with the UN doing something for these kids, which was hopelessly idealistic and self-righteous. Anyway, I wrote a letter to a magazine describing their plight and I got a lot of letters from women who said they'd never thought of children being in Korea. People at home had no idea of the suffering.

✳ ✳ ✳

There were ferocious pitched battles in Korea, with the clashes on the Imjin river and further north on the gaunt hills of Kowang-San and Maryang-San, and the third battle of the Hook, among the most notorious.

In the spring of 1951, 29 Brigade's three infantry battalions – the Glosters, the Northumberlands and the Ulsters – were deployed near the Imjin river above the 38th parallel, protecting the main road to Seoul. Combat patrols probing the scrubby hills reported signs of an enemy build-up. After three weeks, the Ulsters were pulled out, replaced by a Belgian battalion that had been in reserve. That night the Ulsters were watching Doris Day and Gordon Macrae in *Tea for Two* when tracer bullets went through the screen. The Chinese spring offensive had begun. All UN units went back into the line.

The UN forces did not know it, but two divisions – 20,000 troops – had been thrown against them. 'We got hit proper,' says Gloster Albie Hawkins. Thinly spread on a front of 12,000 yards, the British and Belgians repulsed a series of frenzied attacks. Even as the battle raged a reinforcement of national servicemen for the Northumberlands arrived from a transit camp in Japan and was pitched into the line. After three days the brigade had run out of grenades and their casualties were heavy. Albert Tyas, the Northumberland Fusilier with the Ulsters, lost his best friend:

> I carried him down the hill and he died in me arms and that were that. Then the sergeant-major ordered me back up the hill. It were hopeless – the brigade had a seven-and-a-half-mile front to hold, the gaps were too great. We did well. We were almost all national service, with a bit of experience from reservists, who took charge. But it were hopeless.

The retreat began along the floor of the valley. Most Northumberlands got away. The Ulsters and Belgians found themselves in a shooting gallery when the Chinese took possession of the high ground above them. Two tanks of the 8th Irish Hussars came in and tried to help the withdrawal, men hanging on to them. With the Chinese 'spraying the tanks with bullets, which were bouncing off them like hailstones', Tyas saw men fall off the first and be run over by the second.

> As we came down the road, wounded men at the rear of us were screaming and then there was no screaming as the Chinese came along and picked them off where they lay. But the men who'd been run over didn't scream,

they were just a muddied heap. And then there were bloody dozens of Chinks all around us pointing their rifles at us. We were in the bag. They took our weapons off us, we went back up the hill over our positions, over the Glosters' positions, and kept on walking.

The Glosters, surrounded, had surrendered, including Albie Hawkins. 'We couldn't get out and nobody could get in to help. I was taken on Wednesday 25 April about 2.30 in the afternoon. According to the records there were about 400 of us.' Hawkins had been wounded twice.

On the Tuesday a grenade or mortar, no idea, bits and pieces caught me in the right hand and arm. On the Wednesday, same again, but this time hit me in the back and the head. I felt like I'd been given a hefty push, went arse over tip. Didn't realise I'd been hit until my mate pointed out the blood on my uniform. I don't know what was going on in my mind. Blokes were going down hit. It somehow didn't register. I know I was shit scared. No training prepares you for the live situation. After the battle we were like zombies. We came down into the valley, six of us together, and ran into this bunch of Chinks. One was fiddling with an automatic weapon and it went off. It was a mistake – but I honestly thought they were going to top us. In fact they treated us okay.

The Glosters had effectively ceased to exist as a fighting force: 59 had been killed; only 169 out of 850 mustered for roll-call after the encounter and most of them were from the rear elements of the battalion who had not been involved in the fighting. Only Second Lieutenant Denys Whatmore, a national serviceman from Farnborough in Hampshire who before call-up worked in the Admiralty, and three of his men, had made it from 11 platoon. Later, Whatmore was sent back to the Imjin to look for salvageable equipment. On the day after his twentieth birthday he climbed the hilltop, 'The smell of corruption so intense that I – a non-smoker – and all my little party began to smoke cigarettes at an intense rate':

All weapons had gone and the slit trenches had been stripped clean . . . The first man I found was on the ridge near the old Company HQ area, lying on his back, one knee in the air, relaxed, as though sleeping. But he was dreadful close to; as I opened his greatcoat and battledress to get at his pockets for his pay-book, he burst open into a stinking mass of writhing worms. He had, after all, lain there in the hot sun and the rain, for a month. It was very difficult to bury him. We found no bodies in the 12 Platoon position, so we moved down the ridge to my old position. Here, I learned the fate of two men from 11 Platoon. Their bodies lay in or near their trenches, their wounds unidentifiable in their decomposing state, no longer human. We approached them one by one, searched for their identity documents and discs, and got them underground as best we could . . . I hoped I would never be required to take on that sort of task again. But I was, though it was not nearly so bad next time.[9]

All told, the brigade lost about 1,000 men either dead, wounded or taken prisoner. They had inflicted perhaps ten times that loss on the Chinese.

*   *   *

UN prisoners taken at any time during the war were marched, sunup to sundown, to camps on the Korean side of the Yalu river. The march of some 300 miles took up to a month. They were not fed for days – but they were more worried about being hit by their own artillery or being bombed or, worse, napalmed. Americans captured by the North Koreans in the early months of the war were frequently badly treated, but the Chinese adhered to the Geneva Convention. 'The Chinese were all right. The North Koreans were bloody animals,' says Albie Hawkins, who on his way north 'did a runner' three times. 'Looking back, it was just bravado. If I'd had any sense in my bonce I'd have stayed with the column.'

The first couple of times two others went with him

and it was the Chinese who collared us. We got a belt around the ear, a kick up the arse. Fair enough. The third time I didn't know I was going in the wrong direction, north instead of south, and ended up outside Pyongyang – and that time I got nabbed by the North Koreans. That time they put me in an underground prison, tied up, with barbed wire round the walls so you couldn't lean back. There were about twenty of us in there all suffering from dysentery with one shell case and an ammunition case for toilets. The filth and the smell were appalling. Because I was by myself they were convinced I was special forces and interrogated me, during which I got a few beltings. I would have sworn blind they were going to shoot us. When they brought us out they tied every three blokes together, wrists and ankles. We'd been underground six or seven weeks, the fresh air hit us and we collapsed. Another belting. One of the North Koreans drew his finger across his throat and I thought we'd had our chips, but as luck would have it a band of Chinese came along just then, there was a ruckus between them and the North Koreans, and the Chinese told us to follow them. Thank you very much.

After that, Hawkins accepted his lot and even experienced a sense of pleasure when he got to his POW camp. 'The place was full, 600 to 800 of us, other Northumberlands, Ulsters, Artillery, Signals, tankies, medics. I was back among old mates.'

Most men were suffering from dysentery by the time they arrived, from drinking water from the paddy-fields. 'It looked clear enough but the nightsoil on the crops did for us,' says Albert Tyas. Many also had lice, picked up from the straw on which they slept. 'They were the soul destroyer, they got into everywhere, up and down the seams, laying eggs. We didn't rid ourselves until Christmas the first year. You feel rotten when you're not clean.'

In the camps, men were able to fetch wood from the hills to boil their water and do their cooking and, by keeping the hut fires going at night, and with a blanket a man and a padded quilt between two, they were also able to stay reasonably warm. 'It was cold beyond compare,' says Tyas, 'minus thirty, forty, once fifty, and we're talking centigrade. A comb would stick in your hair it were that cold. When you went to the loo you had to be quick!' As prisoners of a military system that could barely sustain its own soldiers, POWs were exposed to extreme hardship and malnutrition. At first in Tyas' camp they got only cabbage with rock salt – 'a small tin, the size of a bean tin, between ten men, which worked out at three–four spoonfuls a man.' Later they got rice, millet or sorghum – often wriggling with maggots – every ten days, then every Sunday and later still, when peace talks were looking promising, every day. Each man also had an issue of loose Chinese tobacco or 'tambi' 'in a box almost the size of a cereal box' that lasted ten days. 'They sometimes missed feeding us, but they never missed the tambi,' says Tyas. 'We had a bible, which we tore up and used to roll – that lasted twelve months. And we got the *Shanghai Times*, which was in English, but which we also used for roll-ups. Very few men weren't smokers and they used tambi for barter – say a bit of soap, but only a bit; one bar had to last three months.'

There were eight main prison camps, with officers and ranks of sergeant and above interned separately from the rest. 'The Chinese thought they'd give us leadership but in truth we survived better without the officers, it's the class system we have,' says Tyas. 'We were better off when we were all equal.' On his march into captivity he remembers about 40 Turkish prisoners including officers – 'and they were being carried in bloody sedans! I was with the Chinese on that one – they made them walk like everybody else.'

Like all the British, Tyas found the Chinese attempt to indoctrinate their captives 'a bloody good joke'.

> They tried to turn us into communists. We had to read out stuff from Engels and Marx and write stuff on subjects like 'What is the cause of war' and read it out – which was a joke in itself as it happens with us, because one of every ten couldn't read or write. The instructors were educated and spoke good English but didn't understand colloquialisms and some of the lads could stick in things fast they hadn't a clue about. They couldn't understand us because when it was our turn we spoke in our broadest Yorkshire, Lancashire, Scouse, Geordie. They had no chance, we just took the piss. But it did keep the mind active.

By the time he was released, Tyas's weight had dropped from 12 stone to eight, Albie Hawkins' from 13½ to under seven.

* * *

The 27th Commonwealth Brigade were withdrawn in April 1951, replaced by the 28th (Kosbies, Royal Fusiliers, Shropshire and Durham Light Infantry). The following October the 28th dislodged the Chinese from the Kowang-San and Maryang-San hills between the Imjin river and

Pyongyang. And here the Kosbies took the full force of a Chinese counter-attack that the troops called 'the Gunpowder Plot' because it came on the eve of Guy Fawkes.

The attack followed hours of sustained artillery fire and bursts of anti-personnel shells that detonated in the air; in the final hour the Chinese poured 6,000 rounds into the position. Outnumbered by more than ten to one, the Kosbies were well barbed-wired in, but the human waves continued to come and hundreds of Chinese got in among the defenders, pushing sections off the features they held. B company was all but overrun and their commander called down British gunfire on his own position for 20 minutes. Willie Purves and his C company platoon, together with one from D company, were on a very high promontory with steep slopes, which they held but became surrounded. He had no idea of the overall battle – communication had been lost:

> The eighty-eight radio sets we had were bloody useless, they covered no distance at all. Eventually I did get through and reported we were still firmly in place but had quite a lot of wounded, including the officer of the other platoon, and what was I to do? I was told to get everybody out, which I did. It was a very tricky situation – at one point the South Korean porters ahead of me with the stretchers didn't turn where they were supposed to and were going towards the position of another company that had been knocked off and was occupied by Chinese, so I had to do some dashing about. Frankly, we got away with murder that night. It was just before light. If it had been light we wouldn't have made it. When I got to headquarters I looked a sorry sight, a great lump of shrapnel in the shoulder, covered in blood, torn clothes, but there wasn't too much wrong with me.

Joe Pyper, 'the man on the wee mortar' in Purves' platoon, was in a much worse state. He had put a dud bomb aside but hours later, running out of ammunition, he tried to use it again by mistake and it exploded in the barrel. Shrapnel went through his eye and took out the right-hand side of his skull. 'I didn't give anything for him,' says Purves. 'It looked to me as though most of his brain was hanging out.'

In the same month of November 1952, on Armistice Day, Second

Lieutenant Nick Harman, who had been in Korea for four months with the Royal Fusiliers, almost died. He went out with a listening patrol just as it was getting dark – and ran straight into an enemy fighting patrol lying in wait. Shrapnel from grenades cut his head and broke his right leg in two places. Harman was down when one of his own men, a few yards in front, got to his knee and fired straight at him with a Sten. Harman took a full burst down his left arm. 'It wasn't exactly a situation which one analysed; I didn't know what was going on. In fact, there was a Chinese officer behind me with a pistol who was about to shoot me in the head. My soldier had saved my life.'

Harman managed to throw a grenade, pulling the pin with his teeth 'as you learn from children's comics'. After that, he was unable to move. There was silence for a while.

> Then some Chinese soldiers came and touched me and then they went away – they didn't carry me with them, which I'm sure they would have liked to do. I think we managed to kill enough of them to prevent them taking me prisoner. Fusilier Tull, my radio operator, was lying badly wounded a little distance away and I could hear our call sign coming from his earphones, along with that particular slushing sound of radio silence. I couldn't answer it, or help Tull, because I couldn't move, with one leg bust, one arm smashed and the other pinned underneath me by my flak jacket. Tull died slowly while trying to put his guts back in his belly. I had two capsules of morphine on me for injecting people when they were dying, which might have eased him off. I suppose that's what I remember with most regret, my inability to help Tull out of his last pain.

The wounded and exhausted Willie Purves was evacuated to the British Commonwealth hospital in Kure in Japan where his wounds were treated and he got fit again by running up and down hills before returning to his unit for the remaining months of his service. For Harman and Pyper, the war was over.

Harman was flown home in a Hercules bomber converted into a hospital plane. The trip took seven days – every time the Hercules landed it broke down.

In Singapore a man at least in his forties, which to me was elderly, joined us, wearing civvies but with a definite air of authority. He turned out to be the Royal Navy captain of an aircraft carrier who had lost his nerve after seeing several of his pilots go into the drink, and I had to comfort him, which was bizarre for a nineteen-year-old who had gangrene and stank.

Patched up at Netley Hospital on Southampton Water, Harman was transferred to the army Millbank Hospital in London (where the Tate Modern Museum now stands) and underwent ten operations in the next nine months, some of it experimental surgery. The nerves and main artery in his arm had been severed 'and it was worth trying to join things up. It wasn't too successful – the hand looks all right, it just doesn't work very well.' Joe Pyper knew nothing of his evacuation: he lay unconscious for 16 days. He was to spend a year in various hospitals – Seoul, Tokyo, Aldershot and then Basingstoke,[10] where they took two or three of his ribs and split them up to insert them into his head, 'and when they wanted a wee bit more finesse they made a skull shape in Perspex. And they made me an eye out of acrylic – in the dental department of all things.' Pyper thinks he was lucky: he was not impaired and was able to go back to his trade as a joiner for ten or 11 years before spending 19 years as a council housing inspector. Today he dismisses the pain he suffered: 'Ah, you get used to pain. I'm used to the tinnitus, too – there's noises whistling away in my head ever since, but I pay no notice.'

*   *   *

Every battalion company had four men trained as stretcher-bearers who went out into the valleys to bring back the wounded, but sometimes other men would go too. On one occasion when a Northumberland patrolling party had walked into a minefield, Terry Brierley was on the rescue team. As there were four injured and only three stretchers, he carried the fourth man.

> The lad was bad, kept passing out. When I had to put him down from time to time and dipped a handkerchief in water in the paddy-field to wipe his face, he whispered 'Immaculate'. I've never forgotten that, a strange word

in the circumstances. Immaculate. I was staggering when I got close to being back, we'd come maybe five miles, and the sergeant said, 'I'll take him from here.' When I got back the officer said, 'Where's your rifle, Brierley?' and I was put on a charge – I'd left it on one of the stretchers. That sergeant was mentioned in despatches and the bugger hadn't offered a hand in carrying the lad until the end. He said to me afterwards, 'I know you carried him but I'm a regular and it'll make a difference to my career, you're only a conscript.'

Treated first at regimental aid posts and then at advanced dressing stations, the wounded were transferred out by train to Pusan and then by plane to Japan.[11]

From the time he was a sixth former Barry Whiting had worked in a local hospital casualty department every weekend ('and sometimes in the operating theatre, just holding things'). In Korea he mostly worked at a field ambulance station as a dispensary assistant, but wanted to deal with the wounded rather than the sick and eventually getting a stripe, went to a casualty clearing post taking in men from the front line. He remembers some horrific injuries, including

a guy very severely injured from a phosphorous bomb – his whole body was peppered with fragments that glowed in the dark and burnt as they dried out and he shrieked and shrieked in agony. The medical officer mixed up a copper sulphate solution in a bedpan, the guy was put in an ambulance and all the time I had to keep his body wet to stop the phosphorus starting to burn again. We went thirty miles on bad roads with the bedpan sloshing about and the solution ran out – so we kept stopping at any unit we found to get water. We got him there, but I never knew whether he survived. If he did he had terrible scars.

Whiting also remembers a young 'catcom' (a member of a South Korean combat casualty unit) 'with half his face hanging off, including his teeth, trying to talk to me as I held his face together' who almost certainly did not survive; and a gunner mutilated when a shell exploded inside the breech of a twenty-five-pounder, 'lying on a stretcher on trestles, the medical officer working on the other side. And trying to find a pulse I put my hand under his arm and my fingers went straight into space, there was nothing there, just skin. And the death rattle: the air expelled from the lungs as they collapse, the first time I really heard it.'

Whiting adds: 'I felt other people's suffering but I could take it on, I could deal with it. You had to be dispassionate or you couldn't function. And, if you're honest, part of you thought, "If it doesn't have my name on it, lucky me." '

At the third battle of the Hook when the regimental aid post could not cope, Whiting went up to help out.

> The injuries were horrendous: one man's buttocks were torn away, another had a foot hanging off – which I was immediately instructed to cut away with scissors. He saw me as I put it under the table still in its boot, and he screamed. Almost all the doctors were national servicemen, straight out of medical school in most cases, with little surgical experience, but they were brilliant.

Once the pattern of the war was established, serious head, chest and other injuries including shellshock were taken out by helicopter to Kure, which is where David Oates – a British Railways employee in the signalling department at Bristol before conscription, who had been a member of the St John Ambulance since he was eleven – worked as a member of the surgical team, his time there covering the last eight months of the war. The two operating theatres of the six-hundred-bed hospital carried out as many as 80 operations a day. When he was night theatre technician, Oates slept on a trolley off one of the operating theatres, ready for incoming emergencies. 'And when we weren't doing anything else we carried out appendectomies, provided a gynaecological service for the Japanese wives of American and Australian servicemen, and did a few circumcisions.'

* * *

During the two years of stalemate from June 1951, both sides were entrenched on top of hills, the valleys below studded with minefields. By day, activity was restricted to irregular shelling, though any movement brought a shower of artillery and mortars. By night, both sides sent out fighting patrols, listening patrols and snatch patrols – prisoners were keenly sought for interrogation[12] – which frequently clashed in fierce firefights. In the British battalions, junior officers, most of them national servicemen, led such patrols. As Willie Purves comments:

There were frozen streams in the bottom of the valleys that you had to cross and you walked very slowly, four or five of you in single file. Sometimes the ice would crack, terrible bloody noise, and you'd freeze while the Chinese put up flares – and down on the ice or in the water or lying on the frozen ground you'd freeze too, if you see what I mean. We had the support of a tank regiment right behind us and they could put a shell on to a target you directed, as accurate as a rifle at 3,000 yards. But by the end of my time our people were trying to save money. When the situation was stagnant the Centurions were only allowed two shells a day.

'It was extremely exciting for a nineteen-year-old with his own platoon,' says Second Lieutenant Tony Thorn, who served with the King's Regiment (Liverpool). 'We were reckless and frightened too. We didn't think about getting killed and, to be fair, we spent three-quarters of our time thinking about our men.'

During this period of stalemate came the third battle of the Hook.

The Hook was a ridge a few miles from the west coast, commanding the route north to Seoul. The Chinese attacked it in October and November 1952, the first time repulsed by the US Marines, the second by the Black Watch. Thorn saw the Black Watch's engagement from his position about a mile away. 'A fellow subaltern who was a friend got hit in the legs and couldn't move. When his platoon pulled back he was left, but he managed to grab the last one, the smallest and slowest, and told him, "If I'm going to die, you're going to die", and made him stay with him. They were okay in the end.' Sappers had turned the Hook almost into a fort by the following May when it was held by the Duke of Wellington's, with the Black Watch and the King's in support. Over six days, the Dukes bore the brunt of the biggest communist assault of the war. Some 20,000 shells, half of them fired on the last night, landed on them, at least one round on every four square yards of the forward company's position, obliterating their trenches. The Dukes were virtually driven underground into the reinforced tunnels and bunkers. The Chinese swarmed on to the position, sealing many of the dazed defenders into the tunnels with satchel charges. Close-quarter fighting raged before the Chinese were beaten back. By the morning the Hook was unrecognisable and the Dukes had lost 29 killed, 104 wounded and 16 taken prisoner. They dug out their entombed men and handed over the position, as they were scheduled to do, to the Royal Fusiliers.

'Because of their casualties the Dukes were never put in a position to face another large-scale attack,' says Reuben Holroyd, who joined them shortly afterwards.

> We still took casualties, men killed by trip-wires in no man's land, men straying into minefields – a favourite trick of the Chinese was to take mines out of the fields and put them on the patrol routes. Some people just went missing – the bodies were never recovered. I was excused patrols because I was a signaller and it took time to train me, so I was regarded as not being expendable.

During the third battle of the Hook, Tony Thorn was in England – chosen to come back in a party of ten to represent the regiment in the Coronation march past in which he carried the colours. 'The Coronation may have saved my life,' he observes.[13]

*   *   *

Formal peace talks opened within a year of the start of hostilities, but dragged on for over two years. At 10 o'clock on the morning of 27 July 1953, the armistice was signed and 12 hours later the guns fell silent.[14]

Before the main exchange of prisoners, known as 'Operation Big Switch', 'Little Switch' three months earlier saw the release of some 700 men (the majority South Koreans) who were in a physically bad way; Albie Hawkins was one of the 32 British among that number. He had been affected by the death from dysentery of a friend he had gone to school with, and he was badly undernourished: 'Less than seven stone and a big potbelly. My legs were paralysed, I couldn't walk, couldn't stand, my mates carried me down to the bogs.' He was to spend the next five months in three UK military hospitals – at Chester, he watched the Coronation on television.

Albert Tyas, who came out under Big Switch,[15] also watched the Coronation with other released men – on their first day back they were ordered down to a cinema for three hours, in eighty-degree heat, when all they wanted to do was sleep. After two-and-a-half years in captivity, Tyas found the entire period of hand-over bizarre. The Americans, having deloused the British prisoners, gave them new uniforms; the British then deloused them again, and gave them British uniforms and burnt the American ones – 'which said we were back in the British army.' For their first meal they were waited on by officers from the Duke of Wellington's and Tyas remembers one saying: 'Now, chaps, what do you think of this wonderful food? Better than shark-fin soup, surely.' 'Silly bastard,' he says. 'Maybe it was a joke, maybe he thought we'd been getting shark-fin soup. They just didn't have an idea of what we might be feeling.' What angered him more was the reception the returning men from the Imjin battle were given by General West, Commander of the Commonwealth Division:

'We were all lined up to meet him, get a welcome back. He pulled each man in with a handshake and stuck ten Senior Service cigarettes into his other hand. 'What regiment?' 'Royal Ulster Rifles, Sir.' 'Good.' The next man: 'Royal Northumberland Fusiliers, Sir.' 'Good.' The next man: 'Gloucestershire Regiment, Sir.' And the general throws his arm around his neck, 'Bravo! What a battle! Well done!' That got right up my bloody nose. I thought: 'We were all in that bloody battle.' A Northumberland lad behind me said, 'What the chuffing hell's going on here?'

What ex-POWs had not known was the extent to which the fate of the Glosters had captured the popular imagination of the people at home and, as Nick Harman observes, 'turned a defeat into a victory'. The glory was all the Glosters', with America awarding them a distinguished unit citation – denoted by a small blue rectangle on the right sleeve – and Bristol giving them the freedom of the city. If the Ulsters and Northumberlands had a right to be aggrieved so, two years later, did the Dukes, whose considerable courage on the Hook was overtaken by news of a breakthrough in the peace talks and consequently received little press coverage.

Albert Tyas worked off some of his anger on the voyage home. Given money to go ashore at Hong Kong from the *Dunera*, he and some of his fellow detainees 'ran around on the beer – we went on the trot for a couple of days'. They missed the boat when it sailed and 'were stuck in the nick for ten days until the *Orwell* came, a good boat, the *Dunera* was rough. And there was a bit of a fracas on the *Orwell* and we were locked up again on board. We were a bit wild.'

Many of the Americans in the prisoner exchange showed considerable emotion, which took the phlegmatic British aback and contributed to their prejudice about their allies. Generally the troops had a low opinion of the Americans. They liked them for their generosity but disliked them for their readiness to abandon positions: to 'bug out' – get into their vehicle and drive like hell away from the enemy – regardless of flanking units exposed by their action. Says Gloster Albie Hawkins: 'Early in January '51 our first major action was on Hill 327 where we lost about twenty blokes and had quite a few injured. We came off the position when the Yanks relieved us. We were still marching to the rear when they drove past us! GIs? We called them generally useless.' Says Northumberland Fusilier Terry Brierley:

> The South Koreans held one position beside us for a long time and in Korea a month was a long time. The Americans took it over, moved in one night with a band playing top tunes. Hello, said the Chinese artillery and ran them off the hill. The SK had to go back and take it. All the Americans seemed to want to do was flatten all the big hills. We had no faith in them – no time for them.

Huge resentment was felt by all Commonwealth forces at the Americans' disregard for basic procedures in the line, and their profligacy. Says Willie Purves:

> You'd take over from them and find muck and litter and half-eaten food tins all over the place. They often didn't dig proper latrines. When they bugged out they'd set everything they couldn't carry on fire. We were attached to an

American division with the Marines, who were very good but a lot of the US regiments were terrible, no discipline.

Above all, other troops distrusted the Americans for their gung-ho attitude. 'The British would decide what minimal barrage was necessary – with the Americans it was maximum everything,' says medic Barry Whiting. 'They were bizarrely careless. We were more concerned about being bombed by the Americans than by the Chinese. I had a few close misses.' The Americans received the greatest condemnation of the war when they attacked the Argyll and Sutherland Highlanders in September 1950 in defence of Hill 282. Called in to strike an adjacent hill, three US Mustangs ignored the fluorescent white recognition panels put out by the Argylls and dropped napalm on them, as well as machine-gunning them. The jellied petroleum tumbled down the ridge, engulfing the defenders, including wounded on stretchers. Ammunition exploded. Thirteen Argylls were killed and 72 injured.

'Gunners and flyers kill the infantry in front of them in all wars,' says Nick Harman. 'In Korea, most of the guns and planes were American, so they did the usual job.' In some defence of the Americans he adds: 'As a mechanised army they were good – they were good going forward. Of course we despised them – British regiments get their strength from despising everyone else, especially their allies. It's good for morale when all else fails.' But some of the guns in Korea belonged to the British and they, too, inevitably, in the chaos of battle, sometimes brought down fire on their own infantry; and the Dukes' John Hollands came under fire from a British tank, which put a dozen shells on to his position:

> The Centurion had changed position in the middle of the night. The front line zigzagged and they were now on top of a hill that was in fact behind us. In the morning they saw us in front of them, diagonally left, assumed we were the enemy and thought 'We'll have some of that.' We got on the radio and were disbelieved up the chain of command to battalion, until we brought in a large piece of shrapnel with WD [War Department] stamped on it. Two of our men had been killed and the whole thing was hushed up. There wasn't even an apology from the tank troop commander.

* * *

From first to last, more than 60,000 British troops served in Korea in 16 infantry battalions, four tank regiments, nine artillery regiments and many supporting units, which got little of the credit. 'But they were there – the quartermaster people with something hot to eat, a truck, blankets, mail from home. Signals . . . repairing radios, telephones, keeping batteries charged from mobile petrol-driven chargers, Royal Artillery linesmen keeping the lines going, Engineers, repairing roads, blowing up roads, sweeping roads of mines . . .'[16] Just over half the men were national servicemen – nearly three-quarters of infantry battalions in the final year. Total British losses were about 1,100 killed, of whom nearly 900 are buried in the United Nations cemetery in Pusan. A similar number were taken prisoner – 50 died in captivity – and there were 2,700 wounded.[17]

John Hollands wrote many of the letters to the next of kin of those Dukes killed in the third battle of the Hook.

> I didn't do them all, I did twenty or twenty-five, but just before I started the padre conducted a burial service for a chap called Brown and all that remained of him was a little brown parcel and I thought, 'How on earth can I tell his family a thing like that?' So the letters I wrote were what you write in such circumstances – clichés: he was a good soldier, he did his duty, he died bravely, he never let his mates down.

Not letting mates down was the ethic shared by British national servicemen almost to a man. Noting that 'the most political army in the world [the Chinese] encountered the least political [the British] and was savagely mauled', Max Hastings commented that 'the regiment, the unit, the "oppo" in the next trench were everything.'[18] It was that sense of comradeship that got men through captivity and which many Americans seemed to lack: 4% of the British died in the POW camps compared with 38% of Americans. As Albert Tyas observes:

> My first day in the camp they carried seventeen Americans to boot hill. Other people said they counted more. The Americans had got 'givinitis': they'd lost the will to live. Americans don't have the British esprit de

corps; that's the marvellous thing about the British. The Americans didn't have that sense of needing to stand together; maybe their country's too big for them to have it. They just willed themselves away. There's no accounting for it.

Albie Hawkins adds:

The first time I was picked up, they held me in a clearing-house until there were enough of us to march north. There were Americans in there and about a dozen Turks. The difference between the Turks and the Yanks was bloody striking. The Turks were hard men, nothing was going to break them. The Yanks just lay down and wouldn't get up in the morning. One just died and there was nothing wrong with him.

In the beginning, the army worried how national servicemen would fare; by the end they wondered why they had. 'My God, those Dukes,' said Brigadier Joe Kendrew, Commander of 29 Brigade after the third battle of the Hook. 'They were marvellous.' It was a tribute that could have been paid to virtually all the national servicemen who served.

The gallantry shown in the Korean War brought many awards for bravery, including a Distinguished Service Order for Second Lieutenant Willie Purves, a Military Medal for Smyttan Common and a Military Cross for Second Lieutenant John Hollands. Purves was the only national serviceman ever to receive a DSO, which was pinned on him at a divisional parade by General Jim Cassels, the divisional commander, when Purves returned from recuperating in Japan. 'An MC is for some action of exceptional bravery – or foolhardiness – which knocks out some key post and shows personal leadership under fire,' he says. 'Now in my case, if there was any of that, was the additional fact that I managed to get all these people out, virtually with all normal equipment, and I was able to give a pretty good rundown on what had gone on.'

Others are less understated. Smyttan Common (who went back to plumbing after national service but rejoined the army in 1958, finishing as a colour sergeant) says:

Willie acquitted himself amazingly well and not just in that action. At twenty-one I regarded myself as one of the older ones but Willie had maturity beyond his years. The old soldiers tried a few tricks on him in the beginning as they always do, but he was up to it. It's hard holding thirty men together and the truth is, a lot of blokes are no bloody good. It's not their fault, they didn't choose to be soldiers. It was bloody hard for some boys from the town, you'd be surprised how many men are scared of the dark. But Willie held the platoon together. You read a lot of shite about national service officers not being able to function without sergeants. All platoon commanders relied on their sergeant if he was a good one – that's what he's there for. As it happens, we didn't have a sergeant for a long time. They were very young, you know, the officers. Some of them were just out of school. And they didn't have that much training themselves. Alaistair Brown who was killed was another. He and Willie were the greatest guys in the world.

John Hollands, whose MC was awarded for a series of patrols carried out in the middle of divisional lines – when he was twice involved in shoot-outs – is forthright about Purves: 'What he did warranted a Victoria Cross, and he might have had one if Speakman hadn't got one in the same engagement.'[19]

As well as his MC, Hollands received the American Purple Heart. He was lying in an American MASH unit, virtually deaf from two split eardrums, awaiting evacuation to Japan, when the UN Commander-in-Chief, Maxwell Taylor, paid a visit:

He stopped at the bottom of each bed, repeating the same words to everyone: 'Have you shed blood for your country, soldier?' Upon an affirmative response, his ADC handed out a medal – scorned in this country but highly esteemed in the States as their oldest decoration. I was lying beside a New Zealander and since we'd both shed blood, rather a lot in his case, we accepted. In the evening, a doctor came round, pointed out we weren't Americans, and asked for them back. The New Zealander replied in forceful terms that he wouldn't, adding that we regarded them as personal awards made by the UN Commander-in-Chief. I backed him up, far more politely, and nothing more was said about it. So I still have mine and wear it with great pride on appropriate occasions.

Joe Pyper, the little Kosbie mortar man, nearly got a Purple Heart too. 'I was in the big hospital in Tokyo when one of the Yank big chiefs came round handing out Purple Hearts. He went to give one to me and was told, "That's a Scottish boy." "Oh gee," he said, "give the boy some candy." '

6

More real bullets

Korea was not a police action as the United Nations called it, but a full-scale war. The counter-guerrilla or counter-insurgency campaigns in Egypt, Malaya, Kenya and Cyprus were police actions or, in military jargon, low-intensity operations – though at times the national servicemen engaged in them might have been more inclined to see them as small-scale wars.

All these campaigns had one thing in common: the British were in the countries of other people who wanted them out and who were prepared to kill them to achieve it. Egypt's case was different to the others. Malaya, Kenya and Cyprus had long been part of the British Empire; Egypt simply wanted to terminate a treaty, signed in 1936, which allowed British troops to be stationed there to ensure free use of the Suez Canal.[1]

Egypt had been swamped by Commonwealth troops during the Second World War; after it, when these had gone, some 10,000 British remained and the Egyptians, sick of their highly visible presence, sought a revision of the agreement. Britain, which seemed to see Egypt as subject to the rule of Empire, refused and there were riots, leading to the death of several British soldiers. Britain withdrew its forces from the cities into the Suez Canal Zone and adopted a more conciliatory approach, but in October 1951, tired of the negotiations going nowhere, Egypt abrogated the treaty. Attacks on British personnel escalated. Commander-in-Chief of the Middle East, General Sir Brian Robertson, wrote in a letter: 'We have got beyond the stage where our clashes with armed Egyptian thugs and police can be classed as incidents, and it has become necessary to mount properly coordinated operations to deal with organised attacks on our troops and installations.' As a significant proportion of the large local labour force defected, pioneer troops from Mauritius and East Africa and civilian workers from Malta and Cyprus replaced them, and the garrison swelled to over 70,000 – most of them conscript soldiers and airmen.

The anti-imperialist campaign in Malaya had already been running for three years, waged by Malay-Chinese communist terrorists – trained by the British to oppose the Japanese during the Second World War – who began by killing rubber planters and tin miners in an attempt to destroy the main economic bases. At any one time there were never more than 5,000 terrorists, but they had the support of the local Chinese – 40% of the population. Not all the Kikuyu – the largest tribal group in Kenya – supported the many-thousand-strong Mau Mau who also used terror tactics to try to drive the British out of the colony and off the land that they had appropriated.[2] But many did, others were coerced, and a state of emergency was declared in October 1952. Three years later the British were fighting Cypriot-Greek Eoka terrorists in Cyprus, who not only wanted the British out but also wanted unification (*enosis*) with the Greek mainland, in pursuit of which they turned on the island's minority Turkish population. For 75 years the British had ruled Cyprus and, despite making soothing noises when approached about a timetable for withdrawal, did not commit itself. Resentment boiled over when large numbers of troops were transferred to the island as part of a finally agreed withdrawal from Egypt – and Britain made it clear that as Cyprus now had increased strategic significance, independence was out of the question.

Having reduced its states of emergency from three to two, in November 1955 Britain was back to three.

*   *   *

The Canal Zone, consisting of nothing but a string of army and RAF camps, installations and munitions dumps was the most hated of all postings. The Egyptian climate was unhealthy, the heat extreme, with cold nights in winter, and in spring a wind blew for weeks, creating sandstorms that covered food with grey grit, got into ears and beds and

106

choked the engines of the vehicles. Men tied down the tents in which they lived as best they could, 'but no matter what we did the occasional one took off,' says Jock Marrs, a CSM's clerk in the 1st Infantry Division transport column.

In the immediate postwar years, men were at least able to go to the three towns along the Canal – Port Said in the north, Ismailiya halfway down, Suez in the south – or even visit Cairo. 'But it was still dangerous, even if it wasn't as nasty as it was later,' says Acker Bilk, who was there in 1948 working at his trade as a blacksmith in a REME engineering depot.

> The first guard I did, I was on the way to stand in a searchlight tower and bullets started coming over. We had a big perimeter, I mean big, four–five miles round, with a bank ten feet high, so the shooting was way over our heads, but we hit the deck smartish. Quite frightening, that. I remember thinking, 'Bloody hell, the buggers are using real bullets.'

From 1951 and the abrogation of the 1936 treaty, things were nasty. The Egyptian nationalist newspaper, *Al Misri*, offered £100 to anyone who killed a British officer. Terrorist attacks, including acts of sabotage, escalated and British personnel were killed or wounded by snipers, by mines disguised in camel dung on the roads and by piano wire stretched at head height across them, necessitating the fitting of serrated metal posts to the front of vehicles including motorbikes. 'At night driving back from somewhere you'd hear the ping as a wire was cut,' says Ron Batchelor, there with RAF Airfield Construction, which built and maintained the airfields. 'It was almost always in the same places. They had a singular lack of imagination.' At periods of relative quiet, men were allowed out in groups, always in uniform, one carrying a Sten with a round up the spout. 'But during Ramadan we went nowhere,' says Batchelor. 'They got a bit excited then.'

Depending on the levels of hostility, it was sometimes possible to go swimming, though there were health hazards. As Royal Artillery subaltern Kenneth Baker (now Lord Baker) remarks, even the Great Bitter Lake, where his light battery was stationed, 'really was an open sewer'.[3] That the source of fresh water to the Zone should be called the Sweet Water Canal the British took to be ironic. The canal came from the Nile Delta across the desert and served many settlements, not just as water supply but also as open drain and it arrived at the Great Bitter Lake dangerously contaminated. 'Occasionally servicemen would fall in and be brought to the British Military Hospital at Fayed, would usually be admitted, and nearly always developed a fever.'[4] The hospital was busy, occasionally with men needing rabies treatment after being bitten by the wild dogs that got through the wire to the food bins, but more frequently with cases of typhus, polio and amoebic dysentery; dysentery itself was endemic. 'Everyone had dysentery. I got it so bad I twice ended up in the military hospital,' says Jock Marrs. 'If that wasn't bad enough, when you were hospitalised your money went down – a private got knocked back to ten bob.'

The levels of sickness were in no small measure due to the sanitary conditions. 'The urinal was a funnel stuck straight into the sand and the toilet was a ten-hole thunderbox where you'd be sat listening to the rats running about below – in one hundred and twenty degree heat,' says Marrs. Dave Garyford, a Catering Corps cook from Wickford in Essex, who served at Fayed with 148 Field Bakery, recalls:

> The shitehawks swarmed around the toilets, which is where the birds got their name. When we served men their meals they'd try to make it to their tents to eat but the shitehawks dive-bombed them all the way, grabbing whatever they could. The squaddies were at their mercy – two mess tins and an enamel mug, all conducting heat, took some juggling.

Before the emergency in Egypt was declared and after it was resolved, it was possible for camps to buy some fresh produce such as oranges, bananas and watermelon. In the years between, when the Egyptian government refused any cooperation, there was nothing to add variety to the compo rations. These came in boxes of already cooked meals for ten men and, according to Garyford,

> 'cooking' involved opening these tins and heating the stuff up. The problem was, all the tins were the same size and had no labels. The only ones that were obviously identifiable were the large, green square ones of dehydrated

Day one in uniform – and the obligatory haircut. One MP remarked in the House that barbers were more fitted to be 'carpenters or metal shearers'. The recruit centre back has escaped lightly.

Lining up for inoculations in basic training – a painful business in the days before throwaway needles. Some conscripts fainted; the inoculations put a few in the infirmary.

REME national serviceman Roger Keight saw this squad drilling in gasmasks at No 5 Training Battalion, Arborfield, Berkshire. His caption: Who farted?

Phil Wilkinson's passing-out parade at the RAF Officer Cadet Training Unit, Jurby, on the Isle of Man. Front right with the bristling moustache: Warrant Officer Cook, the man with possibly the loudest voice in the air force. 'We could hear him from the deck of the ferry as we arrived from Liverpool.'

Few national servicemen made it into the Marines. One who did was Neal Ascherson (centre) who later served as a junior officer in Malaya.

At times the newspapers took the army and RAF to task for using national servicemen as waiters, and some men resented having to do the job. Here the duty squad including Roger Keight (front row, far right) are ready for a 'do' in the sergeants' mess – and are all smiles.

The majority of national servicemen went abroad by troop ships; Eric Michaels went to Malaya on the *Dunera*. 'The lads in the background were in danger of sunburn – and a charge!'

During the years of national service large areas of the world map were coloured red, denoting the Empire – but conscripts were shocked to find that the British were not wanted and some countries resorted to terrorist violence to get them out. Malta was not one – but it still wanted independence.

Almost all men posted to the Med or further east saw Valletta Harbour, Malta, which the trooper *Dunera* (centre) is seen here leaving.

Second Lieutenant Tony Thorn (front, centre) left his King's Regiment (Liverpool) platoon in Korea to return home to carry the regimental colours in the Coronation parade – and missed one of the fiercest battles of the war. 'The Coronation may have saved my life.'

John Hollands' Duke of Wellington's platoon the day before going into the line for the first time. 'The lad with the stick confided that, all things considered, he didn't think he was really suitable for fighting in Korea. He was most put out when I told him it was bloody bad luck and I felt exactly the same way myself!'

Hollands' platoon bunker in a position opposite the Chinese stronghold known as 'The Boot'. 'A rubber tube ran from the forty-two-gallon drum of petrol (left) to a space heater inside the bunker – bloody dangerous, but anything to keep warm.'

Two of Hollands' men 'posing like mad' after the third battle of the Hook was done, 'manning a Browning, which we got from the Americans'.

The army tried to provide some entertainment in Korea, even if the stage was just planks on top of oil drums and the only seating was the ground.

Christmas Eve 1953 at the Rear Division HQ, the Duke's. Reuben Holroyd is bottom right: 'Note the paper hat "to be worn at our Christmas party" sent by the WVS!'

Many men came back from Korea with psychological problems, including Charlie Eadie (centre), here on R and R in Japan: 'You don't come out of a thing like Korea normal.' Northumberland Fusilier Terry Brierley (right) still has panic attacks.

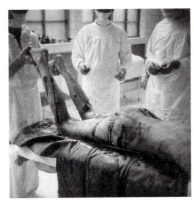

Medical orderlies Barry Whiting (above left) and David Oates (above, back right) assisted at operations on the wounded, Whiting in the field, Oates at the military hospital in Kure, Japan.

Left: A soldier with severe gunshot wounds in a Kure operating theatre.

Below: On 31 January 1951, Albert Tyas (fourth from left) had a drink in Kure, before going to Korea. Three months later he was taken prisoner – and spent two and a half years in a Chinese POW camp, as did three other men in this photo.

Kosbe Charlie Eadie read the Chinese propaganda leaflets and was tempted to give himself up, to get away from the fighting.

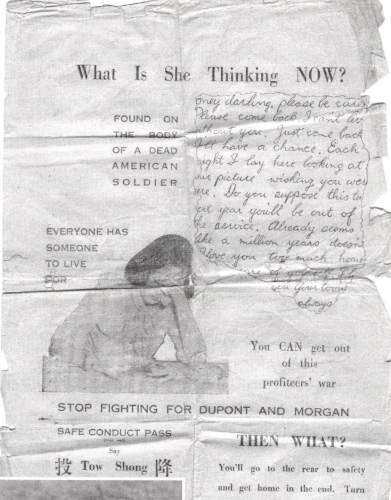

What Is She Thinking NOW?

FOUND ON
THE BODY
OF A DEAD
AMERICAN
SOLDIER

oney darling, please be care. Please come back. I can't live without you. Just come back I'll have a chance. Each night I lay here looking at our picture wishing you were here. Do you suppose this time next year you'll be out of the service. Already seems like a million years doesn't Ilove you too much hone... ...re of yourself I... ...ou. Your lovin' always

EVERYONE HAS
SOMEONE
TO LIVE
FOR

You CAN get out
of this
profiteers' war

STOP FIGHTING FOR DUPONT AND MORGAN

SAFE CONDUCT PASS
(tear out)
Say
投 Tow Shong 降

THEN WHAT?

You'll go to the rear to safety and get home in the end. Turn over see what your buddies say.

John Hollands and the four men in parkas were returning from patrol when they disturbed some Chinese trying to bang the banner into the ground in front of the regiment's position. 'We chased them off and scored casualties, but we'd been out all night in temperatures of around minus 30, so we weren't inclined to give chase.'

HOW THEY WRITE TO YOU:

From relatives of Americans in Korea

"Now my hopes of you being here when our baby is born look mighty glum. My darling, please be careful. I want you and no one else. I'd go without my sleep if only you had a dry place to sleep and did not have to fight. Your loving wife. . . ."

"I soon gave up hopes of your being back by Christmas. That sure was a lousy trick, building up our hopes like that. It must be cold there. Every time I turn on the radio I get the goose-pimples, thinking you are in there too. Darling, I only ask one thing of life. Come back, come back. I cannot face the thought of life without you."

"My Darling son . . . but we were all sad to know you were now going out into all this. Be careful and take care of yourself for Jane and above all of me. Your dear Mom."

"Honey, I cry for you. Does it help any? Everyone here is talking about war. They're scared. I wish old Truman had to fight the next war by himself. I didn't think I'd ever find anyone I would love and then it happened. I miss you so bad tonight. Hurry home to me, my darling, always for you alone. . . ."

"Bill, Dad loves you more than anyone could ever tell you. Sunday he was all heartbroken. He said you wouldn't come back and began to cry. I tried to cheer him up a little but I felt too bad myself. Love you always. . . ."

"Johnnie, This war makes me so dam mad I don't know what to do. Is there anything I might do to help you out. Don't be afraid to tell me. . . ."

"I've been so worried about you the past week. I'm so lost without you. A daddy means everything in a family. Mamma and daughter are so lonely for their loving daddy."

HOW YOU WRITE TO THEM:

From Prisoners of War

From Sergeant William E. Elliott to his wife at Route 2, Vaiden, Missouri.

"Dearest Sweet Wife and Children, I am now a prisoner of war and am being treated very good. So please don't worry about me as I shall be OK. They are giving us plenty to eat and guess that is the main thing. Kiss the kids every day for me, your husband and daddy, Ernest."

From Major John C. Harlan to his wife at 1701, Caroline Street, Baltimore City, Maryland.

"My Dearest Wife Mildred, This is my second letter to you since my capture to let you know that I am well. The Chinese people's voluntary forces are very kind to me. They share their food and tobacco with . . . for lasting peace and a safe return home. John."

From Charles L. Gill to his wife at 7418 Jefferson Street, Kansas City: "I'm a POW but I'm all right. I have a bullet in each arm and one in the leg but they are taking care of them for me. I pray that soon they take me for an exchange prisoner and I'll get back to America. Please don't worry. They aren't bad to us and give us food and cigarettes. They also say we will not be harmed."

WHO ARE THE SMART GUYS?

Those who fought for mad MacArthur and died?

Their letters from home are on the left hand column.

Or those who got out of this dirty war by coming over to us?

Think it over, Soldier.

YOU'RE WELCOME, TOO.

Joe Pyper (near right), the little mortar man in the King's Own Scottish Borderers, lost an eye when a shell exploded in the barrel. For years he did not know how he survived until Smyttan Common visited his hometown as a recruiting sergeant. *Far right*: In the same engagement Pyper's platoon commander Willie Purves won a DSO and Common, seen outside Buckingham Palace with his mother and sister, an MM.

vegetables and powdered potato. The secret of knowing what was what was passed on by the last cooks before they left.

Bacon or sausages for breakfast came ten to the tin in thick, white fat and 'hit the frying pan in a block like a bomb'; when the fat had melted, bread was fried in it. There were also 'thick oatmeal wodges for making porridge, but as nobody on my camp asked for porridge, every man was given a chunk to nibble with his mug of tea.' The main meal of the day at 5 p.m. was 'Irish stew or a meat pie made in the kitchens out of what looked liked dog food' accompanied by dehydrated vegetables and reconstituted potato. For afters there was a choice of tinned fruit, rice pudding or steamed suet pudding topped with jam.

At Jock Marrs' camp, porridge was served. Lining up for his very first breakfast in Egypt he remarked to the man behind him that putting raisins in the porridge was a novel idea, only to be told: 'Raisins be damned, those are dead flies. Just eat round them.' 'Given the food on top of everything else, no wonder morale was pitifully low,' Marrs adds.

For the infantry, Egypt meant constant patrolling and sporadic engagements. For the majority of the huge garrison, life was a constant round of work, guards and pickets, with periodic confinement behind their barbed wire with very little to occupy their free time. Lucky if their camp ran to a cinema, men even volunteered to ride shotgun on vehicles that left the main gate as a respite from the monotony. Guard and picket duty ground everyone down. There was always the possibility of a sniper out in the desert or a drive-by shooting attempt, and at night Egyptians constantly broke in, not in the name of terrorism but free enterprise. The perimeters of all the camps were protected by land-mines and trip flares but 'any Arab wishing to get in just painted his body with oil and added sand so he'd be indistinguishable from the desert, and with care would get through,' says Marrs. 'They took what they wanted, even from the tents in which we were sleeping. We were just grateful they didn't cut our throats.' As preventing such incursions was virtually impossible, the troops, in some places guarding nothing but mountains of furniture and household equipment, let the Egyptians get on with it. Ron Batchelor remembers:

We lost a lot of stuff. When there was night flying we'd put out the landing lights on the landing strips that were outside the camps, which you couldn't guard. You rarely collected them all back in. When we lost something we needed, we'd go into town and buy it back off the stalls. Everything got knocked off, not just equipment but blankets, cap badges, lemonade powder. I did a turn in the drawing office and while I was there one of the Egyptians who worked around the place took a huge light-table home in bits so it wasn't noticed until it wasn't there. Another time an Egyptian was stopped staggering out of camp and he had hundreds of yards of the wire that connected the landing lights wound around himself.

Even the DDT and paraffin that the British provided to the villages to spray on lying water against rising malarial levels found their way on to the market stalls, the paraffin sold as cooking fuel.

Posted to Ismailiya with an RAF aerial photo-reconnaissance unit, the war photographer Don McCullin did three nights of guard duty a week and

Occasionally I would catch people coming into the camp to steal and hand them over to the RAF police who would then phone the local police. You'd see this Egyptian policeman coming along the side of the Canal, complete with fez and cane. We would drive up, salute, and perform the usual courtesies. The offending detainee would sometimes protest that he was only trying to retrieve something that had got on the wrong side of the wire, and the policeman would fetch him a clout round the earhole; much to my pleasure, for I would be thinking that if it weren't for him I would be in bed.[5]

Mike Hollingworth arrived in the Canal Zone with the Grenadier Guards when hostilities were intense:

A colleague was blown up in an ambush and lost both legs, another was shot, I was hit by a ricochet – and suddenly we were locked up in our camps. But then the government changed at home, Churchill was back in early

1952, and we went on the offensive. There was sharp retribution. Regiments of tanks went down the Sweet Water Canal road and flattened the place. Within six weeks we were walking out in Ismailiya.

In that counter-offensive a full battalion of the Lancashire Fusiliers, backed by tanks, stormed the Bureau Sanitaire in Ismailiya, headquarters of the Bulak Nizam, purportedly an Egyptian auxiliary police or paramilitary force but known to carry out many of the attacks. Bren-gunner Eric Pearson was there:

> . . . there must have been half a dozen of us behind the tank as it was going in. There was one big main building and the tank just smashed through the gate, just went through it. As we were going along then, the lad aside of me, he just went 'Ooh', and down he went. So I looked and all his side was out and he was dead. He'd been in the army only a few months. He was a new draft, he came over to Egypt and I should think he'd done about six weeks' intensive training in the desert and then he copped it . . . I don't know what he was hit with, but apparently, what we were told afterwards, was that the police were using dum-dum bullets so that would rip up rather than just going in.
>
> Then we got into the building . . . As we were stood there, bullets came through the wall. Apparently it was our own tanks, they didn't know we were in there. They had armour-piercing bullets and these were coming through a wall a brick thick – right through. Well, I panicked sort of thing. I thought, 'Nobody's coming out of the doors.' So I'm firing at these doors – indiscriminately really, though . . . After that word came round, 'Right, it's all over – out.' Two hours and it was all over.[6]

Forty of the Egyptian auxiliaries had been killed; so had five fusiliers.

Hollingworth left Egypt the following year. He had enjoyed ceremonial duties in London (at St James's Palace he was sent to see off Frank Sinatra who was trying to crash a party at the apartment of the Officer of the King's Guard, although he did not know who Sinatra was) and a spell in Libya ('Tobruk was jolly dangerous – still mined from the war'), but by the end of his time in the Zone 'had had enough of deserts and searching people – it's difficult to forget the smell of unwashed people in a very hot country'. But for two months he was unable to get home.

> Aircraft were grounded and released men had to hitch a ride on passing ships, which were absolutely stuffed with troops coming back from Korea. You'd only get on board if someone had been dropped off at a base hospital or died in transit. We used to go out on a tank landing craft, perhaps a hundred men, and they'd shout down from the deck how many they'd take – and the biggest and ugliest would win. In the end, six of us bribed the Arab helmsman so that at the last minute he swung the craft around to our side, and we were first up the ladder.

The rest of the British were not far behind him in leaving Egypt. In April 1954 the hardliner Colonel Gamal Nasser (one of the band of officers who had overthrown King Farouk two years earlier) became the Egyptian leader; in the October Britain agreed to quit the country within 20 months. On 24 March 1956 the last British troops, the 2nd Battalion, Grenadier Guards, sailed from Port Said. Five years of hostilities had cost 54 servicemen's lives.

∗   ∗   ∗

The communist guerrillas in Malaya were a difficult enemy to engage. They rarely operated in groups of more than 30 or 40, hitting targets before melting back into the jungle and mountains covering four-fifths of the country. To fight them, the British adopted a two-prong strategy: they stopped their sympathisers from providing them with information and supplies, and they took away their initiative in the jungle. To achieve the first they forcibly removed the rural Chinese into new villages that were effectively prison camps. To achieve the second they sent out patrols of about 20 men – over half of them national servicemen led by national service officers – to flush them out.

'Ulu [jungle] bashing', as patrolling was called, in 6,000 square miles of difficult terrain was hard work, even for fit eighteen- and nineteen-year-olds. Cutting their way with parangs [Malayan machetes] along narrow trails of dense saplings, attapalms, creepers, bamboo and trees with roots four feet out of the ground, and with scores of swamps, rivers and streams, sometimes fast-flowing, to traverse, a patrol might cover a mile in four hours. It was hot all year round and in the monsoon season, rain began about four every afternoon and did not abate for up to ten hours.[7] Even when it did not rain, patrols came to rest visibly steaming, their clothes soaked with sweat. It was then that they tended to their cuts and sores, caused by sharp-edged plants, hornets, mosquitoes and vicious red ants that showered from the trees – and some by the chaffing of the 60 lb packs they shouldered. Men were also sometimes bitten by snakes or by the tiny crocodiles that infested the water, or got a nasty jolt from the electric eels. But the leeches were the constant hazard – anything from five to 50 would be on a man's body at the end of the day and they had to be removed with salt or the tip of a burning match – simply pulling the creatures off left the heads under the skin, resulting in ulcerations. Sometimes a man could have so many leeches inside his boots he could work his feet and pump the blood out of the eyelets.

As Hampshire Regiment subaltern Richard Lindley explains:

> Leeches could leave you a bloody mess at the end of the day. But my abiding memory of jungle bashing is of being soaking wet. You'd take off your wet and muddy clothes and hang them on a twig to dry, wrap yourself in parachute silk and climb into a hammock. In the morning the clothes would still be wet, there was no chance of them drying in the humidity, and you'd put them on again and off you'd go. And we lost up to a stone in weight – I came down to eight stone, it was such hard work. I really had a job keeping up, the jungle was so exhausting. And we'd come off patrol and have to play badminton to show how tough we were, when I'd rather have had a lie down. I didn't feel I was natural officer material. At school in Bedford I ran societies and acted, and avoided team games, though I was good at fencing; I was very bookish – though I didn't as much as open a book in Malaya. But I did try to do things right, and I didn't get anyone killed or wounded.

The jungle was an eerie place to be. Twilight green by day, and silent, at dusk it became an orchestra of bird and animal calls before sudden night, and silence once again. Men built shelters ('bashers') out of waterproof ponchos stretched over a framework of saplings, and each did his own cooking on a 'Tommy cooker' that used solid fuel tablets. Many brought curry powder to enliven their compo rations, which improved somewhat from 1954 when self-heating soups were introduced. 'Who but the British would think of providing steamed mixed fruit pudding in the depths of the rainforest, with humidity about a hundred and fifty degrees?' asks Marine Second Lieutenant Neal Ascherson. 'We used to feed it to the centipedes.' No one grumbled about the daily tot of rum, which, as in Korea, was standard issue.

It was estimated that the British spent 1,000 man-hours in the Malayan jungle to achieve a twenty-second contact with the communist terrorists (or CTs as the troops called them, or, more usually, bandits or 'F-Reds' – for which a translation is unnecessary) and 1,800 man-hours to achieve a single 'kill'. Some men, including Richard Lindley, spent a whole year in the jungle and saw nobody; coming across a still-smoking campfire was as close as he got. 'It was hard to be as good as they were,' he says. 'We were noisy compared to them, crashing through the undergrowth, which is why, when we could, we walked along the streams, which are endless in Malaya, because the noise of the water hid the noise we made.'

Battle training in the jungle warfare school set up at Kotta Tinggi in Johore helped the British infantry improve their survival skills and, while they never achieved the standards of the four Gurkha regiments who were operational throughout the emergency, or of the SAS or the Marines (in Malaya acting in an infantry role) who carried out risky parachute jumps and abseiled down trees that could be several hundred feet high, the 30 battalions that saw service achieved a high level of effectiveness. They were helped by the arrival of Iban trackers, brought in from Sarawak and Borneo to accompany many of the patrols. 'We had three of them with us often, and they could be uncanny,' says the Manchester Regiment's Eric Michaels.

> This time they surprised a group of terrorists filling their water bottles, they opened up and got two out of three. When they were on their own the Iban used to cut off the heads to bring them back for identification; we used to bring the bodies back tied to poles. Later I think some units were issued

with cameras to save that. Anyway, we were moving through the jungle and one of the Iban came up to us and was jabbering away pointing to one of the dead terrorists. Not having a clue what he was saying we were nodding and smiling, with which he brings out his knife and scalps him, taking two or three inches off the head. They used to plait the scalped hair on the knife handle; it made them a big hero. 'Plenty bibi,' he said – women.

In the tropics the stomach of anyone killed swells very quickly and by the time we crossed the river that was happening. And for some reason one of the Iban had cut off the hand of the scalped terrorist and stuck it on his head. These were the first terrorists the regiment had killed and the CO wanted to see so he brought his wife and daughter down. When they threw back the sheet there was this scalped fellow with a hand stuck on his head and his guts spilled out. The CO and his family didn't stay long.

Pay Corps lance-corporal Leslie Thomas went into the jungle and was glad he did not have to stay long either. Like many others he was safe in Singapore, 'seeing action with pens and ledgers' until GHQ decided that static units should undergo jungle training and he had to cross the eight-mile Johore Causeway to the mainland and put himself in the hands of infantry instructors.

And then we were sent up country when the CO thought we should know what it was like at the sharp end and we were dumped off landing barges in a camp where guerrillas had been operating. I remember crouching in a swamp with a Malay soldier just in front of me and he was as scared as I was. He kept saying 'Matte, matte, matte' – which means death. I wished I was back in Walthamstow on the local paper . . . One poor chap from the Veterinary Corps was sitting in the latrine, saw a light, thought it was an attacking force and fired his Sten, which got caught in his trousers. The light was just fireflies.[8]

From 1953 when naval and RAF helicopters began to be used to transport infantry into deep locations – reducing what would have been a week's trek to an hour – and RAF DC3s could drop parachute canisters of supplies – allowing patrols to stay in the jungle for weeks rather than days – the CTs were losing the war of attrition.[9] The infantry's success in the jungle would never have been achieved without the first prong of the main strategy: the rounding up of the Malay-Chinese in the countryside, most of them squatters eking out a living on the fringe of the jungle. The policy was ruthless. Communities were surrounded before first light, the inhabitants' homes and crops burnt, their agricultural implements destroyed and their livestock slaughtered. They were then transported by lorry to the new locations, which were surrounded by barbed wire and illuminated by searchlights. By 1951 nearly half a million people had been relocated to nearly 500 new villages and some, at least, were grateful enough for having been removed from the CTs' influence that they formed home-guard units for protection.

The job of moving this mass of people also fell to the infantry who, by and large, did it with good humour. Many national servicemen detested what they had to do; others were indifferent. 'We didn't know who were sympathisers or maybe even terrorists – and British soldiers were being killed by British bullets fired from British guns,' observes the Manchester Regiment's Cliff Holland. In the beginning of his time in Malaya with the Marines, Neal Ascherson perhaps felt no differently; he remembers 'rounding up squatters – and while their now empty homes blazed, we'd eat the fruit off the trees'. But he came to feel that the Chinese were hard done by. 'They were almost half the population but they had no civil rights at all, no vote, no schools, they were not even included in the census. No wonder they felt that communism had something to offer while we were privileging the Malay elite. It did seem obvious.' He started a correspondence with a very radical counsellor in Penang. 'I now realise that all her letters would have been opened by Special Branch and I could have been in the soup.'

He was regarded as being extremely eccentric because he wanted to talk to the Chinese:

Senior officers would roll their eyes. 'Why?' 'Well, why don't the Chinese have a vote?' More eye-rolling. My troop commander was worried that I was not reliable; we had arguments. He was a very nice man and I liked him. He simply said I shouldn't be interested in such stuff and it was potentially worrying. If I was spouting this stuff it could demoralise my men, and he was quite correct.

Ascherson kept his views to himself and tried to be a good officer.

I think I was given considerable respect for my extraordinarily good sense of direction – we never got lost in the jungle. And I was physically tough. But I was a weakie in other ways. To a mutinous sub-section I'd say, 'Yes, you're soaking wet, the situation is dangerous and, yes, Sergeant X has said umpteen times he's never seen anything so fucking silly as this op, but, sorry, we're staying and that's that.' And we would stay, because orders are to be obeyed, mine as well as theirs. But there were times when I gave in to them, for which I despised myself. I could be ruthless towards the enemy, but my fault as a human being was always seeing others' point of view. And a desire to be liked, I suppose.

To his eternal regret, Ascherson accidentally caused the death of two civilian Chinese. A group of CTs walked into an ambush the Marines had set outside the perimeter wire of a resettlement camp and in a frantic exchange of fire he ordered the use of a flamethrower. A hut on the corner of the camp was hit and in the morning it was found that an elderly man and woman had died in it. 'Afterwards nobody said using the weapon was a good idea or that it was stupid, no one said anything either way. But I saw myself as a nineteen-year-old imbecile. I felt terrible about it. I still do.'

There was intense regimental rivalry on achieving captures and kills of the enemy. While the Gurkhas achieved most, among the British regiments the Suffolks, half of them NS country lads from East Anglia, accounted for 198 in three and a half years, 'approaching hunting terrorists in the way that they'd been using to poach pheasants'.[10] By 1960 when the emergency ended, no more than 500 terrorists remained to escape over the border into Thailand. The British had suffered 350 killed and many times that in casualties. Most regiments lost around a dozen men; in June 1952, near a town called Tana Ratah 7,000 feet up in the Cameron Highlands, the Manchester Regiment lost five in an ambush.

A patrol of 13, led by an armoured scout car, commonly known as an AFV (armoured fighting vehicle) driven by Cliff Holland, had gone out to rendezvous with Malay police after a large house was set on fire. When they met up, the police decided the mission was too dangerous and the Manchesters went on alone. A corporal was in charge, Eric Michaels remembers, 'because our officer was on a course and the sergeant had got pissed the night before, fallen in a monsoon ditch and broken his arm'. Cliff Holland says: 'We had a little meeting ourselves and decided we'd been given a job to do and we'd do it. We were all well armed and experienced – we'd been in Malaya over a year and we'd seen a lot of violence.' Like most patrols in Malaya they had a variety of weapons: the short, jungle-issue .303 supplemented by American carbines and Australian Owen sub-machine-guns. The scout car had two Brens.

Holland remembers:

> We set off along this track, me in front driving at walking pace, strung out over maybe a hundred and forty yards. Nothing appeared to be out of the ordinary, we were doing exactly what we'd done hundreds of times before, but I had a little premonition, something not right. The lad behind me, Jimmy Lomas the radio operator/Bren gunner, said, 'You're right, Cliff, I can feel it as well.' Down the track a man was chopping logs, something you'd see all over. But as I approached, he lifted his axe high and when I passed, still higher, and I knew he was signalling. Almost immediately a young Chinese girl and a man passed me, no eye contact – and the terrorists opened up.

The patrol were in a cutting and could go neither left nor right, with the terrorists only yards away, shooting down on them. The girl and her companion were killed instantly.

At the rear, Eric Michaels could not see what was happening:

> I went down on one knee, safety catch off, and a row of bullet holes appeared in the bank in front of my nose, fortunately going away from me. I ran across the track and got a spray of bullets in the leg. Pain, a blur, nothing. I came round down below the track with my gun hanging in the

branches twelve feet above. Joe McKibbon joined me. His eye was missing, he was disorientated and vomiting and passing out. I took his machine-gun. Doc Smith looked after Joe – I never did know his first name, he was just Doc. Someone was always the medic, I suppose he'd been given a bit of training. He wanted to give me morphine but I thought it knocked you out and I refused. Then a figure stood up but I didn't know if it was one of my mates and I didn't shoot. He did, he shot me in the shoulder with a revolver. I was flat on the ground and the bullet travelled up and lodged in my neck. I emptied two magazines in his direction one-handed and he disappeared. We could hear them walking about taking weapons off the lads and finishing them off. It was a long time before help came. I don't know how long but it was long. The villagers along the way had blocked the road and it took time.

At the head of the patrol, Holland had pulled one of his comrades, a regular soldier who was Polish, into the safety of the ATV, which the terrorists now tried to blow up; the vehicle went six feet into the air but landed back on its wheels, shredded by gunfire on the near side. Holland managed to get it moving – and drove straight into a secondary ambush. He drove through that, found a clearing so that the radio would work, and Lomas called for help.

There were three of us, and we had a smoke, I remember clearly we had a smoke. The shooting had stopped. I'd been told to stay where I was and wait, but I decided we were going back. My machine-gun had been hit, it was out of action, and the others had expended their ammunition. 'But we're going back,' I said. And we did. In the killing zone the woodcutter was lying across the track obviously wounded. There was no doubt in my mind that he was one of the terrorists – later it was proved that the group had been in position for forty-eight hours before we came along. I had no intention of leaving the vehicle to move him, so I drove over him. I killed him and I'm very glad I did. Just after, a white man came walking towards me with rugby kit on, carrying a machine-gun. It was the doctor from the local military hospital, which wasn't very far away, where they'd picked up the radio message. And this chap, who'd either been on his way to play rugby or was actually playing rugby, went and got a machine-gun to come and help us.

Holland patched up his vehicle, and was issued with a new Bren. 'The atmosphere in the camp was subdued, no effing and blinding. We were a family of boys who were suffering because of what had happened. The sergeant-major, he called me Cliff, he was like our father, really, sat on the bed with me and told me we were going out at dawn, all five or six hundred of us, to try to catch the gang.' The Manchesters were unsuccessful; but some weeks later they shot a CT carrying the rifle of one of the men killed in the ambush 'and we dangled him on the barbed wire of the town as a deterrent. Yes, barbaric, but it gave me some satisfaction.' Holland continued to patrol; in all his time in Malaya he took no leave.

> I can honestly say I never had a day off, I didn't have an outing. I worked. I swam in the river sometimes and had a couple beers when I could afford it. Those were my only pleasures. The bar was a tent with no sides in it and some local contractor used to dispense bottles of beer from a dirty, filthy zinc bath filled with iced water. A notice in the tent said: *In this bar you'll have a drink, you'll have some more and you'll start to think, you'll think of home and all that's dear, and you'll get yourself another beer.* That got me. I didn't know the -isms, communism, capitalism, they didn't mean much to me, those. I didn't have any shares in the Dunlop Rubber Company that we'd been sent over there to protect, I didn't have any shares in the tin mines. After what happened I don't really know whether I should have been there or not. I just wanted to be done and go home.

Eric Michaels, who almost died from the bullet in his neck, spent over four months in hospital in the Cameron Highlands, 'where millionaires have to pay a lot of money to go these days'. The wounded were usually sent to Singapore

> but the doctor kept me because he wanted to perform a skin graft on my leg, which was shattered. He took the skin from my thigh and I'd say the graft was quite good, though I was left with a big scar five or six inches long, and

the leg is shorter than the other. It was his first graft, so I suppose I was an experiment, but I have no complaints on that score. What I was bitter over were my credits. While you're in hospital you don't get any pay, you're credited with what's owing, and in Malaya we got an extra thirty-three and a third per cent, which was paid by the Malayan government. When I asked for my credits to go on leave to Hong Kong – but I couldn't because I discovered I didn't have the Malayan third – the bloody government didn't pay you while you were in hospital because you weren't fighting for them.

Many casualties in Malaya had nothing to do with the terrorists: amoebic dysentery, malaria, scrub-typhus, encephalitis and ringworm among many diseases took a toll. Troops who went to any of the military hospitals had reason to be grateful for the attention they received, mostly from national service doctors who often had specialist knowledge much in advance of their senior regular colleagues. But those wounded or injured in the jungle had more reason for gratitude. In the beginning, army doctors, almost all conscripts, trekked in with the infantry to treat them, operating wherever they could, and then bringing them out; later they were taken by helicopter or light plane to evacuate casualties. Captain John Heber, a Guy's graduate with an interest in anaesthetics, devised a lightweight anaesthetic pack for jungle use. 'Splendid, Heber,' said his CO, 'you can test it in the jungle.' 'But the jungle's full of terrorists, Sir,' was John's reply. 'Excellent, Heber,' quipped back the colonel, 'I see you read your intelligence briefings.'[11]

Second Lieutenant Peter Duffell arrived in Malaya in the summer of 1960, a month after the emergency was officially declared over, but had a campaign medal pinned on him, although he was not entitled to it. A junior reporter on the *Daily Mail* who had been called up into the Green Jackets, he was impressed by a Gurkha officer at Mons OCTS ('and I'd seen the Gurkhas on the Coronation parade and I'd read John Masters'), applied to serve with a Gurkha battalion and, 'after a formidable interview', was accepted. 'They were incomparable soldiers,' he says. 'The life they led before being recruited made them quite used to the rigours of the jungle, which were so alien to British troops. And they were career soldiers, serving fifteen years at least, a huge number of them from the Second World War

121

with two rows of medals.' Duffell had to learn their language. 'I was no great linguist but all orders were given in Nepali and learning it was the only means of communicating.'

During the 12 years of the Malayan emergency, 134 officers received the Military Cross, including national servicemen Raymond Douglas from Bath (with the Somersets), Leslie Hands of Woodford Green (with the Suffolks) and John Dunton from Isleworth (with the Green Jackets). National servicemen were also among the 264 rankers and junior NCOs awarded the Military Medal. Cliff Holland was promised an MM by his company commander but did not get it. When his patrol was ambushed and his corporal killed he had taken charge of the situation, he had given an account to the military and civil courts of inquiry, and when the ambush position was photographed and measured so that it could be reconstructed at the school of jungle warfare, he was asked to go to Kotta Tinggi to verify its authenticity (it is still in army manuals, described as 'textbook'). And yet the medal 'went to the Polish regular at the side of me, who'd done nothing really and whose English was so poor they only knew his part from what I told them'. Holland adds: 'As a private soldier I had done everything humanly possible, and as God's in heaven, my OC promised me. Not to get the medal hurt. It still does.'

∗ ∗ ∗

In Britain, a widespread belief was that the Mau Mau massacred hundreds of Kenya's white settlers. In reality, they killed 32 – fewer than died in Nairobi traffic accidents during the same four years of the emergency.

The Kikuyu, the largest tribe in the colony, had long sought land reform, which the British refused to consider. Counter-insurgency by the Mau Mau, a secret society of militants within the tribe, was the outcome.

As in Malaya, the insurgents needed the support of the people. Unlike in Malaya, the majority of the Kikuyu were against the terror tactics adopted by the Mau Mau, who obtained their support only by preying on their religious superstitions and binding them with blood oaths and threats. Those who refused were butchered: disembowelled, cut to pieces, buried alive. Some 2,000 Kikuyu died like this.

The British military response was to pour in infantry – the Lancashire Fusiliers were the first to arrive, in October 1952, from the Canal Zone, aboard RAF Transport aircraft – and to mobilise local troops, police and auxiliaries. In April 1954 a coordinated cordon-and-search of Nairobi (Operation Anvil), conducted by eight British battalions, rounded up 16,000 suspects and virtually smashed the insurgents' material supply. By then the strategy used in Malaya was being put in place: the scattered rural communities, compliant or not, were being rounded up into new villages that were protected behind barbed wire and trenches of sharpened bamboo – a million Kikuyu by 1955.

'You read that a lot of them didn't want to go, that places were like concentration camps, but that wasn't my experience,' says Harry Crooks, a cabinetmaker from Whitstable in Kent, who took part in Operation Anvil with the East Kents (The Buffs). 'They were very keen in my view. They were more restricted, but they were allowed out during the day to get food and water, they were just expected back by dusk. They were a lot safer out of reach of the Mau Mau.' His friend George Toms, a papermaker also from Whitstable (who signed on for three years once he started his national service and became a sergeant in charge of HQ transport), agrees: 'It's hard to say what people are feeling when they haven't got a lot, but I'd say they were happy. We moved them lock, stock and barrel, cattle, chickens, the lot. All that was left was the carcasses of the huts.'

As with the Chinese-Malays in Malaya, many of the Kikuyu in the new villages formed a home guard and the British infantry armed and trained them to defend themselves. 'Each soldier in my company had a little platoon of his own,' says Harry Crooks. 'It turned out that in mine two Mau Mau had crept in, which I only found out when they were recognised and taken off to Nairobi. We laughed about it, I'd been training the enemy, but it could have been nasty – I'd taken them all out on patrol on my own.'

Black on black atrocities – the most notorious the Lai massacre in which the Mau Mau wrapped electrical cable around the huts of loyal farmworkers, poured petrol on the thatch and burnt 84 people to death, most of them women and children – added a horrific dimension to the Kenya campaign. In fact, compared with the counter-insurgency demands of Egypt, Malaya and Cyprus, it was something of a sideshow. The Mau Mau were a rabble army with no command structure, operating in ill-organised gangs that were poorly armed with machetes, a few rifles, and homemade firearms that were sometimes a greater danger to themselves than to their enemies. 'I never felt I was up against a fighting army,' says George Toms. 'You had to go on patrols and ambushes, which were sometimes scary, but the Mau Mau weren't. We didn't consider we were in real danger.'

With the local population on whom they had relied for food and shelter gone; with links to the capital broken by Operation Anvil; and badly mauled by the security forces in the early months when they attempted to take them on, the Mau Mau were soon on the run. When raiding parties tried to take settlers' cattle for food as they had done with impunity at the start of the emergency, battalion companies and police units now scattered across the farms inflicted heavy casualties. Troops liked being on the farms: they were likely to be offered a bath and better food than their compo rations or the fresh food served in the base camps. 'The QM claims that the Command supplies are the worst ever,' commented the battalion newsletter of the King's Shropshire Light Infantry (KSLI), 'which is probably true as the Kenya Government are not free with expenditure.'[12]

Indeed, some men in regiments who were in Kenya in the later stages chose to spend the ten days' leave they were given after six months of active service working on a farm, rather than go to the leave centre in Mombasa. 'I liked our units being on farms because I was the battalion plumber and had to set up a safe water supply wherever we fetched up,' says Al Barkley, a painter and decorator from Dudleston Heath near Ellesmere in Shropshire, who was with the KSLI. 'On the farms I knew I had a good supply. In the forests there were a lot of abandoned forestry department facilities I could tap. In some places I had to work miracles!'

Kenya's own forces shouldered most of the responsibility for the campaign: the three Kenyan battalions of the King's African Rifles, strengthened by a battalion from Uganda, another from Tanganyika (present-day Tanzania) and a platoon led by national service Second Lieutenant Tom King, now Lord King of Bridgwater; the Kenya Regiment territorials; and the Kukuyu tribal police. But 55,000 men from 21 rotated British regiments did their share, as did RAF spotter planes and Lincoln bombers in the upland forests. Finally trapped around Mount Kenya and the Aberdares range, the Mau Mau were reduced to rags and starvation.

And in the high forests the security forces picked them off, helped in the last year by 'pseudo-gangs' of ex-Mau Mau led by disguised white Kenyans. Only remnants of the insurgents were left when C company of the KSLI – which had more kills than the rest of the battalion put together – spent three wet and chilly weeks on the 13,000 ft plateau of the Aberdares, seeing nothing but 'herds of elephants, rhino and buffalo, which were far more dangerous than the elusive Mau Mau'.[13] The largest count of kills (290) and captures (194) among British battalions was made by The Buffs very early in the emergency; subsequently the regiment discouraged tally-taking. 'That made all of us happy,' says George Toms. 'It wasn't a competition. I don't like to think I killed another human being, but I fired a lot and I must have. But keeping score wasn't nice.' An estimated 10,500 Mau Mau died and 30,000 were captured.[14] Of the 600 security forces killed, only 12 were with British units.

Men who fought against the Mau Mau had little sympathy for them. 'There were eight of us in my tent and I can honestly say no one expressed such a view,' says Al Barkley. 'They were the enemy – that's it.' Says George Toms: 'I understood what they wanted out of home rule, but I saw some of the things they did – they chopped the legs off their own people's cattle as a warning and it wasn't a pretty sight; the officers had to shoot the poor animals. I didn't feel sorry for the Mau Mau.'

In Britain there were confused feelings about the rights and wrongs of the insurgency and pubs in some places including London and Liverpool had collection boxes for Mau Mau widows. It is going too far to say that the Mau Mau had a clear vision of an independent Kenya, but their failed insurgency created circumstances that made continued imperialism unjustifiable, unaffordable and unviable. The guerrilla campaign ended in 1956; in 1963, just as national service ended, Kenya was granted self-government.

*   *   *

In December 1954 Greek-Cypriot youths on the island of Cyprus tore down the Union Jack over the police station in Limassol and replaced it with the Greek national flag. Two rioters were shot when British soldiers were ordered to fire on the crowd. By the end of the following year Cyprus was in a state of emergency, Eoka terrorists were carrying out acts of sabotage on military installations, throwing hand grenades at army patrols and blowing up vehicles with electrically detonated mines. The dull crump of detonations and the small mushroom-like clouds that appeared against the blue sky became commonplace across the landscape.

The British were hampered by a lack of military intelligence and had no help from the Greek-Cypriot police who, in ratio to the population, were over 80% of the force and were either Eoka sympathisers or were pressured into inactivity; the authorities had to bring in volunteer police sergeants from the UK. In Malaya and Kenya the authorities had been able to isolate a large proportion of the civilian population and win their cooperation; in Cyprus that was impossible: virtually all the 400,000 Greek inhabitants were on the side of the terrorists. What the British did not know for a long time was that the head of the Greek Orthodox Church, Archbishop Makarios, was complicit in recruiting the retired Greek army colonel George Grivas to organise and lead the resistance movement, whose aim was *enosis* – union with Greece.

Grivas was known to operate out of the Troödos mountains in the west of the island or the Kyrenia range north of Nicosia, or both, but, without the information to build up a coherent picture, the British chased shadows. In the three and a half years that the emergency was in place, 14 battalions, sometimes at brigade strength, conducted sweeps, helped by RAF helicopters and spotter planes, fruitlessly looking for 'Uncle George', as the troops called him. On one occasion, when Grivas was thought to be in the hills above Limassol, every available soldier on the island took part in a massive operation, including Roy Battelle, whose usual job was taking his REME mobile workshop anywhere that army vehicles, armaments or optical equipment needed repair. 'The Paras dropped in on the suspect area at daybreak, there were the Marines in a circle around the drop, a second line of infantry in the flush-out – and us down below checking and searching vehicles and passengers. Compared with the fighting troops we were a shambles.'

When he was not on the road doing running repairs, Battelle was at 3rd Infantry Workshop where he saw a lot of written-off vehicles that Eoka had blown up. 'When you saw how bombs ripped through the bodywork and killed or injured drivers and passengers, it made me very sombre. It was heartbreaking to see the sandbags on the floors. Men loaded piles of sandbags in the hope that if they hit a mine they'd take some of the force. In some cases they did and in others they didn't.'

In the day-to-day fight against Eoka, infantry units concentrated on the towns and villages, stopping, searching, patrolling. During rioting they learned to adopt the box formation – first used by the British in India and employed in many places including Singapore, Hong Kong and Aden – with two men holding a banner saying *Disperse or we fire* in the local languages, another with a loudhailer and, when occurrences could be anticipated, an officer's clerk in the middle of the box recording all orders and events. On sentry duty men called out 'Halt' in English, Greek and Turkish, with orders to do so three times before opening fire. Just before Roy Battelle joined 3rd Infantry Workshop 'someone let off a full magazine. When the guard were called out they found a donkey had paid the price for not answering back.' There were many disturbances, most of them orchestrated by women. Eoka frequently put flags on village churches and when soldiers arrived to take them down, the women gathered to throw stones. In the towns, youths threw stones and schoolgirls mouthed obscenities. Soldiers detested being confronted by teenage girls, who were known to smuggle arms under their clothing but who could only be searched by a policewoman or by WRACs. One unit, reportedly a well-known Irish regiment,

> got over the problem of a shortage of womanpower by dressing up one of their young officers as a policewoman to search a bus in which the women passengers were suspected of hiding arms. Thank God he found a large amount of weapons and the women were arrested but, of course, there was a God Almighty row afterwards and everybody was frightfully upset, claiming that this was a foul.[15]

In Malaya and Kenya popular support for the terrorist organisations weakened over time; the opposite occurred in Cyprus. At the beginning of their campaign, Eoka had no more than one or two hundred activists; by the end they perhaps had as many as 700. And, throughout, their grassroots network kept their finger on British activities. 'Anyone in the street could be a terrorist or an informer,' says Adrian Walker, stationed as a corporal in Larnaka with the Intelligence Corps port and travel unit. A friend of his, a national service subaltern in the Royal Artillery (the Gunners), was unhurt when a hand grenade was thrown at his Landrover. A few days later he got a letter, written in good English, addressed to him by name and rank at his billet which read: *Dear Lieutenant Mortimer, sorry about the other night, we thought you were the Military Police.* Walker adds:

Eoka and the Military Police had a war within a war for some reason, a private feud like the Paras decades later in Northern Ireland with the IRA. But that Gerry got such a letter I found quite frightening. They knew everything. The buggers were watching us all the time. Anybody could be an enemy, or, nobody, you just didn't know.

Walker got to Cyprus when the terror campaign was in its third year, but negotiations were going on and tensions had eased. His I Corps unit's job was to watch for terrorist activity in the port, to patrol the coast (in high-speed launches driven by RASC boat section) and go on board the passenger liners. Most of the time he was in civilian clothes, 'a hybrid customs officer, policeman and soldier, with a shoulder holster under my coat – not the average soldier's experience'. In April 1958 the negotiations broke down 'and they started killing us again.'

The previous year, two officers of the Royal Horse Guards were shot within a few days of each other, one the medical officer in his car on his way to attend to a Greek family, the other doing the shopping at a Limassol grocer's where he had been going for a year; the mess waiter died with him. 'I was orderly clerk when the doctor drove off into the town,' says Graham Williams, who was with the Horse Guards' armoured section HQ in Nicosia. 'He was a national serviceman from St Andrews. An hour later they brought back his clothing.' It was a matter of bewilderment to the British that such an intensely religious country could sanction the killings. Williams says: 'We went into the mountains one night and rounded up everyone in a small village for an informer with us to point out the Eoka and the sympathisers – and two of them were priests. On the lorry coming back I asked one of them why and he said, "I believe in the Lord Jesus Christ", and that's all he would say.'

Eoka favoured soft targets – soldiers off duty or out shopping with their wives – and Ledra Street in Nicosia, where there were 19 murders, became notorious as 'Murder Mile'. When such murders occurred, troops often reacted with anger, roughtly treating crowds or people stopped in vehicle searches. When a gunman shot a soldier's wife out shopping with her young child, the Paras' crackdown on Famagusta resulted in four deaths and the local hospital full of injured citizens. 'The gunman's cowardly action could never hope to justify the rough treatment the battalion meted out that night,' says Hugh Grant. 'I do remember feeling guilty on our behalf.' Such incidents – and a confirmed case of ill-treatment of prisoners by two regular army officers, convicted by court martial – played into Eoka's hands. Grivas organised wider allegations of brutality against British forces as part of a propaganda effort that involved the church and the Cyprus press. In the UK, *The Times* acknowledged that 'it was foolish to think it [ill-treatment] didn't happen',[16] but as investigations discovered, most complaints were exaggerated or false – one alleged that troops had buried Greeks up to their necks in sand on Famagusta beach and spread their heads with jam to attract ants – and some were withdrawn even before they were investigated.

The British army were outraged to discover that Eoka's most ruthless killer, responsible among many others for the Horse Guards' losses, was a reporter on *The Times of Cyprus*, who often came back to a murder scene in his professional guise. Nicos Sampson was unmasked as a result of a tip-off. About a month later when Graham Williams was again on orderly duty, the police,

who were now mostly British guys, rang to ask me to get hold of the nearest officer. 'We've got him,' they said. We got off a lorryload of men and they surrounded a farmhouse where Sampson was sleeping with his Sten gun. One of the troopers shot him in the leg when he went for it, and they took him back to police headquarters. The police said, 'You can have the first few minutes with him', and the lads gave him a wee doing. That somewhat delayed his trial.[17] We should have shot the bastard.

When Grivas turned his attention to the Turkish population, attacking little hamlets and burning them to the ground, the situation degenerated into a civil war that the British could barely contain. In the spring of 1958, 120 Greeks and Turks were murdered, the most notorious incident being the Gkuenyeli massacre. The Greek villagers of Skyloura, taken in for questioning and document checks, were mistakenly dropped back outside the Turkish village of Gkuenyeli, whose inhabitants, thinking the Greeks were an Eoka gang, poured out and hacked them to pieces. 'It was a very messy business. Nine Greeks were killed and many others mutilated. Hands and fingers were all over the place and one officer wandered around, rather green in the face, holding a head and asking if anyone had seen a body which might fit it.'[18]

For servicemen caught up in the Eoka campaign, Cyprus was not always stressful. The weather was mostly idyllic and, unlike in Egypt, the tented camps were not unpleasant and the food was reasonable 'though they sometimes spoiled cornflakes, would you believe,' comments Roy Battelle. 'There were few cows on the island and consequently our milk was powder – sometimes in lumps'. At Christmas, however, he adds, the fare was 'slap-up'. When there were lulls in the violence it was possible to go into the towns, although someone in a group was always in uniform and armed, or to go swimming, with sentries posted. 'Most units got to one or two beaches that were considered safe,' says Graham Williams. 'We had a daily lorry that went to Kyrenia, sometimes two. One day we went up there and the beach was closed off. Eoka had mined it and two or three guys before us had been killed.' At times of heightened tension men were confined to camp. In his first four months in Larnaka, Adrian Walker was able to go the pictures; in his last ten months, if he was not on duty, he was unable to leave his tent in the police station compound beside the port. 'We were just the right sort of little outfit to knock off.' He and his seven companions had small oil stoves for warmth but no washing or cooking facilities. 'We heated water from the tap in the yard and went months without a bath. We ate at Nick's café across the road, under armed guard.' Walker remembers 'the general awfulness of life for Cypriots – the breaking into Greek homes to carry out searches, the endemic looting by British squaddies'. A squad led by his friend Gerry Mortimer 'burst into a house one night with guns and started ripping up the floorboards and frightening the children, the grandmother having hysterics – and the householder looked at the disarray and said, "Would you and your men like some coffee?" Gerry said he felt about that bloody tall.' When the ceasefire came the Intelligence unit's RASC driver, Dave Lacey, 'went into town for a walk with a companion who was armed, and came back almost in tears. A little kid, prompted by his parents, had run out of the door, kissed his hand and run off again.' Above all, Walker remembers the curfews:

> Someone would be killed and there'd be a twenty-four-hour curfew. No one was able to go home or get out of their homes to the shops. The curfew might be lifted, there'd be another shooting or bombing, and it would be put back on. The record between one curfew being lifted and another imposed was twenty-five minutes. At times it was as if the town were under plague.

Finally, after over 400 deaths including 105 servicemen's, Britain was forced to reach a diplomatic solution. The Greek-Cypriots were persuaded to accept a compromise: Britain would retain its military and naval bases in Cyprus, which would become independent, with both Greeks and Turks sharing power – and no *enosis*. No one had 'won'.[19]

*   *   *

By 1958 the little island of Malta, awarded the George Cross for its endurance during the Second World War, was also seeking independence, though it never adopted violence to achieve it. But there were demonstrations, the island was plastered with posters and some scuffles with military personnel ensued; by 1960, when Roger Keight worked in REME radio maintenance and repair at 235 Signals Squadron, Mtarfa, some areas in and around the capital, Valletta, were off limits:

> The locals were always friendly and we got on well with the Maltese civilian staff attached to the workshop – we used to visit the home of one of them. The only incident I recall happened one night when we were walking back through the narrow streets rather the worse for wear and we were set upon by a crowd with bottles. One or two or us got cuts and I had a large bump

on my head. We took refuge in the nearby police station and they phoned the camp, who sent a truck to collect us.[20]

* * *

No bullets flew in West Germany, but the possibility of the Red Army rolling over the whole of Europe made the Federal Republic the centre of Britain's military commitment throughout national service and, indeed, for more than 25 years beyond.

The Russians' attempt to blockade Berlin in 1949 and prevent their then allies from unifying the west of Germany made Britain's open-ended commitment inevitable. In the mid-fifties when the French were alarmed at the imminent prospect of the Federal Republic being rearmed, Britain did more, promising to station four divisions – a third of the entire army – and a tactical air force on the continent for as long as deemed necessary. It was a massive commitment, at any time involving up to 80,000 men.

In many respects Germany, where the British zone in the north included the industrial Ruhr, was a curious place to be in the 1950s. In the three years of the Korean War, the tension was great, the likelihood of hostilities breaking out real; that was also true in 1956 when Hungary demanded neutrality and Russian tanks occupied Budapest and overthrew the government; and again in the late fifties when the Soviet Union and the United States were brandishing intercontinental ballistic missiles at each other, raising the spectre of nuclear conflict on the German plains. But peace in Korea, coinciding with the death of Stalin, relaxed the situation to a large degree and a posting to Germany became generally seen as safe, and comfortable, if dull. Indeed, after the Federal Republic was rearmed and BAOR ceased to be an army of occupation, Germany began to be referred to as a 'home posting' – a definition which, given the still potentially dangerous situation, men were always puzzled by; today, the Ministry of Defence is unable to explain satisfactorily how it came about. 'I can only think that describing Germany as a home posting saved the government from having to pay men an overseas allowance,' says Bill Hetherington, for 20 years the honorary archivist of the Peace Pledge Union but in 1952 a Birmingham schoolboy called into the navy to serve at Cuxhaven on the German coast as a monitor of Russian air traffic.

There was nothing of a home posting about the Germany that Alan Tizzard, a tank commander in the 10th King's Hussars at Iserlohn in 1950 remembers:

> Korea was on and communist domination was feared in the West. The Armoured Corps was on forty-eight-hour standby, looking at the Russian tanks looking at them and knowing that war was the squeezing of a trigger away. We didn't have Centurions then, we had obsolete Valentine Archers designed in 1939, and we got numerous calls to arms in the middle of the night, with rumours of Russian panzer attacks. Truthfully there were occasions when we thought we would never see another dawn.

Confirms Tam Dalyell, a tank crew trooper with the Scots Greys at Lüneburg on the Elbe:

> By God I can't tell you how seriously we took it. At the time when things were going wrong in Korea on the Yalu river, the colonel called us all together and said, 'Get your tanks absolutely ready for action.' There was talk of the Red Peril. It was a sinking feeling, thinking that Dalyell was the first line of defence, with the Russians twenty-five kilometres away. Had they decided to roll across Europe we might all have faced a different future – as I sometimes say to older people sitting on park benches.

Glyn Jones, a signaller/wireless operator at Royal Artillery Battery HQ in Düsseldorf, adds:

> Had the Russians come through the Irish Guards whom we were supporting, we'd have had it. In two years I fired ten rounds from a rifle, ten from a Sten, five from a revolver and I'd never been on the field guns. Signalling was my one and only killing trade. I'd been issued with an archaic Piat, an early anti-tank rocket thing with a powerful spring. I didn't know how to load it never mind fire it – I didn't do anything with it except clean it. But the sergeant told me quite seriously that I was an essential cog in the wheel that would roll back the Russian hordes. Made me laugh, that.

The Call-Up

Senior Aircraftsman Gordon Williams, working in air traffic control 30 miles from the East German border at RAF Gütersloh in 1953, 'twice felt war was ready to go'.

The Russian MiG jets had a habit of dashing in to test the radar – they could tell from their scanning equipment what our response times had been. One Sunday morning I was on watch with my mate George when the German police phoned that MiGs were flying over Hanover. Really, this was deadly serious. A run over the rooftops of Hanover was exactly the way an invasion would start, and they'd be on us in three or four minutes. I phoned the duty officer but he'd nipped off to the officers' mess where there was a buffet party. I phoned the mess. The officer who answered was pissed out of his head. Eventually I screamed at him the name of the officer I wanted and he went to fetch him, leaving the receiver swinging against the wall.

It just so happened that the duty driver came up the stairs, so he drove off to the mess and got the duty officer back. It took us just under an hour to get four planes off. The incident was passed off as a bit of a joke. Everybody covered up for everything and everybody. But it was dereliction of duty, except for me and George and the driver.

Had there been conventional war, Alan Tizzard says, the life expectancy of a tank commander was reckoned to be 36 hours. The life expectancy of a Royal Artillery short-range surveyor, Malcolm Higgins found out, was 20 minutes.

A surveyor's job in battle was to occupy the ground between the two front lines, accurately survey the terrain with the help of microphones set up specific distances apart and to a specific depth, linked back to a printer that churned out the information. The gunners were so good they could put a shell into a beer barrel. But they had to know where the beer barrel was, so to speak, and to ascertain that I had to stand up. In Germany I attended a NATO talk where an American general showed a new disposition of forces as three big circles with big gaps between which, he said, unfortunately, they had to leave if nuclear weapons were used. 'Where do the surveyors work?' I asked. He pointed to a gap. So if I wasn't blown up, I'd be nuked.

During the Hungarian uprising in 1956, it seemed that the 'Tripwire' strategy, which had been in place for six years, might go live; had the Soviets' intentions had wider objectives, designated units would have attempted to hold the advance while everyone else pulled back over the Rhine and awaited reinforcements from the UK and America. Briefly, BAOR was mobilised and, Higgins remembers, 'there was a lot of rushing up and down the autobahns – then suddenly we were stood down. Then it was very, very real and one can only surmise what would have happened if the West had gone to Hungary's aid.' He remembers being disappointed: 'We were young, and invincible, and we'd been robbed of our chance to go out and save the world.'

Very few servicemen in Germany gave much for Britain's chances in the face of conflict; Russia had an active army of nearly five million, over 50 divisions, and another two million troops in the satellite countries. 'If the Russians had come it was next stop Dunkirk,' says Glyn Jones.

BAOR trained constantly against the eventuality at all levels and most of the British army ranged across the Sennelager training area, Germany's answer to Salisbury Plain, and Lüneburg Heath, culminating in a big NATO exercise every autumn when, says Alan Herbert, who served with the 10th Hussars, 'the crops were in and we could do what we wanted in our Centurions'. No tankie who served in Germany will forget the tank train to Hohne where the armoured division went every year for a hectic fortnight of open-range firing, but no German who saw the tankies going off on exercise will have forgotten them either. Commanders, often sporting cigarette holders, stood up nonchalantly in their vehicles, slapping the side of them with riding crops, invariably with a dog sitting beside them. According to Second Lieutenant 'Mac' McCullagh of the 5th Royal Tank Regiment:

> The Germans could never understand the British sense of humour . . . each time we drove through a German village, the dog would take its place on top of the turret wearing a Tank Regiment beret with earphone headsets, all the hatches would be closed so none of the crew could be seen and by the time the squadron had passed through, the whole of the German population

would be shaking their heads and saying: 'The crazy British – they have their dogs commanding the Panzers!'[21]

Generally, men enjoyed exercises, which got them out of barracks and broke the routine: they were like the real thing. They grumbled, of course, particularly when the weather was bad and living under canvas for a month or six weeks was no joke – 'and we did things like 'lose' the cookhouse to learn how to go without food,' says Glyn Jones. The infantry thought the Armoured Corps had an easy time of it. Alan Tizzard acknowledges he sometimes pitied the infantry 'sitting in trenches alongside the road, with the barrels of their rifles poking out from under their ponchos in the rain,' but adds: 'They didn't have to dig a tank out of the mud, or change its tracks in the mud, or run the engines at regular intervals throughout the night to stop it seizing up in the cold.' For their part the infantry practised ten- or twenty-mile withdrawal marches in the dark and dug trenches, as did the support units. 'The British army dug hundreds and thousands of holes,' says Glyn Jones. 'I'm sure we moved the Ruhr Valley sideways about a foot.'

The barracks in Germany made up for a lot. Almost all were built in the 1930s for the *Wehrmacht*, *SS* or *Luftwaffe*, were centrally heated and double-glazed, had constant hot water – and men slept two to six to a room. Gordon Williams found RAF Gütersloh 'like a three-star hotel'; Glyn Jones thought Düsseldorf 'Shangri-la'. Posted to Brunswick, Second Lieutenant Tony Thorne, who had left The Buffs for a commission in the East Surrey Regiment, discovered that

> The barracks themselves had been custom-built for some of the Führer's crack Panzer troops and they constituted almost a city within the city . . . We had a camp cinema the size of the Odeon, Leicester Square, an indoor sports complex that included a full-size hockey pitch, and an officers' mess like the Taj Mahal. There was a gymnasium that could have been a venue for the Olympic Games, swimming pools and acres of playing fields.[22]

If anything, the officers' mess at HQ Bielefeld possibly proved to be more sumptuous. 'It was a former Nazi headquarters and it was palatial, it's the only word,' says Service Corps Second Lieutenant Derrick Johns, who was in charge of 91 Company of staff cars. 'All the rooms were individual and en suite. There were tennis courts, a swimming pool, sports room, training rooms, a ballroom – it was like living in the Ritz.'

The food, too – as Education Corps sergeant-instructor Rodney Dale had been told and as he found at No 1 Wireless Regiment in Münster – was excellent in all messes. 'Very different to what was served up in Catterick,' comments Alan Tizzard, 'and the dining hall had tablecloths and waitress service – the first time I went in I thought I'd gone into the officers' mess.' 'As duty officer I had no qualms about asking were there any complaints, which was hardly the case back home,' says Derrick Johns. 'But the food in the officers' mess was beyond belief, the finest food ever eaten in the army, I'd think. And for special functions there were the most fantastic displays – you know, boars' heads on plates. The chefs were superb.'

Berlin was very different to the rest of Germany, an island, in effect, in the communist half of the country. When Don Bullock went there with the East Yorkshire Regiment at the end of 1951 'the city was still in ruins, people still living in cellars. But it was easy for us to travel round, we didn't have to pay fares on the trams. The only setback was the many guard duties – two guards on main gate, guards provided for Berlin HQ, internal security platoon on standby in case of any disturbances, Spandau prison.' Bullock liked guard at the prison, where the seven major Nazi war criminals not sentenced to death at the Nuremberg trials were held,[23] which detachments of the four occupying powers did in monthly rotation.

> The wall had six sentry boxes round the top, each with a fixed machine-gun, searchlight, and tickertape. Outside the wall was an electric fence, then a barbed wire fence. To change guard the sentry would lower a ladder that worked on a pivot, the new sentry would go up, the old one down and then the ladder would be swung up. I felt king of the castle marching between my sentry box and the next.

It was the death of King George VI in February 1952 that caused Bullock a moment of shamed embarrassment:

We were on the city Rhuleben ranges waiting to be trained on using the revolver when two or three German policemen came to our position and had a word with our officer. He told us to get to our feet because we were going back to camp. As we were freezing our asses off sitting on about two feet of snow we gave a loud cheer. The police looked scandalised – but we didn't know at that point.

Many servicemen within lorry-driving distance of the village of Belsen in Lower Saxony visited the Nazi concentration camp, a potent symbol of what war could mean. Derrick Johns took about 40 men who were singing all the way there on a trip of about 50 miles. 'We were there for three or four hours – and hard men were crying. There was no singing in the lorries going back.' On a 'netting' exercise in which field radios were being tuned to the main set at camp, Glyn Jones went to a map reference in the dark 'and the little lad from Cardiff who was driving said, "There are ghosts here." We found we were on the Belsen site. It put the wind up me.'

*   *   *

Men who fought in the Korean War were awarded the specially struck Korean medal from the British government and the United Nations medal (nicknamed 'MacArthur's pyjamas', because of its blue and white striped ribbon); soldiers and airmen who served in the Malaya and Cyprus emergencies received the General Service Medal (the GSM; NGSM for sailors), as they did for service in the Arabian Peninsula[24] and in the short military operation that followed Nasser's seizure of the Suez Canal after the British departure (see *Chapter 10*). Those who took part in the campaign against the Mau Mau in Kenya were awarded the African GSM. But there was no medal for the quarter of a million veterans of the Canal Zone – giving rise to a bitter argument that lasted half a century.

Why Egypt was the only post-1945 campaign for which no medal was given – where more men were killed than in Kenya, the Arabian Peninsula and the Suez invasion (and, in recent years, the first Gulf war and in the Balkans) – is a confused issue.

Initially, it appears that the Foreign Office were reluctant to make the award, when negotiations with Egypt were delicate, although as Colonel

Ashley Tinson, author of *Medals Will Be Worn*, the standard text on medals, says, 'Why they should think that a medal would tip the balance while the arrival of about 60,000 extra troops would go unnoticed, I cannot imagine.' Thereafter, all British governments rejected claims, on the grounds that the Army Council turned down the case in 1952 as did the Honours and Decorations Committee in 1956.

Both assertions were proved to be wrong by a group of ex-servicemen who spent years compiling evidence. Firstly, there was nothing in the records to show that the Army Council had rejected a claim – in fact General Sir Brian Robertson, Commander-in-Chief of the Middle East, applied for the GSM to be awarded and there seems to have been a file in which a recommendation was agreed, although this went missing. Secondly, the honours committee never did consider the matter; it could only have done so had a recommendation come to it from a government department and this did not happen. It *did* receive a proposal from a member of the public – the basis of the government claim for a medal being turned down – but being an unofficial proposal it was not tabled. There was other incontrovertible evidence. In November 1951 Cabinet minutes declared the Suez Zone to be 'active service'; in the House of Commons in January 1952, Foreign Secretary Sir Anthony Eden referred to the conflict as 'war'.

Even then the Zone veterans – who in 1998, after a reunion visit to Egypt, formed an association and submitted a 20,000-signature petition – had other obstacles placed in their path. A full review by the Ministry of Defence deemed that 'no new evidence had come to light', and the government stated that applications could not be considered if an operation was more than five years old, also suggesting that the issue should have been pursued in the fifties. 'As if,' says Jock Marrs, 'lads of about twenty years of age, with no collective clout, and with many of the records closed for years, could have done a bloody thing.' The veterans were able to scotch that one: the rules said nothing about a five-year cut-off, referring only to 'a reasonable period'; more tellingly, they were able to show that the scribbled note on which the MoD relied for saying that the honours committee had said no to a medal in fact referred to *gallantry* medals, not the GSM.

With the government still resisting, the association drummed up considerable public and press support; in a letter to the *Western Daily Press*, Acker Bilk wrote: 'We are all getting older and perhaps that is what the Government wants. If we all die, it can be forgotten.'[25] A number of MPs who backed the claim forced three parliamentary debates in 15 months and on 11 June 2003, in a written answer to a parliamentary question, the medal was awarded, to coincide with the Queen's Golden Jubilee.

The decades of Whitehall opposition remain inexplicable. 'Cock-up or conspiracy?' asked MP Bob Blizzard in the House. 'As I believe that the former was more likely, it gives us more cause to put things right.' Colonel Tinson comments: 'I believe that once the Foreign Office took its original stance, it became a matter of "face". It's as simple as that.' Adds Jock Marrs: 'Fifty years late – but better late than never.'

7

Jammy bastards

To national servicemen wanting to go overseas, Hong Kong was the plum; the 12,000-strong garrison was there ostensibly to prevent a communist invasion, but as China's smuggling through the colony was its only contact with the outside world and its only source of hard cash, the likelihood was remote. Singapore was a good second, and Malaya as long as you weren't infantry; like Hong Kong both smacked of the Orient. Getting anywhere in the Med was considered a fair result, even Cyprus during the troubles. The same was true of Kenya. Austria was popular: unlike Germany, the country had not been completely devastated, the weather was good – the garrisons at Craz, Klagenfurt and Villach were issued with tropical kit in the summer – and Italy was just over the border. By the time the posting ended in the mid-fifties,[1] tensions in Germany had lessened and the possibility of some social life there made it reasonably attractive.

There were postings, too, that men did not even know were possible, like the Bahamas, Bermuda, British Honduras and Jamaica, and postings for individuals that were out of the run of things such as SHAPE (Supreme Headquarters, Allied Powers, Europe) in Paris or the Allied Air Forces Central Europe HQ at Fontainebleau 40 miles away, or, if a man did not get out of the UK, the War Office or Air Ministry in London – civilian digs, perhaps, even civvies at work (definitely excused boots) and uniform only once a week for pay parade. And there were cushy numbers at some supply depots that had so few personnel that there were no parades; and some men were posted down the road from home, getting a permanent living, out pass and going to and fro like any other job – like the Kenyon twins, Norman and John, who, after a vehicle mechanical course, went to a workshop in Eccles near their home in Manchester. 'We used to joke we were posted across the water,' says John. 'The Bridgewater Canal.'

For anyone whose job or posting was regarded as lucky, 'The service expression of the day' – as comedian Bob Monkhouse noted on getting to the RAF central London medical establishment, with promotion to corporal and permission to commute from his parents' home in Beckenham – 'was jammy bastard.'[2]

*   *   *

A national serviceman with musical ability or sporting prowess was likely to fall on his feet; the forces were fiercely proud of their regimental bands and even more fiercely proud of any sporting trophies in the display cabinet. Those who became bandsmen, and sportsmen who might help bring back the silverware, were looked after, drew light duties, got time off for practice – and travelled the world. During the summer months in particular, the bands were out and about, playing at shows, fêtes and concerts.[3]

> In Scottish regiments pipers were very special soldiers indeed ... With the band of the Scots Guards, Drew Bennett ... took part in the Royal Tournament at Earl's Court, the Trooping of the Colour at Horse Guards, and the Edinburgh Military Tattoo; his skills as a highland dancer took him to perform at the Royal Caledonian Ball and at 'countless other memorable engagements'. Nor were these the only benefits: the extra money ... helped to finance his studies at art college when he had completed his National Service.[4]

The national service years were ones of terrific inter-service rivalry at sport – all sport: football, rugby, hockey, boxing, golf, cricket, athletics, skiing. Units vied with each other when outstanding professionals or amateurs were about to be conscripted. 'The CO was boxing mad. He kept an eye peeled for likely young fighters coming up for national service and wangled them,' says Henry Cooper, already British amateur heavyweight champion when, with twin brother Jim – and Joe Erskine – he went into the Ordnance Corps near Aldershot. 'In two years our battalion never lost a match.' A company commander in Germany who owned two horses that he raced, somehow managed to get professional jockeys posted to him. According to Dr John Blair, at the Medical Corps depot at Crookham:

> All the billet orderlies . . . were, or seemed to be, professional footballers. They were absent from Friday afternoons to play on Saturdays, and during the week for training. At least one rugby international spent his entire 2 years at the Depot so that he could play for the Corps team.[5]

Blair himself was taken off a draft to Korea in March 1953 because he played off a single-figure golf handicap and the corps required his services. The novelist Andrew Sinclair, a subaltern in the Coldstream Guards, 'did nothing after basic training except guard palaces and play golf for the regiment, which won the cup that year. Once we won, the general came up to me and said "Andrew, you must play golf for us next year." "Sorry, sir," I said, " 'I'm going to Cambridge." '[6]

If top-class sportsmen hoped to get abroad, most were disappointed – the forces preferred to keep them in the UK; the Leeds footballer Jackie Charlton remained at Windsor during his service with the Horse Guards, but that was because the regiment were not then involved in foreign duty. He was the first private soldier (trooper) to be appointed team captain – and he was well aware of the team's privileges:

> We could have late breakfast, for example, because it fitted into our training programme. In fact every conceivable excuse was dreamed up as to why we should have more time to train. In the end, we were like a professional team, and we duly repaid our debt by going to Germany and winning the Cavalry Cup in Hanover. In army terms, that was like winning the FA Cup.[7]

Another privilege that recognised sportsmen enjoyed was time off to play for their clubs (the Surrey and later England cricketer Peter May in 1947 managed to finish third in the first-class batting averages during national service in the navy). In Jack Charlton's case he got home almost every

Friday to turn out for Leeds, though mostly in the reserves. Younger brother Bobby (now Sir Bobby Charlton), an RASC storeman based near Shrewsbury, got the same consideration, getting home to play for Manchester United. 'I think the club had pulled a few strings to get me posted reasonably close to Manchester,' he says. The army team of his time – including Alan Hodgkinson (Sheffield and England goalkeeper), Billy Foulkes, Duncan Edwards and Eddie Coleman (Man U and England), Stan Anderson (Newcastle, Sunderland and England) Jim Baxter (Rangers and Scotland), Dave Mackay (Hearts, Spurs, Derby and Scotland) and Cliff Jones (Spurs and Wales) – 'was as good as any team in the Premiership today'.

Southampton FC pulled a few strings to ensure that their left winger, John Sydenham, went as a storeman to the Medical Corps not far away at Crookham when he did his stint right at the end of the call-up in 1960 and, he says, 'I was definitely better treated than other people because I was a professional footballer. The only hard thing was there were so many teams to play for: D company, HQ company, the corps, the depot, the army. One week when Saints [Southampton] played Liverpool at the Dell they sent a taxi to get me and that week I played every single day.' The army team 'was fantastic, with the likes of Ron Yates of Liverpool, Alex Young the golden boy of Everton, and Mel Scott of Chelsea, who was at Crookham with me. I have some wonderful memories of travelling to play football around the Far East, Singapore, Malaya. We were so far ahead of everybody it was no contest, we thrashed everybody.'

What a difference being good at sport could make was brought home to Graham Williams when he was at Windsor before going to Cyprus with the Horse Guards. A Paisley schools footballer who had had a trial for Queen's Park, he had just been made team captain (replacing the demobbed Jackie Charlton) and was cutting across the corner of the square with his arms full of kit 'when the corporal-major [sergeant] who was drilling a squad on it shouted, "What are you doing?" Now, I shouldn't have set foot on the square, the holy of holies, but when I said, "I'm the new captain" he turned sweet and nice. Being good at sport certainly took the pain out of things.'

In Düsseldorf, being in the Signals rugby side conferred privileges, 'mainly,' says Glyn Jones, 'because most of the side were officers. We had the regimental bus to take us to matches – the soccer boys bounced around in the back of a three-tonner.' He adds:

> It was outrageous the strokes you could pull because you played rugby, and not that we were that good. One time we played the Welsh Guards and they beat us sixty-three–three, and the only reason we scored the three was because the Guards sergeant-major felt so sorry for us he stood his lot to attention and let us stroll through for the try. We wangled all the time off we wanted. I got out of a guard duty one night before a match because I told the officer 'I'm the blindside wing forward and I need a good night's sleep.'

*   *   *

Skilled tradesmen could hope to get two stripes or even three, but the only national servicemen who automatically became sergeants were graduates or those with A levels who became army or air force educational instructors – popularly known as 'schoolies'. Not only did they get the pay to go with the rank, they largely stood outside the system, setting their own work. Schoolies were considered jammy bastards par excellence.

None were jammier than those attached to the War Office paper unit who were scattered in twos and threes all over Britain to set the tests for soon-to-be conscripts at their medicals. In addition to sergeant's pay they received lodging and other allowances – and only contacted their superiors by phone or letter. But many of them might have swapped with one of their number, Kenneth Small from Perth, who in Singapore taught English to Malay soldiers of the RASC water transport unit and was then posted as art teacher to a European school in the Malayan Cameron Highlands (on Coronation Day in 1953 he paraded with the school Girl Guides).

In the early 1950s when the War Office made the army second-class certificate compulsory for promotion, the schoolies were kept busy; quite a few senior NCOs of war-substantive rank had been demoted, or threatened with demotion, and wanted to regain or secure their stripes, pay and privileges. 'Long-serving staff-sergeants came to me with handfuls of money,' wrote Jeff Nuttall, the schoolie at Central Ordnance Depot at

Weedon.[8] Arthur Main, who transferred from the Green Jackets to the Education Corps and was posted to 16th Independent Parachute Brigade at Aldershot, explains:

> It might have been tempting to take the mickey – I had the RSM and other warrant officers as well as senior NCOs. But I wouldn't have done that, not because they could have made it difficult for me at other times, but because I had too much respect for men who had fought in the war. I worked hard – a fair amount of classes had to be in the evening because NCOs had their daily duties. I also went to teach once a week at the 33rd Light Regiment, Royal Artillery, and with others was responsible for the education of the band boys of the two battalions stationed in Aldershot.

Sometimes, teaching senior NCOs was an uphill struggle, according to Nuttall:

> I started classes in a dusty old Nissen hut at seven thirty in the morning. There they sat, my handful of worried NCOs, battle-scarred and beribboned, chanting the phonetic alphabet. It was a hopeless job. Eventually I did all their papers for them by chalking the answers on the board. Even then some of them failed.[9]

National servicemen who were semi-illiterate or illiterate – as many as three in ten and ten in 100 respectively, according to some estimates that were far in excess of government figures – were also the schoolies' responsibility in the army (the RAF did not have illiterates or semi-illiterates).[10] At No 1 Wireless Regiment, Royal Signals, in Münster, Rodney Dale mostly taught third-class certificate ('twelve-year-old school standard') to regulars and conscripts, as well as second-class and occasionally first-class ('about O level') at the central higher education centre. 'My main work was very elementary, but it had its compensations: in nine months I taught a hundred and sixty men, with only one failure – and he passed on the retake.' Many education sergeants had a cushy time – in many instances they had no other duties and often taught only a few hours a week. One army schoolie stationed on the Isle of Wight 'taught recruits from nine to eleven on Thursdays and spent the rest of the time sunning myself outside the education centre or sailing at Cowes' – but even after all these years is so embarrassed about it that he asked not to be identified.

As might be expected, in some sergeants' messes the schoolies were resented, though that is not the experience of Rodney Dale or Arthur Main. 'It helped that I was good at sport – I played hockey for the depot,' Main says. 'But it helped more that I qualified as a parachutist. So I was accepted – we were all paratroopers.'

It was a different story for Peter Hall at the RAF headquarters for education at Bückeburg in Germany, where he taught economics and business management to airmen going back to civvy street after the Second World War:

> Acting Sergeants of eighteen were not on the whole very popular with their fellows. The next youngest member of my Sergeant's mess was thirty-eight. The older men . . . had sweated for years before being rewarded with their three stripes. They were not at all pleased to see a boy quickly reaching their rank simply because he had passed a few exams.[11]

Hall's fate was to be made mess barman:

> For four months I served drinks from 8pm until three or four in the morning. There was one night off a week. Otherwise I had the torture of listening every night to the Sergeants' wondrously bigoted, reactionary talk as they travelled inexorably into their accustomed drunken stupor.[12]

If the bright did well out of national service, the brighter did better, getting nearly a year of being taught Russian to A level – and the brightest did best of all, being then sent to university to complete in a year the equivalent of a three-year degree.

Once the Iron Curtain rattled down, the armed forces set up the Joint Services School for Linguists to work in intelligence gathering and monitoring – and to create a select pool of interpreters who, if war came, would be able to 'interrogate prisoners and refugees, understand captured documents, administer occupied territory, run propaganda and psychological warfare operations, and listen in to battlefield and higher level radio and telephone conversations'.[13]

To become one of this select band, national servicemen needed at least a school certificate in Latin or a foreign language. Half of those chosen were graduates; almost all the rest had places waiting for them at university. In the nine years that the JSSL existed (1951–60), 5,000 passed through, including John Drummond (later Sir John Drummond, director of the Edinburgh Festival and the BBC Proms), the future Bank of England governor Sir Edward George, the artist Patrick Procktor, the actor Joe Melia, and the writers Jack Rosenthal, Dennis Potter, Alan Bennett and Michael Frayn – who was told by the Royal Artillery personnel officer at Oswestry when he was being sent on his way: 'I suppose you realise that in time of war you could be dropped behind Russian lines?' 'I can't say that deterred me,' says Frayn. 'There were no Russian lines at the time.'

The basic Russian course was run at Coulsdon in Surrey; the camp was attached to the Guards depot and, Frayn remembers, 'we had to go through it to get to the NAAFI, tailor's shop and the swimming pool. No one took any notice of us as we shambled along, but the absolute rigidity of the place terrified us.' The JSSL was supposed to be secret but its existence was common knowledge. Guards' drill sergeants quickly added a new insult for their recruits – 'You look like a bunch of fucking Russian linguists' – and, says Bill Hetherington, who arrived from the naval training barracks in Portsmouth, 'At the nearest bus stop, which was The Flying Fox pub, the conductors used to sing out, "Red Square".'[14]

To reach A level in Russian in nine or ten months was a tall order (even if John Drummond was to write in his memoirs that the Cyrillic alphabet 'soon ceases to be a problem if you are looking at it for about seven hours a day'[15]). Having done so, the majority went on to trade training at various establishments before posting to monitoring stations in Germany and Cyprus, or aboard naval vessels or seemingly innocent trawlers in the Baltic and the Black Sea. The genuinely gifted – no more than a few hundred – who were to be trained as interpreters moved on to Cambridge or London universities and, because Cambridge refused to teach men wearing uniform, were issued with tweed jackets, grey flannels, brown shoes – and green trilbies, denoting their elevation to officer cadet (or in the navy's case, midshipman) status.

If Coulsdon was intellectually rigorous, it was nothing to what was now experienced. 'It was very hard work, not the usual undergraduate thing of being free to go or not to go to lectures,' says Michael Frayn, who was at Cambridge.[16] 'It was nine to five, during which time we read Chekhov and Dostoevsky in the original, for example, then put in more hours of homework and learning vocabulary – I worked a fourteen-hour day. There was a test every Friday and failure meant being thrown off the course and RTU'd. It was quite ruthless in that way.'

As a way of life, however, it was very much preferable to the average national serviceman's lot (in 1967 Alan Bennett, who was at Cambridge with Frayn, told Roy Plomley on *Desert Island Discs* that 'it was one of the happiest periods of my life – much more so than university proper, later'); and they were paid as sergeants, about £5 a week – 'I couldn't believe anyone could be so rich,' Frayn comments. For those who passed the course, six months at Bodmin in Cornwall followed, during which, Frayn explains, they 'learned interpreting techniques – how to interpret prisoners, which is very difficult. A man called Birse, who was Churchill's interpreter with Stalin, was one of the instructors and he was a superb simultaneous interpreter – one language through his ears, another from his mouth. We certainly didn't get that far.'

On leaving Bodmin, most of the JSSL army intake including Dennis Potter spent some time at the Intelligence Corps depot at Maresfield in Sussex, before going elsewhere; Potter was posted to the War Office, where one department read Russian newspapers, noting names of servicemen to build up a file of various units and another dealt with documents, building up intelligence from such unpromising material as scraps of letters found on rubbish dumps in East Berlin. In the early years, the linguistic elite went through officer selection, undergoing, if they passed (Alan Bennett didn't) a truncated officer training course; from around 1956 when Bodmin closed down (Coulsdon had ended two years earlier) and the JSSL moved entirely to Crail on the Firth of Forth in Scotland, the commissioning option was withdrawn. Men were classified as sergeants – creating perhaps more tension in sergeants' messes than the presence of schoolies.

Michael Frayn was commissioned, going from Mons to Maresfield for the last few weeks of his national service. After a physically soft time at Cambridge and 'a very unmilitary existence at Bodmin where we surfed, drove around the county and had rather a good time,' he found Mons 'fairly exhausting' and his final weeks 'immensely embarrassing'. He adds:

> Technically I was in charge of people, but many of those there also waiting for demob had been with me at Cambridge and Bodmin and there were elaborate jokes and mockery. I will never forget a demob piss-up in Uckfield when a bunch of them came back rather the worse for wear and I was duty officer. I really couldn't maintain order and remain a human being.

* * *

Some men made their own luck or seemed to get the armed forces working for them rather than the other way round.

Bob Monkhouse was one. He might indeed have been a jammy bastard to get posted to the RAF medical establishment behind Oxford Street, but in fact he had engineered it, 'After a complicated bit of chicanery' with a warrant officer at RAF Records, Gloucester, 'involving a permanent cash loan from me to a lady of his ulterior acquaintance who was in urgent need of a £200 abortion'.[17] Monkhouse had started as he meant to go on. In basic training he persuaded the station adjutant to let him paint murals on the walls of the sergeants' mess and the station cinema and when he was supposed to go back to basic training wangled on to a secretarial course at Uxbridge. Arriving in central London and failing to get an audition with BBC radio ('professional performers were being demobbed each week as ENSA[18] wound down and its entertainers released'[19]) – Monkhouse again used his initiative. He slipped a letter of his own creation – addressed to the head of radio variety – into a pile that his boss, the RAF's senior neurologist and psychiatrist, had to sign, which said that Corporal Monkhouse's mental balance depended on his getting an audition. Monkhouse duly did and was soon performing for programmes like *Variety Bandbox* – and milking the audience by wearing his RAF uniform.

Ensa (or rather its post-war replacement, Combined Services Entertainments or CSE) took actor Roger Moore's military career out of the realms of ordinary national service experience. Commissioned in the RASC and posted to supply depots in Germany, first at Schleswig (where one of his jobs was nipping up to Copenhagen to buy eggs for all the local officers' messes) and then Neumünster, he enjoyed himself. But when sent to No 4 Training Brigade in Lippstadt, which was far too much like the army for his liking, he rang up the CO of CSE and was smartly transferred. The CSE was a very different world:

> One of my first chores was to take pay parade, which was absolutely hysterical. I was paying out ATS girls who were chorus girls and soldiers who were ballet dancers. I remember one pretty little ATS girl who came in, saluted smartly and I smiled up at her. She smiled back and the RSM standing behind me yelled: 'Don't smile at the paying officer!'[20]

Made up to captain to give him authority as he and his troupe toured Germany, Austria and Italy, Moore was constantly pulled up by senior officers for failing to maintain any semblance of discipline and for allowing everyone to call him Roge. He had just been given another dressing down,

> and I'm walking down the stairs of a hotel in Hamburg with the very fellow who shopped me to the adjutant when in through the foyer comes one of my boys, Sergeant Joey Baker. He flings down his kitbag, rushes up the stairs to me, flings his arms round my neck, shouts 'Roge, darling' – and kisses me. The regimental twit behind me almost became violent.[21]

National service brought out an entrepreneurial spirit in some men. When posted as a filing clerk to RAF Records in Gloucester, with duties that did not involve use of a typewriter, the writer Keith Waterhouse, (not yet a journalist but selling pieces to magazines and hoping to amass 'a bank of cuttings to impress the editor of the *Yorkshire Evening Post*'[22]) overcame the problem when he discovered that if he volunteered to teach an evening class he was entitled to a payment of a shilling a week per head, to a maximum of 14 shillings, out of the station education fund. He offered a typing course – which gave him access to a machine – for which no one turned up, except when there was an announced visit from the education officer, who would then find 14 of Waterhouse's friends (paid a weekly retainer of sixpence each) in attendance. The same entrepreneurial spirit beat in the breast of the identical Hamilton twins, Tony and Geoff (who would become television's most popular gardener), when they were posted as air wireless mechanics to RAF Wildenrath near the Dutch border in Germany. Bored because the station had so little work, they set up a tea and coffee stall in their workshop, also selling cakes and savouries, and patronised by everybody, including the NCOs and officers. It was at this time that they were put on opposite twelve-hour shifts and, Tony Hamilton explains, 'our tea swindle became a twenty-four-hour operation. We put up a notice saying "We never close" and we did a roaring trade.'[23] As their shifts consisted of no more than four or five hours of actual work, one of the Hamiltons would cover both – a deception that depended on their twinness – while the other took off on jaunts across Germany, Belgium and Holland. They even took turns to fly back to Britain and home in Broxbourne, Hertfordshire, by operating a simple scam. Men with leave due were allowed to hitch a lift on flights headed for the UK. What the Hamiltons did was go together to an aircraft scheduled for departure, as if they were carrying out a service. Once inside, the one skiving off removed his overalls (which covered his civvies), which the other brought back in one of the toolbags. Again, the twin remaining did both shifts.

Tony Hamilton really came into his own when he got himself put in charge of the station pig farm. This was in a pine forest a mile from the rest of the camp and he moved his billet into an unused hunting lodge nearby and was allowed to draw any amount of food he wanted from the squadron store. Many parties now took place, enlivened when Hamilton persuaded the officer that sick pigs needed a nip of brandy – he got a chit to draw a bottle a week. All of this, Hamilton admits, sounds impossible to believe, but is nonetheless true.

I sometimes wonder how we escaped the cooler. There's also the tale of my stealing a German pig – though that was by mistake. One of my big sows had broken out and I searched all over for her. Eventually I thought I'd found her in a loose box on a little German farm down the road and got her

152

back to her sty with great difficulty – to discover my pig had already returned and was sleeping peacefully. I should have taken the other one back, but I was knackered. And, I'm afraid, I thought, 'Bugger it, who won the war?'

As he was in charge of meat distribution to the married quarters, Hamilton became virtually untouchable.

Officers who wanted to exercise their authority knew that they wouldn't get their pork ration the next week. One morning I was at HQ for something and a warrant officer not long on the base said, 'Airman, get your hair cut.' I said in a cheeky tone, 'You can't touch me, I work on the station farm.' And he peered at me. 'So you do, very sorry.' He was one of my customers.

Roy Booth was another who got himself into a pretty unassailable position. Posted as a medical orderly to HQ Middle East Land Forces in Fayed, he thought he hadn't done too badly, considering he was in Egypt. But better was in store – he became bodyguard to the director of medical services, MELF. Everywhere Major-General O'Mara went in the back of his old Humber Supersnipe ('he was a big fellow, he couldn't get into the Standard Vanguards that were the new staff cars'), Booth was sitting beside him, armed with a Sten and a rifle.

The beauty was, we never saw any trouble. And while O'Mara was inspecting medical facilities or operating, which he did in complicated cases, we just dossed. O'Mara had a bit of crumpet in Ismailiya and when we went there he used to give me and the RASC driver five Egyptian pounds, which was a lot of money then, and tell us to sod off for two days.

I had a charge sheet as long as your arm. Petty stuff – not being around when I should have been, not having kit ready for tent inspections. But O'Mara was my protector and he got me off everything. Once when I was corporal of the guard I fell asleep – I'd been on the piss the night before. This colonel who hated my guts was duty officer and he caught me, had me arrested and put in clink, but O'Mara stepped in, said he needed me, and the charge was dropped. I'd have lost the stripes otherwise.

After 11 months Booth's good times ended, or at least modified.

Nasser kicked us out of Egypt and O'Mara's tour of duty finished. We set up GHQ at Episcopi in Cyprus and I got Major-General Drummond, the complete opposite, quieter, thinner, definitely no crumpet. I had to pull my socks up, though he looked after me too. I got into a bit of strife over a young lady, the daughter of the quartermaster-major. I used to sneak into the officers' quarters and he caught me and I got charged – for not having my weapons with me. Well, what weapon I did have with me wasn't what the army meant. But Drummond made that one go away. Anyway, most of the time I was in the car, swanning about, and again I saw no terrorist trouble. All in all it was still a bloody brilliant job.

Trevor Baylis's job as a PTI with the Sussex Regiment in Northern Ireland is one he would also describe as bloody brilliant. He loved every minute of it: 'Drainpipe bottoms, red and black bumblebee sweater, working people out in the gym, on the assault course, on runs, chasing them – yes, I was one of the F men of basic training.' At weekends, with Lieutenant The Viscount Enfield and Paddy Lock ('We three were inseparable'[24]), he went canoeing, potholing and rock-climbing – if he wasn't swimming for the army or the combined services. 'Northern Ireland in 1960 was okay – a few black looks but no bombs,' he says. 'For me it was one long outward-bound course.'

In charge of adventure training, Baylis talked the CO into setting up a hut 'where the lads learned some engineering skills, listened to rock and roll, smoked a fag and had some fun. I think some credit came the old man's way for what we did.' The CO might have been less pleased if he had known how Baylis acquired the equipment for his hut.

The secret was to camouflage the big, expensive items deep in the manifest, six pages of boring little items, two hundred half-inch screws, two thousand inch washers, nuts, bolts, that sort of thing, then somewhere in the middle of all this, capstan lathe, one. The CO was a lovely bloke, frightfully posh, and a busy man. And he wasn't mechanical – he wouldn't have been able to tell a jackhammer from a jack rabbit. 'Sign here, Sir, and here, Sir, thank you, Sir.' One day I got a phone call from the guardroom, 'Trev, some stuff here for you' and I said, 'OK, I'll come down.' This consignment for yours truly was three three-ton trucks laden with gear – the lathe, welding equipment, drills, circular saws, and a load of woodworking tools, plus timber and canvas for making canoes, all kinds of gear including aqualungs and diving kit.

Baylis's little factory built a four-seat speedboat (one of the star exhibits at the Northern Ireland Command arts and crafts exhibition – even if it broke up after a hundred yards in Belfast harbour) and then a couple of go-karts out of old motorcycle engines.

The battalion was so proud of our efforts that when the Secretary of State for War, John Profumo, made an official visit to our barracks, my group were wheeled out to demonstrate the karts for him. Me and my mate roared round the parade ground. I then jumped out of my chariot, threw one up [saluted] – the RSM was having a fit – 'Would Mr Profumo like a go?' I said, grabbed him, my mate grabbed the CO and they were off, racing round the square. Next day I was on a charge, cap off, belt off, bonk bonk. 'Who's in charge of this regiment, Baylis?' 'You, Sir.' 'Well it didn't seem like it yesterday. You took over the whole show. Did a magnificent job of it, mind – but don't ever do it again. Dismiss.'

Michael Parkinson's military career was perhaps even more one of a kind than Roger Moore's. It began with him thinking he would not have to do it – and ended with him being promoted to captain during the short, sharp Suez War (see *Chapter 10*).

Yorkshire lad that he was, Parkinson was due to report to the King's Own Yorkshire Light Infantry but collapsed days before in Oxford high street with spontaneous pneumothorax. 'A one in two million chance – my lung collapsed, like being bloody shot by a sniper.' He was taken to the Radcliffe hospital where his lung was reinflated: 'The pain of that bloody needle, I can't tell you, but I thought, "Great, my ticket out". But after a month's convalescence the bastards took me in and put me in the Pay Corps of all things and I couldn't even add up.'

Once in, Parkinson quickly decided that being an officer was preferable to being an other rank and got himself on the track to Wosbe and then Mons – without having the necessary educational qualifications.

I knew you needed five or six O levels and I had two: English and religious instruction. So, frankly, I cheated. They didn't check very carefully. 'You'll have to get your qualifications sent on,' they said. When I was asked where they were I concocted a whole series of lies, like my grandmother was knocked down on the way to the postbox with them or the chief of the education authority had had a breakdown. I just stalled and they forgot about it. I hold the record for being the least educated national service officer ever commissioned in the army.

It took him twice as long as most other officer cadets – he was hardly ever there as he was playing football and cricket for the army and was backsquadded to do it all again. When finally he got his pips and returned to the Pay Corps, posted to Ashton-under-Lyne, he wrote to the War Office:

I said, 'Look, I'm fucking innumerate, give me a job I can do.' It wasn't that I was unhappy. I was enjoying myself, still playing cricket, drinking in The Grapes in Ashton, there were lots of lovely ladies around. But the NUJ [National Union of Journalists] had sent a directive around to reporters doing national service suggesting that they might try to get into army public relations and that's what I wanted. And I got a call, come down and talk to us.

Parkinson did and got the job 'and I sat in the PR unit where a wonderful old captain called Molineux sat opposite me. When he answered the phone he used to say "Hang on a minute," put the receiver in a drawer and shut it. Within a day or two all the calls were coming through to me.'

Posted to Southern Command in Salisbury, Parkinson liked dealing with the press –

and playing cricket for a good side, South Wiltshire, and I had a trial with Hampshire while I was there. But I didn't fit into the mess. Everyone was very nice to me, but I was not only the only national serviceman in the place, but the most junior officer – the next rank above me was colonel. And at weekends I was the only officer, everyone else cleared off.

One night Parkinson brought the cricket team back to the mess and was found next morning under the bar 'as pissed as a skunk and the bar drunk dry. At the time my pay was four quid odd and the bill was forty or fifty quid, which I couldn't possibly pay.' The senior officer had a sorrowful word: '"This experiment isn't working, young man, is it?", and I had to agree. So they arranged for me to live above a pub in Salisbury!'

Derrick Johns might have regarded himself the jammiest bastard of them all. A good proportion of national service medical officers, some eight years older than the normal intake, were married and, being full subalterns or captains, could afford (just!) to bring their wives with them when they went overseas – and they stood a good chance of being granted living quarters. But it was virtually unheard of for the average second lieutenant to be accompanied by his wife. Johns was the exception. He not only had 'a dream posting' but, having married his fiancée Pat on leave in Evesham and returned to Bielefeld,

together we enjoyed social events we had never dreamed of – corps balls at New Year and Midsummer were the society events of the year and everyone who was anyone in the army and out of it was there. As a national serviceman I wasn't entitled to army housing, but we found a flat near the camp and the CO told me: "On thirteen pounds a week you're not expected to do any entertaining, but we do expect you to accept any invitation you get"; we were out almost every evening. On top of that I ran the football team and Pat turned up at every match wearing a knitted hat and scarf in the team colours. I had the dream life.

8

Roll on death,
demob's too far away

Men did not have to get plum jobs or postings to make service life more amenable: there were other outlets. In Germany in particular the sporting facilities were superb, but they were good almost everywhere. In Austria and Germany many men learned to ski – the winter leave centre at Winterberg had been built by Hitler for the 1936 Olympic team – as they did in the winter leave centre in the Troödos mountains in Cyprus where, as across the Med as in Germany, there was also sailing. Even the Middle East offered swimming pools – the lido in Aden, part of a sporting complex run by the NAAFI, included safe bathing protected by shark-proof nets. As well as its on-camp outlets and its town-centre clubs, the NAAFI operated leave centres across the world that were as good as private clubs.

There were other ways to broaden the national service experience. In BAOR leave taken locally allowed a man to travel free throughout West Germany and up to 50 miles into bordering Western countries – Holland, Belgium, France, Austria, Luxembourg – whatever he had saved to spend augmented with a small subsistence allowance (the portion of his all-found pay that was due to him for the period not in barracks). Even in countries riven by hostilities there were some opportunities to try the local food (at a time when other cuisines were virtually unheard of in

Britain) and get to know something of their people, culture and language. For men of a cultural bent there were wonderful possibilities. RAF 'schoolie' Peter Hall (who even in basic training at West Kirby went to the Liverpool Playhouse three times) in Germany got to Hanover's opera house (destroyed by bombs but temporarily housed in the old stables of Hanover Palace) and to Hamburg's (also bomb-damaged but still in residence). On R and R from Korea in Tokyo, RAMC corporal Barry Whiting did not 'chase the pox' like many of his companions but went to the opera house to hear *Carmen,* to the city radio station to see a play being rehearsed, and on an organised trip to one of Japan's renowned artists who taught the art of woodblock printing; he also visited a hydroponics farm and the museum of a large Toyko teaching hospital.

In many places men provided their own entertainments on camp, taking part in amateur dramatics – Peter Hall did at RAF Bückeburg, as did Ned Sherrin, commissioned into the West Kents and the motor transport officer at Klagenfurt in Austria ('providing people with cars and getting the sharp end of their tongue – which made me sympathetic in later life to minicab companies'[1]). Besides doing cricket commentaries on BFN (British Forces Network), Sherrin also acted in plays on air ('Ian Holm, then Ian Cuthbert, had small parts – but he was only a corporal in the RASC'[2]), as did Pilot Officer John Dunn who, once he saw 'the turntables and the other broadcasting toys knew I wanted to be part of all that'. The shift pattern he worked at the NATO airbase at Wildenrath, where he ran a squadron of Ansens that 'did the fetching and carrying', allowed him to get frequently to the radio station in Hamburg where he did announcing and presenting, 'but no programme of my own, sadly'. Putting on pantos at bases where there were service families was popular. Derek Brearley took part in two at the RAF base on the island of Sylt off the Danish coast, where he serviced air-sea rescue helicopters. 'Rodney Bewes was there as an armourer but he didn't indulge. It was a bit below him – he was on his way back to RADA.'

In the late forties and into the fifties, jazz was the thing and around the world men formed groups. In Egypt Acker Bilk discovered the clarinet and spent most of my time with the little band we started – drums, trombone, trumpet, piano, we didn't have a bass, maybe we had a guitar – and me on clarinet. I'd never seen one before. One of the guys called Alfie had a little marching clarinet he didn't want, which is about half the size of a normal clarinet, and I was fascinated. I taught myself, trial and error. We practised every day. We worked from six in the morning but from lunchtime time was your own.

In Cyprus John Barry formed a jazz group from among his fellow bandsmen in the Green Howards, while teaching himself how to compose, by correspondence course, locked away in a storeroom – an endeavour that would one day make him the most prolific composer of film music. Later in the fifties, when skiffle was the rage, LAC William Perks, a transport clerk at RAF Oldenburg [in Germany], went into town, bought himself a cheap Spanish acoustic guitar, learnt a few chords, and formed a group; a national serviceman who after four months had signed on for three years, he was yet to become Bill Wyman.

It was a source of constant irritation to the army and air force that so many men stationed in the UK seemed to think of nothing but their weekend pass home and consequently did not let themselves be absorbed into service life. Those of a different mindset were more likely to do a better job and have a more interesting life. Says Roger Horton, an RAF policeman at Uxbridge in Middlesex:

> I wanted to carry out my duties as demanded, but I also wanted to have a good time. National servicemen hated regimental police: some of them were bastards who took advantage and bullied people, but they were regulars, I think. Others did what they had to do and were ordinary blokes, and I was that. I also had a whale of a time. There was jazz in pubs and clubs, there were girlfriends about. RAF Hillingdon, where I was, was at one end of the Piccadilly line and my home was at Wood Green at the other, but I hardly ever went. My mother used to ring up and I said I'd come but I didn't.

Considering the low level of education among so many national servicemen, it annoyed the army that so few took advantage of the comprehensive opportunities on offer, as indeed it annoyed the air force that the bright men they were able to take showed just as little interest. A huge array of correspondence courses – anything from pig-farming to psychology – was on offer in the forces at a cost of 15 shillings, with three courses allowed at the same time, and the higher education centres in each command catered for men who found correspondence work impossible or impracticable. If a serviceman wanted to register with a local authority for evening classes, the forces paid his fees. If serving in the UK, he could sit any civilian exam set by a recognised body and again his fees were met.

But it was estimated that fewer than ten men in a thousand could be bothered.[3] Undoubtedly many more bothered to absorb something of the world around them outside the service milieu, but they were few enough to make Captain D.J. Hoare RN write in the 1956 *Brassey's Annual* about 'the bored and malcontented':

British youths of this type carry their shells with them and the visual impression is all that is assimilated. My inquiries suggest that a British National Serviceman who has spent a year in Germany knows no more of the people or country than if he had been there for a week's holiday . . .

Why? According to Tolstoy, the chief attraction of military service is that it consists of 'compulsory and irreproachable idleness', but most national serviceman were simply overwhelmed by ennui:

You know, you get so bored you don't seem to have any energy to do anything about it. Do you know what I mean? I was all keen when I first came out here. Get books out of the library, go to German classes, you know. Now I can't be bothered. I don't know. It's just – boring. Some blokes stay in bed all the time. Most of them have even stopped going out of camp.[4]

* * *

A government document in 1953 stated that 'There is very little complaint that the Service man has too little to do, or an unsatisfying Service job, when he is overseas.' It appears that the services did not speak to the men on the ground or, if they did, were not listening. In static garrisons abroad men frequently found there were too many of them for the work to be done – and they had too much time on their hands at the end of the working day. It was as bad or worse on many UK postings. Before going to Egypt with the RAF, Ron Batchelor discovered that the Airfield Construction branch into which he was posted 'had no airfields in Britain to construct' and so was posted to RAF Tangmere, a battery-charging station for RAF jets 'where the RAF took a fortnight to do what could be done in a day'. He preferred Egypt but still did not have enough to do. 'We had a chap nicknamed Amble Stevens because he walked so slowly everywhere. His very walk was a symbol of our service.' Before being posted to Egypt a few years later, the war photographer Don McCullin got the task of painting numbers in a warehouse-full of cans of Second World War air reconnaissance film at RAF Benson in Oxfordshire:

> I thought, I'm not going to do this, and there was wide support for this view in my little group. We mounted a guard on the ridge, to keep lookout for the sergeant who periodically wobbled our way on his bike, stowing the playing cards and grabbing the paint brushes only when he hove in sight. We controlled our output by our sightings, as they say in the RAF. [5]

Ray Selfe, who had been to Pitman's College and had shorthand and typing as well as experience as a cinema projectionist, was made an admin orderly – general duties – at RAF Greatworth, a small isolated Air Ministry relay station between Banbury and Northampton. After lighting the CO's fire in the morning, his main job was helping a civilian employee clean and polish the transmitter hall floor:

> Monday we scrubbed the lino. Tuesday was a day rich in variety – in the morning Bert lifted, with a stick, great blobs of white wax from a large tin and aimed them at the floor and I worked them in with a mop. Wednesday was machine day – we had a mechanical floor polisher with double brush head. Thursday was buffing day. Friday was inspection day when the flight lieutenant would rush in, I would salute, he would say,

'Very good', and leave. I was so ashamed of my job I told my parents it was hush-hush.

After weeks of this, Selfe persuaded the civilian worker to spend more time at home, took an armchair to the transmission hall and installed it inside an unused, shedlike transmitter, and spent his working day reading. Later he was 'promoted' – he was put in charge of the station leisure facilities. His main job was brushing the nap of the billiard table. The leisure centre was little used so Selfe played solitary snooker and darts and did more reading (he had returned the armchair). Every weekend he had a thirty-six-hour pass, which was supposed to start at midday on Saturday, but he was away to Croydon on the motorbike his father had bought him as soon as the flight lieutenant inspected his domain at nine on Friday morning.

> I had such high expectations of national service and here I was growing more melancholic and depressed. I wasn't withdrawn: there was nothing to withdraw from. I went days without shaving and occasionally was charged. Everyone went to see the Festival of Britain except me, because I was on a charge. But because nobody else was there I was in charge of the guardroom!

Trying to keep often large numbers of men – who came and went as their time was up – interested and occupied was a big problem for air force and army. They did try. They provided, at considerable expense, a cheap and very efficient postal service so that men did not feel cut off from home. On bigger camps they set up a cinema and an occasional one elsewhere or in the field (the Army Kinema Corporation had about 150 film units, static or mobile, around the world); they put together entertainment stage shows – in 1953 four toured Austria, eight the Middle East, six the Far East and five Korea. There were innumerable sporting competitions at every level. And, of course, there was the round of exercises and manoeuvres – which sometimes were mounted not for military necessity but to keep men busy, just as in some places treasure hunts were dreamt up that were supposed to show initiative.

Roll on death, demob's too far away

A lack of consistently meaningful employment created a downward spiral that led to skiving – the art of doing nothing intelligently, or spinning out a job, or getting out of doing it altogether. For Eric Brown, with the Royal Welsh Fusiliers in Brecon, skiving started in basic training:

One chap I became friendly with went sick with hayfever – his eye was badly swollen and uncomfortable and off he went into the military hospital at Chester. Now I'd suffered with hayfever since I was a young teenager and I thought this was a good wheeze, so I pulled the same stroke. They put us in blue trousers and a red tie like the wounded men you saw after the war. I didn't mind that though I didn't like that they were second-hand clothes. While I was in hospital my fiancée Shirley came up and we spent a couple of weekends in Chester in a B and B, which was another wonderful skive. When the hayfever season stopped my friend and I were posted back, by which time all the others in our intake had gone to Germany and we had to do another six weeks' basic training. I didn't mind that – we felt we were old sweats and it was six weeks more knocked off. And at the end of that I got married, with a bit more leave I wasn't entitled to, and then Jamaica!

Even men who enjoyed their national service and were conscientiously minded, skived. Says Malcolm Higgins of his time with the Royal Artillery in Dortmund, Germany:

If I could get out of something I would. Skiving became an art, making jobs last longer than they should, prolonging a smoke break. Because I was a surveyor I had to be able to drive – so I was taught to drive all vehicles in the unit, from the motorcycle to the huge Scammels that pulled or pushed the heavy guns around. I had a Champ, which is supposed to be the English version of the Jeep – I drool about it to this day. I was put on the drivers' duty roster and went to pick people up – but I never went or came back the quickest way. A young officer had the brilliant idea of testing a Decca marine radar set with a view to detecting troop movements on the battlefield and six of us were detailed off to test the thing. It was doomed to failure as it was geared to spotting a slow-moving ship some miles away rather than a fairly

165

fast-moving tank, say, a mile away. But it gave us some lovely days sunning ourselves on the hills looking down on the Rhine.

'On a nice sunny day we'd go to a little wood to sunbathe,' says Artillery signaller Glyn Jones, 'or we'd go into a basement supposedly to clean batteries and sit around chatting and having a fag – and you weren't caught that often.' The best skive in Düsseldorf, he adds,

was an official skive – guard of honour on the main gate for VIP visits. When Antony Head, the Secretary of State for War, came and they wanted to put on a good show, they chose fifteen of us, all between five ten and six feet and about the same build, although only eight did the guard. We were measured for a new uniform, which was absolutely unheard of, from a German tailor. We got a day off to be measured – which took all of fifteen minutes – another day for the fitting – another fifteen minutes – another day to take one boot to the guard commander to have it inspected, the following day the other boot, the following day the belt, the following day the bayonet scabbard. And each time we had the rest of the day for ourselves. It took us three weeks to prepare for him. There were other VIP visits and the same fifteen of us were on the skive every time.

Officers and NCOs largely turned a blind eye. A man marching briskly about camp with a clipboard stood a good chance of not being stopped to see what he was doing. A parachute packer on RAF flying stations who shinned up one of the scores of 'chutes in the huge hanging sheds might not be looked for. A language monitor listening for Russian radio activity over his earphones (never knowing whether the snatches he wrote in his log were valuable or not) might not have his frequently checked by his supervisor to see that he wasn't tuned in to Voice of America or Radio Moscow. There were, as Glyn Jones observes, 'scams of every trade. I'd think that most lads with desk jobs read more books and magazines during their national service than they did in the rest of their lives afterwards.'

For some, boredom led to bolshiness, an attitude of minimal contribution or truculence if it could be got away with; but the manner in which men were treated was a large contributing factor. A commanding officer with a good understanding with his senior warrant officer got far more cooperation – and a happier camp – than one who had little time for his national service charges or who imposed bull and discipline with excessive zeal. As a general rule, conditions overseas were more relaxed, but at RAF Gütersloh in Germany, under a new CO, they intensified and, according to Gordon Williams, 'On this operational base, with the Russians just over the border at a time when it was costing the government sixty-five million pounds a year to keep the tactical air force in Germany, the CO virtually stopped all flying practice because he wanted more parades.' The place, says Williams,

became hell – his parades lasted four hours. He literally inspected every man – and there were upwards of a thousand of us – and handed out charges like confetti. I was charged for having the safety catch off my rifle and I got the job of 'bumping' the church floor. The night before his inspections we were up all night cleaning – that in addition to your work. We stopped using most of the showers. The red-tiled corridors on all three floors had to shine and we had to buy the Mansion polish to do it. A friend of mine crossed a corridor at the other end fifty yards away when the CO was on inspection and was charged for not saluting. He got three days. The CO used to hide behind trees at night and jump out in the hope of catching you with a button undone. On one full three-wing Saturday parade he made a young officer take his shoe off because he thought he was scruffy. He was somebody people wanted to kill. Someone in the RAF Regiment fired a rifle into his house, though they never found out who. Honestly. You couldn't make this stuff up. I'd have to say I thought he was mad. Our squadron leader on the other hand was just a bastard's bastard. His masterstroke was to hold a Christmas party for the officers' dogs with paper hats and crackers and little diamanté necklaces for the officers' wives' poodles – and he wouldn't let us off on Christmas Day. On my last day he shook my hand and said, 'I see you're a journalist. Well, you won't be writing anything awful about us will you?' I made up my mind then that if it was the last thing I ever did I'd write a book and put this idiot in it.

Williams eventually got away from Gütersloh by volunteering to go to another station where there had been an outbreak of polio, making men reluctant to serve there.

A decade later, Ivan Churm, a driver at the RASC guided weapons transport company in Wuppertal, found himself on the receiving end of much the same kind of treatment, 'thanks to a new CSM, the youngest CSM in the corps, who'd transferred from the infantry and wanted to make a bloody impression'. Churm adds:

The bullshit was supposed to ease off in a working camp, but it was just like basic training. Once we were getting ready for a bull night, came back after lunch and found our waterbottles thrown all over the billet. The string attaching the cork to the bottle was supposed to be six inches, he said, and not all of them were – but they were as they were issued to us. When he was duty NCO he'd march the guard into the billets at two and three o'clock in the morning to do bed checks, to see we were all in barracks.

I thought, 'I'll get you, you bastard.' I wired the lights so that when he banged into the billet one night and turned them on he blew the lot on all three floors. The switch was black. I didn't intend to injure him and he wasn't injured – but it gave him quite a fright. Towards the end of national service there were only seven of us left and we plotted to get his pace-stick. We wanted to cut it into seven pieces and post it back to him from seven different places in blighty, but we never managed it.

A spirit of rebellion was not unknown among national service officers, especially medics who were older than the run of conscript subalterns and had a professional expertise to which even more senior non-medical officers had to defer. 'Those who'd been working in hospitals and knew that losing two years might mean they'd fail to get on were very indignant and they showed it,' says Dr John Blair who, in his history of the RAMC wrote of 'One Glasgow RMO, angered at the refusal of any officer in a Guards Regiment to speak to him at breakfast, lit the adjutant's newspaper one morning. He was removed next day to an unglamorous destination.' Blair adds:

'At least that doctor was allowed in the officers' mess. In the Black Watch in Perth, the medical officer and the dental officer weren't let in – something that a man who became a major-general in the RADC experienced and was to joke about forty years later. The same thing happened in some rifle brigades, which were equally snooty – my good friend Norman Bradford was at the Rifle Brigade depot in Winchester but lived with the Hampshires down the road.[6]

The services were often nonplussed about how to deal with their national service medical men. In *The Conscript Doctors*, Blair quotes from the memoir of Sir David Weatherall who, while working in the military hospital in Singapore, was dressed in a white coat with just a pair of shorts underneath when he met a general in the corridor. ' "Are you an officer or a doctor?" he asked me. "A doctor," I replied. He was not amused and left instructions that we were to dress for dinner at least two nights a week. We did, but if my memory serves me right it was in sarongs.'

In a number of messes the national service officers were made to sit at a different table to the regulars to emphasise their lower status. But national service officers were quite capable of making their own point. At 3 Training Regiment, Royal Signals, at Catterick, Second Lieutenant Peter Walker, a Londoner who taught operators 'wireless and line – and morse until it was phased out', remembers mess nights 'at the one long table where, as soon as possible after the meal, the four national servicemen opened up a gap so that we were at one end and the twelve regulars were at the other.'

In the Royal Fusiliers Second Lieutenant Anthony Howard (who spent most of his time at Dover where the regiment moved prior to the Suez War and to which it returned) displayed a degree of bolshiness but in subtler ways.

I wrote seven or eight pieces about the army, very much against Queen's Regulations, for the *New Statesman*. One was about courts martial, another about dining-in nights, another that was more sympathetic called 'Golden Bowlers', about the poor majors finished at forty-four years of age. But they were all a bit subversive. I had an idea I would have been drummed out, or court-martialled anyway, if I'd been discovered. Recklessly, three weeks after I came out, I wrote another piece and signed it with my own name – just a bit of cheek, it was me – and I was told they were absolutely hopping with fury. There were some who wanted to pursue me, but the brigade commander Bernard Fergusson said, 'Don't be so silly, leave him alone.'

A qualified barrister, Howard did a good deal of court martial work in the army, always defending.

I don't think I got anyone off – most of them ended up in the slammer, a hundred and twelve days in Colchester or something. The situation was terribly loaded. Doing what I did was, I suppose, some small act of rebellion and I rather revelled in it. To my company commander: 'Major Durkin, would you describe yourself as an experienced officer?' That sort of thing did me no good with my brother officers.

At home and abroad, a popular way in which some men showed their contempt for the service life was to urinate on the camp flagpole – or to cut it down. Some places lost more than one pole and on occasion had to mount a guard. Worldwide, but especially in the Canal Zone, soldiers wore a dark green tie with the letters FTA – their meaning emblazoned on its bottom flap: *Fuck the army*.

There was one kind of bolshiness that was in the mind of only a few, of which few only a handful or two were inclined to make it known to authority: a leaning towards Bolshevism. The national service generation were not politically motivated; what beliefs men had in the main divided Left and Right along class lines and went little further. But the part Russia had played in the Second World War dramatically changed the fortunes of the British Communist Party (sales of the *Daily Worker* in the immediate postwar years reached 100,000), engendering a political idealism in some of the young. At school Michael Frayn was drawn to communism, 'though it wore off fairly quickly, before I went into the army'; Trevor Baylis flirted with communism 'without knowing anything about political theory and my Marxism was closer to Chico, Harpo and Groucho than it was to Karl'; Gordon Williams turned down the chance to be Potential Officer Material at RAF Hednesford, refusing to fill in the papers 'because I was too communist in my outlook then'. Only a man here and there declared radical views against 'military support for the capitalist, imperialist system' – and earned himself a hard time: inevitably the armed forces, confronting communism on a worldwide front, were not disposed to an enemy within, however utopian the motivation. Yet some national servicemen may have made communism work to their advantage. Prior to Nick Harman's departure with the Royal Fusiliers to Korea,

> It was said that two Jewish fusiliers, at the final kit inspection before we went on embarkation leave, left out on display their newly-acquired Communist Party cards – and were promptly returned as security risks to civilian life and their barrows in Petticoat Lane. Whether or not they really existed they were heroes and legends in my platoon, but nobody had the nerve to follow their example.[7]

Sometimes a man's communist reputation went ahead of him – or caught him up. Arnold Wesker belonged to the Young Communist League and sought advice from its general secretary as to whether he should submit to national service; he was told he should and spread the word of 'peace, brotherhood and socialism' among his fellow recruits. When it came to it, Wesker didn't, but he was nonetheless labelled a subversive, as he discovered when 'I got a chance to peep into my records', though all he had done was speak on a British Peace Committee platform a year or so before going into the RAF – 'God knows about what, nothing absurd, just a statement that we all wanted peace, the kind of thing an idealistic youth would say.' The future Fleet Street editor Derek Jameson was another who belonged to the YCL, who while working at Reuters before call-up, was a communist activist – though Stalin's expulsion of Tito's Yugoslavia from the federation of communist states was the end of his Red period. Jameson, in fact, was a happy soldier, an RASC corporal lecturing in current affairs at the Army Training School in Lendorf, Austria, who was not even unduly put out when the war in Korea added six months to his service. But he was less than happy when Headquarters,

171

British Troops Austria, got a pink slip from the War Office revealing his previous association with communism and saying he was no longer to be employed in a position in which he could influence others. He was packed off as an acting chief clerk to HQ Klagenfurt, which turned out to be not so bad after all:

> Q (Movements) is the Army's travel agency, arranging the transfer of military personnel by road, rail and sea . . . Having never been trusted with keys before, I had a good nose round . . . Starting with the Top Secret safe, naturally. As well as returns listing Army strengths in Austria, there was an Order of Battle specifying in detail what would happen in the event of war . . . Imagine what a real spy would have given to get his hands on this lot.[8]

★   ★   ★

Even when they were confined to camp in the Canal Zone, Acker Bilk and his mates would slip out with an Arabic burnous over their uniform and go downtown for a drink.

Bored, but in countries where alcohol was less than half the price back home – in Germany beer was fivepence a pint, a double whisky a shilling and, for most of the conscript era, there was a generous exchange rate of 12 marks to the pound – or, if in the UK, at least being able to buy subsidised NAAFI beer, national servicemen could afford to drink heavily even on their wage at least once a week, and most did. 'Drinking was the only release,' says Gordon Williams. 'My impression is that other than a few goodie-goodies, everyone drank sensationally.' He had one occasion when he regretted his own heavy drinking:

> I was with a pilot officer, another national serviceman, and he asked me to lend him my jacket, because he said he was going into town. He was arrested as a deserter trying to cross the bridge at Cologne. I was pissed when I gave him the jacket and I'd left my wallet in the pocket with my ID. These SIB [Special Investigation Branch] flight sergeants sat me in a chair, accused me of aiding and abetting, and walked round me for an hour. It's maybe the only time in my life I've felt real terror. By the end I'd have given them my mother.

'There wasn't anything to do except drink,' says Ivan Churm. 'Every weekend there'd be bodies all over the billet and up the stairs. Lads threw up on the stairs, in the urinals. Pity the poor squaddie who was on duty on the Monday and had to clean it up, and I had my share of that. That really pissed me off as I was the rare sod who didn't drink.'

There were few Churms. Geoff and Tony Hamilton, in the RAF at Wildenrath, overdid things at times. Tony recalls:

> Whisky by the half tumbler was a shilling and I remember an occasion with Mal Sprinks, a carpenter from Hayling Island, when we got absolutely blotto. Geoff and I found our way back to the billet but lost Mal. About three in the morning the door opened and a large Military Policeman came in with Mal under his arm – he was only a little chap – and said, 'I found this in a ditch', and dumped him on a bed.

There were similar tales anywhere the armed forces were. In Malta, where the local wine was nicknamed 'screech' and cost tuppence for a half-pint tumbler, REME radio engineer Roger Keight woke up one morning after a demob drinking session in Valletta and found a foreign sailor sleeping in one of the beds, and no one had any idea how he got there. 'Demob booze-ups were traditional and always took place in Straight Street – The Gut – where almost every building was a bar and a brothel. As the night wore on we would move down the street getting drunker and drunker and the person who was going home would be so incapable he'd be carried round in a horizontal position.' In Cyprus – where RAMC armed escort Roy Booth and others 'drank a lot of Commandaria wine, fortified wine like port, which we often mixed with white brandy, and got legless' – the authorities attempted to curb excesses by producing a poster that showed a typical British soldier seated in a drunken stupor in a tavern, with the caption: 'Danger – excessive drinking can kill'. On one someone scrawled: *A Para is not afraid to die . . .*

Even in Korea in the line, platoon commanders had to keep a watchful eye – even the daily ration of two bottles of beer could cause inebriation. 'In the winter the beer froze and separated into water and alcohol,' explains Duke of Wellington's subaltern John Hollands. 'Men were warned to thaw the bottles thoroughly but often didn't. I forget whether the water or the alcohol was on top, but one half was extremely potent and some men got absolutely tight.' Overall, the battalions did not have major problems but Hollands had one nasty incident involving his platoon's rum ration.

Going into a forward position, a fellow called Stiles was carrying the rum carboy, which was a hell of a bloody weight, and two of the blokes waylaid him – highjacked it. The bloke who'd had it taken off him didn't say anything until we questioned him, by which time the other two were drunk miles behind us. The sergeant and I went back to look for them and we came under fire from them. We didn't do anything about it: they'd lit a fire and burnt themselves pretty badly so we felt they'd learnt their lesson.

No drinking took place on jungle patrols in Malaya – other than for a rum-tot against the night cold, though some regiments forbade that – but on periods in between 'men did nothing but drink,' says the Manchester Regiment's Eric Michaels.

Over a Christmas and New Year when everyone was in camp I was corporal of the guard and we were out and about picking up bodies and putting them to bed. Most of the guard were drunk too – their mates kept coming in bringing them bottles. It was a chargeable offence, but the duty officer was pissed as well, walking round the camp firing his revolver.

When we weren't working some men were the next best thing to alcoholics. Joe Bailey, one of those killed in the ambush,[9] was a real alcoholic. One time I went into the tent and he said to me, 'Pull up a chair and sit in front of the fire but be careful you don't stand on the dog' – but there was no chair or fire or dog. He was sent off to hospital to dry out. When he came back he complained that when we came to see him in hospital we wouldn't get the little black men off the end of his bed, but we hadn't been to see him, the hospital was miles away.

'I would think that the Canal Zone produced more borderline alcoholics than any other posting,' observes RASC company clerk Jock Marrs. 'If the gippos had ever attacked on Friday or Saturday evenings we would have been hard pressed to stop them from blowing up all the vehicles in the column.'

In the hard-drinking cultures of many officers' messes, especially overseas, national service officers were expected to do their share. It was a considerable shock to the system for many, perhaps half of them straight out of school, who may not previously have drunk or only drank lightly and had not touched spirits. Most, after a hiccup or two along the way, managed. Says the Service Corps' Ned Sherrin:

> The army taught me to drink and eventually not to get drunk. I got very drunk indeed on one occasion when I was messing officer [responsible for catering] and had put on a particularly bad dinner . . . For some reason the next morning we had to be at an air base and I was quite ill. I just got into a car and had it driven round and round until my head cleared. It was a salutary lesson.[10]

A very few national service officers took to drink rather too well and were sent home in disgrace – officers were expected to drink, but they were expected to hold it. From other ranks up, it gave men delight to see if they could get young officers to down more than was wise. 'I will never forget a beach party in Malacca where my platoon got me completely sloshed as never in my life,' says Richard Lindley, a second lieutenant with the Hampshire Regiment in Malaya. 'They put me in the three-tonner and the driver came back at sixty miles an hour and blew up the engine. I got into terrible trouble over that.' Trouble awaited the inexperienced if as duty officer he allowed himself to be inveigled into the sergeants' mess. Strictly speaking, as part of his camp inspection, the duty officer was meant to inspect the sergeants' mess. Anyone who did was likely to be plied with alcohol and to walk out wooden legged. Only the foolish repeated the experience.

* * *

Wherever there was excessive drinking there was fighting. In the UK, things got very lively on Sunday nights at Darlington railway station – where men changed to the branch line on their way back to Catterick at Richmond –

with running battles between the Military Police and those who had been on trains for hours with nothing to do but drink. Weekends were lively in many town centres with national servicemen and Teddy Boys (in a different uniform of drainpipe trousers and long jackets with velvet collars)[11] playing out their own version of the Sharks and the Jets.

When men on their way abroad by troopship got shore passes at ports of call and after a few bevvies ran into other servicemen of any nationality including their own (there was no love lost between certain regiments for reasons no doubt long forgotten), punch-ups often ensued. Once at their permanent destinations many resumed the weekend pattern of drinking and fighting. Hugh Grant, with the Paras in Cyprus, remembers 'the entire company on parade one morning as two bruised and battered American servicemen toured the assembled ranks trying in vain to identify their assailants from the night before'.[12]

Fighting was guaranteed among some servicemen anywhere there was R and R. It was particularly bad in Japan where troops of numerous nations went from Korea. Tokyo, teeming with tens of thousands of men, could be one large brawl, with known animosities between Turks and Greeks, New Zealand Maoris and French Canadians, and the American Marines and the rest of the American army. The Australians and the British had a reputation for fighting anyone as drunk as they were. The much smaller leave centre of Kure had its share of drunken fighting: Duke of Wellington's subaltern John Hollands – for a time given the job of camp adjutant at Headquarters British Commonwealth Forces Korea after spending six weeks in hospital with injuries sustained on the Hook – 'often had to go down to the local police station to bail out squaddies'. There was, Hollands says, a lot of shoplifting and other offences – 'invariably committed when drunk'.

Germany presented a particular problem: the German people, defeated in the Second World War, now had the victors there as occupiers, and many still had Nazi sympathies. Up to the early fifties some locals of both sexes would turn away as servicemen – particularly airmen – passed, and spit very deliberately. Resentments on both sides inevitably led to fist-ups. According to Second Lieutenant Tony Thorne, stationed with The Buffs in Brunswick, 50 miles from Hanover:

For the soldiers there was a favourite recreation at which they could pass many hours. They would go down to the railway station and start a tremendous brawl with the locals. These street battles were always referred to as 'Goodwill Missions' and they would frequently involve hundreds at a time and sometimes last all night. The military police would fly down in their jeeps to see fair play.[13]

'Fights happened in the local bars almost every night,' says Tony Hamilton of his time at RAF Wildenrath with twin brother Geoff. 'We kept out of it. The nearest I got to getting involved, I was rescued by Geoff who bundled me out of a window.' There were so many fights in Iserlohn near Dortmund, burial place of Field Marshal Rommel, that when the Afrika Korps came for their reunions the British had to be confined to camp.

'For my money the Germans I met were friendly and understanding – but I had been on an exchange to Germany before national service and I spoke fairly reasonable German,' says Royal Artillery surveyor Malcolm Higgins of his time in Dortmund. 'I would say most of our lads didn't look for trouble, they just went on a spree. But some lorded it over the population and acted very badly. The attitude was, we won the war, we'll do what we want. The British weren't known for their tact.' But considerable numbers of national servicemen, he remembers,

felt a bit shirty when West Germany in 1955 was allowed into NATO and to have its own army. Suddenly we had troops of terribly arrogant young men – another lot of arrogant young men, I should say – marching around, and we didn't like that. We felt the same aggravation that today makes us think of Germans as people with big towels. Many men refused to salute German officers until they were made to.

If they were not fighting Germans, the British from time to time reverted to fighting each other. In one notorious incident in München-Gladbach the Highland Light Infantry (known as 'Hell's Last Intake') got into a mêlée with the Welch Regiment on St David's Day, the town was wrecked and people were hurt. From time to time, invasions of neighbouring barracks occurred that involved fights with chair legs, but in one incident a bayonet was used, three men were stabbed and one died.

Such drink-fuelled violence occurred sporadically everywhere. In Cyprus, Adrian Walker, a corporal in the Intelligence Corps port security unit in Larnaca, remembers that

> one group of Scots threw a Mills bomb into their officers' mess and blew the legs off the adjutant and another group threw a Mills bomb into the sergeants' mess but someone managed to kick it outside so there was no damage. When quizzed as to why they'd done it, these Neanderthals said, 'We was bored, Jimmy.' That's all they would say.

Walker was in his tent at the police station next to the port

> when there was an appalling burst of automatic firing the other side of the police building, followed by the response of Greener guns, which most of the police were armed with – Greeners were single-shot shotguns with a lever action that fired a half-inch cartridge with six ballbearings in it. We piled into the Landrover, the Turkish police threw open the main gates – we were going to put a road block on. What had happened, it turned out, was that an Argyll Highlander, pissed and armed with the then new Stirling sub-machine-gun, had got into a cab, put the barrel against the cabbie's head, and ordered him to drive along the front of the police station while he shot the windows out. The Turks shot back; the poor cabbie had an armed lunatic inside his vehicle and other armed lunatics shooting it to pieces – it was punched full of bloody big holes. It was a bit like Bonnie and Clyde except, amazingly, nobody was killed.

No one was killed, either, in an incident in the Canal Zone that Service Corps company clerk Jock Marrs vividly recalls, but it was another close thing.

> It was the fault of the orderly sergeant closing up the NAAFI bar one night. Usually what the sergeant would do was go up to the counter and tell the club manager to make a last call for beer and there'd be a rush of those who could still walk. This evening the sergeant banged his pace-stick on the

counter and ordered the shutters brought down immediately. There were a lot of drunken blokes in there who were incensed. One head-butted the sergeant and belted the hell out of him. He limped out the door as windows were broken and a fist and bottle fight ensued involving maybe sixty to a hundred blokes. Meanwhile the sergeant staggered back to the guardroom and the orderly officer – a national serviceman – called out the guard, and sent for the company inlying pickets, and the regimental police sergeant. That was about thirty men in all and they came into the NAAFI, some with rifles and others with Stens.

Most of the mob dispersed except for about twenty hard case Scouses and Scots. The officer asked them to disperse and quoted from the military manual; he was told to F— off, accompanied by some thrown bottles. He moved forward and ordered the guard to do the same with rifles at the port. The idea was for him and the RP sergeant to grab the ringleader, a big Edinburgh Jock. Unfortunately the big Jock grabbed the officer's pistol out of its holster and pointed it at him. Things came abruptly to a halt and you could have heard a pin drop. The officer ordered the guard to help, but no one moved a muscle. At that point the RP sergeant downed the Jock with a kick in the balls. It was then that some corporals from the corporals' mess next door moved in and things were sorted out.

I got my uniform ready for CO's orders which I presumed would happen next day since some of those on guard were from my company and they hadn't done their job. To my amazement nothing happened. There were meetings all over the place and the Jock came out of the company commander's office holding his jaw looking as white as death. The boss must have belted him, with only the CSM as a witness. The whole thing was hushed up or one certain lieutenant colonel's arse would have been in the fire.

*   *   *

Service life was about fiddling. Men fiddled chits to get replacement kit out of stores, fiddled extra weekend passes, got themselves removed from guard duty and picket duty. Most things could be done for a few quid dropped to the appropriate clerk (very likely a fellow national serviceman) who could make it happen. A name could even disappear from a draft – the actor Johnny Briggs would otherwise have spent his time with the Armoured Corps in Benghazi, Libya, not Paderborn, Germany.

The biggest fiddle of all was the black market and it went on everywhere from Egypt ('We were flogging magnetos and Christ knows what,' says Acker Bilk. 'It wasn't big money, but it bought a few bottles of Stella.') to Austria and Germany. More than anywhere, the lackadaisical situation in Austria brought out the entrepreneur in the soldier. Military vehicles were requisitioned to convey illicit goods to and from the distant corners of the British zone and across the Alps into Italy and to the port of Trieste. Military equipment, particularly clothing, got 'lost' – villagers in Styria and Carinthia were seen wearing army-issue greatcoats and boots. In Germany the big black market was in fuel. On winter exercises or on standby, the order was for vehicle engines to be run 20 minutes in an hour, to stop them seizing up; but five minutes might suffice, leaving a saleable 'surplus'. Tanks could be the real moneymakers. They devoured a litre of fuel a minute; if their engines were run for five minutes, not 20, that left 15 litres to flog to some German farmer. During large NATO exercises the German farming population were known to bribe tank commanders to leave the roads and cross their hedges and fields – the British government paid heavily for every acre of damage.

There was also brisk trade in coffee and cigarettes – the weekly cigarette ration was worth more than the average national serviceman's pay.

'If you don't smoke, I'd buy your coupons,' said Harry. 'I flog 'em. Well, I used to do a lot, you know – hundreds of fags going out of camp every week. Thousands. You know, give a bloke five bob for his coupons and then buy them at a bob for twenty and flog 'em for a mark for twenty, eightpence profit on every packet, steady money. But I'm chucking it in. Coffee, that's the stuff nowadays . . .'[14]

At RAF Gütersloh, Gordon Williams says, 'One guy used to buy as many people's two-hundred-a-week cigarette coupons as he could, then buy the fags at a shilling for twenty and sell them at a mark, which was roughly double. My pay as an SAC was seven shillings a day and eleven shillings at the regular rate in the last six. He was making twenty to thirty quid a week.' Once, Williams, who did not smoke, sold his own entitlement: 'You stood at the guardroom window in your best blues to be inspected leaving camp. You could get two or three packs under your beret, a pack in each flat pocket, a pack in the breast pocket to show, two down each sock, one either side. I got them out but was so scared. Everyone was into the black market including some of the officers. But it wasn't for me.'

It was for Artillery signaller Glyn Jones:

I grew a little thin moustache, flattened my hair down with grease and looked like the right spiv I was. Particularly in the winter I used to go down Düsseldorf with my greatcoat full of cigarettes, thousands of them, meet contacts there – the black marketeers were even more of a caricature than I was, homburg hats and long leather coats – sell up, go back and pay the lads out. We were making many hundreds of percent profit. One time waiting for the tram I put the collar of my coat up and two MPs in a jeep screamed to a halt, got out and gave me a right roasting for being improperly dressed. If they'd looked in my pockets I'd have been straight in the detention centre. We got a syndicate going, using a 15 cwt truck, to take hundreds of packs out of camp under a tarpaulin. If we'd been caught, it would have been five to ten years.

In Paderborn Johnny Briggs was also flogging cigarettes and coffee:

We even recycled our used coffee grains after an exercise. We would dry them out, put them back in the boxes, seal them up, and flog them. I could never resist smiling when the racketeers used to complain that a lot of our coffee was very weak. But you could get a camera or a watch for a packet of coffee.[15]

In Wildenrath Tony Hamilton had such a good smuggling racket going that he was nicknamed King Rat.

181

Working on the station farm I was allowed to draw anything I wanted from the food stores – no restrictions at all. Tea and coffee were very short in Holland at the time, so I would draw my contraband, load up my two German workers who lived on the border, and off on their bicycles they'd go. I gave them twenty percent and I was still making forty to fifty pounds a week – which was much more than I was to earn in the next ten years farming.

*   *   *

Some men did time for their black market activitities. Neither Johnny Briggs nor Acker Bilk did – but they got put inside for other reasons. Briggs and a mate borrowed a motorbike to get back to camp – both got 28 days' detention. Bilk fell asleep while on a twenty-four-hour guard, and got 84 days. 'I was about the sixth caught that week and the old man made an example of me. There was a good side to it. Waiting confirmation of sentence they forgot about me for three weeks so I spent my time doing Egyptian PT [lying on his bed], went for little walks with the guard, and the lads passed ciggies and beer through the bars.' The punishment unit, 'where they were a hard lot, eighty to a hundred, most of them in for thieving, some doing a year, two years,' was a harsh contrast. It was run by the Military Police,

> hard bastards, got a grip of you right from the moment you arrived at the gate. 'Drop your kit. Now pick it up' – and put you on a charge for malingering. They had us on twenty-mile bashes. We built an assault course, which wasn't easy in the sand, putting up the posts. We were glad when we finished, but then we had to bloody run over it.

Time inside was added to the end of a man's service. Bilk, in fact, finished up doing two years instead of the 18 months that national service was in his time: in addition to his three months in detention he had already been held back, as was everyone else, for an additional three months because of the Egyptian situation. He did not begrudge that period – 'I was with a bunch of good lads and we were having a ball' – but remembers how lonely he felt when he came out of the punishment unit. 'There'd been sixteen of us in my tent. When I got out my mates were all gone and I was the only one in there.'

Charlie Lewis, a steel-roller from Wigan, who trained as a general driver in the Armoured Corps, 'got into a bit of trouble' when he was posted to the 7th Hussars at Barnard Castle in County Durham. Having been in hospital for seven weeks with pneumonia, he was on light duties working in the sergeants' mess and was laying tables for an evening function when the Hussars' crest on the silver cutlery caught his eye. Two dozen sets went into his kitbag. A couple of nights later he went into town and missed the last bus.

> Camp was six–seven miles off and we started to walk, but then I saw it – the bus from Darlington to Barnard Castle had stopped up overnight and it was there under the trees. So I said, 'Come on lads, we'll have this.' We were flying down the road when I took this corner. There was a grassy bank with a few steps and I hit the bottom one and stalled. Along comes a bobby, the lads do a runner, I'm nabbed and he has me in jail. Eventually the MPs came for me, gave me a bit of a slap, took me back and into the billet to fetch my gear to go in the cooler. I forgot about the cutlery, tipped the kitbag out in the guardroom. Oops.

The civilian court fined him for taking and driving without proper insurance, which 'knocked me down to seven shilling a week, month after month'.[16] The military one put him inside for 28 days. After that Lewis went to Germany with the advance unit to bring out the regiment's equipment and then, because he had only a couple of months to do (including 'what I got for being a bad lad'), he came back and was posted to Mons officer cadet school 'taking cadets out on night exercises, map reading and the like. They used to have to find places and officers would be hiding at one or two of these, but I got to know which, so I used to say, "You needn't bother going there, just tick them off" and we'd all go off for a drink – they used to treat me.'

At Mons, Lewis backed a truck over RSM Brittain's bike but drove off. 'That's one I got away with.'

The reason Malcolm Stoakes went into Portsmouth naval prison was simple enough: he refused to wear his uniform. But his reasons were complicated and confused. The Folkstone ex-apprentice engineer, who

183

did his naval trade training on diesel engines and then got a steamship ('that was good, learning something new'), enjoyed being a stoker – until he went to war at Suez. He went out happily enough.

I didn't have much sympathy for the Egyptians over the Canal, not in a cruel way – just bollocks to them, wogs are wogs. We didn't listen to the radio on the ship and the only things we read were *Reveille* and *Parade*; I had no political understanding. But the experience made me more of a socialist. I listened to what the 7/5[17] regulars who'd been called back were saying. They were bloody bitter and they turned some of us into rebels.

We landed Centurions at Suez and after, I went ashore to the cemetery – I think twenty-five men were killed, most of them regulars but a few national service. And I thought, 'For what?' I got to thinking: there were only thirteen years to run on the lease of the Canal, so what right had we for what we'd tried to do? We said the Egyptians would be unable to take ships through the Canal. Typical British arrogance. And the bloody Canal belonged to the Egyptians, at least it was built with Egyptian sweat and toil.

I think I was very mixed up. They'd fired a few shells at us, that's all; we got a medal, but we weren't bloody heroes. I got more and more depressed and that was made worse because I went back to Malta on a cruiser, the *Kenya*, a 'bullshit ship'. Back in Chatham, I walked into the barracks and said, 'I don't want to wear uniform any more.' They were dumbfounded. They didn't know what to do with me. They put me in the guardroom for fourteen days and tried to cajole me, not nasty. I didn't have a court martial as such, but there were crossed swords on the table. The commodore said, 'Are you going to put on your uniform?' and I said, 'No, I'm not.' They gave me forty-eight hours to think about it, but I thought, stuff you. Forty-eight hours later they transported me to Portsmouth, handcuffed and carrying my hammock with all my stuff in it – staggering down the road, the two escorts weren't allowed to help you. On the train they asked me would I try to escape and I said of course not – in fact I was the one who got off to fetch the teas.

In the prison, run by Marines, Stoakes had his head shaved and was put naked into a cell with his uniform. 'The man running the place was called Tiny he was so huge. "Put it on," he said and I did as I was told. I was terrified. I cried that first night.' The regime was brutal: drill, assault course, emptying slops, polishing ('You had a house brick that you scraped for powder to make your mess tins shine'), and every evening unplaiting tarry ropes to make into mats. The food ration was minimal: men were always hungry. 'And when you went for a shit there were no doors – you sat there with a line of blokes waiting to go, watching you.' But the worst part was 'that throughout your time you couldn't speak to anyone. You were in a cell by yourself. Prisoners today complain about overcrowding – I'd have given anything for a bit of overcrowding!'

Out with seven months left to do, Stoakes was returned in handcuffs to his ship in Malta. He felt relaxed.

All the fear'd left me. I was pleased I made a stand. I'm not a conchie, I'm not a pacifist, I wasn't trying to work my ticket. It's difficult to explain. The funny thing was, the mess deck, mostly regulars, treated me as a hard man, which I wasn't. The master at arms said, 'I'll do a deal with you. You keep out of my way and I'll keep out of yours.' He was OK. I settled down.

Stoakes did an extra 56 days' service – the 14 days in cells plus the forty-two-day sentence. He was discharged on Christmas Eve, 'and as I walked up the harbour I tossed my papers away'.

Guy Bellamy got seven days in the RAF's German field punishment unit at Wahn – now Cologne airport – because he did try to work his ticket. A grammar school boy from Farnham in Surrey, he went to the base as a telephonist, but within a few weeks decided he wanted out. 'I wasn't really unhappy, I just didn't want to stay there.' A friend had been released from his national service by feigning mental illness and Bellamy thought he would try that. 'I didn't go to work, said I couldn't face up to things, hung around in the NAAFI. They sent me to a psychologist who said there wasn't anything wrong with me – I wasn't very convincing.'

His introduction to the detention unit was a shock: a drunken sergeant stood him against his cell door and struck him across the face 12 or 15 times, 'practically falling over at each blow' as he lectured him on 'the Royal Air Force, the Queen and the Commonwealth' and offered him a knife to cut his wrists from which he shaved the hair to show how sharp it was. Later, a sixteen-stone corporal named Alan Macdonald gave him a black eye, a swollen nose, puffed lips and bruised ribs and when he asked Bellamy how he would explain the eye and Bellamy replied, 'I'll say I got it walking into a door,' received another thump 'for being clever'.

Bellamy's ill-treatment was light compared with other men, some of them in the unit for months: they were not only hit but abused in other ways. Macdonald, a regular, forced one prisoner to lick his boots, poured soup over his head and made him eat bread and jam on all fours without using his hands. Macdonald also carried out illegal punishment drills, including making men take their weight on their extended middle fingers leaning forward against a wall, doubling them on the spot holding a rifle at the slope or with a bench form extended over their heads, or doubling them up and down the corridor with a loaded kitbag until they collapsed.

When Bellamy was released from detention, he waited outside the punishment unit to take statements from others as they came out, detailing acts of brutality and abuse. He wrote to MP Michael Foot, who passed the document to the Under-Secretary of State for Air, George Ward. At first Ward 'said the allegations were rubbish – but Foot believed me and said he would raise the matter in the House if an investigation wasn't carried out'. It was. After a series of courts martial in 1954, seven NCOs were sentenced to 560 days. Macdonald got the heaviest sentence – six months. And in the House Foot called for, and got, a tribute to LAC Bellamy from Ward, who somewhat foolishly added, 'but I think it is a pity that no complaint was made earlier when he was in the unit – there were regular visits by medical officers, chaplains and so on . . .' As Bellamy had said in court: 'The reason I didn't complain was because I wanted to get out in one piece.'

Bellamy was moved to RAF Celle to finish his time. Today he says: 'I regret trying what I did. It was silly.'

Londoner Peter Batt spent his entire national service in and out of the glasshouse because he refused to obey orders. 'I just hated it in there,' he says. 'I hated their fucking haircuts and wearing their poxy boots and gaiters. I wouldn't let them take away my personality.' In the Ordnance Corps, Batt was posted all over the UK as an 'undesirable'. He was, he admits, his own worst enemy:

One side of me said, 'Put me in something to do with shorthand and typing' – I'd been a verbatim shorthand writer. But the other side was a nutter, no respect, always showing off. I couldn't even keep out of the nick on the troopship to Egypt. A mob of us got rat-arsed in The Gut in Malta and fought a running battle with the Military Police. I was locked up for the rest of the voyage.

In Egypt, Batt

didn't seem to do anything. I was always on jankers, pissing around cleaning things. I was once on nine charges, one for hitting an NCO – the bastard woke me up. When you're in the nick a lot you get your pay docked. I can't remember what I was docked. I remember a guy called Jacobs, a typical rogue – even by my standards he was completely beyond the pale – and he was docked so much he drew almost fuck all. This time we were lined up and he wouldn't wear his hat or belt and he wouldn't salute. The officer said, 'If you want your pay you've got to salute,' and Jacobs said, 'What do you want for ninepence? A fucking march past?'

Batt should have been out in the summer of 1953, but wasn't until the winter – 'three months, four months over the top. Christ knows. I blanked my mind.'[18]

The services hoped that a spell in a detention unit (the best-known one in the UK then as now the one run by the army in Colchester) would sort a man out. Only those few regarded as being beyond redemption were sent after court martial into the military prison at Shepton Mallet from where, after serving their sentence, they were dishonourably discharged.[19]

* * *

More men than not, probably, got through national service without facing a charge. It was, however, all too easy to get put on a 'fizzer': anyone with a bit of rank had only to decide, fairly or unfairly, to teach a man a lesson – to get a grip of him in service parlance.

Most charges in army and air force were dealt with at company and squadron level, resulting in a sentence of a number of days' jankers. More serious cases were pushed up from officer commanding to commanding officer, who could give a man a maximum of 28 days, either on fatigues or in the guardhouse. If an offence was thought to warrant more, it had to go to court martial, with all the administration and inconvenience that entailed. A favoured way around the regulation was to hand out 28 days, then, as the period ended, press a different charge, resulting in a further 28. 'I couldn't forgive the RAF for what it did to some people,' Gordon Williams says.

> It victimised them. Our barrack blocks were a mile and a half from the guardroom. A man on jankers reported at six in the morning for two hours' fatigues, then went to his place of work, then reported at lunchtime, then again at six-thirty for a couple more hours' fatigues, then again at ten. He was up and down that road, ten or twelve miles, plus four hours' fatigues plus his job, changing into denims for fatigues, back into uniform, into full kit for night inspection behind the guard. It totally wrecked some people. I knew one man who tried to kill himself. Another lad was so insane with that kind of treatment that he wanted to buy a gun.

For the most part an OC's or CO's[20] morning 'orders' was a miserable catalogue of petty cases of disobedience, insubordination, lateness, being improperly dressed, going AWOL (absent without leave), drunkenness, fighting and stealing on camp and out of it. But it was a process not without gallows humour. At RAF Hednesford before going to OCTU, John Dunn sat in a corner of a squadron leader's office sticking amendments into Queen's Regulations and listened. 'An NCO, in that peculiar way they had of talking, would give the evidence – something like "Where is your rifle?" I asked, and he replied, "Up your arse." Knowing this not to be true I cautioned him and charged him." Honestly, I don't know how the officer could keep a straight face.'

9

It must be the uniform

Adventure, travel, danger: national servicemen wanted to go abroad for different reasons, but the majority had hopes of sex. 'Germany or Egypt, or Hong Kong if they liked,' thinks the hero of Leslie Thomas's *The Virgin Soldiers*, 'somewhere where you could have a good time and have some women.' Whether the period covered by conscription was a moral one or an inexperienced one is open to debate. A good proportion of men believed in saving themselves for marriage; the majority, in any event, were virgin soldiers – and airmen and sailors. 'Sex was the great mystery in those days,' Thomas told a radio audience:

> I mean, I gather they all do it now by the time they're 14, but I certainly never had any experience of sex when I went in the army . . . I would say that in the barrack room of 40, I bet 30 of them hadn't either. You used to take a girl home and kiss her on the doorstep, that was the normal thing.[1]

It was the chance remark of a fellow conscript in Singapore who said, 'I hope I'm not killed before I find out what it's like,' that gave Thomas the idea for his novel.

Home and abroad, sex was the most common topic in the barrack room. Middle-class lads with a cloistered upbringing were amazed by some of the conversations that went on around them concerning what men did with their girls and their worries now that they might be doing it with someone else. They were equally taken aback by open conversations about masturbation, in the services a constant source of humour ('Hands off cocks and on socks'), even though the physical act was a fact of life for men of all backgrounds ('the regular creaking of an iron bed might indicate that one of us was on the way to orgasm,' the art critic Brian Sewell wrote in an article on basic training),[2] and a few were truly shocked by the occasional frank hoisting of erect penises. As with everything in national service, men discovered that theirs was not the only standard of behaviour.

> Sometimes in the evenings, particularly on a Tuesday or a Wednesday when they did not have any money to go out, Tasker and Lantry would lie on their beds and see who could think the dirtiest thoughts and get the biggest and best erection.
>
> They pursued this activity with fetid enthusiasm, sometimes beneath the sheets and sometimes above them, and viewed their finished achievements with academic, even medical, pride.[3]

That the services put bromide in the tea to dampen men's urges was something that many national servicemen believed right through their service career, despite the impracticalities of doing it – and its conspicuous lack of success. 'It was an old army joke that somehow came to be believed,' comments Dr John Blair, himself conscripted into the Medical Corps. 'How that happened, possibly, is because sedatives at the time included bromide and were as popular as Prozac today, and bromide does depress all physical activity. It would have had very little specific effect on sexual activity – far less, shall we say, than the rigours of basic training.'

Basic training was not a palliative for many young men's desires to have sex and, removed from parental influence and emboldened by a sense of manliness – and of anonymity – bestowed by the uniform, many went in pursuit of it. There was enthusiastic cooperation to be found around most of the camps in the UK. At the naval base at Wetherby, the girls from nearby Leeds who arrived at weekends were dubbed the Leeds commandos, 'because they were in action in all weathers'. At RAF Hednesford, where Gordon Williams did his basic training,

It must be the uniform

The squadron leader said there was a notorious pub in each of the three villages of Hednesford, Rugeley and Cannock, where the local girls, apparently, were at it for five bob a time. These pubs, he said, were to be avoided, and he named them. Come the weekend there was a drumming of feet as the lads made a beeline for you know where.

In Aldershot

there was this female called Myrna. She was going with some bloke in C Company until he got demobbed. By this time Myrna was obsessed with all things military and used to haunt the Havelock Arms where C Company hung out ... she used to bestow her favours on any C Company Tom who glanced in her direction. They used to smuggle her into the billet at weekends and she would move from bed to bed like a bloody mobile hot water bottle. So, needless to say, she ended up with one up the spout! Even in her advanced pregnant state she would sail into the Havelock like a ship in full sail and it was a real laugh to see C Company personnel down their pints and scarper. Nobody could say with any degree of certainty who the actual father was – not even Myrna. When the baby was born ... she called it Charles! Somebody even put a sign on their noticeboard saying 'To C Company and Myrna – a son Charles born 12th February 1957.'[4]

As ever in life, there were double standards: some men with serious girlfriends, fiancées or wives played around, as Malcolm Higgins, with the Royal Artillery in Dortmund, Germany, remembers:

There was this three-year man, tough guy, with a couple of stripes, who had a way of swaggering round. One day I came into the billet and he was crying his eyes out. 'I'm going to kill her,' he said, and gave me a letter from his wife to read. She'd met an American back home, they'd got together, in modern terms they were an item. I was feeling genuine pity when this guy suddenly looked at his watch, said, 'Got to go and meet Greta now' and was off, full of eager anticipation. I thought, what sort of morality is this?

193

The fifties were a decade in which men and women began to go steady, become engaged or married very young. The enforced separation caused by national service intensified many men's feelings about a relationship, sometimes unrealistically; in some cases it had the opposite effect back home. A 'Dear John' letter was painful to receive in basic training but even more painful abroad. Eric Michaels was in Malaya with the Manchester Regiment when he got his 'Dear John', and he remembers 'quite a few others'.

> It happened to me at eighteen, which wasn't too bad. Most of us took it in our stride, we'd pin them on the pole in the tent and go and get pissed. But some of the guys were really upset. Some of them were twenty-one, out of their apprenticeship, been with the same girl five or six years. They didn't put their letter up, just sat looking at their photos, and you heard them sobbing during the night.

When Tony and Geoff Hamilton first arrived at RAF Wildenrath in Germany and were marched to their billet, the corporal at the door asked each man as he entered:

> 'Girlfriend?' If the answer was 'Yes', we were told, 'Right, choose a bed at the far end.' When we asked why we were being separated like this, he explained that he didn't want the rest of the troops kept awake by the weeping when the 'Dear John' arrived . . . We nearly all got them eventually, even the handful of airmen who were married.[5]

'The corporal knew what he was talking about,' Tony Hamilton observes.

> I remember a solicitor, a lot older, who got one and cried himself to sleep. There were others. I remember mine. I was very upset. I was working on the station farm by then and Geoff came up to see me. He said what I needed was a good fight and we wrestled in the snow. 'Now do you feel better?' he asked. I said 'Yes'. 'Right,' he said, 'now you fly home and pin her ears back.' I did, on another of our illegal trips – and the relationship started up again. Christine became my first wife.

In Cyprus, Dave Lacey, the RASC driver attached to Adrian Walker's port security unit, got a 'Dear John' from his girlfriend in Plymouth and

> he started to wake up punching out. We knew, so when we woke him up we prodded him with something, keeping back out of harm's way. This day he was asleep and the figure of Second Lieutenant Graham Howes appeared and grabbed him by the shoulder, whereupon Lacey smashed him in the face. Howes was national service himself and he just laughed it off – but another officer mightn't have and striking an officer could have meant a long time inside. What was funny was that Dave said, 'Christ, I'm sorry, Sir, I thought you were Corporal Wybourn' – as if thumping a corporal was all right.

∗   ∗   ∗

An old army adage says that men prefer to fornicate than fight, but even when they were fighting in Korea some men found time for fornication.

Korea was laid waste, its rural areas largely abandoned by the people, but brothels sprang up here and there in the devastated villages. When they were pulled out of the front line into reserve, men determined to have sex found ways of getting to them. The majority of troops were not prepared to risk leaving camp illicitly and many were convinced there was never a brothel anywhere near where they were engaged in the war, 'but it was possible to have women up and down the peninsula,' maintains John Hollands, a subaltern in the Duke of Wellington's. 'When we were in reserve one man went to a brothel, got the clap and was so angry he went back and burned it down – and got twenty-eight days in Pusan detention centre.' When troops arrived in Japan on R and R it was not a case of seeking sex out: sex was all around. In the aftermath of the Second World War millions of Japanese lived on the verge of starvation and the country teemed with prostitutes – 80,000 of them in Tokyo alone – offering their services for a handful of yen:

> Tokyo was the entertainment centre of the UN Forces. There were other leave centres but none matched Tokyo. It had its own special buzz. Nothing had been seen like it before or since. So many dollars were changing hands

195

that the re-floating of a defeated and bankrupt nation was underway, all based on man's insatiable desire for alcohol, female nudity and sexual intercourse.[6]

It was a similar story in war-ravaged Germany, with brothels everywhere. In Hanover the whorehouses were in a street that ran parallel to the five platforms of the station and was known as 'Platform 6'; Hamburg, with its Winkelstraße red-light district, turnstiled at either end, was described as the biggest brothel in the world. At the time of the Korean War, sex in Germany could be had for a tin of Nescafé, a bar of chocolate or perfumed soap – even for as little as two cigarettes. By the mid-fifties it was more expensive – 20 cigarettes – and by the time the last national servicemen packed their kitbags in 1963 it was strictly cash only.

Sex was as cheap and readily available virtually everywhere men served. In Malaya the price was five to ten Malay dollars, about five shillings at the lower end of the scale. 'Some kind person had introduced him to the night-life of Kuala Lumpur and he could not get over the miracle of being able to sleep with a woman for five dollars,' noted RASC sergeant Peter Gaston about a colleague called Alex. 'He did a lot of C.B. through staying out late with the girls.'[7] In Hong Kong the going rate was two Hong Kong dollars (about two shillings and sixpence) or half that for manual relief, which was usually performed by old women. On his way to 18th Field Ambulance in the New Territories north of Kowloon, Oliver Reed opted for the second

and was led away by an octogenarian woman whose appearance and clammy hand were so frightening he was unable to manage an erection. 'Tommy have too much beer,' she hissed in disgust before waddling off. Oliver, still a virgin, was left to pull up his trousers and gingerly return to his mates.[8]

Across the Spanish border from Gibraltar in La Línea, where all the bars and brothels were strung along one street, it cost the equivalent of four shillings for a 'short time' – though the prices went up when the American navy was in harbour. 'I never had a go with any of these women,' noted Peter Sharp, stationed in Gib with the RAF as an air gunner. 'They were a

196

horrible-looking lot, as clapped out as the Lincolns we used to fly at Leconfield.'[9]

Not all sex was with prostitutes. In Germany, RA signaller Glyn Jones observes, 'a lot of German girls wanted to marry British lads to come to this country and were prepared to give their all. Naturally, as far as the squaddies were concerned, it was pure sex – chasing women for a bit of nookie.' It was possible, of course, simply to enjoy women's company. Adds Jones:

> We learned some working German from the newspapers and we were able to do quite a bit of chatting up. We used to book in at night, then slip out through gaps in the perimeter and go into town until the early hours. The perimeter was guarded by displaced persons caught on our side of the border – Russians, Poles – who wore army uniforms dyed black and cap badges with a big 'DP' on, and you had to lob them a few hundred cigarettes so they knew your face and not shoot at you on the way back in. And we went to carnivals. If the women fancied you they slapped you on the head – we came back with lumps.

At the beginning of his time, fraternising was supposedly not allowed and men could only go out in uniform; later it became civvies with boots and only later still, when the ban was lifted, civvies and shoes. 'But even then women weren't allowed into camp, not even the NAAFI.' Which is not to say that men did not bring them in – they were certainly doing so before the end of the decade when Ian Carr, a national subaltern, noted that 'some of the more enterprising other ranks simply cut a hole in the perimeter fence and under cover of darkness smuggled in women from the town. Patrolling the camp at night with the duty sergeant, I often had to make short detours to avoid the writhing bodies.'[10]

There were few writhing bodies in the Canal Zone, the most desolate of national service postings. 'Sex – none, absolutely none,' says RAF Airfield Construction branch tradesman Ron Batchelor, who adds cryptically: 'We did have an outdoor cinema. Even then it was surprising how often the RAF decided to drop flares so the brightness obliterated the screen.' Grenadier guardsman Mike Hollingworth remembers 'nothing but an occasional pair of eyes – just like Libya.' Peter Batt, in Egypt with the Ordnance Corps, comments:

> The Egyptian women were covered from head to toe in black, so they were a waste of time, and there were a handful of WRACs that the likes of us couldn't get near. But what blokes used to do was get a fix on one of them, get a good image, and rush off to their tents for a wank. I've always thought that stories of wanking in basic training were exaggerated. I mean it happened, but it wasn't an everyday occurrence. But in Egypt I saw rows and rows of tents and blokes wanking in full view of everyone going to and from dinner. And what do you expect, healthy young blokes with no women and nothing to do?

So many men who got from the Zone to Cyprus on R and R craved sex that many others on their way to the Golden Sands leave centre were surprised to find they had been delivered to a brothel; the taxi drivers assumed everyone wanted to be. Sapper Robert Grettan did:

> The brothel itself was just like an ordinary suburban house that you might find in Sidcup and perfectly civilised. You went in just an ordinary sitting room with three or four women sitting round and the madam. We were warned that if the Military Police came, it was like fire drill, being told how to get out – and sure enough there was a raid while we were there. So the first trip was ignominious in that nothing happened and I was arrested running away pulling my trousers up. I was just taken to the local Military Police HQ and warned and let go.[11]

⋆   ⋆   ⋆

Right from basic training the services tried to head off men's inclination towards gratuitous sex by scaring the daylights out of them with films and lectures about the potential dangers of venereal disease. No one who did national service ever forgot the films. 'Psychologically they were very effective,' says Malcolm Higgins of what he saw at Catterick. 'The women they used in the films were secretaries, typists, respectable people – the point rammed home was that you couldn't tell who had VD and might give it to you.' The possible consequences of contracting VD was another stark factor. At RAF Hednesford the film Gordon Williams saw 'showed a lad walking down to a red-light district and later wearing dark glasses because he was blind. That was a horrifying prospect.' Says the Sussex Regiment's Trevor Baylis: 'The close-ups showing the various stages, bits dropping off, ding-dong. As a kid I knew about all the asylums around London and that they'd been filled with people in the final stages of syphilis. "Shit," I thought, "I'll never have a woman again." Well, for at least five minutes.' Perhaps the majority of men watched with the mixture of revulsion and startled enjoyment they would have got from a horror movie. The Royal Fusiliers aboard the trooper *Halladale* on the way to Korea were shown a very scratchy film and, says Nick Harman, 'most people laughed, if they weren't being sick – the ship was rolling and pitching like anything'.

Medical officers did their best to convince servicemen to stay on the straight and narrow, lecturing them when the lights came up or in separate lectures, often accompanied by slides. The MO at Hednesford when Tony Hamilton was there did not, he thinks, believe it likely they would heed his advice. 'It was just before Christmas and he finished by saying "I wish you a happy syphilis and a merry gonorrhoea."' Lieutenant John Donald, aboard the *Fowey* with the Royal Scots, thought his lecture had been very convincing, until soon after he got an inkling of what easy temptation men had to weigh his words against. He had spoken about the sexual dangers ashore at Gibraltar before the troops went down the gangway, telling them that the women 'were poxed up to the eyeballs and doing dirty things to them would cause them great anguish and their balls to drop off'. Going ashore himself he was stopped at the bottom of the gangway by a small boy: '"Hey, Johnny. You like jig a jig? Come and see my sister. She is very beautiful and her skin is brown but she is pink inside, just like Queen Victoria." I reeled back in disbelief. I could not believe what my Presbyterian ears were hearing.'[12]

Morality was not a medical officer's business, but one Welsh national serviceman – promoted to the coveted role of MO on a different ship – considered that it was; he not only refused to issue condoms to the troops when the ship berthed in Malta's Grand Harbour, he had the entire supply thrown into the water. He was transferred to Aldershot.

Fully aware that film, lectures – and morality (the padre was sometimes called on to have a say) – would not deter a lot of men, the services tried to lessen the chances of them contracting VD by issuing free condoms, setting up self-treatment prophylactic centres and holding FFI (free from infection) inspections. These were normally carried out by MOs, but in extreme circumstances by platoon commanders, just as they conducted foot inspections. 'I'm not now sure whether I was instructed to inspect my men's private parts, but if I was, I certainly didn't,' says Richard Lindley, who served as a second lieutenant with the Hampshire Regiment in Malaya. The services also put red-light districts out of bounds but, as many men were prepared to risk military wrath as well as VD (and got into many confrontations with army and air force police), they frequently raided the brothels. After six weeks in hospital in Kure recovering from the injuries he sustained in the third battle of the Hook in Korea, John Hollands for a while became camp adjutant at Headquarters British Commonwealth Forces in the town and 'used to accompany the provost marshal – an Irishman from the Ulsters with one arm – and his MPs once or twice a week'. From time to time the authorities shut the brothels down, though they reopened quickly. As a belt and braces operation, they tried to ensure that the prostitutes were free from disease by issuing permits to those who passed the regular medical examinations. But a prostitute given a clean bill of health could contract VD from her next client and pass it on to her next; and, of course, many prostitutes did not work out of brothels. Received wisdom among servicemen was that the surest way of avoiding VD was to wait outside the pox clinic until one of the girls came out with her all-clear card, and grab her.

In many units men could get condoms (in naval terms called 'sports gear') from the guardroom as they booked out. At the Royal Artillery Battery HQ in Düsseldorf, Glyn Jones says, they were issued by the MO's clerk: 'You held out your beret and he dropped them in.' According to Gordon Williams, at RAF Gütersloh 'the prophylactic room had a table stacked with French letters. We used to take them by the handful, spit in them and throw them in the officers' gardens hoping they'd think they'd been used.' Standing orders throughout the armed forces stated that any man who had sexual congress should go to the PAC (prophylactic aid

centre) that was on every static camp – in Malayan cities like Penang and
Kuala Lumpur, cabins were erected in the streets – squeeze the provided
ointment on his penis, and sign a register or collect a chit verifying he had
carried out the procedure. If he had and still contracted VD, he would not
be charged.

The instructions in Düsseldorf, Glyn Jones remembers, were on a notice
on the wall of the PAC. 'The first bit was "wash penis, bracket, nob, bracket."
That wasn't added graffiti, it was part of the instructions – there were lads
in the regiment who didn't understand the word penis.'

Despite the many precautions, a considerable number of men at home
and abroad caught venereal disease and MOs were kept busy treating it –
not to mention the matter of pubic lice ('crabs' or, in naval argot, 'minge
mice' or 'mechanised dandruff'). While these were harmless and quickly
killed with insecticide lotion, they caused their hosts considerable irritation
and MOs lengthy queues, although some men sought to remedy the
infestation themselves. At the RASC guide weapons transport company in
Wuppertal, Ivan Churm returned from home leave to find

> one of the lads bollock naked on the floor having a shave and Old Spice
> poured on his tackle. You've never seen the like of the crabs on him, like
> little missiles. I asked why he didn't go to the MO. The gist of it was, he
> worked in the canteen with the German staff, could speak a bit of German,
> and he'd been screwing his head off. He wanted to keep it quiet.

The incidence of VD was high in Malaya and Hong Kong, a little less in
Singapore and considerably less in Germany. In Malaya, the highest rate
was among the soldiers of the most successful terrorist fighters, the
Suffolks: just as they stuck together in the jungle so they did in the brothel:
they patronised the same girl and when one caught VD, they all caught
VD. In the Manchester Regiment, which also served in Malaya, Eric
Michaels remembers 'One lad caught VD five times off the same prostitute
and I can only say she was very good or he was mental. He got 112 days
inside. One little lad who'd never been with a woman, they got him drunk
and brought him to a brothel and he was the only one to catch the clap.'
The incidence of VD was greatest in Korea and Japan. It was picked up in

Seoul, on short leaves in Pusan, Inchon and elsewhere – including village whorehouses – but, in the main, during five-day R and R in Tokyo and the much smaller Kure. 'I remember one little lad coming back sick from Kure,' says Smyttan Common, in Korea with the King's Own Scottish Borderers. 'He hadn't got a dose, but it was his first time and in his enthusiasm he'd torn his G-string.' To a large extent the high rate of venereal disease resulted from Japanese women's dislike of using condoms. 'Jap bints don't stand for rubbers. They reckon it makes it like trying to strike a damp match.'[13] Among men at HQBCFK, John Hollands thinks, 'at least thirty per cent got a dose at one stage or another. We did, of course, keep a strict record of all those reporting sick with VD. We also tried to trace who they'd last had sex with – impossible in most cases.'[14]

Korea was the only place where conscripts served that those who contracted venereal disease were not charged: the army took the decision because every man was needed to fight the war. The writer of an army report on VD, who described it as 'a scourge', commented: 'I cannot see the logic of court martialling a man for a self-inflicted wound but not allow any action against him if he gets VD.' Prostitutes in their hundreds swarmed around soldiers as they left the barracks in Tokyo urging them to come and live with them during their leave, he noted, adding, 'The temptation must be tremendous and certainly their results are almost 100% successful.' The writer complained that the treatment for VD was too 'painless and quick' and suggested: 'The medical cure must be more unpleasant in some way. I suppose we can afford and must use penicillin . . . but surely it could be accompanied for "safety's sake" by some of the pre-war methods which were so efficacious in preventing a man ever getting it again, and of discouraging his friends.'

Medic Barry Whiting remembers the queues outside the ST (special treatment) tents in Korea: 'Every unit had one and there were queues every day. There was a brisk business in stolen penicillin – we had big problems trying to keep supplies secure. Those who nicked it sold it to the other guys and to the Koreans too. When it was sold to the gooks, it was frequently watered down.'

The occurrence of venereal disease rose when the war in Korea ended – British troops stayed in the country for another four years. 'Obvious, really, men had more time on their hands,' points out medical orderly David Oates, whose national service at the British military hospital in Kure extended eight months beyond the 1953 ceasefire. 'My friend worked in the large VD clinic and he was kept very busy. Most men came to Japan for treatment, but he made several trips to Korea with the medical officer to do work there.' The standard prophylactic aid centre in Kure, which happened to be attached to the hospital was, he remembers, for some reason always referred to as 'the pie and coffee shop'.

The only consolation to the British army in Korea was that VD among Australian conscripts was even higher – but then they were paid over £11 a week compared to the less than £3 a British national serviceman was paid even in his last six months.

While penicillin cleared up most men's conditions without complications, some became seriously ill and spent an extended period in hospital. Coming home, the Duke of Wellington's Regiment stopped off at Kure, where Reuben Holroyd found that 'one of the lads who'd been on general duties at HQ there and had never left Japan, was in hospital with some rare form of VD. It was some time before he followed.' Any man with the clap who came to the end of his service had to stay where he was until he was free of the condition. As national servicemen around the world chanted, 'Blobby nob stops demob'.

VD was of professional interest to Captain John Spence, who was in the last national service intake into the Medical Corps at Crookham in 1960 and who worked in the special treatment clinic at the British military hospital in Singapore:

At that time we saw very few new cases of syphilis in the UK; it was quite exciting to find a primary chancre and see the treponema pallidum (called 'the stately spirochete') under dark-ground illumination. We were the first place visited by many naval ratings after landing, people who had dallied unwisely in Burgis Street, and subalterns who traditionally spent their first leave visiting Bangkok and picking up some exotic infection. I remember one unfortunate who had achieved the grand slam, having syphilis, gonorrhoea and lymphogranuloma inguale.'[15]

At the military hospital in Fayed, Raymond May was less enthusiastic. A medical technician from Birmingham who had been given the same job in the army, he had to obtain the blood needed to carry out VD tests. 'Normally sheep's blood is used for this and other tests. In Eygpt there were no sheep and we had to use ram's blood – and I collected it at source.' The source was Reesa, who lived in a small pen at the end of the laboratory. May recalls:

> The blood-taking procedure involved the ram having a large needle inserted into his neck artery. Knowing this, and not being keen, he would retreat to the opposite diagonal corner. Head down he would then paw the ground before gathering sufficient anger and speed to hurl himself at me, at which point I would wrestle him to the ground by the horns, cowboy style, and a colleague would jump into the pen and tie his legs together. My previous work with laboratory animals – rabbits and mice – had not prepared me for this. I was engaged to be married and hopes for the future included children. Taking blood from Reesa posed serious threats to such ambitions.

How many men had sexual encounters during national service, whether they paid for it or not, can only be guessed at; men in different places at different times have different recall. 'Absolutely certain, most lads were virgin soldiers coming in, almost all,' says Glyn Jones. 'Very few were coming out – ninety-nine per cent, I'd say.' Yet in Cyprus with the Horse Guards, Graham Williams' memory is that 'the ones who did were few and far between. The prostitutes sat out on the pavements with their legs blatantly open and no knickers, but the only guys tempted were the ones who couldn't live without it. Everyone got a weekly supply of condoms – I gave mine to some sex maniac in exchange for beer.' 'Geoff and I didn't indulge, but a lot of blokes did,' says Tony Hamilton.

> I took a trip to Amsterdam with my pal Mal. Along the Kanalstrasse the women sat in the windows and I wouldn't have touched them with a bargepole. But Mal said, 'I really fancy a basinful of that.' He was back in ten minutes. All the time, he said, she was smoking a cigarette. He didn't feel

he'd had value for money, so he'd rolled up the hall rug and stuffed it up his jacket – and he sent it home to his mother.

The services' constant warnings about venereal disease did get through to many. 'We would head for the red light area [in Hamburg] and boast about how many women we would score with,' tankie Johnny Briggs says. 'But, truth to tell, I was always a bit frightened of catching something.'[16] The same fear kept the Medical Corps' Roy Booth, a self-confessed ladies' man, out of the brothels in Cyprus, 'except once when we went in for a laugh. I was sitting there on a long wooden bench with all my mates and this big, fat mama in a dirty dressing gown came towards me. I was so scared I ran like bloody hell.' Royal Fusilier Maurice Mickelwhite (Michael Caine) was another who steered clear on R and R in Tokyo and warned others to do the same. They were back in Korea and Mickelwhite was in the latrine when one who had ignored his warning

> ... came rushing in after me. 'What does the clap look like?' he demanded in a terror-stricken voice, dragging out a very sad tearful penis for my inspection. 'Just like that,' I said, rather cruelly... Word of my correct diagnosis ... spread almost as quickly as the disease, and the latrine was turned into my surgery ... some became so paranoid that they would think that the end of it was changing colour. I would tell them purple was supposed to be the colour of the end of it but they in their fearful imaginings could see other hues that no one else could spot. It eventually got so bad that I had to produce my own organ as a colour match for what a perfectly clear penis should look like. If a military policeman had ever interrupted my impromptu surgery two guys standing there matching the colour of their penises would have been quite difficult to explain.[17]

Comments Eric Michaels: 'There were stories that in hospital they stuck a thing like an umbrella[18] up your penis, opened it up and scraped it down to cure VD. That was frightening – but I was frightened by the films.'

Fidelity kept many men out of harm. If some married men played around, they did not include the newly wed Roger Keight in Malta and Alan Herbert in Germany. 'Every bar in The Gut[19] had a brothel over it and the prostitutes filled the bars, so you could hardly avoid them,' says Royal Engineer Keight.

> I used to chat to them, ask them why they were doing what they did. Many said it was because, despite Maltese girls being chaperoned when they went out, a lot became pregnant from 'secret liaisons' with servicemen and as a result had a young child to bring up. They were officially licensed and they'd proudly show you the medallion round their neck that indicated they'd been cleared at their annual health check.

'Sex didn't come looking for me and I didn't go looking for it,' says Herbert, in Germany with the 10th Hussars. 'But the squadron clerk, Danny Shayler, who provided condoms for those requiring them, looked kindly on married national servicemen going on leave, so on the two occasions I got home from Germany I came laden with half a day's production of the London Rubber Company, which Zita and I did our very best to exhaust.'

Many national servicemen are happy to admit they were sexually inexperienced when they went into uniform and came out the same way. 'I was a pure young man, I really didn't chase after women,' says Malcolm Higgins. 'I did manly things like snooker and darts and cards.' 'I really was a virgin soldier,' says Richard Lindley, as does Eric Michaels: 'Me, a virgin in and a virgin out. In Penang, where the regiment's main headquarters was, and Kuala Lumpur, these fellows would come up beside you in their trishaws. "You want a nice woman, Johnny?" But the five-fingered widow was fine by me.' Says Nick Harman: 'There were no Korean tarts at the front line, otherwise I'd probably have had a go, which would have been my first.' The only use he remembers for condoms, 'which were as thick as gumboots, was to keep rain out of rifle barrels'.

Both Harman and Lindley remember the pleasure of once again discovering the company of the opposite sex as their national service ended. Lindley came home from Malaya through the Suez Canal on the ss *Cook*, 'which brought back families including a teenage daughter. Having been starved of female company I had never seen anything so gorgeous. Those romantic walks on deck in the moonlight!' For Harman, badly wounded in Korea and flown home to hospital in the UK, the abiding memory is of the Queen Alexandria nurses, 'Starched caps, red capes with little badges of rank, light blue uniforms – and they *rustled*. Not having been near a woman for so long, it was the most exciting thing sexually.'

Sex, of course, remained in men's mind as some kind of initiation into manhood. Those who left the forces inexperienced were prepared to let it happen in its own good time. The television presenter Michael Aspel, coming to the end of his service as a radio operator with the King's Royal Rifles in Münster, decided he could no longer wait. 'I was nineteen, looked about fifteen, and hadn't had a chance to try out, shall we say, my more vital working parts. I knocked on this door. They wouldn't let me in. They thought I was too sweet and innocent to be corrupted.'[20]

Not all sex was merely 'nookie'. There was love or, perhaps, what men took for love. Leslie Thomas in Singapore fell in love with the girl he slept with and who became Juicy Lucy in *The Virgin Soldiers*:

> If you like, it was a teenage love affair . . . We used to go swimming and go to the pictures and ride around Singapore on those little trishaws, but she was a professional girl, I mean she had many other men a lot better than me and a lot richer than me, I should think. But I really felt it was the first time I'd ever known a girl, this was the real thing, albeit I had to pay ten dollars just the same as anybody else. When I came away from Singapore on the last night I went down to see her for the last time and I walked into the cabaret where she worked and I saw her sitting at the edge of the floor. You used to have to buy a book of tickets and you gave the girl a ticket every time you danced with her – ten cents a dance idea – and I saw her sitting at the edge of the dance floor and she was by herself. She was Chinese, she was very beautiful in my memory, and I just didn't have the ability to go in and say goodbye to her. I just turned around and I walked very sadly away.[21]

Some men did not want to walk away: they wanted to get married – and they presented their commanding officers with a dilemma. Some COs were paternalistic and worried about the men in their charge, most really not much more than boys; others simply considered such young men to be foolish fellows. Either way, invariably, their decision was the same: to post a man out as quickly as possible. That remained the way of things in the Middle and Far East right to the end of national service – rightly or wrongly the services' view was that the cultural clash, taken into consideration with a man's possible infatuation, gave no relationship any hope. In Germany from the mid-fifties, COs were likely to grant permission, once they had ascertained that a man was serious and that a girl came from a respectable background. Before the country's recovery, however, when there was a likelihood that a woman was trying to use a man to escape her circumstances, there was little chance. Brian Fisher had to struggle to marry his Siegrid.

Called up in 1951 while working in a printing stores in Watford, one of four brothers who did national service, Fisher joined the RAF Regiment and first went to RAF Celle near Lüneburg then to RAF Faßberg. On this massive base, 5,000 men 'lusted away after the very few women – a few regulars' wives in married quarters and the very nice girls who staffed the Malcolm Club.'[22] Siegrid worked in a little shop at the club through which men had to go on their way in 'and she picked me out'. Their relationship caused a rumpus in her family ('the war was still an issue between us and them') and an even greater one with the RAF when Fisher sought permission to marry.

> 'Unfortunately – well, fortunately, but unfortunately at the time – Siegrid had fallen pregnant. The squadron commander, wing commander, station commander – right the way up they tried to talk me out of it, and they talked of sending me back to England. My time was nearly done and I said, 'If you do, I'll only have to come back when I'm discharged, because I'm going to get married.'

The RAF contacted Fisher's family to get their approval, then sent him home to think about it. When he returned still determined, he was allowed to go ahead. With two friends from the squadron as witnesses he married in the local register office, in uniform. 'I was proud of my uniform,' he says.[23]

✳ ✳ ✳

It must be the uniform

Homosexuality in the armed forces during the national service era caused considerable – unwarranted – anxiety. This was largely a backwash from American paranoia worked up by Senator Joseph McCarthy's equation of 'deviancy' with communism; but in Britain, which had equally punitive homosexual laws as the US, there were the added worries stirred by the defection to the Soviet Union of the homosexual spies Guy Burgess and Donald Maclean, and the high-profile trial of Lord Montagu and two co-defendants in which the principal witnesses were a couple of regular airmen. In the 1950s when homosexuality was understandably closeted, there was much ignorance, misinformation and bouts of hysteria. Some politicians not only feared Reds under the bed but in the beds of national servicemen, too.[24]

The reality was that the overwhelming majority of conscripts saw not a trace of homosexual relationships, which, where they did exist, were mostly between regular servicemen. The only place that Peter Sharp met any homosexuals in the RAF was in Gibraltar:

> There were a couple of nancy-boys on the station who were notorious. I never knew what their real names were because everybody called them Gladys and Marlene. Both were married, but that did not make any difference. When they went into town at night they used to doll themselves up a bit with rouge and lipstick. I think they were warned once or twice by the Military Police but they were never actually caught.
>
> Anyway, Gladys and Marlene were harmless enough. Homosexuality never seemed to me to be a problem in Service life. [25]

What little and mostly anecdotal evidence there is suggests that any homosexual relationships between conscripts, as between the 'two strange friends who held fingers because they were in love' in Leslie Thomas's *The Virgin Soldiers*, were at least tolerated, and with good humour. On the other hand, a smattering of national servicemen were administratively discharged every year, usually for predatory behaviour – or if a case involved an officer and another rank. Sergeant Robin Ollington, The Royal Warwickshire Regiment:

> We had a very handsome PT corporal called Corporal Ryan, wonderful

physique, and we had passing through us as a recruit a young man who was obviously gay. And he was nicknamed Dolly from the start. He went off and got a commission, and he came back to the battalion, which he shouldn't have done, because we all knew him as a recruit . . . Anyway, he fell in love with Corporal Ryan and we never knew anything until one day he appeared very briefly with a black eye, and then he was posted to another regiment. And it transpired . . . that when he was orderly officer one night, he'd gone round and climbed into bed with him in his bunk, and protesting his love for him in the dark. Corporal Ryan didn't know who this person was and belted him.[26]

10

Bollocks!

The 1956 conflict known in contemporary British history simply as Suez led to the unfrocking of the then prime minister, Sir Anthony Eden – and to the beginning of the end for national service.

Within four months of Britain's agreed withdrawal from Egypt that year, President Gamal Nasser had nationalised the Canal and Eden had ordered the service chiefs to prepare an invasion with the French. When this proved impossible due to a lack of aircraft, warships and landing craft, Eden fell back on a plot involving the Israelis. Israel would attack Egypt, and Britain and France would occupy the Canal Zone on the pretext of separating the combatants and keeping the waterway open. More complex issues were at play: France did not just want the Canal back, it also wanted Egypt to drop support for guerrillas in Algeria who were fighting for freedom from French rule; Israel had a regional agenda and wanted to force Egypt to the negotiating table.

Against the likelihood of repercussions throughout the Middle East, Britain recalled 20,000 navy and army reservists – men who had done their national service, some as recently as six months earlier. Their collective reaction was anger and defiance. Some just ignored their recall notices. Others returned them with 'Bollocks' scrawled across them. Second Lieutenant Brian Sewell, RASC, rather more politely wrote back saying: "'I'm not coming. This is not a legitimate war." I was so angry. I had been an enthusiastic soldier. But this was a moral issue, and the government was profoundly wrong. I heard nothing. I could have been imprisoned, yes, but I didn't care.'

The Royal Engineers 25th Port Operation Regiment reported to a camp in Southampton docks but stayed scruffy and refused to parade. When a general stood on a chair in a tent to address them, they booed and jeered and showered him with stones. The general retreated.

The planning did not go smoothly:

Britain's strategic reserve – 16th Parachute and 3rd Commando Brigades – was already committed to Cyprus and had to be withdrawn for regrouping and retraining; landing craft had to be taken out of mothballs and the techniques of amphibious warfare relearnt; and when it was decided in September to add armour to the invasion force, the Centurions of 1st and 6th Royal Tank Regiment had to be transported to their embarkation ports in southern England by the removals firm Pickfords because of a shortage of Army tank transporters.[1]

September became October. New mutinies broke out at camps at home (from which some 14,000 reservists did not move) and among reservists shipped abroad. On 1 October, Service Corps reservists were put under close arrest after a disturbance in Cyprus. On the 5th, Grenadier Guards held a mass protest meeting in Malta. On the 8th, Medical Corps reservists caused trouble at the depot in Crookham. On the 9th, men of the Royal Artillery in Malta took part in a protest march. At the end of the month a batch of reservists sent to Germany were granted a week's home leave and were brought from Rotterdam to Southampton aboard the *Asturias*; on the return leg, 381 of them were missing. At the Artillery Paras camp at Barton Stacey where the Pay Corps' Les Wiles was attached, 'The guardroom and cells were packed with reservists who had failed to report or had gone absent from the camp or Germany and had been hauled back to await trial.'[2]

Insubordination among recalled men was nothing new, though the scale of it was. During the Korean War, more than 200,000 Second World War veterans and early national servicemen had been recalled and many were resentful. REME mechanic Norman Kenyon and his twin John, attending their first camp on the reserve, had some recalled men train with them. 'It was a shambles,' says Norman. 'Now, looking back, I understand. They'd done their stint, they had families. But at the time I thought it was shocking. They wouldn't soldier – they just sat behind buildings and smoked.' Nick Harden, a carpenter from Liverpool also doing his national service with the Engineers, saw similar behaviour among the Suez reservists. Having trained in mine clearance in Dorset, he was sent to a field regiment in Kent and 'hung around for several weeks of absolute chaos'. He adds:

> If the national servicemen were resentful of what was going on, we were angels compared with the reservists. More or less to a man they refused to polish boots or press uniforms or even do guard duty. They spent most of the time abusing the career soldiers for being idiots. The army could do nothing – it would have meant starting a fight with more than half the contingent.

It was more of the same when the regiment arrived in Malta. 'We were training over obstacle courses, running up and down hills. These people just lay down on the grass and told the officers, "Bollocks to you." Our training was farcical.'

In fact, Harden never left Malta. But Peter Batt never even left England. How Batt, 'the world's worst fucking soldier' (as his troubles with the Ordnance Corps in Egypt proved), was ever called back was, he thinks, 'Astonishing. Total bloody mystery.' At the time he was a reporter on the *London Evening News* and he was 'a thousand percent against invading Suez – though what really pissed me off was the idea of having no money. I was on fifteen quid then, which was good money.' Still, he went 'with a good heart'. When he got to his camp in Hampshire, however, he had 'a flashback of the horror of it all when they started bunging all this tropical gear at us – and I scarpered'. His father made him return, where he was duly charged and put in detention. 'When I came out, everyone was gone. Five months I was on that poxy camp, languishing, going potty. I was going to write to my MP, to everybody, but being me I didn't do anything. All I remember were the Presley hits.

I never went on a parade, nothing. I don't remember anything about my going.'

Another who missed Suez was Second Lieutenant Andrew Sinclair of the Coldstream Guards. He already had doubts about whether he would go should he be called back but as it happened he was on a scooter riding round Italy when his papers arrived and he did not get them for two weeks. 'I rang up regimental HQ and said, "Sorry, I'm a deserter, I'll come back straight away." "Oh, don't bother, Andrew," they said. "We called up somebody else instead of you, do have a happy hols." So my great moral crisis over Suez, well, that was rather a joke . . . all I did was write *The Breaking Of Bumbo.*'[3]

Michael Holroyd also missed the campaign. Just commissioned at Eaton Hall, he was on leave, sitting in a cinema watching Pathé News, when he saw his regiment, the Royal Fusiliers, embarking at Southampton. Reporting to HQ at the Tower of London he was told he had been sent a telegram, which he had not received. It seemed he was in trouble until the telegram resurfaced: 'it appeared that the adjutant, in the heat of war, had addressed it to himself'.[4] Holroyd was sent to Connaught Barracks in Dover, empty since the Fusiliers set sail, to make them ready for refugees from the Hungarian uprising.

Suez was a brief affair: 'Malaya lasted 12 years, Suez not many more hours as far as the ground forces were concerned.'[5] Allied air attacks destroyed the Egyptian air force on the ground. The Egyptian government armed civilians in the Canal cities and blocked the waterways with sunken ships. On 5 November British and French paratroopers dropped into the Canal Zone in defiance of a resolution of the UN Assembly, which had adopted a US resolution. On the 6th the allied troops landed at Port Said – at which point both the Americans and the Soviets threatened reprisals against France and Britain if they did not withdraw. Simultaneously facing a run on the pound, Britain made a humiliating exit at midnight (though elements of the army stayed behind to clear the waterways and make it operational again). The problem of the Canal was passed to the UN.

In his army public relations role, Michael Parkinson was sent to Suez, partly to keep an eye on Robin Day, then working for ITN – 'they were convinced he was a Red subversive'. He landed with 40 Marine Commando and 'it was all this John Wayne bit, Iwo Jima, guys armed to the teeth, bullets going zing, zing, and me armed with a Remington typewriter.' Soon after Britain drew stumps on the whole affair, Parkinson was made up to acting captain unpaid ('nineteen years old, three pips, ridiculous'). He was in a Landrover escorting four press photographers in Port Said when a hostile crowd surrounded the vehicle:

> It looked very nasty. This big guy stood on the hood. Officer Parkinson, who had never fired his revolver in his life, was frozen with fear. But the driver, a little Cockney reservist named Krevitsky, said, 'I've had enough of this', took the gear handle, went round and hit him with it smack in the face, and I really mean hit him, bang. And he went down and I thought, 'Oh my Christ, what now?', but the crowd fell back and Krevitsky calmly drove through them.

When Parkinson got back to England, landing at Southampton with a convoy of the PR unit's three-tonners, Krevitsky asked him if they could take a little detour on their way to Aldershot. 'His idea of a little detour was via the East End of London, where I lost two lorries for a while and had all the stores in them nicked. The episode was probably orchestrated by Corporal Krevitsky. He no doubt opened a lapdancing club or something on the proceeds.' For some reason Parkinson had to go to Mons OCS to disband his unit. As he was walking across the parade ground, 'the first person I saw was my training captain, who had taken an instant dislike to me in training. And here I was, a captain, acting, admittedly, and about to be demobbed. He looked at me in disbelief, shook his head and walked on. Which somehow summed up my national service, really.'

One Royal Fusiliers national service officer who did make it to Suez was Anthony Howard – who went to war with a suitcase. The night the embarkation order came through he had been to a 'rather good restaurant with other subalterns and was rather drunk. I remember looking at my kitbag and thinking, "I'm not going to take that." And I didn't, which was crazy. But the whole thing was crazy. Like most people I didn't think the invasion would happen. I didn't think the government would be so stupid.

There was no legal justification and that was obvious to the whole world.'

Howard waded ashore from a tank landing craft with his Sten above his head, though this was after the fighting was over. Egypt had suffered heavy casualties and material damage, the native quarter of Port Said totally destroyed. 'I only fired once. Someone was moving about in a cinema and my commanding officer ordered me to tell whoever it was to come out, and to give him a burst. I fired at the roof. He came out, understandably alarmed, the caretaker probably, and was taken prisoner.'

The homecoming he remembers as being 'ghastly'. He adds: 'The blow to the pride of the professional soldiers was devastating. They had been humiliated. They'd gone to knock Nasser off his perch. We were still the British lion. Then our tail was well and truly tweaked.'

In the short encounter, 22 British servicemen were killed and 90 wounded.

* * *

Suez was the final nail in the coffin of British imperialism. But, within the broader context of what kind of armed forces Britain should have for the future, it also raised the question of whether national service should continue, with all the old arguments about its effects on the economy, industry and the very fabric of the country. On 4 April 1957, Duncan Sandys, the new Minster of Defence in the government of Harold Macmillan (Eden having departed because of 'ill-health'), delivered the White Paper that settled the issue. Britain's defence policy would shift to nuclear deterrence and long- and medium-range missiles, the armed forces would be cut almost in half, with an entirely professional, mobile and newly equipped army doing away with the need for huge static garrisons like Hong Kong and Singapore – and national service would end in 1962.

There were those who, ten years earlier, had said national service should never have begun. Lieutenant-General Sir Gifford Martel advocated the creation of a Territorial Army reserve of four million war-trained veterans. 'Instead of this,' he wrote, 'we choose to spend the most stupendous sums on our National Service army... This is the sorry position in which we are left to-day.'[6] The military commentator Captain Basil Liddell Hart advocated what Sandys was now instigating: a professional force, standing by like a fire brigade. He pointed out that the countries rolled over by the Nazis had had conscription at the time, but 'so-called trained reserves' were so slow to mobilise as to be useless. What answer, he asked, did France have to 'the opening stroke of attack by about 15 hundred tanks covered by a thousand aircraft?'[7] But the most persistent critics of national service were the Labour Party. They had instigated it in power; nevertheless, they opposed it in Opposition, with Manny Shinwell (the man who raised the period of service from 18 months to two years during the Korean War) the most vocal. His continued attacks on conscription caused Field Marshal (now Viscount) Montgomery, essentially the architect of national service as Chief of the Imperial General Staff, considerable annoyance.[8]

Ending national service, or reducing the time men spent doing it, was a row that had rumbled on and on long before Suez. In a television broadcast in 1955, Clement Attlee as Leader of the Opposition, said there was a 'strong case' for reduction; Prime Minister Eden responded by saying it would be 'criminal folly to weaken ourselves'. Yet later that year Eden announced that the armed forces would be reduced from 800,000 to 700,000 because Britain no longer needed such a large strategic reserve, and national service registrations were to be cut from four a year to three, a move that would take some 35,000 men off the list annually; in December 1956 – post-Suez – came the announcement that BAOR was being decreased from 77,000 to 50,000 men.

Still the government could not bring itself to say that national service was ending, though the signals were clear enough. Then Macmillan arrived at Number Ten and told Sandys to get on with it. As far as Britain as a whole was concerned, it was not before time. In 1949, 57% of the population thought conscription was a good thing; after Korea in 1953, the percentages were reversed; by 1957 three-quarters of the country wanted to see the back of it.

Defence spending – which doubled in the NS era to 8% of GDP – was an albatross around Britain's neck; the Korean campaign alone represented a loss of £200 million a year from industrial production.[9] Industry was hard hit by national service. Because of its overlapping nature, every year 300,000 men were taken out of the job market – many of them just as their apprenticeships finished and their employers had a right to expect a return on their investment – leading throughout the fifties to an acute manpower shortage that was blamed for spiralling inflationary wage demands as firms chased too little skilled labour.

In the beginning, some enlightened firms had cooperated with local military authorities in running one- or two-day courses for those about to be called up; others had set up their own pre-service courses; one even sent its lads to an outward-bound school. But by 1957, industry was fed up. A good proportion of men returning from their spell in uniform did not come back to the jobs that by law were held open for them; others, who had not been employed by the forces in their trades, were found to be deskilled; and, worse, as a 1957 survey of 70 companies found, many who had done very little during their service had lost the capacity to do a day's work. National service was even proving to be a problem in getting youngsters to take up apprenticeships in the first place: with the prospect of two years' conscription hanging over them, they preferred to take dead-end jobs that paid better.

The voices of many who had done their time overseas also contributed to public opinion turning against conscription. Almost without exception, men had gone off without a thought as to the morality of colonial rule; most would have agreed with Don McCullin (who moved from Egypt to Kenya to process film for Bomber Command in Nairobi during the Mau Mau campaign), who considered himself 'a super-patriot, well to the right of Alf Garnett. My country could do no wrong.'[10] The hostility of local populations to the British presence made them think otherwise. Many of those who served in Germany reached a different realisation. They had witnessed a country that had risen from its ruins because it invested in the *Wirtschafswunder* – the economic miracle – and not, as Britain had done, in international policing.[11]

The Sandys plan downsized all three services, but the army bore the brunt. It was to be cut from the existing 330,000 to 165,000 by the time the last national servicemen was due to go home in 1962, five years later. Infantry was to lose 11 battalions (there were also some amalgamations), armour would lose seven regiments, artillery 20, engineers four – and a lot of regular officers, no longer sustained by the national service pyramid, would be shown the door. At the peak of conscription in 1952, there were nearly 30,000 army officers, almost one in every six regulars. By 1962 over two officers in every five would have been forced into retirement. In the immediate aftermath of Suez, Michael Holroyd, promoted to the rank of temporary unpaid captain, spent the last four months of his national service at the War Office where, with a subaltern who was also a conscript, he was in charge of officers' redundancies:

> We divided the country up, the two of us, and went to work. Since our recommendations were invariably accepted this was, I suppose, real power. Majors and colonels of all conditions would send us their forms giving reasons why they should stay or go . . . It was ironic that the breed of person who had made much of one's life uncomfortable over the past two years should apparently . . . be at one's mercy.[12]

$$* \quad * \quad *$$

The army was shocked by the depth of the cuts imposed upon it; it had anticipated a professional force of 200,000. Yet at the same time it was sick and tired of national service. The navy took so few conscripts (an average of a few thousand a year) that its training framework was not disrupted by their presence. The army (and to a lesser extent the RAF) had to change the framework to accommodate the conscripts. From the beginning, the navy refused to take men who did not meet its standards of intelligence and the RAF quickly followed, leaving the army, as it complained, 'to continue to take the dullards'. In both the army and air force, national service tied up the best men in carrying out the training, most intensively at the officer cadet training schools (there were 85 officers and 650 NCOs at Mons). National service also seriously reduced the morale of regular servicemen who found their promotion path blocked by cleverer or better qualified conscripts and who, into the bargain, had to endure the constant round of exercises that the new conscripts, delivered by the national service conveyor belt, had to be given – and listen to the constant moaning of many of them. Even when conscripts were trained, which, including trade training, took an average of nine months, the armed forces were lucky to get 12 useful months from them once leave, embarkation leave and travelling to and fro were taken into account. In cases where men served in the UK and then in another country or two, or moved between a number of camps, the usefulness was even less. It was estimated that for one reason or another some 30,000 national servicemen were on the move at any given moment.

For the army, certainly, the national service tail wagged the military dog[13] and the flood of recruits fortnight after fortnight overwhelmed the training camps, never giving them the breathing space to develop a method less reliant on drill and bull. No one denied that both instilled discipline. But Lieutenant Colonel E.H. Tinker of the 13th/18th Royal Hussars considered 'Much valuable time is wasted in teaching unnecessary movements with the rifle, still banged on the ground as though it were a pike.'[14] He also pointed out that drill had originally been practised for the way soldiers were deployed on the field of battle: 'It was training for war. Since the beginning of the 20th century drill has ceased to be a warlike exercise.'[15] A damning case against bull – the services' obsession with order and cleanliness, as much a part of the RAF's basic training as the army's – was made by playwright Arnold Wesker in *Chips With Everything*:

> I'm your pilot officer. You'll find that I'm amenable and that I do not stick rigidly to authority. All I shall require is cleanliness. It's not that I want rigid men, I want clean men. It so happens, however, that you cannot have clean men without rigid men, and cleanliness requires smartness and ceremony. Ceremony means your webbing must be blanco'd, and smartness means that your brass – all of it – must shine like silver paper, and your huts must be spick and span without a trace of dust, because dust carries germs, and germs are unclean. I want a man clean from toe nail to hair root. I want him so clean that he looks unreal. In fact I don't want real men, real men are dirty and nasty, they pick their noses – and scratch their skin, I want unreal, super-real men.[16]

At the beginning of 1956, the published findings of Sir John Wolfenden's inquiry into national service in the army – commissioned by the Army Council – had more to say about bull. Acknowledging that it was necessary from time to time to see that kit was serviceable, 'excess of zeal' led to too-frequent inspections, and 'stiffening clothes with cardboard, blancoing pull-through cords, blackening the soles of boots and burnishing the tops of boot polish tins should be forbidden'. More crucially, the Wolfenden committee concluded that national service was wasting men's time: 'Our overwhelming impression is that, with few exceptions, the national serviceman regards his two-year period of service as an infliction to be undergone rather than a duty to the nation.'[17]

The army would have shuddered if Wolfenden had investigated reserve training.

In the early years – when the commitment was 15 days' camp in each of the three years' liability, plus the equivalent of 15 days of spare-time training – most men did it willingly enough, though Albert Tyas was not one of them. The Yorkshire plumber, a Northumberland Fusilier taken prisoner in Korea fighting with the Ulster Rifles, had spent two years and four months in captivity and thought that being expected to do any reserve training after his experience was 'a bloody imposition', though in his case it was only four days: 'They very kindly said that for every month in prison camp they'd knock two days off – fifty-six days. So for the extra four I had to go to Scarborough – and I'd only been married a week. We were quite bolshie, about ten of us, and we refused to do any soldiering. They kept us locked up in a tent – but they made us tent orderlies!'

The Territorial Army, a volunteer force after all, was not geared up to running reserve training efficiently and were in despair about subversive elements. As early as November 1952 the GOC-in-C of Anti-Aircraft Command wrote to the Under-Secretary of State at the War Office asking what was to be done with 'men of bad character'. (He had, apparently, a particular problem in Glasgow.) 'If a TA CO awards a man detention, only that portion of it can be put into execution which can be served before the end of the training period,' he wrote. 'The alternative is a court martial and it is not considered feasible for TA units to run courts martial.'

The War Office decision was to send such men for their annual stint to ordinary training units. But that solution would not have been possible later. With time, more and more men grew bolshie about something that seemed pointless (employers grew more discontented, too). For the infantry, it was more of the same: drill, bull, exercises – and they had had their fill of that; men in skilled arms like the Royal Engineers who could

221

have benefited from upgrading to newer technology, invariably found the equipment even less up to date than it had been during their service. Men's hearts simply were not in the reserves – and many who turned up quietly slipped away. One was Charlie Harris, a Service Corps supplies storeman at Woolwich Common during national service. 'We used to go over the fence for two or three days. When I was sent to Crowborough in Sussex we sodded off to Brighton, drinking. They didn't catch us. We buggered off on the Wednesday, came back on the Thursday – and went home for the weekend.'

Harris did his three annual camps, but many men were not called. Some were ordered back for one or two, others for none. The navy recalled most of those who could serve on ships but not many others, and the RAF, other than expecting aircrew to continue flying with the auxiliary or volunteer reserves, recalled hardly anyone. 'I sometimes used to think, when I was farming and standing in the middle of a field in my old RAF greatcoat covered in muck, what they'd have thought if I'd turned up in it,' muses Tony Hamilton. That was another anomaly: some men who were not recalled received instructions to return their kit (and had to pay for any losses); others heard not a word.

Sandys reduced the reserve commitment to 20 days in a single year, but hundreds now did not answer the call. Units began to release men from their obligation if they had a halfway decent reason. Back from Cyprus and his stint with the Horse Guards, Graham Williams went to work for a newspaper 20 miles away from his home in Paisley and told his commanding officer 'I couldn't be training on Tuesday night or Wednesday or whatever it was, I'd be out on jobs. As it happened he was my old German teacher and he quietly forgot about me.' By 1958 reserve training had disappeared altogether.

* * *

Dukes and dustmen, tradesmen and toffs did national service. The government always emphasised that national service was universal – but it never was that.

Under the various Acts, only clergymen, the blind and the mentally incapacitated were specifically exempted from doing it. Indefinite deferment, however, was given to underground miners, some agricultural workers and merchant seamen,[18] as well as to sea-going fishermen and a few scientists and engineers engaged on high-priority projects. But what about other key workers in the docks, steel, power, the building trade in the years that Britain was chronically short of housing? What about the railways? In 1951 the Railway Executive sought the exemption it had had during the Second World War. Having lost 2,400 firemen and cleaners to conscription, the railways had been forced to bring men south from Scotland – and accommodate them in old sleeping cars – to keep freight traffic moving.

The government refused the request, as it did all others, less on the basis of how essential the railways were to the country than from nervousness of undercutting national service's apparent equality. Which industries were key and which were not caused constant rows and the exemption granted to the merchant navy was never far from the centre of them. In a debate in the House of Lords, Lord Cherwell said there were no doubts about exempting 'genuine' merchant seamen, but thought it 'abominable' that 'a dishwasher, bar tender or hairdresser on a luxury liner was allowed to escape entirely . . .'[19]

While the arguments about exemption could not be anything but public, there was, over time, an inequality in who was or was not called up on medical grounds that was surreptitious. Some men were medically unfit for national service in any circumstances. But, as both the government and service chiefs knew from the beginning, the national service age group continually delivered far more men than were needed or could be handled – and the flow could best be controlled by adjusting the medical standards, depending on circumstances. During the Korea War years of overstretch, these were lowered to take more men; during the rundown of national service they were raised, to take fewer. As one example, in the late forties, Acker Bilk served with the Royal Engineers in Egypt despite having taken the top off a middle finger in a tobogganing accident; in the early fifties, George Younger (later a Conservative member of government who became Viscount Younger) served with the Argyll and Sutherland Highlanders in Korea despite having lost two fingers in a shooting accident. Yet in 1958 Howard Winstone, who would become world featherweight boxing champion, who had lost the tips of three fingers while working in a toy factory, was discharged from the Welch Regiment after two weeks.

From 1955, when the end of national service seemed inevitable but the government still dithered, it nonetheless broadened the categories of exemptions. Police cadets were added (there was a shortfall of 10,000 policemen); university graduates in science or engineering with first-class honours who took jobs in the UK requiring degree qualifications in their subjects; first- or second-class honours student graduates in science and mathematics who went into teaching. The public welcomed the first of these moves but, comprehensively against national service though they now were, widely resented the other two. As E.P. Danger from SW1 wrote to *The Times*: 'It will be very hard to persuade any ordinary person that a young scientist of, say, 20 is so vital to the country that he cannot be spared for a couple of years.'[20]

The liability for conscription continued to be whittled away. From 1956, those in medical grade three were exempted – cutting another 5,000 from the annual intake[21] – as were men under the height of five feet two. During the Second World War, the British army had not taken men under five feet six[22] but during national service, again in the name of universality, had done so, in some cases, perhaps, unfortunately. Sent to 6 Driver Training RASC in Yeovil, RAMC Doctor Martin Leadley's

> eyes were opened when I saw the sort of dwarfs who were posted into the RASC. Many from Glasgow and Manchester were under the 5 feet and 100 lb requirement for training to drive a 3-ton lorry. They could not reach the steering wheel nor were they strong enough to handle the heavy vehicle. Was I supposed to stretch them?[23]

Nineteen fifty-six also saw the government, 'impressed by the thousands of cases affecting small businesses dependent on one man', amend the National Service Act to exclude one-man businesses[24] – a decision that three years later allowed Michael Heseltine, who in 1983 would be the first national serviceman to become Defence Secretary, to bring his time in uniform to a halt after only eight months.

After being commissioned, Heseltine had been back with the Welsh

Guards at Pirbright for 61 days when the 1959 general election was announced. The following day he applied to resign from the army to fight a seat for the Conservatives in the Gower constituency in south Wales, which under Queen's Regulations he was entitled to do. Having lost (his opponent polled three times as many votes) he should have returned to Pirbright. But the manager of his business affairs had been found to have had his hand in the till, and, claiming there was no one to pick up the pieces, Heseltine got his solicitor to write to the War Office 'asking whether they really wanted me to return'. He cited the problems that had arisen with his business and eventually got a reply saying that, in the circumstances, he would not be recalled.

> This outcome, I'm glad to say, confounded the teasing statement made by a left-wing newspaper columnist, Tony Howard, during the election that my colleagues in the officers' mess at Pirbright were so convinced of my defeat that they could hardly contain their excitement at the prospect of my return and listening to my campaign memories. 'Oh Lord, yes,' my adjutant was even quoted as saying in response to a question as to whether I'd be back, 'and we're longing to hear all about it.'[25]

By 1957 when there were 330,000 men of call-up age, only 130,000 were actually called up.

*   *   *

Whatever the imperfections of the national service system, parliament, press and people wanted at least to feel it was as fair as possible. It angered everybody that an estimated 1,000 men a year skipped the country – in the main to southern Ireland and Canada where there was no call-up, or in the case of some research scientists to lucrative jobs in America – intending to stay away until they were beyond the cut-off age of 26. The government closed this loophole in 1954: a man spending 28 days abroad in the last year of his liability could in future be conscripted up to the age of 36.

The issue had come to the top of the pile because in 1955 the first group liable for call-up under the 1947 Act were now reaching 26. One of these was the racing driver Mike Hawthorn – who was in Italy with the Ferrari team. There was a lot of adverse newspaper coverage and the name of

Stirling Moss was quickly dragged in. In a debate on national service deferment in March 1954, an MP in the House asked: 'How about the speed merchants? How do professional motor drivers escape?' The former War Minister Manny Shinwell sarcastically referred to Hawthorn and Moss saying: 'When I hear of these young, daring, courageous people going abroad racing round tracks to the danger of their lives, and when I hear of their physical incapacity, I wonder.'

In fact, the kidney complaint nephritis[26] made both men unfit to be conscripted, though Hawthorn would only prove that following an operation later in the year, after which he was examined by consultants on behalf of the Ministry of Labour and National Service. Moss, the most famous British sportsman of his era, had nothing to prove – he had volunteered for the RAF at seventeen and been rejected at his medical in High Wycombe on 19 August 1947. He sent Shinwell a photostat of his medical card. 'The accusation was hurtful and upsetting,' Sir Stirling Moss says. 'I couldn't be more proud of my country and I desperately wanted to join the RAF. There was no public hostility towards me – I never received a nasty word or letter from anybody. Quite frankly we'd got the record straight and that was that.'

Politicians did not like sportsmen getting away without not doing national service, as cricketer Colin Cowdrey was another to find out in June 1955. He had passed his medical and reported to Cardington for kitting out, where huge letters were painted on the side of a hangar: *The RAF welcomes Colin Cowdrey*. Within days, the RAF said goodbye, rejecting him because of flat feet.[27] In the House Labour MP Norman Dodds – who claimed to have 'a long list of boxers, tennis players, jockeys, racing motorists, cricketers and footballers who, so far, have dodged the column in a most blatant way' – pointed out that there were grade three men in the RAF who could only wear canvas shoes, and called the Cowdrey case 'a wangle'.

Four years later, as national service was winding down and more and more men were being exempted, politicians were still riled by the famous who escaped the net. Now the issue focused on the pop singers Terry Dene, discharged within weeks from the Green Jackets after a mental breakdown, and Marty Wilde, medically rejected with fallen arches and severe corns. A number of MPs raised protests, Conservative Gerald Nabarro fuming that 'There is really no excuse at all for Terry Dene, Marty Wilde, Colin Cowdrey and the remainder being able to evade military service simply on grounds evidently that they earn large sums of money in civil life or are prominent sportsmen.' Cowdrey invited Nabarro to make his comments without the protection of parliamentary privilege. 'I did not try to get my discharge and no one in high places attempted to pull any strings for me,' he said. He sought, and received, an apology.

As an important footnote to 'universality', a widespread misconception in recent years is that non-whites did not do national service, because the armed forces did not want them. The main confirmation for this is, vaguely, that few national servicemen remember seeing non-white faces in the ranks, and, more specifically, an apparently xenophobic government report in 1949, not published at the time, which concluded that making Indian citizens liable to conscription would result in 'a good many unwanted persons . . . who are difficult to absorb and are not much value in the UK forces'.

The view is wrong on both counts. The reason there were so few non-white conscripts is that, up to the mid-1950s and the sudden rise in immigration, the non-white population in the UK was measured only in tens of thousands (the statistics of the time are as imprecise as that) – there were few such men to call up. Where the government report is concerned, the context needs to be understood. In 1949 India had just been given independence, the possibility was that considerable numbers of Indians and Pakistanis holding British passports would be flocking to Britain, and the last thing the army in particular needed, as it struggled to handle the national servicemen already overwhelming them, was an influx of more young men from a different country, bringing with them complications of culture and language.[28]

In fact, at the very least, some hundreds of 'men of colour' (the argot of the period) were called up – men like Billy Boston, whose father came from Sierra Leone. The then unknown Wigan and Great Britain rugby winger went from his home in Cardiff's Tiger Bay to the Royal Signals in Catterick, where he stayed as a PTI – when he wasn't playing rugby.[29] 'And as it happens *I* never saw another man of colour,' he remarks.

A point also put forward as additional evidence of racial prejudice is that from the late 1950s the authorities readily considered those with 'Asiatic' names to be either temporary residents or engaged in full-time education and therefore not required for national service – but, again, this is to ignore the context: post-Sandys the authorities were finding as many ways as they could to squeeze as many men as possible, irrespective of their ethnicity, out of the system.

Until Sandys, men whose origins were in the subcontinent but who lived in Britain were expected to go into uniform like everybody else – as a test case in December 1954 clearly shows. John Ullah, who arrived in the UK from Pakistan in 1951 to help an uncle run a drapery business, appeared before the Birmingham stipendiary magistrate for refusing to submit to a medical. He claimed he was only a temporary resident and that Pakistan was an independent country. The magistrate found him guilty. An appeal was heard in the High Court in April 1955. It was dismissed.

*   *   *

It was possible to appeal before a tribunal against doing national service on the grounds of conscientious objection, and every year some 700 men did so (a peak of 945 in 1952, during the Korean War) – about four in 1,000.[30]

A man who opposed his conscription – on religious, humanitarian, political or other grounds – could expect one of four verdicts: unconditional registration (acceptance of his case), conditional registration (ordered to do civil work), non-combatant military service, or rejection of his position and therefore normal call-up. If a man refused to accept any of the three options against him he could go to prison – and every year between 30 and 100 men did.

Refusing to attend a medical was a civil offence and resulted in an appearance in magistrates' court and a fine of between £2 and £5. Jail sentences (a month to a maximum of a year) were not usually handed out until a second or third appearance but were not automatic[31] – the playwright Harold Pinter, in 1949 a student at the Royal Academy of Dramatic Arts, made two court appearances and escaped imprisonment, though both times he took along his toothbrush, just in case.[32]

In 1955, described in *The University Libertarian* magazine as 'a typical year', 38.9% of objectors had their appeal dismissed outright; 17.9% were ordered to do national service in a non-combatant role (usually the Medical Corps); and 40.6% went to work on farms or in hospitals or, in some cases, continued in their current employment such as teaching – on a national service wage in all cases. Only 2.6% had their appeals upheld.

It is commonly believed that only those whose case was based on religious conviction succeeded in getting unconditional registration but that, according to the Peace Pledge Union archivist Bill Hetherington,

> is a myth. Nothing was as black and white as that, it depended entirely on the tribunal, and tribunals could be perverse. Probably the majority who got unconditional were Quakers or had Quaker-like beliefs, but a very few who were politically motivated did too. Jehovah's Witnesses were generally harshly treated; they were regarded as cranks who knocked on people's doors.

The artist David Hockney – who objected to doing national service because he disapproved of what he saw as a 'colonial war' in Cyprus – was given a conditional judgement at his tribunal in Leeds in 1957 and went to work as a ward orderly at St Luke's Hospital in Bradford and then St Helen's Hospital in Hastings. Three years earlier John Dixon's tribunal in Fulham had also sent him to work in a hospital – as a porter in the Royal Free in London. 'I had a brother four years older who'd had a bad time with REME in Egypt and I was predisposed not to like national service,' he explains. 'But I happened to pick up a copy of *Peace News* and it gave me a principled objection to war.' After a year Dixon decided to go to India – he was interested in the Gandhi movement's policy of passive resistance – sought permission, was refused but went anyway. On the way his ship called at Cyprus and 'a couple of conscripts came on board and we got chatting. They had sympathy with my stance. In fact they rushed off and brought us back some tinned food.' On his return Dixon reported to the Ministry of Labour for whatever fate awaited him, but was told: 'Get married, find yourself a job,' about which he says: 'At the time I thought this very nice guy was letting me off. Later I realised I was more trouble than I was worth.' Mike Randle was a conscientious objector ordered to work on the land – as he was already doing on his father's farm in Sussex. Although his father had been a conscientious objector during the Second World War, Randle believed that some wars were just and had no intention of refusing his conscription. 'What tipped the balance was the nuclear issue. War couldn't be like that. It was against all proportionality.' Most people, he thinks, were reasonably disposed towards conscientious objectors. 'They saw our case. In fact many wondered why more men being called up didn't go our route.' Only once was he confronted by personal abuse, 'when I went back to my Catholic boarding school in Berkshire for some reunion and one of the other fellows, hearing I'd been a CO [conscientious objector], said, "Oh, you coward." '33

Some men became conscientious objectors after completing their call-up and refused to serve on the reserve, like Londoner Gabriel Newfield. He had gone into the Medics, become chief documents clerk at Crookham, and for his last eight months was a sergeant-tester at the Ministry of Labour and National Service medical centre in Wanstead. But while at the London School of Economics he considered his position, decided it was no more morally right being in the RAMC than being a fighting soldier in a tooth arm, and wrote to the army to say he would not do part-time service. Unfortunately there was no procedure for this kind of stance – Newfield could not appear before an appeals tribunal before being given at least three months' detention or imprisonment. When his papers came, Newfield reported to Crookham in civilian clothes, carrying his kit. He spent all day trying to get someone to listen to him. Eventually he persuaded an NCO to arrest him and put him in the cells. The next day the adjutant placed him under open arrest, so he could come and go as he liked, and was then allowed home for a week on promising to turn up for his court martial. Newfield got his three months, after which his application to the tribunal was upheld. Later he received an official communication from the Army Emergency Reserve, RAMC: 'Services no longer required.'

Bill Hetherington's personal journey towards pacifism was unusual. He not only did national service in the navy as a Russian-language decoder, but also fulfilled his three recalls on the reserve, fitting them in during vacations at Oxford where he read politics, philosophy and economics.

> I was a conscientious objector at heart when I did national service, but I didn't know there was a movement. During my reserve service I was scared that coming out would get me court martialled. But shortly after I'd done my final fortnight, Suez happened. There were half a dozen in my college who'd been in the navy with me and I was horrified, when there was a protest march of town and gown, to see them standing on some steps in Oxford shouting 'We want war'. I knew I didn't belong among them.

A little later, at home in Birmingham, he joined a nuclear disarmament vigil on Hiroshima Day and when soon after he got his papers for his next five years on the non-active reserve, he sent them back. 'They wrote to say it didn't matter whether I kept them or not, I couldn't get out of my legal obligation – and they enclosed my next theoretical posting. I returned that too – covered in CND stickers.' He still wishes he had had the courage to be 'a stand-up conscientious objector,' but adds: 'Having done national service, I know what they rejected. And down the years of dealing with cases of conscientious objection when I've found myself faced by some supercilious bastard I've been able to say, "I know what I'm talking about".'

The few Welsh and Scottish nationalists who appealed to tribunals got short shrift – as did Irishmen from south of the border when they appeared in front of magistrates' courts, having been caught working in England and claiming that they were exempt as England was not their permanent home. When a warehouseman from Dublin living in Fulham appeared in court on a charge of theft, the magistrate asked Detective Sergeant E.R. Grant: 'They come over here and I see a lot of them, but I rarely hear of one who has done any military service. Are they not liable for it?' 'Yes, if they stay long enough,' replied the policeman. 'The difficulty is they keep moving from address to address and suddenly decide to make a visit back to Ireland.' To which the magistrate responded: 'Now would be an excellent time for the military authorities to look a little alive about him.'[34]

* * *

In the wind-down of national service, the government tried for an element of fairness by targeting those who had been deferred for professional or trade training before the Sandys announcement, leaving those deferred from 1957 to slip the net. But even this was inequitable: men who finished their apprenticeships but continued part-time study for qualifications 'not essential to such men to follow their occupations but of use to them in their careers' were not called up. The government got more men off the books by widening recognition of full-time courses beyond those at universities, university colleges and agricultural and technical colleges; by extending to arts graduates the dispensation that already allowed science graduates to bypass conscription – and by allowing many at university to take a second degree.[35] Before this, a first degree only was the rule. In 1951 David Findlay Clark had a degree in psychology and a scholarship to continue doctoral studies at several American universities, 'But the "Men from the Ministry" were not . . . to be moved from their view that no further deferment could be allowed and the call to arms was an immediate imperative.'[36] Clark headed for the RAF and the scholarship, only available in that year and the next, went to a female student, the next in line.

The government took other measures to reduce intakes. It spread exemption from underground miners to all miners. It quietly struck off those with police records and known delinquents. It broadened the hardship rules, instructing hardship committees to look sympathetically on men who were the only support of widowed mothers and younger brothers or sisters – between May 1959 when the new guidelines were made known and December, there were a record number of applications and 7,000 had already been granted; few married men with children, the government admitted, were now being turned down. Without prominence being given to the fact, the medical was possibly the prime control, with the standard of physical health and the IQ requirement being raised. In the first three years of national service, 11% of men examined were declared unfit; in the last three years it was 26% – a remarkable level of physical decline among young men if taken at face value (the average across 13 years of medical examinations was 17%).

Before the mid-fifties, over 20% of the national service age group were not conscripted for one reason or another. From 1955 it rose to around 30% – and after Sandys to 46%.

In December 1959 the army announced that it was releasing many national servicemen up to three months early – something the other two services had been doing for some time. In the RAF a lot of aircrew, surplus to requirement, were going six months early. Mike Watkins, who had trained as a NATO navigator in Canada, sailed home on the *Empress of France* in 1958 to find, to his disappointment, that he was headed for civvy street.

Had my national service continued I would have gone to an operational conversion unit and trained on whatever aircraft I would have flown – Shackletons, Hastings, Lincolns. Above all I would have liked to fly the Canberra twin-engined bomber, my favourite aircraft since I'd made models of it as a child. But they had no need of me. One of my contemporaries insisted that the RAF had a duty to allow him to complete his two years. They found him a job in the MoD.

For the navy, the passing of national service was of little significance – in 1960 it had only 500 conscripts in a strength of 98,000. For the army and RAF it was a different story. It wasn't a question of total numbers going: it was that among them were skilled tradesmen and specialists, who could not easily be replaced. Additionally, the end of national service stemmed the flow of conscripts who converted to three-year engagements – a quarter of all three-year men in the army and 29% in the RAF. The army had another headache: almost two-thirds of its NCOs were national servicemen (in comparison, the RAF in 1959 had only 19 national service sergeants out of 13,000 and 393 national service corporals out of 23,000) and the majority of officers at platoon level.

After a slow start, RAF recruitment of regulars progressed but, despite television advertising, better pay, pensions, plans for more and better family accommodation, recruitment of overseas nationals – even promises of a relaxation of discipline – at a time of full employment, army growth was marginal, especially of men with qualifications. In April 1961, when the army still had over 80,000 national servicemen in its ranks, the possibility was that conscription might have to be continued, a contingency that Sandys had made provision for if recruitment fell short.

Voices raised against the end of national service from the time of the White Paper had become a clamour during 1958 when Britain was obliged to send troops to help with trouble in Lebanon and Jordan and a coup d'état in Iraq, as well as deploy reinforcements to places as widely separated as Cyprus, Libya, Bahrain and Aden. When the Irish Guards were sent to Cyprus they had to take with them a company of Welsh Guards to bring them up to strength, such was the strain on human resources. Yet at the time the army was 320,000 strong, prompting the worry: how was Britain supposed to cope with an army of only 165,000? In 1961, when that figure was being discussed as a 'floor' and recruitment was 20,000 short of a 'ceiling' of 180,000, impasse seemed to have been reached. The regular army was too small; a national service army was too big.

The answer seemed to many to be either selective service or ballot, to begin in 1962. One estimate was that 12,000–25,000 men would be needed each year until regular recruiting reached critical mass, probably in 1965 or '66; others talked of the need being one man in two or four. But how should these men be chosen? By the American model of 'selection by exclusion'?[37] By ballot? But that would not give the army the skilled men it needed; as the *Sunday Times* had already fulminated: 'our crying need is for technologists, not tank crews; scientists, not soldiers.'[38] It was apparent that any kind of selective process would have the bright and the skilled in its sights and, as the army itself phrased it, 'put a premium on ignorance'. There was huge public hostility to both options: either there was national service or there wasn't. Both options were shelved.[39]

The government position was that men born up to June 1939 were to do national service in the normal way. The call-up of those born in the third quarter of '39 was 'uncertain', from October '39, 'unlikely', with those born in 1940 being told they 'need not expect to be called up'. It was an uneasy period for those in these groups and there was considerable activity in the various channels of exemption that the government had introduced.[40] In the final analysis, after services' pay was again improved (on a par with what had successfully bolstered enrolment into the police), recruitment to the armed forces in 1962 was 27,800, the highest figure since 1939, and the army scrambled over the line, helping the government stick to its forecasts.[41]

It was just as well. Had national service continued it almost certainly could only have been as a 'universal' imposition, however many get-out clauses were engineered, and it could only have headed towards chaos. In 1956, 330,000 men had reached eighteen. Thanks to the postwar baby boom, between 1960 and '65 that yearly figure was calculated to rise to 470,000 . . .

∗ ∗ ∗

Would it end, wouldn't it? Men had been going into the services at a later and later age since the annual registrations were reduced from four to three: in 1959 it was theoretically at nineteen and three months. But there was a backup of those waiting for their papers – a wait that increased during 1959 when the government was treading water. Peter Duffell, who was to serve as a platoon officer with the Gurkhas in Malaya, was working as a junior reporter on the *Daily Mail* when he registered on his nineteenth birthday in June 1958. After waiting 16 months – and having contacted the Ministry of Labour and National Service several times, on each being told he would be called up in the next two months – he wrote a letter to *The Times*.

> In it I said my career was being hampered. At one end my employers couldn't consider me seriously because I was supposed to be off any day; at the other, the longer the delay the older I'd be before I got back. Quite unbelievably a few people sent me white feathers. One said, 'We know about chaps like you, we had them in the war.' It was a complete travesty – all I'd said was I wanted a date so I could get on with it. Anyway, shortly after, the old *Daily Herald* ran a leader with a headline like 'Wake up War Office'. Five days later I got my papers.

The national service experience in the last two years varied enormously. For many, it was no different than it had been for those who had gone before. Many a man, however, found he was treated with indifference, 'regarded as an obsolescent creature who is not really worth training properly'.[42] Men like Duffell who served across the Med and Middle and

235

Far East probably had the best of it, those in Britain the worst. It did not help any of them that accelerated demob of national servicemen ahead of time starkly indicated that there was no real job to do.

The Southampton footballer John Sydenham, called up in July 1960 to the Medical Corps at Crookham where he stayed, in the early weeks 'felt shot to pieces, a total wreck' because 'it was a waste of time, everyone knew it was a waste of time – and it was putting my career in jeopardy. Ted Bates [the Southampton manager] had bought Harry Penk to take my place. If Harry set the world on fire I knew I might never get back.' The one thing that kept him going, he says, was knowing that the call-up of Terry Paine, the team's outside right, was imminent and the likelihood was that Bates could swing it for him to come to Crookham. Paine (ultimately capped 19 times for England, including a World Cup) failed his medical because of a perforated eardrum. Whether he really had the condition he does not know.

> Six weeks before my medical I got boils in my ears and was in a lot of pain. The club doctor sorted me out. At the medical when I came to the ear doctor I said I had constant earache and running of the ears – I was streetwise enough to lay it on a bit. He cleaned my ears out, stood at the window and told me to stand at the door. He called out different words, brown, now, cow, and I pretended not to hear every sixth one or something, though I reckon I could have heard a pin drop and still can. He sent me to Winchester County Hospital to see the specialist. Now, I come from Winchester, don't I? 'Terry Paine, what are you doing here?' the specialist said. I told him, 'It's this national service.' He took out a long thing with a feather on it and stuck it in my ear and said, 'Oh no, you're not fit enough for national service.' That was it. Whether he was a Saints fan or not, I don't know. I was out of the place and down the road doing handsprings.

At Crookham, Sydenham was 'distressed and desperate' and, Paine remembers, 'he rang me up to say he was going to jump ship.' When it came to it, Sydenham didn't. 'Football saved me. Most of the time I was playing football for the army. But if it hadn't been for that I really think I would have gone over the wall.'

236

Some men had less-than-ordinary national service experience. They included the writers Alan Bennett and Michael Frayn (right) who learnt Russian at the Joint Services School for Linguists and John Lyon-Maris (below left), the first national service officer to serve on secondment with the Royal West Africa Frontier Force in Nigeria. Mike Watkins (below right) was one of the few national servicemen chosen to go to Canada to train as aircrew with NATO; and Michael Myers (bottom left) one of the few chosen to be a pilot – most had to sign on.

Doctors (and dentists) were the only conscripts assured of a commission, like Captain John Blair, whose first child was born during his service in Aldershot. Blair was also taken off a draft to Korea – because he played golf.

Some men made more of their service than others. Trevor Baylis (left, kneeling), a PTI in Northern Ireland, canoed, potholed and rock-climbed: 'Life was one long outward bound course.' For medic Roy Booth (bottom right, homeward-bound on board the *Asturias*), life was one long skive in Egypt and Cyprus as bodyguard to a major general: 'A bloody brilliant job.' For Lawrence Bell (bottom left, centre, aboard HMS *Vanguard*), life, as an electrical artificer in the navy, was well paid and had privileges. In Germany with the RAF, identical twins Tony and Geoff Hamilton (below) often stood in for each other, allowing the other to illegally take off on jaunts – and even fly home to England.

Some men were definitely unhappy. Guy Bellamy (left), an RAF telephonist in Germany, tried to get a discharge by feigning mental illness – and was put in a detention centre instead. Southampton footballer John Sydenham (middle), thought about going AWOL – 'but playing football for the army saved me'. Ray Selfe (right) was so ashamed of his RAF job polishing floors that he told his parents his work was secret.

6 MORE MONTHS OF THIS PRISON LIFE - 25 MORE DULL NIGHTS NATIONAL SERVICE IN GERMANY

MISS. J. PHILLIPS
8, NEW ROW.
ELDON
D.P. AUCKLAND.
Co DURHAM,
ENGLAND

Ivan Churm (above) and John Keenan (below: back row, left) had to do another six months on top of their two years because of the Berlin Wall. How Churm felt is clear from this postcard to his fiancée. 'If I wasn't on duty I was asleep.'

In the Suez Canal Zone, Acker Bilk (front right) got 84 days in detention for falling asleep on guard – but he also discovered the clarinet.

Jock Marrs (second left, standing, as a member of the 1st Infantry Division modern pentathlon team) loathed his time in 'the God-forsaken hellhole', but helped in the fight to get Zone veterans the campaign medal denied for 50 years.

In Malaya, Cliff Holland (above left), driving the armoured scout car, was part of a jungle patrol ambushed by terrorists. Five of his comrades were killed – and Holland has suffered what he was to find out was post-traumatic stress disorder ever since. His friend Eric Michaels – above right, front left, returning from an earlier patrol – was badly wounded. He, too, endured years of nightmares.

Men lost considerable weight in the Malayan jungle. Second Lieutenant Richard Lindley, centre front row of his platoon, came down to eight stone – 'and we'd come off patrol and have to play badminton to show how tough we were, when I'd rather have had a lie down'.

In Cyprus men lived under canvas, and Roy Battelle (left of group and, right, working under a three-tonner) and his mates at 3rd Infantry Workshop enjoyed the sunshine.

The food, as in most places, was variable, but Battelle remembers the Christmas fare as being 'slap-up', though the mess hall looks spartan.

Some of the vehicles that came into the Cyprus workshop were beyond repair, blown up by Eoka terrorists. But like national servicemen elsewhere, those in 3rd Infantry Workshop did not let the terrorist threat rob them of their sense of humour (left). *Above right*: A patrol of the Horse Guards armoured section HQ, with Graham Williams holding the Sten.

A popular misconception is that non-white British citizens did not do national service, but hundreds did, including Ken Carter from London (kneeling front right), caught in the final draft to serve with Ivan Churm in the RASC.

When Glyn Jones joined the Royal Artillery in Düsseldorf no fraternising was allowed. Later, the instruction was to make friends with the locals – which Jones is doing here, with very small locals.

Visiting Belsen was a sobering experience for all. Jones (centre, front) was told by one of his group, 'There's ghosts here'.

The army tried hard to keep its conscripts away from excessive drinking and from sex; few heeded at least half the advice. But some, like Malcolm Higgins (front, fourth from left) joined a Christian leadership course in Iserlohn.

The forces frowned on national servicemen wanting to marry locals, and invariably posted them elsewhere quickly. Brian Fisher (centre) had to fight to marry his Siegrid.

Many national servicemen kept demob charts, ticking off the days. Most were simple calendars. Some, self-made, ticked off mornings, afternoons or even hours until demob. Some were ingenious – none more so than the one Roger Keight kept in Malta.

Most units gave the last national servicemen mementoes. Ivan Churm and two colleagues received a small shield and a cigarette lighter – 'Two of us didn't smoke, but it's the thought that counts.' Despite his feelings about his national service, Churm still has the lighter.

Demob meant demob parties – and usually prodigious drinking. Here at RAF Wunstorf, SAC Gordon Williams (bottle in hand) gets ready for civvy street. Self-caption: 'Black eye from fighting another Scot, Bill Colligan, from Dundee.'

Bollocks!

The very last national service draft was on 17 November 1960 and 2,049 men were caught up in it; 1,999 went to the army, 50 to the RAF.[43] Among the army's allocation were John Keenan, the Blackpool butcher sent to the Catering Corps, and Ivan Churm, the Bishop Auckland bricklayer sent to the RASC. Even after they had reported to their Aldershot depots both thought they might be released. Says Churm:

We were in the billet two hours and were already bulling when a corporal came in and said it had just been announced that this was the last day of national service. There'd been no indication that it had been on the cards. 'Champion,' I thought, 'we're going home.' Only we weren't – and we knew we were redundant before we set off. What made it worse was that a TV crew turned up to get reactions and interviewed the last two through the gates – and as a PR exercise the army released them. If there's a word beyond devastated, that was me.

Over in the Catering Corps Keenan's intake had only been issued with knife, fork and spoon and for a couple of days held out hope of going home, 'which went up in smoke when they kitted us out'. Discontent among the last national service recruits was so great that on 8 December it was reported that at Pontefract Barracks near Doncaster the commanding officer had banned the television sitcom *The Army Game* as an unsettling influence; two days later the cast turned up as a publicity stunt and the army, with pained expression, let them in.

National service staggered to the close. In barracks everywhere there was a sense of desolation as conscripts were demobbed and no one came to replace them. John Sydenham, who had become a storeman at the RAMC depot, had nothing to do.

They had to find things for us. They got me and my mate Reg to move a lawn from where it was to the top of the camp behind B company, an area that was totally useless. They gave us a handcart and said it should take us three or four weeks. I had my car on camp, we cut the turf, loaded it into the boot, took it up and finished in three or four days – and then there was nothing to do again.

He was shocked on bonfire night when he was given the key to a store that was supposed to be full of old furniture but which, when he opened it, proved to be full of furniture that was brand new. 'We were still told to smash up what we needed and we did. The furniture wasn't wanted any more than we were.' So bored was 2nd troop, B squadron, 10th Royal Hussars during five days off duty at Paderborn in Germany that, says Alan Herbert,

> as the regiment had more or less given up on providing any social activity, we formed Fart – the farters association research team. The purpose was to investigate the combustible properties of the fart, which involved sitting in a darkened room around a lighted candle awaiting the arrival of a specimen, when the trousers would be dropped and the candle held in position to see if it would ignite. As I recall only Scouser Pye actually succeeded. You don't get more bored than that!

Also in Germany, transporting 65-foot missiles out of Wuppertal, Ivan Churm 'could feel the whole place running down. One platoon was closed – we spent a month with scrim cloth cleaning the vehicles before they were put into mothballs.' No national servicemen were flush, but Churm was worse off than most, which added to his sense of futility. His father, crippled down the pit, was unable to work and the family needed more than the £3 the army gave them. Churm babysat for NCOs and regulars and cut hair so he could send money home:

> I drew five marks a week – ten shillings at the time. I didn't drink, I didn't smoke, I didn't even go to the NAAFI. If I wasn't on duty I spent my time asleep, except on Saturday afternoons when half a dozen of us used to go into a department store in Wuppertal. They had a jukebox-type machine that people fed with pfennigs, and toy bears and other animals played their hearts out on different instruments to oompah music. It was our ritual. We must have looked a sad bunch of plonkers – but that was the measure of our aimless humdrum lives.

With two months still to push, fate delivered a bitter blow to some 10,000 men,[44] almost all in Germany – they were kept back for another six months.

In August 1962 the East German security forces had sealed off 68 of the 80 Berlin crossing points to stop East Germans escaping to the West. The situation had worsened when the Russians reinforced the barbed wire barriers with concrete – the Berlin Wall, which was to stand until November 1989. Struggling with recruitment and stretched by new trouble in Brunei and Sarawak, the army considered that it had no other option but to keep the national servicemen left in Germany where they were. Churm's unit were called to the gym, not knowing what was going on.

> The CO and his entourage came in and told us to sit down. 'I have bad news for you,' the CO said. 'Due to the Berlin Wall you are being retained for another six months.' Wall? This was the first we'd heard of a wall. Then he told us that lads in Berlin were being demobbed because Berlin was being classified as active service. I stood up and asked could I ask a question. 'Yes, Corporal.' 'What chance is there of being posted to Berlin?' The CSM shouted, 'Office!' but on the way out the CO said to him, 'Joke' – which it was and it wasn't.

Like many national servicemen throughout the conscript years, Churm had a demob calendar (sometimes called a chuff chart), marking off the days left to do. Some men began theirs from the beginning of their service; the majority, like Churm, only started in the last six months and his 'was almost complete, turning a nice blue. I had to extend it – and again it was white, like my face. It was worse for some of the lads, they'd already handed their kit into stores.'

For Alan Herbert, Germany and the Hussars were over and done – he had been demobbed in January 1962. But John Keenan was still there, cooking in the officers' mess, and he remembers the reaction to the news as being 'hysteria'. He adds: 'Some of the lads were in danger of losing their wives. Several went AWOL. We had to sign a bit of paper and most of us refused point blank. The officer said that was senseless, he'd told us and a second officer would witness that he'd done so, but we still wouldn't sign.' For Keenan the extra time was a body blow. He had married on leave the previous year and his wife Delia was expecting their baby in the December, when he should have been demobbed. He did get compassionate leave for the birth and was grateful for that (whatever criticisms there were of the armed forces, their willingness to grant compassionate leave was never one of them). 'And, ironically, once I'd got used to the idea, the last six months when I was left in charge of all the cooking and had civilian cooks under me, turned out the best time of all, I enjoyed the work so much.' It was a different story for Churm, who considers his final six months

the worst in my life. The CSM kept up with his bull. He even got a grip of the officers. The way they used to do duty was one would take orderly officer for a week instead of day by day and he'd oversee morning parades on his own, giving them all an easier time. But he wasn't having any of that. He made them all stand on the parade ground. We had a national service officer, Lieutenant Geary, who was a canny bloke, who looked after us, but he got demobbed, so we were on our own. There was bitching between everyone. The night our original conscription ended there were five of us living in the same room. We sat up until midnight – it was like New Year's Eve gone sour – and when midnight arrived we all shouted 'Bastards', and put the light out.

Churm came home on his second paid leave from Germany before Christmas and on 22 December 'was kneeling in front of the altar in our local village church' getting married to Joan, whom 'I'd been courting from the age of fourteen'. On his return he decorated a tin from the cookhouse, planted two gladioli bulbs in it and secured it to his second-floor windowsill. 'As they grew they looked like a two-fingered gesture against the rendered concrete. The lads emptied their tea dregs on them and they flourished. They were my symbol of freedom.' The scandal of War Minister John Profumo's affair with the prostitute Christine Keeler broke and Churm and his mates were delighted at his predicament. 'He'd been shagging her and then she shagged him just like he was shagging us,' says Churm. 'Believe me, she was our Vera Lynn, the forces' sweetheart. If I'd had a picture of her I'd have stuck it up.'

When finally about to be released, Churm was called in by his CO, told he was a good soldier and was asked if he would consider signing on if a married quarter was offered. 'I said, "Can I speak freely, Sir?" "Of course."

"I wouldn't sign on if you offered me a half." He laughed. He was a decent man.' On his last pay parade Churm gave the paying-out officer 'the insolent old left-hand salute. He never twigged or he saw and thought sod it, he's on his way home.'

In April 1963 there were only 2,500 national servicemen in uniform, all in the army in BAOR; in January the last airman, SAC Jim Wallace, a joiner from Glasgow, had gone, from the Coastal Command station at Kinloss in Scotland; the last naval conscript, a Russian linguist whose name is unrecorded, had departed in late 1961. The national serviceman with the last-issued number (23819209), Private Fred Turner, a cook with the 13th/18th Hussars, flew home from Germany and became a civilian on 7 May. Released from his unit on the same date, Second Lieutenant Richard Vaughan of the Pay Corps chose to cycle back from Germany across Europe and it was another nine days before he was demobbed.[45]

And then there were none.[46]

11

Paying the price

How many men died doing national service, or died prematurely because of national service, is something no one can know. Official records show that between the end of the Second World War and the termination of conscription, during which Britain was involved in 57 recognised actions around the world, some 2,000 lives were lost as a direct consequence of enemy engagement and 395 of them were national servicemen – over 200 in Korea, over 100 in Malaya. The figure might be marginally lower if John Hollands, a subaltern with the Duke of Wellington's in Korea, is right: 'A young bloke called Hepple drowned in the Imjin when we were in reserve. He was carried away by the current and was listed as killed in action. I presume many who died in accidents of one kind or another were similarly listed.' The figure would certainly be higher if killed national servicemen who had signed on for three years were added, though what it would then be is difficult to estimate – the armed forces listed these men as regulars. Whatever the total killed in action is arrived at, thousands more national servicemen died in accidents[1] – unintentional discharges of weapons, overturned vehicles and collisions, crashed aircraft – and through disease. Many thousands more were wounded or injured. Adds Hollands:

> The best disciplined battalions had their share of what might be considered avoidable accidents. With every soldier on active service carrying a loaded

243

personal weapon day in and day out, accidents were inevitable. Some were very nasty. I was in 12 platoon in D company; in 10 platoon one fellow was cleaning his rifle with one up the spout and it went off. The bullet went through the door, but his friend was walking by outside and it went through his head. The poor fellow who shot him was hospitalised and I think went out of his mind. During our major battle of the Hook, the commander of 10 platoon, a national service Harrovian, heard someone running down this right-angle trench when the Chinese were swarming all over us and shot him as he came round the corner – and it was one of his own blokes. I think he was scarred for the rest of his life.

There were many incidents in Korea of night patrols from one regiment running into others from different regiments and firing at each other, or sentries firing at returning patrols, something with fatal consequences. In an official report an officer wrote:

> There are an almost incredible number of genuine accidents. In my own regiment we had six men in hospital with accidental wounds and the CO was certain that none were self-inflicted. Indeed from the types of men concerned, the tasks they were employed on and the way the accidents happened (four done by *other* men) it was pretty clear they were genuine.

He listed the factors as: the intense cold, which made fingers slip; the unreliability of Stens; jumpiness in night-fighting against the Chinese 'who are apt to appear from any direction'; and lack of sufficient practice in handling weapons.

Two of these factors, together with the enclosed eeriness of the jungle and the sense of isolation in it, caused other such incidents, particularly in a battalion's first year when men were raw and nervous and, adds Eric Michaels, who soldiered there with the Manchester Regiment, 'when lads are cold and wet and hungry they can do stupid things'. Even men who should have known better died in shooting accidents. Adds Michaels:

> We had a sergeant who ordered a patrol, before he went off on a recce, to shoot anyone coming along a particular path – and got killed when he came

back along it. We had map references to know where people weren't supposed to be, so if someone *was* there it was a terrorist, supposedly. Once we ran into what turned out to be a patrol from a Scotch regiment who weren't supposed to be there and we started shooting at each other. Then the officer heard voices in what seemed to be English. He was a national service second lieutenant and he stood up and shouted out, 'Are you friend or are you foe?' It was brave and stupid and hilarious. I'll never forget the words.

Nor will Michaels forget the day the driver of a three-tonner in which he was travelling in the back was shot dead. 'You weren't supposed to unload until you got out. This time one of the lads started to unload while still in the vehicle. For some reason the driver stamped on the brake and the rifle went off – he fell dead out of the cab.' Michaels also remembers a new recruit getting his arm shot off. 'The set-up was, new recruits were taken out to some part of the jungle where there wasn't any trouble. One of them started shooting. The lad went home on the troopship he'd just arrived on.'

'Frankly, I was much more worried about shooting the guy in front of me than being shot by the enemy,' says Richard Lindley, who served in Malaya with the Hampshires. 'In fact I'd rather they'd shot me than I'd shot one of my own men. Against orders I never had one up the spout.'

Fooling around with revolvers caused the death of a number of men in recorded instances in Egypt, Malaya, Kenya, Cyprus and Korea, where Terry Brierley, with the Northumberland Fusiliers, saw a regular killed by a national serviceman.

We'd pulled back into reserve. I was a lance corporal in charge of the guard – all the sergeants were at a party. A regular called Karl, married with three children, had just come from Hong Kong to join us. Two of the lads were pissing about with a Luger and a Smith and Wesson, acting cowboys. Both were meant to be unloaded but the Luger wasn't. It put a hole in Karl's chest. At first we didn't know the seriousness of it: it was only a small, neat hole. We were laughing and joking and made him lie down while someone got help. I only realised why he was such a grey colour when I saw where the bullet had come out his back like a sledgehammer; I could have put my fist in it. He died. The lad who shot him got twelve months.

In Cyprus with the Intelligence Corps, Adrian Walker was almost shot by a tent mate in a similar situation. 'He had one of these trick holsters and he was farting about with an unloaded pistol practising quick draws. Then he reloaded and like a fool pulled the trigger. The pistol was one of those issued to tank and aircrew, low velocity. In one of those freaks of ballistics the bullet hit the flap of the tent beside me and bounced under my bed.'

Also in Cyprus, Auberon Waugh wasn't so lucky; an ensign (second lieutenant) with the Royal Horse Guards, he put six bullets into himself. Immediately following the Gkuenyeli massacre in which Turks had murdered Greeks, his troop of armoured cars were sent to guard a road between the opposing villages. In England his armoured car training had been on a medium machine-gun called a Bisa, which needed two cocking actions to slide a round into the breech; in Cyprus the armoured cars had Brownings, which needed only one. It was probable, he thought, that he had cocked the gun in a moment of absentmindedness. In any event, when he gave the barrel a wiggle from the front, it put four shots through his chest and shoulder, one through his arm and another through his left hand. He had to have a lung removed as well as his spleen and two ribs:

> Feeling quite happy as the morphine took effect and fortified, as they say, by the last rites of the Church in the shape of an Irish priest to whom I took an instant dislike I said [to the surgeon]: 'Tell me, Colonel, what chance do you actually think I have of pulling through?'
>
> He fixed me with his cool blue eyes and said: 'I think you've got a very good chance.'
>
> I felt as if an icy hand had been placed over my heart, but more even than terror I felt fury.
>
> 'What do you fucking *mean* I've got a good chance? You're supposed to say I will be out of bed the day after tomorrow.'[2]

Waugh, who had been in Cyprus only two months, later learned that no one thought he would survive. In February 1959, nine months and 12 operations later – one to remove a finger that had not healed – he was out of the army.

Carelessness cost lives. In Korea, John Hollands says, 'some platoons lost up to half their strength to what is laughingly called friendly fire, accidents with munitions and accidents with homemade fires.' During their stint in Cyprus, the Norfolks lost 18 men – most of them national service – but only two were killed by Eoka. In Malaya, Marine subaltern Neal Ascherson remembers 'only three or four killed by the enemy but many, many more died in road accidents, driving into monsoon ditches in the dark or in heavy rain, or sliding on red-mud roads and meeting Chinese lorry drivers head on.' Road traffic accidents, on and off duty, were responsible for many deaths and injuries across the world and were high in Kenya and in Germany, where Roger Moore, while at Neumünster supply depot and on his way back from running a quiz night, hit a tree in his jeep. He was unconscious for a week in hospital in Schleswig and was then moved to Hamburg for treatment to severe head and facial injuries. 'My face was a ghastly mess. No scars are left from that little encounter but it could have finished me . . . Who wants an actor with no face?'[3] There were a number of incidents, remembers Alan Tizzard, a tank commander with the 10th Hussars, 'where men slept under tanks on manoeuvres and died when it rained and the tanks settled into soft ground'. In the UK, on his way back to camp on his motorcycle, airman Ray Selfe crashed on a country road and was found unconscious with compound multiple fractures of the skull. When he regained consciousness four weeks later he was in hospital at RAF Halton, Buckinghamshire, and had lost his sense of smell and had a reduced sense of taste. After several more weeks he was transferred to the psychiatric unit and given a number of tests.

Early in 1952 I sat with a young doctor in the consulting room. 'How do you feel about your service in the RAF?' he said. I replied with great vehemence, 'I've hated and detested every fucking second.' He sat back and said, 'You know, I don't like it very much either. I'll recommend you for a medical discharge.' The following week I was weighed, measured, given further medical checks, then told to pack my service clothes, don civilians and report to the hospital's commanding officer at 1400 hours. I did so, he mumbled something insincere about being sorry the RAF was losing me, signed a form, shook my hand and I left.

Selfe asked a passing RAF policeman where the return stores were and was directed to a shed with double doors on which there was a sign: *Returned uniforms and RAF equipment will only be received between 0800 and 1200 hours. No exceptions.*

There were clear windows above this sign and I could see a counter where a sergeant was directing the activities of admin orderlies. I tapped on the window and held the kitbag up. Angrily he looked at me and mouthed, 'Read the notice, airman.' I mouthed back, 'I've read it, shithead,' and turned the kitbag upside-down, then draped the drawcord across the door handle and started the long walk down the drive from the hospital. I heard the double door open and a bellow, 'Come back here, airman.' I turned and said, 'I'm no longer an airman,' and gave him the two-fingered gesture. He screamed in rage, 'You'll be back, I'll make sure you'll come back.' He couldn't and I didn't.

Accidents in training at home and overseas also caused deaths and injuries. In basic at Catterick with the 3rd Carabiniers, Alan Herbert saw two companions die on an initiative test when they were swept away in the river Swale. Attempting to beat another squad, his tried to cross the river at Downholme, which was in spate.

The regular corporal with us said it was okay. We linked arms in file and went into the water, which was up to our hips. Suddenly the bottom dropped, those in front stumbled and about ten of them were washed away. The verdict was misadventure. One of the two lads who died was married and his widow at the inquest screamed out, 'You killed him.'

The deaths have been on Herbert's mind ever since and in March 2003 he tried to get access to the records but was told they had to remain confidential for 75 years. 'Without access to the full records I can't say, but forty-three years in the university of life tell me that the inquest had all the hallmarks of a whitewash. Judged by the standards of the time the regiment got away with it, but by today's standards it's clear they failed palpably in their duty of care to their recruits.'

The Hara Mura battle school in Japan, where many men went before Korea, 'was supposed to be more dangerous than Korea,' says Reuben Holroyd, who trained there with the Duke of Wellington's.

> It was battle conditions training with live ammunition and there were casualties. There was a large siren in the middle of the area and if it sounded everyone had to stop firing and stay where they were while jeeps with stretchers came out. There were definitely some men killed and more wounded and injured – there were a lot of mortar bombs that hadn't gone off lying around and if someone kicked one it sometimes did.

Holroyd was hurt earlier, more badly than he knew, when the troopship bringing his regiment stopped off at Hong Kong and they had a few days fieldcraft training.

> I was leader of a section sent ahead to establish a position to give fire cover. We dashed to the edge of this paddy-field – and there was a sheer cliff. This officer rushed up, jumped up and down, threatened me with a court martial if I didn't jump. He was a funny sort of fellow, a national serviceman straight out of England, too enthusiastic, wanted to show he was in charge. Anyway, this drop was twenty-five feet or so, like being on top of a house, and the officer was saying, 'Jump, the water will break your fall.' So I jumped.

The water was two feet deep. What Holroyd broke was his back – more accurately he got a compressed fracture of the spine. For days he could not see properly or move his neck. It wasn't until the 1970s that he found out what he had done. 'I'd been complaining for years and the doctors talked about slipped discs and torn muscles. Eventually they asked if I'd been in a bad accident like a car smash. The only thing, I told them was jumping off that cliff. 'Ah-ha,' they said, that's it.' Since then, Holroyd has had several operations and is 'held together with plastic and wire. The bones are so pressed together, they're crumbling away. But I get a forty per cent war pension. It's tax free. I'm not complaining.'

The officer who ordered Holroyd to jump was posted to Hara Mura where he was killed when a three-inch mortar misfired. 'There's a procedure when that happens,' Holroyd explains.

> You wait, the shell might have a delayed fuse. Then two of you slowly turn the barrel horizontal, tilt it enough for an NCO to catch the shell and carry it to a specially dug hole, if there is one, for dealing with later. Well, this officer decided he would have a go, he would catch it. Except he dropped it and the mortar was standing on a concrete base. The mortar crew were wounded but he copped it. I know that's true because some of my friends were at Hara Mura at the time before coming on to Korea.

Injuries and death through accidents were so common in the army that they seemed to be treated almost casually, as *Back Badge*, the newsletter of the 1st Battalion of the King's Shropshire Light Infantry, during its tour of duty in Kenya, perhaps indicates. In the December 1955 issue, following an item about a farmer and his wife providing baths and teas to C company every day, this:

> Corporal Middleton was seriously wounded when his patrol was mistaken for Mau Mau by a farmer. He is now in England where we wish him a quick recovery and a speedy return. Private Collins was accidentally wounded in the foot by a member of his patrol. He is now on the coast recovering and we shall be welcoming him back soon.

And under news of the three-inch mortar platoon: 'We were sorry to lose Private Gardiner as the result of an accident while firing on Kipipiri, where he lost his right hand. He is back in England now and we wish him the very best of luck.' And under news of the assault pioneer platoon: 'Another task given to us was transporting poles and wire to farms in the Gilgil district and the erecting of farm fences. During this task a most regrettable accident occurred when a lorry loaded with heavy poles overturned and

Private Lanchbury was killed. He was buried with full military honours at Nairobi.' In the June 1956 issue, A company reported: 'On 12th March the tragic deaths occurred of Lieutenants Hazell and Gordon in a car accident. A strong contingent of A company attended the funeral and every man in the company mourned the loss of two popular officers.' D company reported:

> On 12th March 2nd-Lt Evans was killed in a motorcar accident between Nakuru and Gilgil. He was one of the most popular officers and a great loss to the company. 2nd-Lt Lapage-Norris, who had only recently joined us, was badly injured in the same accident, but is making a good recovery. In addition we wish Lance Corporal Caines a speedy recovery from his accidental wound received during Operation 'Full Stop'.

Back Badge in December '56 reported that the regiment had left Kenya for Aden. It had had no battle casualties in its tour of duty but in total had lost seven men, all accidentally killed.

And what of men killed in flying accidents? Barry Purcell, a national serviceman who signed on in the RAF and served as a flight lieutenant, has compiled some statistics and 'I have been amazed at the number of aircraft written off and losses of aircrew plus passengers, particularly in the earlier postwar years. I have no separate figures for national service aircrew losses, but it's certain that a fair number were killed in training accidents when solo on Vampires or Meteors.'[4] He adds:

> The big bulge in accident rates in the early fifties was due to rapid expansion of jet aircraft numbers and the learning curve not keeping up. I was lucky to join in 1956 when the training methods were taking effect. Nearly all the friends who were with me on the five-year engineering course at De Havilland at Hatfield who'd gone into the RAF and Fleet Air Arm ahead of me were dead before I joined.

'At first I liked the idea of the Fleet Air Arm,' says Nigel Lawson, 'but my then wife said it was too dangerous – landing and taking off from a heaving deck is a dicey business. I'm not sure of the figures, but something like half those who took the course were killed!' Dr Michael Myers, one of the few national servicemen to become an RAF pilot – in 1949 – and remain a national serviceman, adds:

> Flying was dangerous. While on Prentices and Harvards, two men out of twenty-six were killed and one seriously injured. The two who died were national service – there were eight of us. Donald Byron died when his Prentice failed to recover from a spin; Alan Hooper appeared to succumb to carbon monoxide poisoning: his Harvard was seen to enter a gentle dive into the ground without any attempt to recover. Meteors were crashing all over the country, as I remember. I seemed to be always on the phone telling my mum and dad it wasn't me.[5]

Diseases and parasitical infections picked up in Egypt, Malaya and Korea plagued considerable numbers of men for months or years after their demob, and even for the rest of their lives. RASC clerk Jock Marrs was one of the many who came back from the Suez Canal Zone with intestinal problems. 'I was so bloody skinny my old man said I looked like something out of Belsen and my mother cried. It took a good six months to get my system back to anything like normal.' In Malaya and Korea, malaria was prevalent. 'My back wasn't the problem when I came out of the army, it was malaria,' says Reuben Holroyd. 'We took Paladrin tablets every day and when we left we were given three months' supply and told we'd be all right. But for years it was the same: I went down with the symptoms – temperature, sweating gallons, shaking. It happened two or three days every three months, then every four–five months, eventually it stopped. But it was years, years.' A virulent strain almost killed Michael Caine who, soon after his release, lost 40 lb, collapsed on stage, and was initially told he would be lucky to see out his forties. The army gave him a disability pension of three pounds ten shillings a week ('only half the normal pension, I was told, because although restricted by my now weak and permanent physical condition I would nevertheless be able to work at some jobs'[6]), though subsequently he was called back to Roehampton military hospital for successful treatment.[7]

According to the records, 2,498 British servicemen were wounded in

Korea; a high percentage of them were national service (in the second and third years nearly three-quarters of infantry battalions were conscripts). A few came back paralysed, a few with double amputations, many with lost limbs or disfigurements. Many received shrapnel wounds, some still retaining fragments in them and setting off airport detectors when going on holiday years later. But, as David Griffiths – a regular soldier with the Royal Engineers in Korea and for 25 years the welfare officer of the British Korean War Veterans' Association[8] – points out, many injuries were insidious.

> The intense cold of the first winter in particular cost a lot of fingers and toes, but later in life many men developed circulation problems and heart disease directly as a result of the strain the conditions put on their bodies. Then there are the medical problems of unknown origin. There's a lot said about chemical damage these days; no one said anything about that in Korea where we used to get a weekly spray-down with DDT to try to keep us free from lice. DDT was banned in the seventies because of its links to cancer, so it's quite likely that some problems are due to that, but nothing is proved. And a hell of a lot of men were made deaf to various degrees by artillery fire, mortars, tanks, incoming munitions. It's now an offence not to wear ear defenders, but that wasn't known to be necessary until the 1970s. Tank crews weren't normally at risk but in Korea when the line became static they were – they often fired from fixed positions with turrets open and visors down.

'A grenade went off beside my head and I am deaf-ish,' comments Royal Fusiliers subaltern Nick Harman, 'But I'm okay in one-to-one conversations.' John Hollands – blown off his feet by friendly fire from a British Centurion – is rather more affected: he usually wears two hearing aids, and headphones to watch television. Like Harman he is fine in a one-to-one situation, 'but haven't a clue in a room of people talking'.

Hollands receives a 50% war pension for the damage to his hearing. Men who have developed deafness in later life have rarely succeeded in making a successful claim. 'The government acknowledges that many men have lost their top hearing due to gunfire, but take the position that once it happened it didn't get worse and subsequent deterioration is due to age,' says David Griffiths. 'The British Legion is still fighting to say otherwise.'[9]

Winning claims for men injured in their service has never been easy. It took the British Legion until 1989 to get a 50% pension for the Glosters' Albie Hawkins, who came out of a Korean prisoner-of-war camp so malnourished that he did not physically recover. 'I can walk round the house and out the door and that's about it,' he says. For years claims were dealt with in the DSS and, says David Griffiths, 'they got lost between a dozen different in- and out-trays.' Now they are the responsibility of the Veterans' Agency set up inside the Ministry of Defence[10] and 'the attitude to the way veterans are treated, especially the disabled, has been transformed'. Inevitably, numbers of men have not received satisfaction and may not do so. One is Terry Brierley, another who served in Korea with the Glosters. He got shrapnel in his leg in a forward position. By the time his platoon retreated his boot was filled with blood. 'The officer said it was just a scratch and he got the sergeant to take this lump of metal out with a penknife. It hurt a bloody sight more coming out than going in. The officer said, "If you try to get out disabled it'll go on your record and you'll never get a job." That would have been a slight in those days, a leper-like thing to happen.' When he did come out, Brierley went down the pit for 17 years, but his injury prevented him playing cricket and walking – 'and I loved walking'. When he applied for a pension,

> a doctor from the pensions people at Pontefract came here to assess me and in this small room he got me to go to and from the television, four paces maybe each way. In five minutes he was gone. They refused the claim. The trouble is, I didn't have a discharge medical though my discharge papers say I did, so there's no record and I can't prove it. But I'm angry and I'm still trying. It's not the money, I'm not bothered. It's the recognition.

*   *   *

Among those who lost their lives during national service were the small number who took their own because they found the demands beyond them. In the late 1940s the military commentator Captain Basil Liddell Hart warned that 'not all men are the same' and urged more stringent psychological tests to filter out the inadequate. Given the pressured nature of the conscript process, it is not surprising that it was impossible to institute such tests – and some men who could not cope killed themselves.

One was a friend of south Londoner Roy Booth when he was in training with the Medical Corps.

> He was a lad from Worcester Park and we used to get the train together and part company at New Malden. This time we had a forty-eight-hour pass and I waited at the station but he didn't turn up. I waited two or three trains and eventually had to catch the last one. At the guardroom they said, 'Where's your mate?' My mate, it turned out, had put his head in the gas oven. His mum and dad weren't home when he got there and he was so depressed he just decided to end it. I remember thinking national service was okay for most of us; it was for me, stockily built, a bit of a jack the lad. But he was terribly quiet and he couldn't handle it. There was another one a couple of weeks later; he hanged himself in the barracks and that's a fact and all. It's always seemed to me that some sort of screening process should have told them.

Derrick Johns, later a Service Corps officer in Germany, lost the man in the next bed during training in Aldershot. 'He was a delightfully cultured lad called Jimmy Wands from Edinburgh and sometimes he was filled with despair. Finally it overtook him: he went home on leave and shot himself. He just didn't want to come back. If only he'd been able to accept that things really would get better. It should never have happened but I don't blame the army.'

On Ray Selfe's first night in the RAF at Padgate – where he had been made senior man in his billet – he was shaken awake by another recruit who told him;

> 'There's a bloke hung himself in the shithouse. You'd better do something about it.' I hurriedly dressed and went out to the ablutions building. The WCs had no doors and a body hung from the flushpan – metal chains had long disappeared to be replaced by cords. This one was fashioned into a noose. I vomited into the nearest washbasin, then ran to the roadway between the huts where I found a sergeant, who took over.

After breakfast, Selfe and the senior men from the other billets were ordered to a meeting hall where an officer advised them to try to prevent the men from writing home about the suicide.

'It would upset the parents and we don't want members of parliament unnecessarily concerned about our well-being,' he said. Asked why the boy killed himself, he said the man was obviously mentally unstable and had somehow slipped through the medical net. Asked by another man on the incidence of suicide, he said it was less than one a week, which was good considering the number of airmen processed each month.

It is almost impossible to read a biography of anyone who did national service without finding at least a passing reference to suicide. The fear in the minds of many men, coming apprehensively to basic training, that they might not be up to it and could find themselves pushed over the edge, was fuelled by stories that in most cases were apocryphal. A suicide that did occur would almost inevitably be said to have happened in the previous intake, although countless intakes had come and gone since. The subject was such a part and parcel of national service basic training that it was widely half-believed that anyone witnessing an attempted suicide would be instantly demobbed.

No records of those who died by their own hand have been put into the public domain. The army said the figures were comparable to those in the wider population. The near-certainty is that they were a little higher – on a level, say, of that among university graduates, another cohort displaced from home and subject to the pressures of a different way of life. In 1959, according to the *British Medical Journal*, the suicide rate in seven universities studied was 8.5 men per 100,000, compared with 6.1 per 100,000 elsewhere in the same age group – suggesting a suicide total of 140 among 2.3 million national servicemen, or nine a year across all arms and units.[11]

It has been alleged that some cases of suicide were covered up as accidents. One can speculate that this is possible, certainly where a firearm was involved. One would like to think that if this happened it was to save a family's feelings, not simply, in the graphic phrase used by Jock Marrs about an entirely different sort of incident in Egypt, to keep someone's arse out of the fire.

* * *

National servicemen knew that in certain circumstances they could be killed or injured. What they did not know was that their government would put some of them at risk as human guinea pigs. But that is what happened during the Cold War development of chemical and nuclear warfare.

What went on throughout the 1950s at Porton Down research establishment in Wiltshire only came to light in 1999 when the present government kept a re-election promise to allow those who had taken part in experiments there to have access to their records – something that those who suspected a link with their deteriorating health had previously been denied. The men had all volunteered to take part in tests to find a cure for the common cold, or in psychological experiments, or as observers in gas tests. What the records showed was that they were exposed to deadly nerve agents: sarin in particular, but also to mustard gas, tabun and soman.[12]

The story began to be pieced together. In the 15 postwar years to 1960, 2,644 men – the majority conscripts – went to Porton Down for an additional payment of up to 15 shillings and a few days' leave. At unit level where volunteers were sought, they were assured that the experiments were carefully planned under medical supervision and there was not the slightest danger. What in fact happened was that they breathed in nerve gases or had them dripped on their skin in liquid form, or both. In the wave of anger that followed, a former national service airman, Gordon Bell from Sunderland (who now lives in Canada), came forward to say that in 1953 a fellow volunteer, Ronald Maddison from Consett in County Durham, had died at Porton Down, and accused the government of murder.

More details emerged. In 1953, at the height of experimentation at the establishment, 531 men were involved in various tests, 140 between 25 April and 5 June. Maddison, a twenty-year-old regular, was one of these. Scientists, seeking to determine the amount of sarin applied to clothing and bare skin that would cause incapacitation or death, administered what they considered sub-lethal doses and 200 milligrams were dripped on to a double thickness of army uniform over Maddison's arm. He collapsed and died within 45 minutes. An inquiry decided that the tests were too important to halt, but the amount of sarin that could be applied to bare skin was set at 5mg. The inquest into Maddison's death was held in secret and his father, who was allowed to attend, was bound by the Official Secrets Act from discussing it. In August 1999 Wiltshire police launched an inquiry into Porton Down's activities among unconfirmed reports that 25 suspicious deaths were involved. In July 2003 it was announced that although the investigation had revealed criminal liability on the part of three scientists, the Crown Prosecution Service had decided there was insufficient evidence to bring a prosecution. The three scientists were themselves deceased.

The matter has not rested there. In November 2002, the current Wiltshire coroner applied to the Lord Chief Justice, Lord Woolf (himself once a national service captain in the army legal branch), who ordered a further inquest into Maddison's death.

Ken Earl, a national service airman who was in the same experiment as Maddison, began the Porton Down Veterans' Support Group in 1999 from his home in Maidstone. The group has over 450 members, who suffer from a multiplicity of symptoms including skin and eye disorders, breathing problems, heart, lung, liver and kidney complaints, deafness, growths, motor neurone disease and spinal deformation. 'And I know of men who have died as young as twenty-six directly because of Porton,' Earl says. 'I know, too, of several suicides.'

Earl, a medical orderly at the RAF hospital at Wroughton near Swindon who flew all over the world from RAF Lyneham to bring back the badly wounded and the very sick, volunteered for nearby Porton Down after seeing on the noticeboard they were seeking help with common cold research – as did some 40% of his group's members. His exposure to sarin, he believes, damaged his memory and his immune system.

I was about 30 when I began to notice symptoms. I'd always been incredibly fit, played rugby, was a sprinter and an amateur weight lifter. But I began to get very painful areas in my spine, which was diagnosed as ankylosing spondylitis.[13] I was suddenly in and out of hospital: painful heels, dead leg to the knee, duodenal ulcers, multiple cysts, recurrent polyps in the bowel – a dozen operations on these alone, they just keep appearing – embarrassing skin problems. I come from a very strong family, my brothers have no problems, my mother lived to ninety-two. None of this should have been happening to me.

What was worse was that in his forties Earl, an actor who was a regular in *No Hiding Place* and has appeared in many television series from *The Avengers* to *Minder*, began to lose the ability to learn his lines.

I'd always had an absolutely magnificent memory for scripts. You needed that in repertory, playing one part while learning another for two weeks' time. But the ability went, I simply couldn't do it. Of course I carried on, but with a monumental effort. I grew increasingly nervous about it and I couldn't take on leading roles.

Earl never associated his physical problems with Porton Down until the Maddison case. 'I simply didn't – the fifties was an era when you trusted people.' Laconically he adds: 'At least I never get a cold. But I never got a cold before I went to Porton either.'

Peter Carpenter, a plumber's mate from Twickenham stationed in 1950 as a radar operator at the Royal Artillery 37th Anti-Aircraft Regiment in north Wales, was another who went to Wiltshire to take part in what he thought was an experiment to find a cure for the common cold.

The sergeant came on parade one morning and asked for a couple of volunteers. 'Where is this, Sarge?' I asked. He told us and I asked: 'How do you get there?' 'Via Paddington.'' Well, that meant I could nip home to see my girlfriend before I went and afterwards for the bit of leave that went with the deal. 'Thank you very much,' I said.

At Porton Down Carpenter had rubber patches of different colours put on his arm; when he asked what they were for he was told it was to help with the development of children's gas masks. ' "So what's that to do with the common cold?" No answer. Now I know it was sarin – sarin with GB stabiliser it says on my records, whatever that is.'

In another test, Carpenter was given a rabbit in a cage and a perforated can of flies, and with seven others was sent into a field where a controlled explosion took place. He was told to go towards it, write down on the clipboard he was given if he could smell anything, and put the flies on top of a post.

By the time I got to the post the flies were goners, on their backs, and the rabbit was bouncing about demented. I turned round to tell these scientists and officer that there was something wrong with their rabbit – and they were all wearing gas masks! Bloody hell! Next thing I remember is waking up in bed. One of the blokes was extremely bad. A high-ranking officer with a beard came round and asked this lad how he was. 'Why don't you fuck off and let me die,' he said. He was really bad, raving. The officer was good. He put his hand on his shoulder and said 'You lie back.' When he came to me I told him I was all right but my wrists and knees and ankles ached like hell.

In a day or two Carpenter and the others went to a building shaped like a threepenny bit and were instructed to enter wearing gas masks.

There was an electric fire in the middle. This bloke came in, broke a glass phial over it and disappeared bloody fast, telling us to remove our gas masks. By now alarm bells were ringing. I took my mask off but I held my breath. The others were choking. When I couldn't hold it any longer I shot through the door. I don't know what that was about, the records don't show, maybe mustard gas, but some of the lads were rolling on the floor.

Before he was thirty, all Carpenter's teeth were loose.

I went to a dentist in Hounslow, an Aussie. He had a look and said, 'There's nothing wrong with your gums, so I don't understand.' Eight teeth had to come out for a start and the rest after that. It broke my heart – I had a beautiful set of teeth, pearly white: the lads used to call me Mr Maclean. Other blokes who went to Porton had the same problem. My mate Ken

Paying the price

Ward from Sheffield says his teeth just crumbled to chalk.

In his forties, Carpenter was troubled with bad circulation and pains in his feet. Subsequent examinations showed he needed replacement knees but would first have to have vascular by-passes in his legs before he could be operated on,

> and the specialist said I was in such a right old mess that if I had that done there was the danger of having both legs amputated. They said, 'It's crutch time for you', but bollocks to that. [Carpenter can only walk 50 yards.] My garden shed's only twenty paces but it's up a gradient and I have to stop. The pub's only a hundred yards and it's all downhill and they say why don't I come down, but as I say, coming down's fine, how the bloody hell do I get back?

All things considered he thinks he has been pretty lucky. 'A lot of fellows are bad and I mean bad. And it's down to Porton, not that you can prove anything. They say my knees gave out because of the plumbing, or it's my age. So, again, thanks very much.'

A three-year 'extended' national serviceman, James Kelly from Burton-upon-Trent went into the Ordnance Corps and was posted after technical training to 18 Battalion at Bicester. In 1953 he saw a notice looking for observers for a gas course. 'I thought I'd be sitting in a class taking notes on identifying different gases,' he says. 'I didn't know I was going to have sarin splashed on me. Maddison died from two hundred milligrams. I had two hundred and fifty – and some men had three hundred.'[14] He remembers 'feeling a bit dozy' during a dexterity test that followed

> I had to follow these lines on a revolving drum with a pencil while they interrupted me with questions. 'Eight sixes?' Forty-eight. But I became less able. 'Seven sevens?' What the devil are seven sevens? And by the time the answer came I'd missed a number of lines. Afterwards I was wheezing, like I had a chesty cold. When I went home for the few days leave I was really quite ill.

261

Between his mid-twenties and early thirties everything seemed to go wrong.

> I was in and out of hospitals with obscure symptoms. I had a tooth removed and ended up in hospital. Appendicitis, tonsils out at thirty-two, kidney stones, jaundice, hepatitis B. They got to know me quite well in Burton hospital, but they could only stand round scratching their heads. At one stage I was asked if I'd spent time abroad – which I had, two years in Suez – when I think they were looking at tropical diseases. Then in my forties I noticed deterioration in my hearing; I was having to ask people to repeat things. I was working in sales and marketing in the textile industry and doing quite well. But the industry was going through a bad time and the company closed down.

Kelly found it difficult to get another job – he couldn't hear at interviews. Eventually he did get a job but in the end was unable to handle meetings. Suffering from depression he enrolled at Manchester University for a national diploma in the management of thoroughbred horses ('I'd always ridden and if I worked with horses I wouldn't have to talk to people a lot'), but his marriage broke up and the family home sold. He moved to Bicester where he bought a smaller house and got employment looking after hunters and dressage horses, also teaching children and adults to ride. 'But I was living on a pittance and couldn't afford the house. I rented it out and lived in a mobile – until I met someone and was able to move back.'

If the men who went to Porton Down were lied to – or at the very least misled (in 1961 an official at the establishment wrote: 'Experience has shown that detailed descriptions tend to deter the servicemen, so now very little is said') – the many thousands who, in the fifties, witnessed Britain's nuclear bomb explosions in Australia and the south Pacific were simply told nothing. Between 1952 and 1958 Britain conducted 21 nuclear tests in Australia and on Christmas Island (now Kiritimati) in the south Pacific.[15] Around 22,000 British servicemen, a high proportion of them conscripts, were involved, 15,000 of them as observers – and none of them knew they were being exposed to radiation fallout.

Nick Harden, who returned to barracks in Maidstone after failing to get to the Suez conflict, went with the Royal Engineers to Christmas Island in

January 1957 and remembers the regiment being told it was where atomic bombs were tested, and nothing else. 'But as far as we were concerned what else was there to know? After Hiroshima we were all curious to see. I don't recall anyone not being happy.'

After ten months helping to build an airstrip and roads, he witnessed the explosion of a megaton hydrogen bomb 1,000 times bigger than Hiroshima. 'There was almost a carnival atmosphere before the event,' he says. 'They showed *Gunfight at the OK Corral* in the cinema. We had a life-sized cake in the image of Brigitte Bardot. It was one big holiday on a Pacific island. Set off your bomb, we'll watch, a great privilege, and then we'll go home.' On the day, men were taken in vehicles to the point of the island furthest from where the detonation would occur and told to sit down on the ground under a cluster of palm trees.

Everybody had a pair of sunglasses and a groundsheet, which we were told to put over our heads, and close our eyes. A cheerful voice from the tannoy in the trees started the countdown from 50. Halfway through he stopped because there was a technical hitch and we were told to stand up and stretch our legs. After about ten minutes the countdown started again: ten, nine, eight–zero. At zero I got the shock of my life. There was a light. I've read that in earlier explosions men just covered their eyes with their hands and some of those who opened them could see the bones in their hands like an X-ray. My eyes were closed and I was wearing sunglasses under a groundsheet. But I was aware of this light, like a camera flash only brighter than that by far and sustained for half a minute. And silence. It's the only time in my life I've heard silence. You take it for granted, the warbling and chirping of birds, but the whole thing stopped, shocked into silence by the light. It was as if all existence was petrified, as if it was turned to stone and frightened to death.

With the light, the temperature started to rise, hotter, hotter. I started to panic, I thought something had gone wrong, something to do with that technical hitch. I thought we were going to be roasted alive. Somebody close to me sobbed. The light went out and the temperature began to fall rapidly. We were ushered away to the vehicles. The southeastern sky was just a bloody mass moving towards us. When it was almost overhead came a bang to end all bangs and a great wind, which threw us off our feet and overturned vehicles. This wasn't the first megaton bomb but they didn't seem to have anticipated this. I turned around and where we'd been sitting the ground was littered with coconuts lashed from the trees, and dead birds. Everybody was very quiet. It wasn't carnival day any longer.

No one, Harden says, was medically examined. Some men were sick or had diarrhoea and a few were taken into the medical block. 'We thought those who were sick were wimps. We'd never heard the word radiation. Even if we had we wouldn't have understood it as being dangerous. We would have understood a bullet or a bayonet – but radiation would have been an abstraction.' Subsequently a number of men were sent home to England and the rumour was that they had developed leukaemia; Harden knew one of them who quite certainly had the disease and later died of it. Harden himself remains in good health, yet for years he regularly dreamed about the explosion. 'The gist was always the same. I'm in the middle of a big city. People are going about their business when suddenly the whole place goes quiet as this enormous light lights up the sky – and I'm the only one who knows what's happened: a nuclear attack. I wouldn't call it a nightmare exactly, but it used to wake me up feeling afraid.'

In 1946, the Medical Research Council reported: 'Radioactivity of all kinds causes an increase in mutation rates in all animals and plants,' and went on to warn that 'radiation produces genetic effects'. When Prime Minister Churchill was told of the risks that men were being exposed to he said: 'A pity, but we cannot help it.' A report to the Chiefs of Staff, on atomic weapons trials dated 20 May 1953, stated: 'The Army must discover the detailed effects of various types of explosions on equipment, stores and men with and without various types of protection.' Undoubtedly a similar report sanctioned activities at Porton Down.

In the ensuing half-century the other countries involved in the nuclear test programme – Australia, America and New Zealand – have accepted responsibility. The present British government, like all previous British governments, says that studies have shown no evidence of excess illness or mortality of nuclear test veterans.[16] And the Ministry of Defence continues to maintain that it has not seen any scientific evidence that Porton Down volunteers suffer 'unusual patterns of ill-health because of their participation'. However, an independent epidemiological study by the Medical Research Council has been instituted to compare volunteers' health with a sample group of other ex-servicemen. The Porton Down Veterans' Support Group is cooperating in the study, which will not be complete before 2005, but, having already been frustrated in bringing test cases to the High Court, they fear a whitewash. And men like James Kelly remain disgusted.

This government kept its promises to let men see their records, then slapped a Section D notice on so we're unable to sue them. I'm also sure the MoD lent on Wiltshire police. I'm angry. I don't want to be bitter. Bitterness poisons people's lives and I don't want to live the rest of my life like that. Whatever the outcome, it seems wrong to me that stuff used during the War in concentration camps should be used in this country on volunteering servicemen – who were lied to.

*   *   *

A few years after Malaya with the Manchester Regiment, Cliff Holland, then a policeman in Salford, was sent to deal with a dispute in a rundown part of the city. Afterwards, the elderly woman who lived in the house invited him in for a cup of tea.

It was a poorly furnished two up, two down, very sad, no floor covering – there were thousands like it in Salford at the time. On the sideboard were a series of photos of men in uniform, obviously relatives of hers, and I took an interest. When she was telling me about them, she opened a drawer and took a picture from it, polished it with her apron and gave it to me saying, 'This is my youngest boy, Tommy. He was killed in Malaya.' I was looking at the face of Tommy Traynor, one of the men who'd been killed in the ambush. I was absolutely stunned. What upset me was that she was living in such dire straits and the son who could have come home and brought her comfort was dead. She began to cry. The photo wasn't on display, she said, because she couldn't bear to look at it.

I went back to the police station and spoke to an older man who advised me to go tell the old lady I was with her son when he died. That's what I did the next day. I told her Tommy had got a bullet in the head and it hadn't hurt him. I showed her a series of photos of the military funeral of him and his friends. I told her a bugler stood under a tree and blew the last post with tears running down his face, two big black stains on his shirt where the tears formed. I told her that the following day the whole battalion, hundreds of men, had gone into the jungle to try to catch the people who'd killed Tommy. She stopped crying. The years lifted from her face. She polished the picture again, moved the other photos on the sideboard and put Tommy's in the middle. 'I can look at him now,' she said, 'because I know it didn't hurt.'

A 'big, strong, hard twenty-five-year-old copper', Holland found the encounter hard to deal with. He had had nightmares ever since his return: about the ambush, about a pregnant woman that a notorious terrorist, Ah Hoi, had killed by knifing her, and her unborn child, through the stomach – Holland and three other soldiers had been sent to recover the body from its shallow grave. The nightmares worsened but Holland kept the lid on his emotions until 1987, when he met the Queen Mother.

> I received a call saying the Queen Mother was coming to the regiment and would like to speak with me and two other men who'd been in that ambush. When I went to meet her and she asked me directly what happened, there was a plaque behind her with the names of those who'd died. And while I was answering her I was looking at this and I was bloody living it again, the noise, the shouts, the bugles, the screams and moans of the men. And from that day on I became quite unwell. I found it difficult to find my way home; I'd leave my coat behind. The incident had opened a can of worms. I can't explain why it didn't happen until thirty-five years later, except it had always been there. I suppose it's because you're older, your children have gone, there's space in your head for these things to get hold. I saw my GP many times. He didn't know what was wrong and neither did I – I had no problems, marital, familial, financial.

Holland was watching television when he happened to see a doctor who had been in the Falklands with the Paras speaking about how ill he had subsequently been with post-traumatic stress disorder. It was the beginning of a kind of salvation. Having contacted the doctor, he got in touch with the Combat Stress organisation[17] and had his condition medically confirmed. 'Really, there wasn't any advice to give me – basically, get on with it. But it helped that there'd been someone to listen. I wasn't looking for sympathy, just understanding – and people who understand are few and far between.'

Holland has his demons under control but, he thinks, they will be with him forever.

I haven't slept properly since Malaya. When I was first married, I jumped out of bed and smashed the dressing table mirror into a million pieces. For most of our married life we've had single beds, so I disturb her less. Sometimes even now when I'm asleep panic fills me and I wake up. There's no medication, nothing they can give you. They say avoid thinking about it, avoid anything that might bring it back, and try not to think about it, but you can't. I watch the news, and it's Iraq. How can you avoid this? You have to live in the real world, you have to know things. You can't forget, you can't. It'd be like forgetting your own name.

His Manchester Regiment colleague from Carlisle, Eric Michaels, had his nightmares too, 'terrible, enough to make you crap yourself'. When he came out he could talk about his experience in the day quite happily, but at night 'I'd fight and kick, lashing out. If the dream went to the end before I woke up I'd be frightened, sweating, scared to get out of bed for a bit, frightened someone was after me. If my wife woke me up before the end, it was okay. She used to say she deserved a medal for sleeping with me.'

He did not seek help. 'I'm not one for running to the doctor's,' he says. But in 1992 he got hold of a leaflet, realised he was entitled to a disability pension, and contacted the British Legion. He also, finally, saw his doctor, who organised some counselling. Michaels also saw a psychologist, 'a young woman, who told me to close my eyes and picture I was back in the ambush. It amused me really, such a daft thing to suggest. I can talk about it but I still can't shut my eyes and let myself picture it. She said she was afraid that there was nothing else she could do. Anyway, I got my thirty per cent disability.' He talks of Joe McKibbon, also wounded in the ambush: 'Joe got into a bad way, turned into a hobo, drinking, sleeping rough in doorways. That was post-traumatic stress, in all likelihood. Some lads set him on fire and he died.'

Michaels' bullet-wounded leg cost him dear. At first he was unable to go back to his trade as a painter and decorator because his leg used to swell so badly; he had to get a job in a factory, though afterwards he went to work for British Rail 'painting as it happens, anything to do with the signal system, signal boxes mostly'. But worse, the injury ended any chance he had of a career in football.

I had a trial with Arsenal after I was demobbed, outside left, but nothing came of it. Despite the trouble with the leg I hadn't slowed up – I just wasn't as willing to go into a tackle as I'd been. Maybe I wasn't good enough, but I probably would have played for Carlisle. In Malaya I used to think, okay, if I have to get shot, then anywhere but the leg, the left, my working leg. I should have known better – the terrorists favoured shooting people in the legs because that put you down and they could come along later and finish you off.

For the last two years he has been free of his nightmares but at a price he would never have paid: 'I lost my wife after thirty-three years and I've had her death to think about. No nightmares now, aye, but a lousy trade-off.'

Numbers of men who were in Korea also came back to have their sleep filled with bad dreams. To this day Northumberland Fusilier Terry Brierley suffers, though not as badly as he once did, and he continues to have panic attacks: 'I feel anxiety in my chest as if it'll burst. I've even passed out.' Albie Hawkins, taken prisoner with the Glosters, tells a similar tale: 'Asleep one minute, bolt upright the next, sweating, visions in my mind, them coming at me. I saw my local doctor and got sent to a trick cyclist, but nobody could do anything.' Like Cliff Holland he finds talking helps:

It's nice on the second Friday of the month when my local Korean veterans' branch meets. A good old chinwag – nice. They're the only people who understand. My wife who's dead now, used to listen to me, but it was two different worlds, she had no idea and she couldn't have. There's a bloody mile of difference between the reality and what you see on television. The latest Gulf thing brought that back to me. What you see on telly isn't real. You don't know what it's like until you're on the receiving end.

Albert Tyas, captured with the Ulster Rifles, took over 40 years to excise his nightmares. When he was a PoW, letters from his fiancée Joyce 'kept me right in the head'. But Tyas wasn't right in the head. He got accustomed to sleeping in a bed again (for months he preferred the floor) but 'I never, ever, left that bloody hill. Night after night I was back in the battle, or sometimes in the camp, and I never left, never.' In the early nineties he went to Catterick to see a psychiatrist, 'when the place was full of soldiers back from the Gulf' and was told to talk about his experience or write about it. Soon after he was asked to give a lecture to the British Korean Veterans' Association 'and I gave them a lecture all right. And I went home and slept like I'd forgotten it was possible to do. For the first time in forty years I wasn't back on that hill.' Tyas has spoken, and written, about Korea ever since.

Charlie Eadie returned from Korea to his native Glasgow a very disturbed man, as he admits:

> I was wild, in the jail a few times, drunk and incapable, fighting. People thought I was a nutcase. They'd say, "Dinna have anything to do with him, he's trouble, a bad 'un." I went back to my job as an electrical winder but I lost that. I lost maybe six jobs. I wasn't interested in work. I wasn't interested in anybody telling me what to do. I just kept drinking and running about. I felt people were looking at me strangely, you know? My mother and father didn't know what was wrong with me and finally put me out of the house. But you don't come out of a thing like Korea normal. I wasn't the only one – other lads turned into down and outs. I bumped into them in town – I wasn't much better myself. I'd seen a sergeant shoot a badly wounded Chinese soldier to put him out of his misery. I'd been ordered to shoot another man who'd had his leg blown off and was signalling for a cigarette. I refused and the sergeant shot him, too. I got hardened. There was a tiny house in no man's land we were keeping watch on in the middle of winter and I saw the wee figure of an old peasant woman. I aimed and shot her. A man came rushing out of the house to get her and I shot him too. It didn't mean anything to me.

At home, Eadie had no idea what he was doing a lot of the time. 'A plane would come over and I'd be under the table automatically. It was back around the time that Chinese restaurants were just starting opening. The first time I went in one I was looking at them like they were the enemy, you know? I was insulting them, saying things loud like "I've killed people like that", calling them gooks.' And, he says,

> the nightmares were frightening, shelling, we were always being shelled, and I'd dream they were out to get me. But I couldn't talk to anyone about it. I looked forward to the weekends with the TA and the two weeks' camp a year, not for the soldiering but because I was among soldiers again. Some of them looked up to me as a hero type and there was a lot of heavy drinking. I was a fool – fooling myself.

Eadie stopped fooling himself when he met his wife Irene. 'She had a wee struggle with me, but she sorted me out.' He got a job with the Singer sewing-machine factory on Clydebank and left 23 years later as chief inspector. The nightmares are long gone. 'But often before I fall asleep I think about Korea. It's always with me.' Recently he went for a spin from Prestwick where he now lives and stopped off in a place called Monkton, 'so tiny, so quiet, just one street and a pub. And I was looking at the cenotaph for World War Two and at the bottom it had: Korea, Lance Corporal Jackson, King's Own Scottish Borderers. It made my heart jump: I was with him when he died. It didn't cause me trouble, reading that, no, no trouble. Just sadness.'

That other men who saw harrowing service did not develop obvious symptoms of post-traumatic stress did not mean that they were un-changed. Royal Marine Neal Ascherson, whose order in Malaya to use a flamethrower in an encounter with terrorists led to the accidental death of two elderly Chinese, is not haunted by the incident, but it is always there. He believes he could have done with some support and says, 'I did have re-entry problems', adding: 'Somehow, ever after, in the back of my mind, I felt terminally disqualified to live in the second part of the twentieth century.' Comments Nick Harman, whose wounds, sustained in Korea with the Royal Fusiliers, left him with 'a paralysed hand, a sore arm and a weak leg' and put paid to the promise he had showed at Eton as a oarsman: 'I dare say the experience made me an odder character than I would have been.' For years he did not allow himself 'to think about any of it – which seems a good thing to me'. KOSB corporal Smyttan Common also prefers not to remember. 'You didn't hear about post-traumatic stress in those days. Now that you do, you realise you had it but I wouldn't like to say any more. Keep the demons under lock and key, aye.'

> All I need is a pint and a comrade;
> You can 'stuff' all our trouble and strife.
> 'Counselling'? You can forget it,
> I already get that from my wife![18]

Barry Whiting, a medic in Korea, thought he had escaped unscathed,

yet when I got home people said to me, you're not the nice guy who went away. Something had happened to me. I was intolerant, hard to get on with, pretty nasty. A few years ago I met up with one of my old school friends who'd been with the Royal Artillery in Korea and came back on the same ship, the *Fowey*. A friend of his in the Artillery had lost a foot on a mine – we had a lot of them – and I was looking after him on the voyage; I worked all the way back, in the sick bay. Apparently I'd told this chap to stop wallowing in his suffering and get on with it. I was, and am, a religious man and if pushed I'd say the job I did in Korea was an extension of Christian ethics. I didn't specifically remember the incident my friend told me about, but I was horrified that I'd been so callous. Fortunately that period of my life didn't last.

Fellow medic David Oates, who served in the military hospital in Kure, also thought he was unaffected and, indeed, remained so for over 40 years – until he put a record of his service on paper.

The RAMC Museum, the Imperial War Museum and the National Army Museum had virtually nothing on the medical side of Korea, so I wanted to contribute something. But doing it created a state of acute anxiety. For the first and only time in my life I had to go on to tranquillizers. Once I'd done that the feeling passed, but obviously I'd stirred up something deeply unpleasant.

Cyprus, too, had its victims. Adrian Walker speaks of a friend with a degree in classical Greek, who became 'a kind of referee' at interrogations of suspected terrorists 'to try to see fair play and stop the more aggressive things that happened – torture was commonplace and the Turkish special branch were absolutely ruthless'. After a prisoner under interrogation died, Walker's friend was posted away from the island in case attempts were made on his life. 'You can imagine the sensitive kind of man who'd become a Greek scholar – psychologically he was suffering badly, he was going off his head. I never saw him again.'

Walker himself is unsure to what extent he was affected by his own experience, which includes an incident he describes as 'squalid':

I used to do duty in the post office with two Turkish policemen as bodyguards in case someone came to kill me. These two were like a homicidal Laurel and Hardy standing behind me muttering in Turkish and fiddling with the mechanism of their Greeners; I used to worry, those things could blow a hole in you the size of a dinner plate. One day just before Christmas 1958 a woman in traditional black came in. Her son or nephew working in London had sent a few Christmas presents. I had them ripped open; inside were a couple of little plastic water pistols that wouldn't have fooled a child. But there was an embargo on anything that looked like a gun, so I told Laurel and Hardy to bust them up, and these buggers really enjoyed it. So I'm sitting in the post office watching my colleagues busting up the Christmas presents of poor children and I've never been so disillusioned in my whole life. Whatever I was doing, it wasn't soldiering.

An incident he tries never to think about occurred at night in the police compound in which he lived.

An old Ford Consul had been brought in and the police were standing round looking at it. There was something black, a liquid, coming out under the door seals. What I saw was so horrific I no longer know what I saw. Three Greeks had been caught in the open by the Turks, who'd beaten them to hamburger meat. And because of this religious thing that a believer can't go to paradise if he's mutilated, they'd chopped off their arms and legs and I think beheaded them, and they'd stuffed their cocks in their mouths – quite a common Middle Eastern and Mediterranean custom.

After Walker was demobbed, 'a little box from the MoD' arrived containing his campaign medal and he remembers thinking: '"I don't want this" – and I dropped it into the bin in the bathroom.' Recently, in a London chip shop, he was talking to the Greek-Cypriot owners

> about those times, the curfews, and the infantry clumping about outside their homes, and the woman told me her mum used to wash the socks of the Scottish soldiers in funny hats who'd been maintaining the curfew near her village. I thought that was bizarre, and touching. What was more touching was that when I got home I found she'd put something extra in with my chips, a couple of sausage rolls or something like that. That was typical of the kindness of the Greek-Cypriots and I thought: 'I'm the one who should be making reparation'. Perhaps that's why I chucked the medal, I don't know, residual guilt, a medal for behaving like a hooligan.

RAF admin orderly Ray Selfe's legacy from national service went deeper than the injuries he sustained in the motorcycle accident that led to his medical discharge: he remained scarred by the whole experience until his death three years ago. Selfe went on to a career in film and television as a producer and director, in the seventies owned a chain of cinemas in the West End, and finally ran a film archive business providing clips for BBC and ITV programme makers. But, while he was able to isolate national service in a pigeonhole of his mind, it was always there as a marker that nothing in his life would ever be as bad. The material in this book relating to his experience comes from an unpublished memoir he wrote in 1996, angrily entitled 'How I learnt to polish a floor for king and country'. His son Howard, who now runs his father's business in Margate, gave permission for its use because he felt it was a story that should be told. 'At dinner parties Dad would talk about his national service and get very emotional about it,' he says. 'National service blighted his life without a doubt.'

12

How was it for you?

Ten years after finishing his national service, Gordon Williams was staying with his wife and children in a hotel at Shanklin on the Isle of Wight and found himself looking at a couple sitting in the corner of the dining room. The man seemed familiar but it took Williams a little while to place him as one of his drill corporals from basic training at RAF Hednesford. Williams went over to speak to him. 'He was now a bus inspector in Watford and he said that when he was on a bus going down the street he looked at the passers-by and could tell those who'd done national service from those who hadn't just by their bearing. I thought that was a nice conceit. But I thought maybe there was truth in it.'

'The majority benefit from National Service at least in physical fitness and character development,' was the conclusion of a report issued by the King George Jubilee Trust in 1955.[1] The following year a War Office survey showed that 80% of men said they had enjoyed national service, 93% said it had developed their confidence and resilience, and 60% said they had not wasted their time; the same year, the forces' yearbook, *Brassey's Annual,* quoted an army survey indicating that '15% like the life, 10% hate it and are bad soldiers and the remaining 75% do their best but long for the day when all will be over.' Most national servicemen would say *Brassey's* had it about right.

Not all the men who liked service life served in the earlier years, but most of those who did had a sense of duty: national service seemed a seamless extension of two world wars. 'My dad[2] was in World War One – wounded and three years a prisoner,' says Nick Harman, himself badly wounded in Korea.

> As a boy I watched bombings in Britain in World War Two and cheered on our lads. I expected to fight somewhere. There was quite a choice of places to get killed during national service and several of my school contemporaries were killed. There seemed nothing unusual about that. The question often arises whether it was fair to subject nineteen-year-olds to war. Of course it wasn't fair. But perhaps it's even more unfair to subject married thirty-year-olds with children.

John Eason from Nottingham, who fought with the Black Watch in Korea, had no equivocation about the value of the call-up, not just in Korea but in the wider perspective:

> Individually National Servicemen may complain that they are wasting their time and that they could employ the two years more profitably. So they could – or, rather, perhaps they could. But from the nation's point of view their service is vital . . . Any man who will not give up two years of his life for his country should be thrown out of it.[3]

Whenever or wherever they served, most men took the rough with the smooth and came out the other end of the process with a sense of pride. Even many who moaned about service life surprised themselves with the vehemence with which in arguments (and sometimes fights) they stood up for their flight or squadron, corps or regiment or ship. Many developed a sense of belonging, particularly in the infantry, which has never left them. 'When you join the infantry you become part of a family,' says Cliff Holland, who went to Malaya with the Manchester Regiment, 'and I'm still part of that family to this day.[4] My grandfather served with the regiment, my father served with the regiment, I've stayed with the regiment all my life. I have a soft spot for soldiers – I even visit them in prison. I regret nothing about my national service. I'm proud. And why shouldn't I be? I was a soldier.' Glyn Jones, who went to Germany with the Royal Artillery, comments:

> I see national service as one of the most wonderful experiences of my life. I remember everything as clear as a bell. They were the best years of my life as a single man. Not as a married man: having our daughters, both of them at university getting their degrees, them getting married – national service isn't comparable to those. But as a single young man – definitely.

The overwhelming majority of conscripts – most, perhaps, of *Brassey's* 75% – needed time to put their service into perspective. 'I resented national service, it interfered with my career and put me two years behind,' says Ron Batchelor, who went to Egypt with the RAF. 'But I look back with regret at my attitude and wish I'd made much more of my time. At the time I didn't appreciate how much I enjoyed it.' To which Alan Herbert, who served in Germany with the 10th Hussars, adds: 'I think I hated virtually every minute during it, but I wouldn't have missed it for all the tea in China.'

'You read that distance lends enchantment, that with the passage of time men only remember the good bits about national service, and for some that may be true,' comments Adrian Walker, who was in Cyprus with the Intelligence Corps. 'But if it's possible in a single phrase to cover what the majority of national servicemen feel about their time in uniform, it's rueful affection.'

Some, however, were to remain unequivocal in belonging to the 10% with little or nothing good to say about their time in uniform. One was Auberon Waugh, who was in Cyprus with the Royal Horse Guards (the Blues) and who was vituperative about it until he died in 2001. In a television interview he described national service as

> rather like being summonsed to the headmaster's office to be beaten, and beaten for two years. I went to Caterham Guards centre . . . which, really, if it had been visited by the International Red Cross, would have been closed down immediately. It was a sort of Buchenwald horror . . .[5]

In a newspaper he wrote:

> I well remember that on the last day of my basic training at the Guards
> Depot, Caterham, our commanding officer asked us who had found the
> experience disagreeable. My hand shot up, and I expected everyone to follow,
> but mine was the only one.
>
> Then he asked who had found it tough but stimulating. Two hands went
> up. Then he asked who had found it entirely useful and beneficial. A forest
> of hands went up. And that was when the misery, terror and boredom of the
> preceding six weeks were fresh in everybody's mind.[6]

Another who loathed his call-up was the political journalist Paul Foot,
who served with the West Indies Regiment in Jamaica. 'My strongest feeling
about national service is that I bitterly resent having had to spend two
years at that time of my life for Her Majesty. Again and again, I am tempted
to write to her to demand those two years back.'[7] He expanded on that
some years later in another radio programme. Asked whether the army
turned boys into men, he said:

> I absolutely reject that. I mean, really resent the notion that these people
> shouting at me and . . . being able to properly polish something turned me
> into a man from just a weed. I feel that not only was it a waste of time, but
> also of my resource, you know, it is a precious time that, a really precious
> time 18 to 20, to swipe that away from a young man was a terrible crime,
> really.[8]

Few men who became officers, as Waugh and Foot did, remember their
service with such hostility. It is less surprising that Peter Batt, who spent so
much of his time with the Ordnance Corps in Egypt on jankers or in
detention, says: 'National service was a total waste of fucking time, no
glamour, no nothing. It left me as flat as a pancake. The only thing the
army gave me was a pair of boots. I went for a job interview on a newspaper
wearing those boots.' And yet others who clashed with services authority
do not see their past in such black and white. Malcolm Stoakes, who
served time in the glasshouse for refusing to wear his naval uniform, says:

Okay, I had my problems, but I like the idea of national service – though I prefer conscription, national service sounds like you're doing your country a favour. You should be prepared to fight for your country and your family. Not for anything silly, not for Falklands' sheep dung or in Iraq, which had nothing to do with us. That was just a Blairite spin thing. Laurie Lee wrote, 'Beware those waving flags' – how bloody true that is.

Guy Bellamy, who spent time in detention for feigning mental illness while in Germany with the RAF, also has some good to say:

National service gave me time to think. In the eleven months before it, I'd worked in a shop; I wasn't going to stay there but there was no point in thinking about the future. In the RAF I began to think, about being a journalist, maybe a novelist. Being a telephonist wasn't frantic – that's when I started keeping notebooks. I'm reluctant to admit it, but national service did me good – I grew up a bit.[9]

For some men, the sense of time lost and of boredom remains the legacy, especially among those whose service did not take them out of the UK. The novelist David Lodge, one of the relatively few men to come to national service after university, served as a clerk at the Armoured Corps driving and maintenance school at Bovington in Dorset, and, like the narrator of his national service novel, *Ginger, You're Barmy*, thought

National Service was like a very long, very tedious journey on the Inner Circle. You boarded the train with a lot of others, and for a while it was very crowded, very uncomfortable; but after a while the crowd thinned, you got a seat, new faces got in, old faces got out; the slogans on the advertisements got tiresomely familiar, but you sat on, until, after a very long time, you got out yourself, at the station where you had originally boarded the train, and were borne by the escalator back into the light and air.

Men felt what they felt, but this is a way of thinking with which Willie Purves, who, with the King's Own Scottish Borderers in Korea won the only DSO ever awarded to a national serviceman, has no patience.

In the days I joined the bank in Hong Kong it was compulsory to belong to the Hong Kong Regiment. As a lance corporal I was given the job of punishment training for four men senior to me in the bank, who had been national servicemen and who refused to turn up for training or parades. This did not endear me to them, but it gave me the opportunity to talk to them. They hated the army, they said, they'd had bad experiences, they were bored. I felt sorry for them. There may be greater opportunities for some, it depends on how the cookie crumbles. Well, it crumbled for me and I took my opportunities. But if I had been an orderly clerk in an orderly room somewhere in Catterick – and that's probably was where someone like me who had just moved up from licking stamps and keeping the fire going was likely to have fetched up – I would have got something out of it.

A lot of men have complicated feelings about their service. The Southampton footballer John Sydenham went in, smarting that he was among the very last to have to do it and resentful about the interruption to his career. 'I'd just played two games for England Under-23s and Saints had just been promoted from the Third Division. Everything was going for me – and there I was, knocked back, two years taken from a career that was only going to last ten, twelve, maybe fourteen years.' The army came as a big shock to him. 'I'd led such an undisciplined life. I was a scruff. If you didn't want to shave in the morning, you didn't, who cared? I'd just about manage to crawl out of bed at ten to go for training, then down the snooker hall in the afternoon. What I had to do in basic shot me to pieces. I was a total wreck.' Yet the army did him good. 'It taught me I was spoilt, if I'm honest, and knew nothing. It taught me how to deal with people. It gave me discipline in life – shoes clean, shirt pressed. And I've never had trouble getting up in the morning since. As I found in business after football, getting up at the crack of dawn gives you the drop on most people.'[10]

Jock Marrs loathed his time in 'the God-forsaken hellhole' that was the

Suez Canal Zone. He came back to Scotland disillusioned, 'having forgotten whatever I knew about accountancy before I went in', and in 1955 – after a row with his TA commanding officer who said he could not leave the country until he completed his third year in the reserves – he emigrated to Canada. In the employment office he ran into a Canadian army recruiting sergeant who asked if he might be interested in signing on. 'My reply was "Not bloody likely." He said he wasn't surprised – a lot of ex-British national servicemen had emigrated and come through his office but he hadn't been able to convince any of them.' Marrs was to remain 'a happy civilian', yet his feelings about national service are ambivalent. He is proud of his efficiency as a Service Corps company clerk, has in recent years joined the Royal Canadian Legion, and was one of the moving spirits in finally getting a campaign medal for Suez veterans – something denied for 50 years. And he spends a lot of time amassing material for the Britain's Small Wars website and answering queries: 'You'd be surprised how many come from young folk who want to find out something about what their dads did.' Why national service still dominates his thoughts is not a question to which there is a straightforward answer. 'I guess you could say it's a love-hate relationship,' he says.

Gordon Williams is no less ambivalent. In *The Camp* he wrote such an angry, and real, novel about national service – about the RAF in Germany – that it might suggest his own service was disheartening; yet his certificate of discharge says his conduct was exceptional, his ability good, his personal qualities good, his bearing smart, that he was keen and had a prominent sense of humour. He still has it (as until recently he had his issue fork 'until somebody nicked it') which suggests this was not the case and, indeed, that he still feels some kind of attachment. 'Maybe it's not possible to give a coherent, rounded picture,' he says. 'Some of the times were marvellous, some were horrible. I guess fifty/fifty. What I think is that the principle of national service was great – it was the practice that wasn't.'

National service changed many lives – directly for those who decided to make the armed forces their career, including some who rose to high rank like Field Marshals Sir John Chapple and Richard (The Lord) Vincent, who both served in the Royal Artillery as conscript subalterns, as did Lieutenant-General Sir Peter Duffell with the Gurkhas and who, after the

281

battalions were amalgamated in the nineties to form the Gurkha Royal Rifles, became the commanding officer. Brigadier Johnny Ricketts – commissioned in the same intake as Michael Heseltine – commanded the Welsh Guards in the Falklands where Colonel Tom Seccomb, one of the few national serviceman to rise high in the Marines, was Brigadier Julian Thompson's deputy. Conscripted Pilot Officer Phil Wilkinson (who spent most of his service in fighter control at Seaton Snook between Middlesbrough and West Hartlepool), rejoined the RAF after taking a modern languages degree, and rose to Air Commodore, his last post in Moscow as defence and air attaché.

Ninety percent of my colleagues arriving at Oxford in October 1959 had been through the national service mill and most, if not all, were the better for the experience. Mine had included being a station commander for three weeks – on a remote outstation on the Yorkshire moors, which had seven or eight airmen and a couple of NCOs. I had my own chef, wrote my own station routine orders, popped to the bank in Whitby, with armed guard, once a week in the real station commander's personal vehicle – actually a one-ton truck and the station's only vehicle – to collect the payroll, and issued it to the eager outstretched hands, especially an unfortunate cook with inappropriate marital and discipline habits whose stoppages meant he drew sixpence every other week. I had to wait nearly thirty years before I was a station commander again.

What struck all men who went to university after national service was how young and naïve the eighteen-year-olds seemed, even allowing for the gap of two years. 'They were just schoolboys,' observes Malcolm Higgins, who did his time with the Royal Artillery in Germany.

I couldn't believe how different I felt from them – how I'd changed. At eighteen I was an arrogant little oik who was going to set the world on fire. Had I gone to university straight from school I'd have been a little swat, straight into the books, without any understanding of how the world ticks. National service smoothed off a lot of my rough corners and made me understand wider issues and look at people differently – and certainly made me a better officer than I would have been during my national service.

In fact, Higgins first became a teacher and taught English in France and then in Islington in London ('a sin bin school then as it still is') before rejoining the army, in the Education Corps, in 1962.

> I was head of department but my income was eight pounds thirteen shillings. gross, five pounds something net. It wasn't breadline but it was bread and thin marg. I saw an ad offering short-service commissions, at the end of which there was a gratuity of a hundred and twenty pounds, which was exactly the deposit on a house in Hemel Hempstead. But I enjoyed the life so much I stayed for fifteen years.

He rose to major, dealing with re-selection in the northwest.

What he calls 'the grown-upness of being an Education Corps sergeant' made Rodney Dale decide he was out of place at university, after national service. He went up to Cambridge to read natural sciences in October 1955 but 'was desperately unhappy' and left at Easter 1957 to become a 'bucket and spade' chemist with a firm manufacturing camera tubes, before turning to writing books, mostly on the history of technology (and a biography of Clive Sinclair). 'National service had thoroughly upset my equilibrium,' he says. 'Everyone was bitterly disappointed, including me. But the army had given me independence – I just had to find an independent life.' He was not the only man whose expectations, or the direction he should take, were radically changed by their call-up.

Anthony Howard, who had done university and his bar exams before becoming a second lieutenant in the Royal Fusiliers, had every intention of practising law until his subversive foray into journalism, at the army's expense, mapped out a different future; after some broadcasting with the British Forces' Network in Germany – away from his day job as a transport air movements officer – John Dunn gave up ideas of an acting career, tried to get a full-time post with BFN and, having been told he didn't have enough experience, listened to the advice 'to try the BBC'; David Oates returned to British Rail after serving in Kure military hospital during Korea, but 'national service had made me one hundred per cent committed to general nurse training' and he switched into the NHS; Roger Horton had worked in insurance and got his professional qualifications, but after serving as an RAF policeman 'never wanted to go back to sitting in an office all day' and eventually got into the jazz scene and became proprietor of the famous 100 Club in Oxford Street in London – 'and if there's a better life than forty years of mixing with jazz musicians and running a licensed jazz club, I have yet to hear of it.'

'I was a carpenter before I went in,' says Nick Harden, who returned to Liverpool from service with the Royal Engineers on Christmas Island.

> For three years I worked on the docks, but I was discontented – national service had put into my head that there was a better world than labouring. So I went to evening classes, eventually got a state scholarship to Christ's College, Cambridge, to read English, and became a teacher. University was another excellent experience, but one I don't value as much as the army. I haven't anything like the memories. Rationally it did more for me, but the army did something vital for my internal self that Cambridge didn't.

Derek Brearley is another who became a teacher and thanks national service for it. While he serviced RAF helicopters on the island of Sylt, he took advantage of the educational opportunities on offer to add four O levels to his existing two and, though he went back to Halifax and finished his apprenticeship as a machine tool-fitter, his qualifications then got him into teacher training college, which led to 'thirty happy years teaching maths and computing'.

For John Keenan, a butcher who became an officers' mess cook in Germany,

> national service raised my sights. It was the best thing to happen to me. As a young lad I thought nothing about the future; I supposed I'd carry on working for somebody else until I was sixty-five. But the army showed me I could do better. I became manager of a failing business in a village in County Durham, got the place back on its feet – just me and the lady who baked the pies. Eventually I bought the place, and another.

Moreover, Keenan became president of his butchers' association, then

Master of the Company of Butchers of the City of York, where he hosted a dinner for Lord Slim,

> the son of the famous one. We were chatting and he asked if I'd been in the services. I told him I'd passed through Mons officer training school, spent a little time at Sandhurst, and was then in the 10th Hussars. All true . . . At Aldershot I'd passed over that little bridge between the Catering Corps and Mons each day, and I went to Sandhurst when they were playing some army games to carry messages to the control room. And I was in the Hussars, even if I was only a lance corporal in the Catering Corps. I met one of Slim's party years later and he told me he often told that story.

Keenan adds: 'It's a sad time of life for me because my wife died of cancer four years ago. But national service gave us a brilliant life, and I really do mean it was all down to national service.'

For some, national service opened up unexpected opportunities. At a prosaic level, it helped many men get jobs – a lot of employers, especially in the earlier years, regarded a good certificate of discharge as the highest kind of reference. But their period of call-up did more for Eric Brown and Adrian Walker. 'What national service showed me was that I didn't want plumbing any more,' says Brown. 'Then I saw an ad in the old *News Chronicle*, looking for ex-national servicemen for various opportunities with Rolls-Royce. I went to Derby in 1957. From a little lad I could draw and I trained as a technical illustrator. I'd never have had the chance but for national service.' Walker was lying on the floor of a friend's bedsit wondering what to make of himself when his friend came in and threw him the *Telegraph*

> and in the personal column it had in those days was an ad looking for anyone interested in being a trainee diamond prospector in Sierra Leone. I think it said public school but certainly said someone who had seen active service. Well, I'd read *King Solomon's Mines*. So I spent five years in West Africa at the fagend of the Empire – and was a temporary officer in the Sierra Leone police during the diamond wars. National service was absolutely pivotal in my life.

285

Men as different as inventor Trevor Baylis, Labour MP Tam Dalyell and broadcaster Michael Parkinson regard national service in a similar light. For Baylis, his time in the army with the Royal Sussex Regiment 'toned me up intellectually'. For Dalyell 'it did a hell of a lot of good – because I was from a background that simply made me unable to talk to those from other backgrounds. A question of shyness, which national service helped me overcome.' Had he not failed as an officer cadet and become commissioned in the Scots Greys rather than serve in it as an ordinary trooper

> I would have remained among my class – and I say that not as an elitist because, while I have many other faults, that is not one of them – and would never have learned to deal with people, coalminers, lorry drivers, car plant workers, as I have had to do. Were it not for national service I would never have developed the confidence to deal with my first job, a tough school in a mining area, and I would never have been selected as MP for West Lothian.

It isn't likely that without national service Michael Parkinson would have remained 'a little local reporter from a pit village who'd never left home before, other than holidays in Scarborough' but, he says,

> National service changed me. I'd seen men fighting, I'd seen dead men for the first time, I'd been in a situation where I could have been killed. All of that and everything else opened up life's possibilities and taught me there's nothing to be frightened of in life, though that needs qualification – when I got to Fleet Street my Suez experience qualified me to be a war correspondent and I went to the Congo for the *Daily Express* for three months and was mostly terrified. I slept in a bath rather than in my bed, because they had a habit of entering a building and shooting up through the ceiling. I also covered the Six Day War in Israel. But when the BBC wanted to send me to Vietnam I said 'No bloody way.'

If they have made it into *Who's Who*, most men commissioned during national service include it in their entry. Parkinson hasn't. 'Looking back, national service seems strange, surreal. I behaved in a way I have never done since. Somehow, it no longer has anything to do with me.'

Among its myriad influences, national service in all likelihood turned around lives that otherwise might have been wayward, like those of self-confessed jack-the-lad Roy Booth, who as bodyguard to a very senior Medical Corps officer first in Egypt and then in Cyprus took more than a few liberties because of his position, and Charlie Lewis, who nicked the regimental silver from the 7th Hussars. 'National service straightened me out,' says Booth. 'I didn't enjoy every minute of it, but I enjoyed most of it. And if I hadn't done it I would have been in real trouble, I'm absolutely convinced of that.' Comments Lewis: 'I was a bit of a tearaway. I don't think there was harm in me, but I had a habit of getting into trouble. I think I'd have done something stupid if national service hadn't given me a bit of personal discipline. I'm proud to have served. I went to work in me beret for years and still have it in the garage.'

It is salutary to hear the number of national servicemen who say, without embarrassment, that national service made men of them. Lawrence Bell – who after his time in the navy had no desire to go back to engineering instruments for ICI, spent 20 years in Customs and Excise before going to university, taught English, and then at fifty-seven did a degree in psychology before setting up practice – puts it differently: 'If I hadn't done national service I think I'd have been a kind of non-person; only three-quarters of a person.'

*   *   *

By and large, men did not resent the state taking two years of their lives, however unwillingly they went into uniform. But if they ended up kicking their heels, they questioned why they were there.

> I slowly grasped the nontechnical meaning of entropy. They were substantially tradesmen, and one of them, a Cockney, engendered the thought by asking, 'Look at us! A painter, four plumbers, a carpenter, two motor mechanics, a platelayer, two shipbuilders . . . and what do we do? . . . And look around any town in Britain – slums, broken-down buildings, chaotic railways and buses, and where are we, who could fix it all up into a decent country?'[11]

'I was sixteen stone and built for the building game, not a sentry box,' says Ivan Churm. 'Britain was getting on its feet in 1960 when I went in to waste two years, but I'd have willingly got stuck in to help make things better. That would have been brilliant, that.' In the early years many men found satisfaction in helping to alleviate the hardships caused by the worst of the industrial strikes that bedevilled the country (electricity, for example, in 1949, docks in 1950, petrol tankers in 1953–4) and during the East Coast floods.

> On one single occasion in the RAF I did a physically useful thing. I helped to repair the flood-breaches in the disaster of 1953. We did not do much exactly – we filled a lot of sandbags with mud and laid them all wrong. But such was our enthusiasm at having something constructive to do we would have built a wall a hundred feet high if we had not been stopped in time.[12]

What a number of men bitterly resented was not just wasting their time but being made to do what they saw as demeaning jobs as waiters or officers' batmen (soldier-servants in elite regiments). Intermittently, stories surfaced in the press:

> The general idea behind National Service for which the taxpayer finds the money is two years training in the Forces, for the nation's benefit . . . Right or wrong, it's a fairly simple straightforward programme.
>
> Until you come to cases like that of Brian Holland. In his two years' National Service, Mr. Holland appears to have spent nine weeks learning the art of warfare, one year and forty-three weeks (involuntarily) as an RAF batman.
>
> His most vivid memory of the formative period learning to guard this country's shores will be the night when he was dressed in silver wig, lace collar, knickerbockers and buckle shoes as footman at an officers' ball. This was out of hours, and he received ten shillings. But he did not volunteer: he was detailed.
>
> Other batmen, he claims, did no training at all, though they learned to dress children for school.[13]

When he first went to Cyprus with the Royal Engineers, Roy Battelle was made a batman for some weeks. 'I was furious at the stigma. I was a fully qualified tradesman.' In Germany with the Royal Artillery, one of Glyn Jones' friends from back home in Wales also served as a batman. 'That upset me. I would have objected to that; I could not have been called that. Not only did he look after his officer in the barracks, but he had to clean the home where the wife was. Mind, we had a lot of fun reading their letters to each other.'

The caveat should be entered that, with more men than they could usefully employ, the army and the RAF had to find something for everyone to do; but, equally, in the new, socialist, postwar Britain where the old, rigid class structure was being whittled away by egalitarian social, economic and educational policies, the armed forces continued in a kind of time warp. 'We discovered we had fallen through a hole and landed in the eighteenth century . . . the game we were playing was gentry-and-mob, with touches of knights-and-serfs.'[14] Numbers of men have memories of being on manoeuvres and having to put up the officers' mess tent in pouring rain before being allowed to erect their own bivouacs; of officers who in the field should have been eating compo rations like the troops but who brought hampers or stopped off in village shops; even of officers who did not sleep under canvas as they were supposed to do, but who retreated to the nearest guesthouse or hotel. Many more talk angrily of being ordered to tend officers' gardens, beat coverts for shooting parties, or walk the CO's dog. 'The Royal Fusiliers, in which I served, was not a smart regiment,' comments Anthony Howard.

> But the first thing handed to me were instructions to officers joining the regiment which said, 'Every officer must be able to ride a horse with confidence whether or not he intends to hunt.' That, in a nutshell, tells you how socially behind the times the army was in the mid-1950s. The people in the officers' mess were living on borrowed time – after Suez the shake-out caused the most tremendous convulsion.

A lot of the regular officer class seemed to think of those under them, whether national service or otherwise, as lesser beings. Once, the actor Johnny Briggs drove his commanding officer to a gymkhana in Germany:

> There were three entrances to the event, suitably signed. The first said 'Officers and Ladies', the next, 'NCOs and Wives', and the third, 'Other Ranks and Women'. I was so amazed, even in those days, by such blatant discrimination, that I took some photos. Sadly, the pictures never survived. I was parking the car after dropping Lt-Col Ramsey off, when a Royal Military Police officer came up to me and demanded my camera. Then, despite my protests, he ripped the film out and destroyed it.[15]

This was no isolated instance and the *Daily Mirror* once printed a report about a regimental ball in which the order of proceedings was announced in this manner.

The very few national service wives who were able to accompany their husbands – virtually all in the Medical Corps – on postings were not immune from the military mindset. One RAMC captain was told by his CO in Singapore that his wife must not socialise with the wife of a brigadier (they had become friends because their children were the same age); in Germany another army doctor was carpeted because his wife was seen talking to the wife of another rank in the NAAFI shop. Such hierarchical strictures, the wife of another national service captain noted, extended to the queue for the Ladies, which sorted itself out according to husbands' ranks.

For a lot of men their feeling that the officer class was indifferent to them was exacerbated on their return from abroad to their depots for demob. 'We hadn't seen officers during basic training, except on the firing range where regulations said they had to show up, and we didn't see any now,' says Alan Anderson, who returned from serving with the Royal Artillery in Germany.

> I wasn't looking for a welcome mat, just a bit of 'Well done lads' sort of thing. What I got for the two weeks I was there was GD [general duties] – painting posts and the rocks around the front of the guardroom, emptying dustbins and delivering coal to married quarters. We weren't looked on as men who'd come back from doing their bit for their country, but outcasts.

A lot of men had already been made to feel like that because of their treatment by Customs, who had searched their kitbags, broken open their boxes, unwrapped their gifts and charged for watches and cameras, and in some cases confiscated goods. 'That was our bloody awful welcome back,' remembers Adrian Walker.

The armed forces, and the government, were no more considerate in offering practical help to those it was returning to civilian life, and men still remember a sense of resentment. 'A lot of men came back with no job to go to,' says Cliff Holland. 'What were they supposed to do. They couldn't go to the Labour Exchange and say, "I'm very good with a gun, do you want anybody killing?" ' 'Some sort of pamphlet of advice would have been useful,' Adrian Walker suggests. 'I came out of the army knowing what a fourteen-year-old probably knows today. I didn't know whether or not I was entitled to the dole or how to find a doctor. And the assumption was that everyone went home to a home. Some didn't. How did you go about finding accommodation?' He adds: 'Just a piece of paper saying "Thank you" would have been nice.'

'Dragged in and chucked out,' remarks Glyn Jones cheerfully.

Looking back across the years, the most common criticism men have of service life is the disparity in pay with regular servicemen who, according to *The Economist*,[16] cost four times as much to pay and twice as much to keep as their conscript counterparts. Among some who served in the army, a major criticism is that they were lied to, to induce them to sign on. 'Some men on draft for Korea were told they could choose a different regiment if they did the extra year and not go – and then got sent anyway,' says John Hollands, who served there with the Duke of Wellington's and highlighted the issue in *The Dead, The Dying And The Damned*. 'That was morally disgusting.' Similar stories surfaced in the newspapers concerning drafts to Malaya and Cyprus – in the House in 1956, after Emrys Hughes, the Labour MP for South Ayrshire, complained that 'men in certain Scottish regiments were lined up and told that if they signed as regulars they would not go to Cyprus,' War Minister Antony Head asked for particulars, saying: 'That form of recruiting is wrong.' In one instance, certainly, a senior officer condoned the practice; in other units officers may not have known what was, in effect, being done in their name, which is an indictment of their command.

It was not the services' fault that, reaching home at last, their time done, many men felt a curious sense of deflation. It was not that they expected to be treated like heroes here any more than at the depots; rather, perhaps, they would have liked a greater display of affection than an emotionally undemonstrative age often gave. 'I walked into the house with my mother and sister,' says Reuben Holroyd, back in Yorkshire from Korea.

> My mother had gone to the railway station to meet my sister from Liverpool University, saw some Dukes waiting to pick up lads from the London train, and waited on the off-chance. My father was in the bathroom having a shave with a cutthroat razor. He heard us come in and wandered into the hall. 'All reet?' he said to me. 'All reet,' I said. And he went into the bathroom and back to shaving.

∗　∗　∗

There were, of course, many regular officers who played by the rules and who gave their men proper consideration, and were well liked and respected for it. In training depots some attended passing-out parties (and on occasion drove the inebriated back to barracks); in working units others knew the names of all their men – even going to the lengths of having photos of new arrivals on their office wall as reminders. Many officers were quick to give a man who had a family crisis a thirty-six or forty-eight-hour pass, or allow him to take leave to deal with it;[17] in some cases those with places booked at university were granted early release to take them up. When national service was raised from 18 months to two years in 1950, Arthur Main, an Education Corps sergeant-instructor attached to the Airborne Forces depot in Aldershot, was worried that he would lose his place at Aberdeen. 'I'd been accepted on the divinity course on the strict understanding that I'd be there in January '51; now I wouldn't be out until the June. The CO was very understanding as he'd been throughout – I'd even been given special leave to go to Aberdeen to sit the entrance exam.' There was little that officers could do to help married national servicemen with accommodation (there was insufficient for regulars), but the adjutant at RAF Swinderby found something for RAF policeman Bryan McDonough. Turned down for a deferment by a tribunal while he tried to settle his wife in London, McDonough got a more sympathetic hearing from the adjutant.

> I told him my wife was unhappy being apart and at first he gave me permission to live out so me and Olive could be together – we rented a room in a cottage in the village. But then he offered us a billet on an ex-WRAF site not used since the war. It was sub-standard, with single-brick walls and a hardboard partition to the bedroom, and bloody cold. But it was better than being separated. I've never forgotten what he did.

What kind of time national service officers had of it also depended on the consideration or otherwise of their commanding officers. In some units, COs made no concessions, insisting on their conscript officers purchasing dress uniform – which in elite regiments could be so ornate as not to be out of place in Gilbert and Sullivan and were beyond the ordinary means of a man unless he had private money – and making them pay full mess bills. More sympathetic COs, however, set reduced tariffs for them in the mess and waved the dress requirement, allowing men to appear at dining-in nights in number one uniform or even in dinner jacket. Many national service subalterns had reason for gratitude. But while the majority enjoyed the pomp and tradition of mess nights, they thoroughly disliked the way such occasions frequently ended, with games like high cockalorum and British bulldog, rugby with the chair cushions and junior officers mounted on the backs of senior officers trying to unseat each other. 'I've never been a very physical person and I didn't enjoy it,' says Alan Protheroe, who left the Welch Regiment on commission for the Catering Corps and became assistant adjutant at the Aldershot headquarters. 'I joined in of course – peer pressure.' 'I remember a game of Are You There, Moriarty? – a sort of blind man's bluff with stout rolls of newspaper,' says Brian Sewell, who was a Service Corps transport officer in Blandford, Dorset. 'I would have preferred to back off, but one didn't want to be put down as a prig. I have heard of messes in which the instruments they used were more brutal.' Protheroe knows something of that.

I went as a guest to a Parachute Regiment dining-in. First, everyone got drunk. Then it was bread rolls being thrown, then bottles, then God knows what else. To my amazement there weren't any injuries but there were chaps there with scars, with missing teeth – they were very tough men. I kept out of proceedings, which, as a guest, I was entitled.

Matters were no more genteel in RAF messes. 'There was a huge amount of drinking,' says John Dunn of his time in Germany,

all sorts of drinking games like Cardinal Puff, repeat what someone had said and if you didn't get it right, drink another pint or whatever, there were always traps like that. It was all quite juvenile – the spirit of we won the Battle of Britain, a hangover of that. If there was to be flying the next day, things were rather more subdued, but if there wasn't, all hell broke lose. Once someone drove a Volkswagen up the steps and into the dining room; I remember it sitting there the following day. On another occasion someone set fire to the furniture. The nice thing about going down regularly to BFN at Cologne was that it got me out of a lot of dining-in nights, which I truly hated.

At one UK air force station, David Findlay Clark's CO, when the worse for wear, signalled that the night was over 'by making as to shoot out all the Anteroom lights with his Service revolver. 0.45 calibre bullets have a tendency to ricochet alarmingly after hitting the inside of a Nissen hut's corrugations so there would ensue an immediate retreat to one's bedroom or a dive to the floor.'[18] Nothing so exciting when Richard Lindley had to leave his Malayan jungle base to dine at the Hampshire Regiment's HQ in Kuala Lumpur – 'but I do remember we had to wait until the colonel was boozed up enough to go to bed and we couldn't go back until the old bastard had bored the stripy mess-kit pants off us.'

What many national service officers remember of life in the officers' mess was that it seemed to be an intellectual no-go area. 'I can't remember any discussion about literature or the arts or science,' says Lindley. 'As to politics, there was none of that – regular officers were rabidly right-wing and that was that.' 'Only in Anthony Howard did I encounter someone to whom books were a part of life, and our conversations were like a private language,' wrote Howard's fellow Royal Fusilier Michael Holroyd.[19]

Senior officers who gave their conscript juniors their trust in carrying out their duties were in the main rewarded, as Korea and Malaya in particular proved. 'I can only speak from my experience, but in my belief the national service officers were generally better than the regulars,' comments John Hollands.

> When you think about it, they should have been, they were drawn from such a wide spectrum of the population. Other ranks I've met subsequently invariably say national service officers were better to serve under in Korea. The Sandhurst man I think went by the book, as though on a field exercise and not in the front line, which requires flexibility. And he had an inability to relax, which you have to have; when you're living in the same bunkers with men, fighting the same enemy and the rats, you have to have that. They may still call you 'Sir', but there's a closeness there, an understanding, which regulars couldn't achieve.

Inevitably not all national service officers were good officers; in some respects it was harder to be so outside active theatres. As Glyn Jones says:

> Some were among the finest people I've ever met. One Welsh officer I played rugby with – I used to sit in one of the thousands of holes we dug, him and me and the radio set, and we talked for hours. Before I went in I didn't know such an animal as a national service officer existed. But I felt sorry for some of them who had no authority or just couldn't play the part. On guard one night, this little lad was orderly officer and he'd obviously borrowed the dress uniform, which was miles too big for him. When he went to draw his sword he couldn't get the last two inches out of the scabbard, his arm wasn't long enough. He had to pull the scabbard behind his body to do it. The guard tried to stand there and not laugh. The one to titter was the sergeant.

Comments Malcolm Higgins:

National service officers had a lot of responsibility. Some rose to it. Others were absolutely abominable. At Larkhill a national service officer told me to get my hair cut on the very day I'd had what today would be called a number one – virtually shorn to the bone – and his hair was curling around his ears and collar. Once I was charged with having dirty boots by another who strolled late on to the parade ground, unshaven, with his pyjamas showing through his gaping gaiters. Some threw their weight around in the name of rules that didn't apply to them.

And Anthony Howard: 'I remember a nineteen-year-old Etonian having a man run off the square into the guardroom, and being deeply offended. I make no pretence of having been a good officer, in fact I was pretty idle, but I certainly never treated men as though they belonged to a different race.'

*   *   *

The best part of half a century on, almost every national serviceman without exception remembers those he served with. National service engendered a comradeship so deep ('It was an honours degree in comradeship,' Grenadier Guardsman Mike Hollingworth asserts) that anyone who did not do it could not understand. 'I made comrades the like of which I have never done ever again,' says Trevor Baylis. 'I looked forward to demob for two years but when the day came, "Christ, hey, I'm going to miss you guys." ' Says Tony Rees, who served with the Pay Corps in Singapore: 'It was customary for people going home for demob to tour the barrack rooms and bid farewell, which almost always involved tears. I could never understand that until it was my turn – and boy, did I blub!'

'You missed the comradeship when you came out: maybe a bit of you always would,' says Glyn Jones.

It's not easy to explain to women. It's everything when you're in. You're a little unit and you'd do anything for it. You'd pinch off another little unit but not your own. You shared everything. The deep feeling inside you was, he's my friend, what happens to him happens to me. That sharing and closeness of men – when you've experienced it you can understand how men rush out under fire to bring back a colleague even though he might be dead.

The alchemy was so great it made some national servicemen due for release sign on, and a huge number thought fleetingly, if unrealistically, about it, including Jones.

> The kit and blankets were handed in, my friends came to the main gate and through it I went, everyone waving and shouting good luck. Then I rounded the corner and all went quiet. Relief. Free of restrictions. Apprehension about what I was going to do. Sorrow. A collection of these things – and this emptiness. I was tempted to sign on. An illusion, really.

Jones joined the fire brigade, ending a thirty-year career as senior staff officer for Oxfordshire. 'Akin to the army in lots of ways,' he observes.

Roy Battelle, married not long before national service and anxious to get home from Cyprus to his wife, baby daughter and not-yet-seen new council house, was another who had confused feelings. 'When eventually your name gets on the order list, you can't really believe it. And you get into a situation where you're reluctant to go, to leave your pals. I wanted to go, but I didn't want to leave them. However silly it sounds, I wanted both.' Even Gordon Williams felt confused when his release came upon him. 'The night before demob I got into a great card game and almost didn't get my chitty of release for the train or something,' he says. 'All the lads came out to the bus. I'd never had mates like this before and I was overwhelmed. I almost signed on, honestly.' He cannot help adding: 'It was a good card school.'

'I couldn't wait to be off, get back to London, Pimlico, see the old crowd I knew from school, youth clubs, dances,' says Ron Batchelor. 'But a lot of chaps had married, or moved on. Life had moved on. You have no idea how lonely I felt, how suddenly I missed the comradeship of the RAF. I thought about going back in – how seriously is another matter.'

As much as he loathed the army, Service Corps driver Ivan Churm felt the loss of comradeship. Like the three musketeers they thought of themselves as, he and his friends Keith and Dougal were released together,

297

but Dougal was turned back at Düsseldorf airport – he had inadvertently handed in his ID card at camp. Churm was 'choked'; and his emotions got the better of him when, later, he parted from Keith.

> Düsseldorf, Gatwick, Waterloo, King's Cross – we got the train together, me to Darlington, him onwards to Gateshead. As the train rolled into Darlington station I felt a mixture of euphoria and sadness. We could only push each other on the shoulder as a final goodbye. As I walked along the platform tears rolled down my face. People were looking, but I didn't care. I felt like I'd just lost someone as close as a brother.

For some men national service formed a bond that has lasted a lifetime, like that between Cliff Holland and his Manchester Regiment comrade Eric Michaels, and in some cases cross the officer-OR divide. Willie Purves has kept in touch with two of his KOSB platoon from Korea, Joe Pyper and Smyttan Common, and they exchange Christmas cards; when Common and his wife went to Australia for their daughter's wedding and came back via Hong Kong, Purves (not only very senior in the bank but a member of the Hong Kong ruling Executive) put his Daimler Sovereign at their disposal. But most men forgot their promises to keep in touch: getting on with life took precedence. 'Nobody wrote to each other,' says Gordon Williams. Yet the impulse to see old faces remained for others and, in retirement, they have done something about it. In 1987 when he left the insurance company in Bristol where he worked his entire career, Tony Rees was looking through his old army photo album and 'I was unable to shake off an uncontrollable urge to see some of my old pals again.' He started writing letters to local newspapers and traced 24 men he served with at Nee Soon – where the pay of all soldiers throughout Singapore and Malaya was dealt with and on which Leslie Thomas based *The Virgin Soldiers* – as well as 600 more who, across the national service era, served there. Every year since, about 150 have attended a reunion in Birmingham,[20] and groups have made a number of nostalgic returns to Singapore. Rees, who invited Thomas to a reunion but who 'declined politely saying it wasn't his cup of tea', is still tracing names:

It's like being a detective. Sometimes I've made two or three calls to the same name across the country. When I get the right one, if it's someone I served with, I recognise the voice immediately. Most of us don't look the same any more; most of us have spread and lost hair. But every now and then a newly located guy will come along who doesn't seem to have aged a minute – it isn't fair, is it?

Don Bullock saw his own departure from national service with the Yorkshire Regiment in Germany like this: 'You knew you might never see these friends again, but you never forgot them, not really forgot. As you grew old, in your memory they stayed young and always would. And they'd be there until lights out.'

So, too, the memory of those who died, and their burial: the slow march with rifles reversed and the drums draped in black, the volley of shots over the grave, the strains of the Last Post.

> We've just stopped here to say goodbye,
> We're on our way back home;
> We wish that you were coming too,
> At least you're not alone.
> Your cross is one of many, Bill,
> In rows so neat and straight;
> Your loss is one of many, too,
> Goodbye, – Our dear old mate.[21]

* * *

National service was abandoned over 40 years ago but has left behind a curious nostalgia. As early as 1970 public opinion had swung back in favour of it, with three adults in five (65%), according to an Opinion Research Centre poll, saying they would support its re-introduction. More than a little surprisingly, nearly half the young men in the age group that would have been affected were in agreement. That percentage increased a few points (to 52%) in a Gallup Poll among sixteen- to twenty-nine-year-olds, taken before the 1987 general election, when the question of whether Britain should or should not have a non-nuclear policy was an issue and, if so, what should stand in its place. As recently as 2002 when reality TV turned its voyeuristic eye on army basic training,[22] the bring back national service debate was trotted out again.

The 1970 poll ascertained that people's call for the return of the call-up was because they saw it as a means of restoring discipline, giving aimless young men something to do, keep them off the streets, and put a stop to vandalism, violence and hooliganism. Only 2% of the survey gave Britain's defence needs as a reason for their support, rather overlooking the fact that national service was to serve the country, not a custodial sentence.

Yet many national servicemen would today welcome the return of conscription as a social prophylaxis. In his autobiography, Arnold Wesker (who now admits to thinking that his time in the RAF did him good – 'Something I never thought I'd say') wrote: 'I have a dark and heretical suspicion that conscription kept crime and violence to acceptable levels,'[23] and 'I still have a hunch that that remains true.' Says Derrick Johns, who served as an officer with the RASC in Germany:

> There should still be some form of conscription as part of the education process. A lot of young men today have no direction, no standards, they don't come into contact with those they don't want to come into contact with. I knew guys like that, I promise you, and they came out of the forces different people, better people, with improved lives.

Brian Sewell adds:

> National servicemen turned louts on the streets into responsible men. Boys learned what there is no way of learning now: respect, interdependence and compassion for the group. Learning to live together, to give and take, to expect support and give it. And society is breaking down because it has no mechanism as effective for teaching these things. A gap year in Uganda is hardly the same thing at all.

Alan Protheroe (who enjoyed the army so much he eventually became a full colonel in the TA) says: 'Whether they liked it or not, national service gave people self-discipline and self-respect – there were people who came in who honestly couldn't even do up their shoelaces. That and pride in personal appearance was something that spilled back into civilian life.'

No national serviceman realistically thinks national service could come back, of course. The large, low-tech army of the 1950s could not gainfully employ all the young men who entered its embrace; the small, high-tech army of the 21st century would simply seize up. National service no longer has military purpose. And Lawrence Bell makes a blunt additional point:

> If there was conscription today, they wouldn't go. During the years of national service ninety-nine percent turned up, and they sent out the police for the other one percent. It's easy to round up one percent. Now it might be fifty percent – tens of thousands of men – and the authorities couldn't do anything about it. Today, society is ruled by sentiment and emotion. As a nation we've gone soft and the sexes have moved closer together. National service was a very masculine thing and the general run of chap took it in his stride and national service tightened him up. They'd just unravel now – an anarchic situation.[24]

But deep in the British psyche the idea that young men should do some form of compulsory service for their own good has never gone away and which Trevor Baylis articulates: 'There should be some contingency, something short and sharp. It doesn't have to be a boot camp. Young people have it so easy, they don't understand hardship. A bit of pain administered under threat of punishment would do them good. And God knows they could do with some physical fitness.' Others have called for a different kind of service that would be useful to society. In 1987 Prince Charles, in an article for the Economic and Social Research Council, proposed some kind of service 'in conditions approximating to those in the armed forces'; he returned to the proposal seven years later on television,[25] saying: 'In Germany you can do community service instead; we are the only country in Europe that does not have this approach – it's a pity we don't.' The House of Lords has expressed similar thoughts. In a debate on the voluntary sector in 1995, the Viscount of Oxfuird suggested that young people of both sexes should be required to give 12 months service between leaving school and the age of twenty-five that was 'something short of military conscription but service to the nation'. Earl Attlee, son of Britain's first postwar prime minister, supported him, though he veered towards an expansion of the Voluntary Services Overseas, 'because the youth of today has been raised on such a diet of television and screen violence, they should be made to do something that shows respect for their fellow men.'

Charles and their lordships were some decades behind the *Daily Worker*: it campaigned to replace conscription with a year's voluntary service to the state in 1958.

⋆　⋆　⋆

Suddenly feeling he wanted to contact his old 10th Hussars tank crew from his days in Germany, in 1995 Alan Tizzard posted an inquiry on Channel 4's Service Pals teletext service, and heard nothing. He was not surprised: all the messages seemed to relate to the two world wars. Wondering where all the national servicemen were, he posted another message: *Did you do national service and were you proud to do so?* When that appeared 'we wore out the letterbox, we were shovelling up letters.' The National Service Veterans' Association (NSVA) was born. One member wrote a letter to the *Daily Mirror* and in five days the alliance got 2,300 replies.

Ever since, the alliance has been campaigning for an official medal in recognition of what national servicemen did for Britain. 'It's not a question of those killed or wounded, it's a question of having served, of being there,' says Tizzard. 'As far as I am concerned, there is no difference between the hero and the poor erk who pushed a broom on a deserted airfield where the last Lancaster bomber landed in World War Two. And what kind of cost are we talking about? A medal the size of half a crown – which would cost no more to produce.' The association is also lobbying for a national monument.

The NSVA has won a number of MPs to its side and has presented a 10,000-signature petition to parliament but has not convinced the government of its demands. In a written answer in November 2002, Lewis Moonie, then veteran's minister in the Defence Department, replied to a question asking were there plans to award national service medals: 'None.

It has never been the government's policy to consider service in the armed forces as the sole justification for the institution of a medal.' The answer to a question asking were there government plans to erect a monument was again: 'None.'

In fact, a national service medal is available and there is also a national service memorial, which was commissioned as a private initiative and was dedicated at the National Memorial Arboretum in Staffordshire in June 2003. Neither satisfies Tizzard. 'The medal is unofficial, a bauble,' he says. 'The monument looks like a giant traffic cone.[26] What we want is a government-backed monument.'

Many national servicemen, whether they belong to the NSVA or not, have strong feelings on the medal issue. It is something that Bob Van Mook, the managing director of Award Productions, the international medallists that strike the unofficial award – and has underwritten the memorial in Staffordshire – recognises. 'I have spoken to a lot of national servicemen who want official recognition, but it is not likely to be forthcoming,' he comments. 'Some men are sniffy about the commemorative medal because it is not official, which we make very clear. But we have sold over 100,000. Men wear their medal with pride.' Van Mook emphasises that the dozen different medals his company issues have benefited veterans groups or charities by a sum rising towards half a million pounds – over half of that, from the sale of the national service medal, going to the Royal British Legion poppy day fund.

Quite aside from Tizzard's viewpoint, the matter of unofficial awards has caused considerable uncertainty in recent years, as Colonel Ashley Tinson, author of the standard text on medals, explains:

The ruling is that on parades, veterans shouldn't wear them and Legion standard bearers shouldn't wear any. However, people can't be prohibited from wearing jewellery – and that is what unofficial medals are – and it has become accepted that they may be worn below the official row on the left breast, or on the right. The drawbacks are that if worn on the right they take the position allocated to prestigious gallantry medals; if worn on the left by those with no other decorations, they take on the appearance of an official row. The Legion are, I think, sorry they backed the national service medal, though the income must have been welcome. Some at RBL Pall Mall would like me to say that unofficial medals should be prohibited, but I find that difficult when they sponsor one. My own view is that unofficial medals are a pain in the butt.

Tizzard and his organisation soldier on. They have won the right for national servicemen to march on Remembrance Sunday as a body, and have succeeded in getting a number of local authorities to erect commemorative plaques (Buckinghamshire County Council has plaques in High Wycombe, Marlow and Princes Risborough). Tizzard still has hopes of winning official sanction on both the medal and monument fronts; it took Australia until 2001, he points out, to strike a medal for its peacetime conscripts. The NSVA's campaign for a government-endorsed monument – which Tizzard personally would like to see within the precincts of Parliament itself – receives the support of Brian Sewell, who has suggested that a sculpture dedicated to national service could be considered for the empty plinth in Trafalgar Square.[27] 'Two million eighteen to twenty-year-olds, give or take, served in whatever way they were asked to frighten the Russians for twenty-eight shillings or whatever, and deserve enduring recognition – it was a tremendous gift to the nation.'

*   *   *

Had Korea not happened, national service could have been a transition from war to an uneasy peace, with Britain prepared to live with the threat of communism in Europe without the need for continued conscription; and Manny Shinwell might have achieved his aim of ending it by 1953–4. Had Britain understood the lesson of Indian independence – that, as Mike Hollingworth puts it, 'other countries didn't want to belong to our gang any more' – national service equally might have been drawn to a swifter conclusion, as it might had Britain not dithered on the nuclear option. 'It took a long time for that penny to drop,' observes Anthony Howard. And after Sandys, national service could have been wound up in a year or two – by 1958 or '59 – had the government raised a better equipped and rewarded army more quickly and been less keen (despite the problems of overmanning, which it addressed in other ways) to catch those who, before the White Paper, had been given deferment. 'That didn't make a lot of sense,' adds Howard. 'Having made the decision, they should have called it a day. It was unfair on the army. It was unfair on the last generation of national servicemen too.'

National service began robustly in the forties and petered out in the sixties, but it was overwhelmingly a phenomenon of the fifties, as much a part of the decade as steam trains, coal fires, smog, prefabs, ballroom dancing, Brylcreem, Old Spice, Teddy Boys, Radio Luxembourg, *The Goon Show* and *Dick Barton – Special Agent*. Things changed across the national service years, naturally. Consciousness of war receded and CND marches flourished. Lyons teashops gave way to espresso coffee bars. Frankie Laine and Guy Mitchell were ousted from the hit parade by skiffle and rock and roll, and the last conscripts came out to the Beatles and the beginning of the youth-dominated culture of garish clothes, long hair and alternative lifestyles that would hardly have been possible without the ending of compulsory military service. The Standard Vanguard, seemingly once the only new car on the road, gave way to other models, and there were fewer flat-capped workers, off to factories and docksides on the smoke-filled upper decks of buses, or on their bikes, an old service pack containing their Thermos and sandwiches across their shoulder. A lot of men first started to smoke during national service; the majority, who already did, smoked far more than they would otherwise have done. 'Stress of combat made men smoke, just as it did those on whose hands time hung heavy,' says John Hollands. 'It does amuse me in a cynical way, now that the government makes the tobacco companies carry warnings on their packets, that with free and subsidised cigarettes they got men to smoke like chimneys.' 'I got to be a sixty-a-day man,' says Albert Tyas. 'You can't blame national service, it was society then.' He stopped smoking in 1967: 'The doctor gave me twelve months and I'd be dead. He said, "Take these", and handed me a book of death certificates. "Fill in your own", he said.'

In the early years, national servicemen frequently got into dancehalls and cinemas free, and men who had served in the Second World War or who had been in and out of national service themselves, were pleased to stand them a pint in pubs. These gestures of generosity had gone by the mid-fifties, but, across the country, in those pre-motorway days, drivers still regularly stopped for men in uniform thumbing a ride.

Many of the hundreds of camps which men hitched to and from are gone, or abandoned; even the sprawl of Aldershot and Catterick has been cut back and the Catterick Flyer has not run along the Darlington to Richmond branch line since Beeching. Victoria Barracks, the navy's basic training depot in Portsmouth, has gone. The Guards' depot at Caterham has gone. The Intelligence Corps has moved to Bedfordshire and the Maresfield site in Sussex, now split by a by-pass, is part leisure centre, part housing estate, and part East Sussex fire brigade training school. The Joint Services School for Linguists in Bodmin is an industrial estate, as is RAF Bridgnorth in Shropshire. RAF Watchett in Somerset, home of the RAF Regiment, has disappeared; RAF Norton is being used by a driving school; RAF Hednesford, used to accommodate Hungarian refugees after 1956, is now incorporated into Cannock Chase County Park.

The drill corporal that Gordon Williams bumped into in an Isle of Wight hotel told him he had made a nostalgic return to Hednesford with another corporal. '"The place was derelict," he said. "But we could hear the boots" – and when he said that, there were tears in his eyes. I was touched – despite remembering thinking at the time I'd have to kill him.'

The oldest national servicemen are now in their mid-seventies; the youngest began to draw their old-age pension this year. Many still have bits and pieces from their service: a cap badge, a shoulder flash, a few photos, perhaps their discharge papers; others have displays on their walls; one or two have their complete uniform polythened in the wardrobe.[28] And they all have their stories. Men like to talk about their national service, at least to someone else who did it – the attraction of shared experience. Most other people today have little idea of what national service entailed – the majority of young people have never even heard of it – and perhaps have gleaned what they know from *Lads' Army* or reruns of *Carry On, Sergeant*. 'When I have tried to talk to my wife and son about national service,' Williams says, 'they've laughed, as if national service was some kind of Boy Scout thing.'

Lying on a Cyprus road with six machine-gun bullets in his body, Auberon Waugh could not resist saying to his Corporal of Horse, Chudleigh: 'Kiss me, Chudleigh.' At least Waugh later thought he had made the Nelsonian reference. 'I have told the story so often now that I honestly can't remember whether it started life as a lie.'[29]

If Waugh did not say it, it was not a lie: it was an embellishment on a truth. Perhaps some of the stories in this book have embellishments on other truths. All I can say is that I have listened to men tell me tales so absurd – and tell them with such relish – that I cried with laughter; that I have listened to men tell me tales so harrowing – and tell them with such distress – that I turned away while they controlled their weeping; and that all these tales are stamped on the memories of these men as ineradicably as once they stamped the last three digits of their national service number on their service-issue eating irons.

Notes

Introduction

1. During the war men were called up between the ages of eighteen and forty-one. Release depended both on how long a man had served and his age, with older men with the same length of service getting preference.

1. For gawd's sake don't take me

1. *Caught In The Draft*
2. *As Much As I Dare*
3. Frederick Holmes Dudden, master of Pembroke College, Oxford, strongly believed that students should go to university before national service.
4. A number of writers have erroneously stated that national servicemen in peacetime could volunteer to go down the mines as 'Bevin Boys' instead of serving with the armed forces.

   At the beginning of the Second World War the government made the mistake of allowing miners to be called up or to move into other – better paid – essential industries. By 1943 there was a severe shortage of coal workers and in the December Minister of Labour Ernest Bevin devised a scheme of recruitment. Each month his secretary drew one of ten numbers out of a hat; men (with some specialist exceptions) whose registration number ended with that number were directed into the pits. The scheme lasted 20 months, but the last Bevin Boys were not demobbed until 1948, which is how the confusion may have arisen.

5. While army and air force interviewing officers were present at examining boards, those from the navy often were not – the navy had little need for national servicemen. It was rather different during a period in the middle fifties when the first of the postwar seven-year regulars were leaving in large numbers and were not being replaced fast enough. For three years the navy doubled its intake of conscripts – but the peak was still only 6,500. The navy did recruit some men without skills to be shipboard stokers, who did the dirty jobs like chipping rust and cleaning and red-leading the bilges.

6. *A Game of Soldiers*

7. *Ibid*

8. Pulheems, which with adaptations is still used, is an acronym: p for physique, u for upper limbs, l for lower limbs (the pelvis down), h for hearing, ee for left and right eye, m for mental capacity (intelligence) and s for emotional stability. Each of the seven boxes was numbered 1 to 8; an 8 in any box indicated unfitness for military service. Every man was given an overall grading or P (for profile) coding, numbered 1 to 6; those with a 4, 5 or 6 were ineligible to serve in hot climates.

9. According to a 1953 War Office memorandum to the Select Committee on Estimates, 70.5% of men were graded 1; 11.1% graded 2; 7.5% graded 3; and 10.9% graded 4. Prior to 1951 only those placed in grades 1 and 2 were called up, but the Korean War created such a shortage of men that the net was widened 'to bring in men with minor disabilities or ailments, such as would not prevent them from doing, for instance, clerical work'. (*The Times*, 22 July 1953)

10. *The Peacetime Conscripts*

11. *The Best Years Of Their Lives*

12. *Second House*

13. *The Dynamite Kid*
14. *All Bull*
15. *Grinning At The Edge*
16. *Start the Week*

2. Am I hurting you?

1. *Loitering With Intent*
2. *Called Up: Impressions Of National Service*
3. Between the Second World War and the mid-1950s, nearly 400,000 Irish came to Britain.
4. For example, the Ulster Rifles, Irish Fusiliers and Enniskillen Fusiliers made up the Northern Ireland Brigade; the Black Watch, Highland Light Infantry and Argyll and Sutherlands the Scottish Highland Brigade; and the Devonshire, Gloucester, Berkshire, Wiltshire and Hampshire regiments the Wessex Brigade.
5. The late forties and fifties had more than their share of bad winters. In March 1947 the RAF suspended call-up for a time because there was insufficient fuel not only to heat the barracks, but even for cooking.
6. *Life In The Jungle*
7. In the House Mr Simmons (Brierley Hill, Lab) asked the Secretary of State for War what proficiency regimental barbers were required to attain. The appropriately named Mr Head referred to Paragraph 1003 of Queen's Regulations, which stated that hair was to be kept short. There was laughter when he continued: 'A soldier may please himself what style he wears provided this rule is observed.' There was even more laughter when he added: 'There is no establishment for regimental barbers and, although units usually provide civilian or soldier barbers, the army man may choose his own civilian barber.' (*The Times*, 6 July 1955)
8. From 1952 the services issued mattresses (or paliasses in service-speak). Before that, men got three thirty-inch-square 'biscuits' filled with straw, and frequently lice, despite fumigation. Until 1952 sheets and pyjamas were not issued.
9. *Writing Home*

10. The RAF were the only service to differentiate between the majority who had not been in the cadets and those who had, giving each group a number beginning with a different digit. The RAF at all times knew who had previous experience, and those who did found it could confer small privileges.

11. An inquest was held in Birmingham in January 1953 on John Hughes, twenty-two, who died in hospital after being in the army 18 months. He had been called up and graded A1 although for seven years he had suffered from a rare disease, angioneurotic oedema, from which his mother and grandfather had died and of which the medical board had been informed. In July that year the case of a man suffering from tuberculosis was raised in the House. He had shown the medical board scars on his back and had still been graded A1. Discharged after 45 days, he had subsequently died and his widow denied a pension because his service had not been long enough for an entitlement.

12. Two years later the government claimed that they had and that since the introduction of the measures there had been only 2,671 appeals – 0.8% of examinations. In 42% of cases the grading was confirmed and in 11% the grading was raised.

13. The army took about three-quarters of national service doctors and the air force a quarter, with only a very small number going into the navy. Some 90% of army MOs were conscripts and only slightly fewer of the RAF's (in 1953, 413 of 534 doctors and every dentist – 81).

14. One was playwright Alan Ayckbourn, let go at RAF Cardington in 1960 because of a knee problem. 'When he got to the gate he started running. Someone called out that there was a bus to the station every 20 minutes but he wasn't risking any of that.' (*Grinning At The Edge*)

15. *My Autobiography*

16. What men cleaned equipment with and when is a confusing area. In 1953, *Soldier* magazine announced that the four khaki-green shades of blanco, used since around the turn of the century, were to be phased out, replaced by what Army Council Instructions referred to as 'Renovator Web Equipment', which was rather like waxy boot polish, and waterproof (which blanco was not). But right to the end of national service, men saw nothing of the new product and continued

blancoing in the old way. In the late fifties Duraglit – an impregnated wadding – took over from Brasso in some places, but not in most. Staybrite buttons and cap badges, requiring no cleaning, began to appear from the middle fifties. Such buttons were of no interest to the Rifle and Light Infantry brigades whose buttons were black. It is always assumed that before Staybrite, all cap badges were of brass but this is not so – in the immediate postwar years a lot of men were issued with ones made of plastic.

17. A trained soldier in the Guards was a lance-corporal. There were some curious ranks at the old, posh end of the army – a corporal of the horse in the Household Cavalry, for example, was a sergeant-major – but this is a subject outside the scope of national service. What did surprise most of those going into the army without any knowledge of it was that they were not always called privates: they could be troopers, guardsmen, fusiliers, signalmen, sappers, gunners, rangers, riflemen – but privates all.

18. The navy (unlike the army and air force almost entirely a regular service with comparatively few national servicemen) was criticised for the food it served in the large dining halls of shore establishments. Aboard ship, men ate well. On large ships the food was prepared and cooked in the main galley, a couple of men from the different messes detailed at mealtimes to bring back the dinner trays. Smaller ships operated canteen messing: the navy made an allowance based on the number of members in a mess who purchased food against this allowance, generally from ship's stores, although buying ashore was permissible. This was prepared on the mess deck by the mess itself and taken to the ship's galley to be cooked by the ship's cooks. If a mess went over budget, a subsidy was levied on individuals. Canteen messing was highly popular.

19. *Life Without Armour*

20. *Younger Brother, Younger Son*

21. *Red Rose Blues*

22. Imaginative cuisine was not always appreciated. During a period when the issue of service food was again in the headlines, a correspondent to *The Times* wrote on 23 December 1954 to say that when he had

been in charge of an RAF station in tropical Africa during the Second World War, American rations, consisting of a lighter diet with a high proportion of fruit and vegetables, were flown in during the hot season. 'My troops soon asked me to receive representatives who claimed they were half-starved. When asked what they would prefer, with sweat rolling down their faces, they asked for steak pie and suet pudding.

'This week I was told of the long-suffering committee at an RAF station in East Anglia which has striven to increase the attractiveness of the airmen's menus by items including *chouxfleur mornay*. A vigorous complaint was made that it tasted of cheese. With a sigh the committee arranged for cauliflower in future to be unadorned.'

Further correspondence indicated that at one army camp a raisin pudding had been prepared with a sauce containing cinnamon and nutmeg, which remained untouched because the men said 'We don't like gravy with our puddings. Sauce ought to be white.'

23. *Called Up: The Personal Experiences Of Sixteen National Servicemen*
24. Established in 1921, the Navy, Army and Air Force Institute has traditionally run canteen shops on many camps.
25. *Army of Innocents*
26. In the army every recruit had to 'mill', or box against, opponents of roughly his own height and weight.
27. *Halcyon Days*
28. After four raids in five years on barracks in Northern Ireland, the IRA turned to the mainland, where they first hit the Royal Engineers Training Centre at Arborfield near Wokingham, Bucks, on 15 August 1955. Overpowering the night guard, they escaped with 24,000 rounds of .303 ammunition in bandoliers; 24,000 rounds in cartons; 30,000 rounds of 9mm ammunition; and 1,300 rounds of 0.380mm. They also got away with 55 Stens, ten Brens, two rifles, and one .38 pistol.
29. Men stayed on their national service rates for their entire service until conscription was increased from 18 months to two years in 1950, when the last six-month regulation was introduced. In 1950 a regular private's pay was £2 16s; in 1960, £4 11s. A national service army corporal in 1950 earned £2 12s 6d (regular rate £3 13s 6d), a sergeant

£3 13s 6d (regular rate £5 5s 6d). In 1960 these rates were corporal £3 3s (£5 19s) and sergeant £4 4s (£9 2s). Rates in the RAF and navy were broadly similar.

30. *Clock This*
31. The average person swings arms and legs contralaterally – that is, left leg with right arm, right with left. A few recruits marched with left arm with left leg, right with right, and were the despair of training staff, who sometimes spent hours drilling them on their own. Such cases of neuromuscular incoordination, nicknamed tick-tock men, were not as rare as might be supposed.
32. *Guardian*, 21 December 2002
33. Talking about national service, most of the men interviewed in this book slipped back into the speech patterns including the vulgarity of those years, almost as a conditioned reflex.
34. *Making An Exhibition Of Myself*
35. *Called Up: Impressions Of National Service*
36. In the immediate postwar years when fuel was scarce, the forces had coal heaps whitewashed so that servicemen would be less inclined to steal from them and, if they did, the theft would be evident; in time painting coal become a punishment. On 2 March 1956, in answer to an MP's complaint on behalf of one of his constituents, the Minister for National Service, Antony Head, said that in this particular case the coal had been dumped in the middle of a very dark yard and the army had had it whitewashed because soldiers 'were always falling over it' (Laughter).
37. The armed services recognised Church of England, Roman Catholic and 'other denominations' – but as only CoE and RC had padres, other denominations such as Baptists were told they were CoE, as were most atheists and agnostics.
38. *Brasso, Blanco & Bull*
39. *A Game of Soldiers*
40. *Guardian*, 30 September 1986

3. A class act

1. *The Peacetime Conscripts*
2. *Ibid*
3. *Called Up: The Personal Experience Of Sixteen National Servicemen*
4. *Life In The Jungle*
5. *Younger Brother, Younger Son*
6. In 1954, the ex E-boat took the then Home Secretary, Gwilym Lloyd George, to plant the Union Jack on two reefs off Jersey.

   Half a century ago the International Court of Justice in the Hague heard counter-claims to ownership of the virtually uninhabited Ecréhous and Minquiers reefs, breeding grounds for grey seals and colonies of terns. Making the argument in favour of British sovereignty, Sir Lionel Heald said that if France won title 'Jersey and Guernsey would be in danger of being claimed at a later date'. The court upheld the rights of Britain and Jersey in its judgement at the end of 1953.

   Of the Home Secretary's action Lawson says: 'A curious incident. But I can claim to have been part of perhaps the last act of enlargement of the British Empire.'
7. Flying was officer-only except for a very few national servicemen immediately after the war who flew as sergeant-pilots. Non-commissioned aircrew posts were phased out until, in 1950, there were only five sergeant-gunners, and they were gone by the following year.
8. When the Fleet Air Arm was fully stretched by the Korean War, the navy, for a short time, commissioned some national service RNVR pilots and observers. The scheme was unsuccessful: the wastage was very high and only a very few who got their wings went on to make deck landings and join a carrier group.
9. Canada trained all NATO aircrew as its contribution to NATO. Navigators went to Winnipeg and pilots to Alberta in the West, Saskatchewan or Ontario – where Barry Purcell spent nine months on pistons before four on the American T33 jet. Belgian, Dutch, Norwegian and Portuguese were on his course; Greeks and Turks, because of the Cyprus troubles, were posted to different camps. At Winnipeg Mike Watkins won the award as the best recruit on his

intake. What British aircrew found galling was that they lost their rank of acting pilot officer (the Canadian air force did not commission its aircrew until after they had finished training), having to revert to the officer cadet's white disc – and having to salute Canadian pilot officers. But it was a small price compared with the experience, which included sailing to and from Canada on the luxury liners of the day, first class.

10. Barry Purcell left the air force as a flight lieutenant. Mike Watkins applied for re-entry after reading economics and law at Cambridge and exchanging his navigator's brevet for a flying officer's with the university air squadron; he finished a thirty-year career as a group captain. After 16 years' operational flying, Ian Wormald left as a squadron leader, for three years from 1976 was a contract pilot for British Aerospace, returned to RAF flying in 1979, and for six years from 1985 was a British Aerospace test pilot. David Piercy rose to flying officer and was chosen to take part in the Coronation flypast. He signed on after becoming the youngest flying instructor in the RAF at twenty-one, but was discharged at twenty-three with diabetes. He became a haematologist.

11. *Stand By Your Beds!*

12. *High Hopes*

13. *Called Up: The Personal Experience Of Sixteen National Servicemen*

14. *Called Up: Impressions Of National Service*

15. *Skip All That*

16. *The Peacetime Conscripts*

17. *730 Days Until Demob!*

18. *The Peacetime Conscripts*

19. *Will This Do?*

20. *Blanco, Brasso & Bull*

21. *Evil Spirits*

22. One of the final tests for upper yardsmen was a lecture, or viva, for which candidates chose their topic as at Wosbe – but of which they had to give due notice. Hopkin Maddock and his fellow upper yardsmen 'reduced the odds on being asked searching questions by selecting obscure titles. One was "A roof over your head", chosen by a newly qualified estate agent. Mine was simply "C_2H_5OH". The session, we were told, was the briefest on record.'

23. In 1951 Grenadier Guardsman Mike Hollingworth was on the last rehearsal parade for the Trooping the Colour, which brigade regiments did in rotation and that year was the turn of the Scots Guards. 'The youngest officer of the battalion, who had the honour of being the standard bearer, was Second Lieutenant The Master of Napier, Lord of the Isles, and he cocked up – didn't get his sword into his scabbard in time. The RSM screamed across the parade ground: "Second Lieutenant The Master of Napier, Lord of the Isles, Sir, you are idle, take his name." He got six extra orderly officers.' (Being orderly officer is a daily duty that officers do on rota, which means being responsible for what happens in camp. An officer can be punished by being given 'extra orderly officers' – though usually such a punishment can only be given by a senior officer.) Later, Lord Napier was Princess Margaret's equerry. Hollingworth eventually became a BBC producer and when he met Princess Margaret, he told her the story.

24. Warrant Officer Cook at RAF Jurby was a foot shorter than Brittain and Lynch but was a contender in the loud voice department. Officer cadets on the ferry rounding the harbour wall at Douglas swore they could hear him two miles away.

25. *Life In The Jungle.* But in *Michael Heseltine: A Biography*, Michael Crick suggests that Heseltine's 'overconfidence, or, more bluntly, his arrogance' cost him the senior post. He quotes Christopher Madden who was elected SUO: 'He made everyone assume he was top dog. He may have rather overdone it with the company commander – making him feel he reported to Mike and not the other way round!'

26. There is a recorded case of a graduate in economics at Eaton Hall who refused to get out of bed on his first morning. A series of NCOs, warrant officers and officers threatened and implored him to get up but he refused, saying he felt like a lie-in. Eventually carried off to the guardroom, he was discharged from the army.

27. In his autobiography, *Will This Do?*, Auberon Waugh admitted to faring rather worse: 'Put in command of four armoured cars with thousands of square miles of Salisbury Plain to drive on, I contrived to crash all four; they paired off to crash into each other.' Nevertheless, he went on to get his commission in the Royal Horse Guards (the Blues).

28. The military standard in Nigeria was 'about school cadet force standard,' says Lyon-Maris. 'We soldiered on the British pattern but they were a bit dangerous with rifles – if there was a weapon stoppage they were inclined to turn round and point the thing. They were very frightened by grenades – some silly ass would invariably drop one and we'd be diving for cover. It didn't help that 50% failed to explode, as did the 25 lb shells – munitions deteriorated very quickly in the heat and were probably old stock anyway; West Africa was a backwater. That did present dangers because the officer and white NCO had to gather up the duds.'

29. *The Peacetime Conscripts*

30. In the Guards, the POM squad trained alongside other ranks, 'the rest of this vast National Service population of the Depot – whom we met intangibly on parade and were advised not to associate with during our brief minutes in the recruits' N.A.F.F.I.' (Tom Stacey in *Called Up: The Personal Experience Of Sixteen National Servicemen*)

31. With the end of national service, Mons contracted to a quarter of its former size and for some years turned to making short-service officers from rankers and school-leavers (who remained civilians during training and could leave at any time). Eaton Hall was knocked down, save for the clock tower.

32. *Skip All That*

33. In 1950 a national service second lieutenant's pay rose from 11 shillings; it remained at 13 shillings until conscription ended. As a full lieutenant, a national serviceman earned 16 shillings (against a regular's 19s 6d – which incrementally rose to 34 shillings by 1960). Like other national servicemen, all conscript officers went on to regular rates during their last six months.

4. Now what?

1. British troops were stationed in Bermuda from 1946 to 1953, when the garrison was withdrawn. Later that year a detachment of the Welsh Fusiliers were sent there to provide internal security when Churchill and Eisenhower attended a Summit conference.

2. A lucky handful of writers got to sea on big vessels as captains' clerk-secretaries.

3. In 1954, on the way back from Korea with 1,700 servicemen, it sank off the Algerian coast after an explosion in the engine-room killed four crew; the passengers were rescued by a nearby Norwegian vessel.

4. *What's It All About?*

5. A large tank ship, the *Lofoten*, went to Egypt in the wake of the 1956 Suez débâcle to help with the clearing-up operations – the Egyptians had sunk a number of vessels in the mouth of the Canal. The *Lofoten* carried three gross of condoms in the sickbay in case the crew got ashore. As they did not, the national service surgeon lieutenant disposed of half the stock one afternoon by having them inflated for the crew to shoot at with revolvers. On decommissioning back in Malta the fleet pharmacist questioned the excessive use and was told that the items had been lost overboard in a gale . . .

6. *The Conscript Doctors* is a book of the edited reminiscences of some of the doctors who did national service in the three armed services, collated by Dr John Blair from a unique archive that he compiled, with the assistance of the British Medical Association and the Wellcome Institute. In its entirety, the archive will remain closed in the Institute and will be made public 20 years after the death of the last contributor.

7. *Ibid*

8. 'Baffs', British armed forces vouchers, were an all-paper currency in denominations from three pence to a pound.

9. 'The cultural atmosphere at Beaconsfield was several orders of magnitude more elevated than that at Bury St Edmunds . . . the profanities of our basic training units were exchanged for such adventurous orders as: "As you were – let's have it homogeneous this time" and: "Get fell in properly, no more bloody parallelograms".' (*Halcyon Days*)

10. *Ibid*

11. BOAC – British Overseas Airways Corporation – became Britain's state airline at the end of 1939. In 1975 it merged with its sister airline BEA – British European Airways – to form British Airways.

12. Men in Germany were entitled to take two leaves in the UK during their time, for which their fares were paid. Before air flights became the norm, the trip entailed train and boat. From the mid-fifties men who had used up their entitlement but still had leave owing could fly on BEA at a special services rate of £26 return – still two or three months' money for the average conscript.

5. 'Some bloody police action'

1. Other countries to send combat forces a little later were Canada, Australia, New Zealand, South Africa, The Netherlands, Belgium, France, Turkey, Greece, Ethiopia, Thailand, Colombia and the Philippines. Countries that were not members of the United Nations – Sweden, Norway, Denmark, India and Italy – sent non-combatant support, mainly medics.

2. At the outbreak of the conflict the British sent 22 Royal Navy ships, which happened to be on summer exercises in the Far East, to Korean waters. Throughout the war Royal Navy, Commonwealth and Allied warships launched constant air attacks, causing immense damage to rolling stock. So did the bombardments from such vessels as HMS *Belfast* (preserved in the Pool of London), which in 404 days patrolling fired over 8,000 shells from her six-inch guns and steamed more than 80,000 miles. A few national servicemen saw naval action off the Korean west coast. The government decided not to commit the RAF, although it permitted pilots to be attached to American fighter squadrons (and shipped out 17 Meteor twin-jet fighters for the Australians). Two flights of RAF light observation planes in Korea were piloted by army personnel.

3. In the summer of 1951 doubts were expressed as to whether the government had acted legally in recalling men under the 1939 and subsequent wartime legislation. The law officers decided that they had acted illegally – the postwar National Service Acts has superseded the earlier legislation. The Opposition was informed of the ruling but, like the government, felt the issue was too sensitive to be revealed. Among reservists who became prisoners in Korea were men who had

been taken by the Germans or Japanese during the Second World War. The government subsequently introduced new and more limited powers enabling them to call up reservists by issuing a proclamation without the prerequisite that there must be a 'great emergency' or 'imminent national danger'. Such a proclamation was used for Suez in 1956.

4. A form of cold injury resulting from standing in freezing water for lengthy periods, trenchfoot or immersion foot can result in permanent loss of sensation and in severe cases, gangrene.

5. *A Call To Arms: Interlude With The Military*

6. *The Dead, The Dying And The Damned*

7. According to an undated army document in the National Archives, 'such incidents are very difficult to catch out, and it is a catching complaint. Unlike VD it is not a thing to lecture about as that gives men who had never thought of it the idea. The answer is for a constant watch on morale to be kept by leaders at every level – CO to section commander.'

8. From *The British Part In The Korean War* by General Anthony Farrar-Hockley, quoted in *The Korean War*, Brian Catchpole

9. *One Road To Imjin*

10. In Basingstoke, Pyper was lucky to find himself in the hands of the New Zealander Sir Archibald McIndoe, the plastic surgeon who earned an international reputation for physically and psychologically rehabilitating aircrew in the Second World War.

11. In the first months of the war, the British hospital ship *Maine*, the only hospital ship in the area, went back and forth to Japan carrying 300 wounded at a time, with doctors working round the clock performing operations – typhoons permitting. Only one ward had air conditioning, used for the dangerously ill, and Randolph Churchill in the *Daily Telegraph* wrote scathingly of the conditions, in which the temperature was as high as 116°F. As America does not bury its dead on foreign soil or at sea, US personnel who died were laid aft, with ill-afforded ice covering them in the heat. At Pusan hundreds of white-painted coffins were offloaded to store ships returning to the USA. The *Maine* left the war zone when replaced by three larger American hospital ships, taking

seriously burnt soldiers from the Argyll and Sutherland Highlanders – injured in a misdirected American napalm attack (see p. 99) – as well as wounded Glosters to Hong Kong.

12. Chinese soldiers about to be taken more often than not blew themselves up; in some instances they did so after they had become prisoners, also killing or injuring their captors.

13. Thorn had converted to a short-service commission and then a regular commission when, in 1954, he contracted a near-fatal attack of polio on an exercise in Hong Kong ('crawling through a paddy-field on which they chuck everything') and came home in an iron lung. He spent two years in hospital, eventually becoming a teacher. He retired in 1995, 'when I was falling over too often' and now has a stairlift and a pavement buggy.

14. The armistice halted the fighting but did not officially end the war. Barbed wire, tank traps and manned guardposts still form the frontline defences of South Korea.

15. About 76,000 enemy POWs, mostly North Koreans, and about 13,000 UN were repatriated. Some 22,000 Chinese and North Koreans preferred not to go home and most were resettled in Formosa (now Taiwan) or stayed in South Korea. Twenty-one Americans and one Briton chose to remain with their captors, most drifting back over the coming years. The single British defector returned to Britain in 1962. But 100 British servicemen taken prisoner remain unaccounted for, and 7,956 Americans. British, American, and other allied troops were known to be in Chinese, North Korean and Russian hands at the end of the war in 1953.

16. *A Barren Place: National Servicemen in Korea 1950-1954*

17. Total United Nations forces killed were over 14,000. The Chinese and North Koreans lost something like 750,000 men. Upwards of 3 million Korean civilians perished.

18. *The Korean War*, Max Hastings

19. Private Bill Speakman, a Black Watch regular attached to the King's Own Scottish Borderers, was one of five Victoria Crosses awarded during the Korean war, all to regular soldiers. There were 40 DSOs to regular soldiers in addition to Purves'. Other national servicemen were

recipients of some of the 177 Military Crosses awarded in addition to Hollands' and the 217 Military Medals in addition to Common's.

6. More real bullets

1. The 100-mile artificial waterway linking the Mediterranean with the Gulf of Suez and the Red Sea was built by the French in ten years, opening in 1869, but in 1875 the British government became the major shareholder. The Suez Canal Company had offices in Paris controlled by a council of 33, ten of them British.
2. About 30,000 white settlers occupied 12,000 square miles of the best farmland; 250,000 Kikuyu occupied 2,000 square miles of the worst.
3. *730 Days Until Demob!*
4. *The Conscript Doctors*
5. *Unreasonable Behaviour*
6. *730 Days Until Demob!*
7. The average annual rainfall in Malaya was 98 inches; in the wettest part near Ipoh in Perak, scene of some of the hardest jungle fighting, it was 232 inches.
8. *Called Up: Impressions Of National Service*
9. Malaya was overwhelmingly an infantry campaign, but the RAF continuously flew voice aircraft and dropped 15 million propaganda leaflets a month, as a result of which activities many CTs defected. The RAF also destroyed enemy crops by spraying, and ran bombing sorties.
10. *Jungle Green*
11. *The Conscript Doctors*
12. *Back Badge*, June 1955
13. *Ibid*, December 1955. Unlike in Korea and Malaya, troops on active service in Kenya, which in the uplands at night could be distinctly cold, did not receive a rum ration – but the mules did!
14. These figures were published in 1956. More recent data refer to 30,000 Mau Mau dead and 80,000 captured; another recent source puts the total number of Africans who died at 114,000.
15. *The Savage Wars Of Peace*
16. *The Times*, 12 June 1957

17. Ironically, at Nicos Sampson's trial the judge said categorically that he disbelieved the allegations brought by the defence.
18. *Will This Do?*
19. Archbishop Makarios, exiled by the British to the Seychelles for two years, became President of Cyprus in 1960. He was briefly deposed in 1974 by the Greek military junta in Athens, who staged an invasion of the island with the aim of achieving *enosis*. Nicos Sampson – whose 1957 death sentence had been commuted to life imprisonment but who was then freed under an amnesty agreement – replaced Makarios, Turkey invaded Cyprus, taking possession of the north, and the Greek coup collapsed after eight days. Sampson was sentenced to 20 years but was released in 1990. Cyprus remains divided to this day.
20. Talks on independence began in 1962 and it was realised two years later. Malta became a republic in 1974.
21. *730 Days Until Demob!*
22. *Brasso, Blanco & Bull*
23. They included Rudolf Hess, Hitler's deputy, Albert Speer, his armaments minister, and Grand Admiral Karl Donitz.
24. After the loss of the Suez Canal, Aden, in the Arabian Peninsula at the foot of the Red Sea, became the main base for Britain's Far and Middle East interests. The colony – 70 square miles of rock and sand around the port, and the inland protectorate, about the size of England – had kept the large garrison that had once secured the Canal's southern approaches. By 1961 Nasser was encouraging the Arabic peoples to cast out the British colonial rulers. Before the end of national service, there was more bloody violence, with the murder of off-duty British officers and policemen, as in Cyprus. The situation worsened after the end of NS with terrorist attacks; in one, in June 1967, 22 British soldiers were killed and 31 wounded in Aden's notorious Crater district. Britain finally withdrew from the Arabian Peninsula in November that year.
25. 13 December 2001

7. Jammy bastards

1. Like Germany after the Second World War, Austria was divided into four zones, occupied by the Russians, Americans, French and British. Like Berlin, Vienna was similarly divided. The British occupied the southern zone and stationed a battalion in Vienna for ceremonial duties, withdrawing with the other powers when an international agreement guaranteed Austria's neutrality.

2. *Crying With Laughter*

3. The Scots Guards pipe band in 1959 went on a twelve-week, 24,000 mile tour of America and Canada, giving 65 performances in 56 cities.

4. *The Best Years Of Their Lives*

5. 'The National Service Era in the RAMC', Mitchiner Lecture, 1994, given by Dr John Blair

6. *Second House*

7. *Jack Charlton: The Autobiography*

8. *All Bull*

9. *Ibid*

10. In a written reply on illiteracy among servicemen, Harold Macmillan, when Minister of Defence, said: 'The terms "illiterate" and "semi-illiterate" are not used in the Services, but in the army the following number of national service entrants and the percentage proportionate to total intake who have been found unable to write their names, addresses, etc, on a form are: 1952, 1,400 (1.2%); 1953 1,027 (0.92%); 1954 (January to September) 653 (0.84%).' (*The Times*, 17 February 1955). On 21 May 1956 the newspaper quoted General Sir Gerald Templar, Chief of the Imperial Staff, as saying: '. . . we are sometimes somewhat appalled by the standard of education, or rather lack of it, which some of our recruits possess when they join.'

11. *Making An Exhibition Of Myself*

12. *Ibid*

13. *Secret Classrooms*

14. Whatever humour attached to the existence of the JSSL, the government took the secret nature of its work seriously. In 1958 two Oxford undergraduates who wrote in *Isis* about incidents that occurred

on the East-West boundary during their national service, were imprisoned for three months under the Official Secrets Act. Things changed after the collapse of communism in 1989-90, but as late as 1987 the BBC was forced to pull a radio programme on the school under threat of prosecution. This prompted a letter to the *Guardian* (16 May) from Michael Sheldon in Norwich who remembered an officer explaining that his JSSL group would be signing the Official Secrets Act. 'I have long since forgotten any "secrets" he imparted to us . . . What I do remember is that our solemn initiation took place in a classroom full of electrical equipment and that, at the end of the proceedings, a technician in overalls crawled out from under one of the benches . . . What to do? The technician was removed under guard and, for all I know, may have had to be shot or made head of MI5.'

15. *Tainted By Experience*
16. Frayn returned to Cambridge as an 'ordinary' undergraduate' in 1956 to read French and Russian (later changing to moral sciences – now more straightforwardly called philosophy). As he was still on the reserve he had to seek permission from the War Office to go with an exchange group to Moscow University 'and there were "conversations": would I report on people we would meet? I refused point blank, and I never heard from them again. Evidently I was not the kind of person they were looking for.' Frayn's Russian came in useful as a journalist on the *Guardian* when he covered Harold Macmillan's visit to the USSR. In 1986 the National Theatre staged his translation of Chekhov's *The Cherry Orchard.*
17. *Crying With Laughter*
18. ENSA was set up to provide entertainment to the troops during the Second World War and many men in uniform served with it. Almost all the top entertainers of the day also appeared in its shows, though the standard was not always high – ENSA was dubbed 'every night something awful'. Nevertheless, ENSA was staging 3,000 shows a week by the time it ended in 1945.
19. *Crying With Laughter*
20. *TVTimes* Extra

21. *Ibid*. The comic Kenneth Williams was called up towards the end of the Second World War and was not a peacetime national servicemen, but he served with the CSE in South-East Asia, based at Singapore. In his autobiography, *Just Williams*, he wrote: 'In the middle of a huge army barracks, accommodation was provided for an assortment of performers, musicians, writers and designers, who possessed little or no regard for military discipline or protocol . . . though they were servicemen and sometimes wore uniform . . . Officers and NCOs drilling troops on the parade ground didn't relish the sight of actors in casual shirts and silk cravats swanning around the perimeter in animated conversation; six o'clock reveille was not observed by itinerant thespians who performed at night and rose late. Long-haired flamboyancy contrasted strangely with martial stiffness and there were dark mutterings about "These arty-crafty CSE fairies". The playwright Peter Nichols, a postwar conscript who served in the CSE with Williams – and Stanley Baxter – based *Privates on Parade* on his Singapore experience.

22. *City Lights*

23. *My Brother Geoff*

24. In October 1997 Baylis went to the Palace to collect an OBE and was surprised outside by Michael Aspel with the *This Is Your Life* red book. Viscount Enfield, now Lord Strafford, and Lock were guests on the programme.

8. Roll on death, demob's too far away

1. *The Peacetime Conscripts*

2. *Ibid*

3. According to Major F.L. Lee writing in *Brassey's Annual* , the armed forces yearbook of 1954, 1,068 candidates from the Forces in July the previous year took General Certificate of Education exams, with 731 achieving a pass in one or more subjects; in the December, it was 1,052 out of 1,678. In 1953 there were nearly 300,000 national servicemen in the three services.

4. *The Camp*

5. *Unreasonable Behaviour*
6. When Blair was a full colonel in the TA commanding a cadet corps unit he went to the Black Watch barracks in Perth and 'when it came to lunch a major said, '"I think we'll go to lunch now", and left me standing, though I outranked him. As far as he was concerned I was designated a cadet officer and, like national service medical officers had been, I was not socially acceptable.'
7. *All Bull*
8. *Touched By Angels*
9. Described in Chapter 6
10. *The Peacetime Conscripts*
11. GOC-in-C Western Command, Lieutenant-General Sir Lashmer Whistler, forbade soldiers walking out in Edwardian clothes. If a man had no other civvies then he was to wear uniform. He reminded soldiers that for rank of corporal and below the wearing of plain clothes off duty was a privilege. *The Times*, 27 July 1955
12. *A Game Of Soldiers*
13. *Brasso, Blanco & Bull*
14. *The Camp*
15. *My Autobiography*
16. Twenty-seven of the 68 prisoners who appeared before Hampshire Quarter Sessions at the beginning of 1949 were servicemen, making the deputy chairman, Ewen Montagu, write to *The Times* to say: 'Our impression is that in the Army there is a great lack of sufficient work or organized or guided leisure, with the result that "Satan finds some mischief still for idle hands to do", and crimes are committed from sheer boredom or for excitement or adventure.' On 11 February Field Marshal Sir William Slim, Chief of the Imperial General Staff, told a press conference: 'I am expected to do with the National Serviceman in 18 months what his parents should have done with him in the previous 18 years. If a man is a thief I did not make him a thief . . . most crime is committed by youth and at the moment most youths are in the services.' In newspaper discussions of the problem it was suggested that the special training units instituted during the Second World War to deal with men 'who

had defeated all the normal resources of the Army' might be re-introduced.

17. Seven-year regulars, who served five years with the reserve.

18. Batt became a sports journalist after national service and was sports-writer of the year in 1973; he was an early scriptwriter on *EastEnders*. His wild ways did not abate: he worked for a number of Fleet Street newspapers and was fired from all of them – more than once. He also became an alcoholic (now reformed), 'but I don't blame the army for that, that happened after'.

19. The most notorious inmates of Shepton Mallet were the Kray twins. Called up to the Royal Fusiliers in March 1952, they duly reported to the Tower of London, laid out an NCO and went home for afternoon tea. Arrested next morning, they got seven days in the guardhouse and again absconded as soon as they got out. AWOL on another occasion, they sent a rude postcard from Southend to the personnel selection officer at the Tower. After various other incidents and a month in Wormwood Scrubs for assaulting a policeman, the Krays served nine months in the military prison.

20. The CO is the most senior ranked officer in a unit, whatever its size. In an army regiment, for instance, he would normally be a lieutenant-colonel. The officers in charge of the companies making up the regiment would normally be majors and would be known as OCs, indicating the difference in authority.

9. It must be the uniform

1. *Caught In The Draft*
2. London *Evening Standard*, 18 June 2002
3. *The Virgin Soldiers*
4. *A Game Of Soldiers*
5. *My Brother Geoff*
6. *The Exposed*
7. *Called Up: The Personal Experiences Of Sixteen National Servicemen*
8. *Evil Spirits*
9. *Called Up: The Personal Experiences Of Sixteen National Servicemen*

10. *All Bull*
11. *730 Days Until Demob!*
12. *The Conscript Doctors*
13. *The Exposed*
14. Information about the incidence of VD is contradictory. In 1953 the army claimed that the rate in the UK had dropped by 28% over three years, by 46% in BAOR, 70% in MELF and 41% in FARELF – but an army report in the mid-fifties found a far higher incidence of VD among men than in the Second World War.
15. *The Conscript Doctors*
16. *My Autobiography*
17. *What's It All About?*
18. This was the kind of treatment that the writer of the army report on VD in Korea and Japan had in mind when he suggested that men should be subjected to something more 'unpleasant' than penicillin. The umbrella treatment had long been abandoned.
19. Straight Street or 'The Gut' of national service memory has long since changed, as any holidaymaker who has been to Malta knows. There is even a Mothercare shop there.
20. *Caught In The Draft*
21. *Called Up: Impressions Of National Service.* The novel *Key To The Door* by Alan Sillitoe, who served as an RAF wireless operator in Malaya in 1947–8, also features a love story between a national serviceman and a Chinese hostess.
22. The Malcolm Clubs in Germany, which were rather like posh NAAFIs, were instituted by the mother of a British pilot shot down during the Second World War.
23. In fact Fisher then signed on, quickly becoming the youngest sergeant in the RAF Regiment. He and Siegrid celebrated their golden wedding in 2003.
24. In a debate about National Service in the House, Mr McGovern (Glasgow, Shettleston, Lab) said he objected to people saying National Service was a great moral force in young people's lives. When he was a boy he went to Chatham barracks for five months and found he was being chased around the lavatories and everywhere by men in the

Navy who wanted to commit unnatural offences for which noble people had been charged in the last few months. He had seen young men packing and unpacking their hammocks for five hours in the night because they refused to submit to petty officers' demands . . . which was why he objected to boys of 18 being called up. *The Times,* 18 November 1953

Arthur Lewis (West Ham North, Lab) asked the Minster of Labour to introduce legislation to permit National Service men on registering to claim exemption on grounds of conscientious objection if they believed they were liable to corruption from the practice of homo-sexuality in the Armed Forces. Before the Minister could reply, Brigadier Medlicott (Norfolk, Nat.Lib & Con) said there was no evidence that homosexuality in the Armed Forces was more prevalent than in the country at large and this was an 'unwarrantable reflection on the Armed Forces of the Crown'. The Minister, Mr Watkins, entirely rejected the imputation. *The Times,* 3 February 1954

It might be pointed out that servicemen sometimes took advantage of homosexuals. As Jack Charlton noted in his autobiography of his time in the Royal Horse Guards: 'Windsor was also full of gays – we used to call them queers. It was quite a well-known thing that young soldiers would go off with businessmen and suchlike, and we used to exploit this to a degree that was criminal at times. We used to go to a certain pub where they would buy you drinks all night. They would become very friendly at closing time, but we'd just say, "Well, thanks very much, see you now," and walk off.'

25. *Called Up:The Personal Experiences Of Sixteen National Servicemen*
26. *730 Days Until Demob!*

10. Bollocks!

1. *The Guinness History Of The British Army*
2. *All Bull*
3. 'Bumbo' is an old Etonian national service officer in the 'Redstone Guards' who attempts to convince the battalion rugby team that they should disobey orders to go to war at Suez. Unsurprisingly he fails and is made to resign his commission.

4. *All Bull*
5. *Six Campaigns: National Servicemen At War 1948–1960*
6. *The Army Quarterly*, July 1949
7. *Birmingham Post*, 1 September 1947
8. On 6 September 1952 Montgomery (who had become Deputy Supreme Commander of NATO) wrote to Churchill saying he had given lunch to Shinwell in a private room at the Savoy and explained 'why National Service was necessary, and always would be necessary'. He told the Prime Minister that Shinwell 'had got hold of some very unsound ideas from somewhere' but he, Montgomery, had put him straight and Shinwell had promised to 'lay off'. In fact Shinwell did no such thing.
9. Britain had such trouble meeting the bills for the war that final debts were not settled until 1964.
10. *Unreasonable Behaviour*
11. Before it was allowed to re-arm in 1955, Germany spent the $1.7bn it received in American Marshall Aid on re-equipping its industrial base – helped by the labour of the age group of young men who in Britain were absent, doing national service. By 1955, while Britain was still cloaked in drab, post-war austerity, the German economy was vigorous, people were well dressed, and the shops full of quality goods (which many servicemen brought home as presents).
12. *All Bull*
13. The figures speak for themselves. Between 1949 and the end of the call-up in 1960, the navy took 90,700 men, the RAF 388,907 and the army 1,132,972. In 1954 – at about halfway through the NS era – the navy had 126,000 regulars and only 7,800 (5.8%) conscripts; the RAF 187,000 regulars and 69,900 (27.1%) conscripts; and the army 220,000 regulars and 224,000 (50.8%) conscripts. In 1952 and '53, the army consisted of 61% national servicemen. It is worth pointing out that one of the reasons why the navy placed less reliance on conscription was that it was shrinking: the number of cruisers, destroyers and frigates in commission fell from 113 during the Korean War to 77 in 1960.
14. *The Army Quarterly*, June 1950
15. *Ibid*
16. Wesker first put his RAF experiences into an unpublished novel, *The*

Reed That Bent, while an admin orderly at RAF Spurn Point, which was on a tip of land near Hull; he later adapted the play from it. 'I loved Spurn Point because of the lighthouse beyond the camp. I don't remember how I came to meet the lighthouse keepers, whether it was in a pub, or in the street, or whether I knocked on the door and said, "Please can I come here to write my novel" – but that is where I wrote it.'

17. In the House, Minister of War Antony Head said that 'the army were not blameless in the matter' (Opposition cheers) and announced that he had instructed the Army Council to issue all units with instruction to reduce bull. The Army harrumphed and said it would comply with the directive, but defended bull. At a press conference at the Royal Signals Training Brigade at Catterick, Colonel H.B.L. Smith, senior admin staff officer to the GOC-in-C Northumbrian District, said somewhat absurdly: 'We are not prepared to live in a military slum.' Lieutenant Colonel E. Belliott, CO of No 7 Training Regiment, Royal Signals, added that the average national serviceman came into the army 'naturally untidy and had to have his mentality changed'.

What at least one soldier thought of the remarks made by officers at Catterick was demonstrated a few days later when a large sign was erected outside the camp entrance saying, 'Beware of the Bull!' A national newspaper offered prizes of half a guinea for the best bull stories.

The army claimed that polishing tins, cutting grass with knives or scissors, and painting coal had not occurred after 1954 – which many a national serviceman would contest. The army also told Wolfenden that they were issuing labour-saving devices such as electric floor scrubbers and polishing machines and 'a new type of barrack table with a top which does not need scrubbing'. No national serviceman remembers ever seeing such items.

18. In April 1955 exemptions in the three categories were 70,877, 54,526 and 47,574 respectively – a total of 171,337.

19. *The Times*, 6 July 1955. The debate arose out of an unofficial seamen's strike in June 1955, which stopped liners sailing from Liverpool and Southampton. The government issued letters warning men eligible

for national service that they would be called up; 200 immediately requested to be re-registered with the merchant shipping pool. The strength of the merchant navy at this time was 148,000 of which 43,500 were catering ratings.

20. 12 August 1955

21. About 9% of men were graded three each year but – another inequality – only a third of them were called up. At this time there were 10,000 grade threes in the army and 3,000 in the RAF.

22. Even during the Peninsular War when demand for men was desperate, the minimum soldier's height was 5ft 3in; in the Boer War it was 5ft 6in. During the First World War it began at 5ft 6in, was reduced to 5ft 2in and to 5ft in 1917.

23. *The Conscript Doctors*

24. As with everything to do with national service, there were winners and losers under the legislation. Tony Addis from Birmingham, who had joined the Royal Artillery as a regular but bought himself out after 11 months to carry on his family's removal business, was called up for national service – for one day. Gerald Dawe of Berrow near Upton upon Severn in Worcester, a blacksmith in partnership with his father who was in ill-health, sought exemption under the hardship rule – supported by 150 local farmers who used his forge – but was turned down by a military service hardship committee, which also refused him leave to appeal.

25. *Life In The Jungle*. In his biography of Heseltine (now Lord Heseltine), Michael Crick wrote: 'Three years later the election loophole, which had enabled Heseltine to leave the Army, was closed. It was being widely exploited by disenchanted regulars who could not afford to buy themselves out. The rules were such that, absurdly, a serviceman only had to apply for the papers necessary to stand for Parliament; once discharged, he could promptly abandon any political "ambitions" without forfeiting an election deposit. The rules were eventually tightened when hundreds of servicemen applied for nomination papers to contest several forthcoming parliamentary by-elections.'

26. When the body produces insufficient antibodies to deal with bacteria,

the kidneys can become inflamed. With acute nephritis the urine is scarlet because of an overproduction of red corpuscles. Symptoms are headaches and loss of appetite and can include vomiting and fever.

27. Cowdrey's orthopaedic specialist issued a statement, saying that when sixteen the cricketer had spent seven weeks in plaster and had many courses of treatment that kept him going but did not cure his condition: 'He plays cricket now in special boots, but his big toe joints will cause him discomfort and impede his speed in running. These joints are likely to become progressively stiffer and one day he is going to need an operation on both feet.'

28. Considering the service that India and the West Indies had given Britain during the Second World War, a racial policy in relation to national service would have been indefensible. At the end of 1945, there were three million Indians in the armed services who had fought in south-east Asia, North Africa and Italy, many of whom became prisoners of war. Of the war's 182 Victoria Crosses, 29 were won by Indian soldiers. Some 20,000 West Indian volunteers served in the British armed forces, 6,000 of them in the RAF. A little-known fact is that many West Indians went to the United States to work in the munitions factories to help the war effort.

29. In his first game for the Signals, Boston scored 37 points and in another game racked up eight tries. Signals won the army cup in 1953, Boston scoring six of his side's eight tries against the Welsh Guards. Watched by Wigan, he was signed virtually on the spot. In one full season during his national service Boston amassed a staggering 126 tries. He was touring Germany with an army XV when he was picked for the Lions – the first coloured player Britain took to Australia.

30. Between January 1949 and December 1960 when the last tribunal sat, 8,284 men registered as conscientious objectors, against 16,000 in the First World War (from 1916 when conscription was introduced) and 60,000 in the Second.

31. If a man was to be sent to prison rather than fined, defending solicitors asked that the sentence should be for three months – less than that and he was not entitled to a hearing before an appellate court. At this stage, almost all conscientious objectors accepted the earlier judgement

of their tribunal, their sentence was commuted to time served and they were immediately released. Men who still refused invariably got another three months and were then discharged.

A man who underwent his medical and then refused to answer his call-up papers was taken by the police to his designated barracks; if he refused to put on uniform he was punishable under military law. Most conscientious objectors refused the medical and stayed in the hands of the civilian authorities, but some took the medical and then refused, determined to make their stand in the bitterest way. They served their sentence in a military jail.

A very few men who did their national service refused to do their reserve training for reasons of conscience and again were subject to military law. On 8 February 1956 an MP raised in the House the case of Roger Hobbs from Bristol who, having declined to attend his annual camp and been sentenced to 56 days in Colchester detention unit, was 'forcibly dressed in a canvas suit, which was screwed at the back'. In reply Minister of War Antony Head said that Private Hobbs, who completed his conscription period in November 1954, reported on 24 September 1955 but would not put on his uniform. 'He could not be left in civilians and the canvas suit was the only other clothing available that was neither civilian nor military dress.'

The sting in the tail for conscientious objectors who did civil work instead of conscription was that it was for the 18 months or two years of national service plus 60 days – the equivalent of service on the reserve.

32. Pinter also appeared before two tribunals before getting exemption. He was, as papers released in December 1999 by the Public Records Office (now the National Archives) show, fortunate: two teachers at his old east London grammar school did not support him. While his housemaster, James Medcalf, wrote to say he did not doubt Pinter's sincerity, he added that 'a spell in one or other of the services would do Harold Pinter a world of good'. Headmaster T.O. Balk wrote that Pinter 'has always been prone to select the pleasant, the attractive and the easy in his life and to discard the drab, the unattractive and the difficult. If some other form of national service is to be done by him,

it should be of a nature which will compel him to exercise much self-control and self-discipline and which cannot be easily evaded.'

33. Randle and Dixon continued to work for the peace cause. In 1962, having been among demonstrators at the American airbase at Wetherfield, they appeared at the Old Bailey among 'the Wetherfield six' who were charged under the Official Secrets Act with conspiracy to enter a 'prohibited place'. All got 18-month jail sentences. In Wormwood Scrubs Randle met George Blake and was instrumental in 1965 in helping him escape to East Germany – which led to another Old Bailey appearance in 1990, with another of the 'the Wetherfield six', Pat Pottle. After defending themselves, Randle and Pottle were acquitted.

34. *The Times*, 15 September 1955. In some cases the Irish government made representations and men were 'freed' if they agreed to go home.

35. In 1959, 50,000 men were being exempted from national service under the broad banner of education.

36. *Stand By Your Beds!*

37. In the American conscription system, the country was divided into about 4,000 county areas, each with a local election board appointed by state governors. All young men registered, with practically no exceptions, and were medically examined. If fit, they were liable. Each year Washington decided the total number of men required. This total was divided up between the boards according to the number of their registrations. Volunteers were deducted from the total and the boards then selected the call-up from the remainder according to their qualifications as required by the services.

38. 24 February 1957

39. There was nothing new in these suggestions. In 1949 the first postwar defence review recommended selective service; Churchill proposed a ballot system. The Cabinet also looked at a two-tier system of call-up: one category of men would do six months, followed by a lengthy period in the reserve; the other category would do two or three years and then be released without any reserve obligation. In 1950 the government toyed with imposing compulsory military service on the colonies.

In *The Army Quarterly* of January 1950, Lieutenant Colonel H. Franks, noting that 'more and more youths are becoming delinquents', suggested that a 'Regular Boys' Service Corps' be formed 'to produce in the next decade an adult population that would see in National Service something it is eager to undertake, not avoid'.

Local boards would select suitable cadets, aged twelve upwards, who would be boarders of two types: conscripted boys 'who are or have been, or who, on account of their environment, show every likelihood of becoming juvenile delinquents (from these, such as are considered as being beyond the pale, will be rejected)'; and volunteers from families of service and ex-service personnel 'and from other families of all classes; the former should have priority in selection should the number of volunteers exceed that demand'.

The corps, Colonel Franks adamantly stated, 'will *not* be another Hitler Youth Army'.

40. There was activity in illegal channels too. At Maidstone Quarter Sessions, Michael Charteris, 22, of Crawley, East Sussex, was charged with obtaining £2 by false pretences from the government. In prison in Liverpool, Charteris had agreed to join the army instead of Donald Muddiman, 21; Charteris had been in the army for a short time before being discharged on medical grounds. He went to the Queen's Own Royal West Kent Regiment at Maidstone on 17 December 1959 and was paid £2 in Charteris's name on pay parade. The pair might have got away with it except Charteris went absent without leave – and Muddiman was arrested. Both got 12 months.

41. What helped army recruitment was the projected introduction of new equipment, which promised excitement. The air-portable 105mm howitzer replaced the 25-pound gun, the general-purpose machine-gun replaced both the Vickers and the Bren, and the Chieftain tank replaced the Centurion. There were also new anti-tank missiles, the first British radar device to locate enemy mortars, and the first armoured personnel carriers. The Belgian FN self-loading rifle – adopted by the army and NATO in 1955 and tried out in Malaya and Kenya – was now coming on stream, after years of modification. The Stirling sub-machine-gun was already replacing the Sten.

New uniforms were coming, too: khaki worsted battledress blouses and trousers, thick woollen shirts, and Second World War webbing were out, as were studded boots in favour of boots with rubber soles; and men were to be issued with suitcases, not kitbags.

42. Captain R.I. Raitt, *The Army Quarterly*, October 1961

43. After the last batch of air force conscripts left Cardington – the reception centre from 1953 – on 1 December, reception and basic training were combined in one place, Bridgnorth in Shropshire.

44. Of the 9,912 men retained for the additional spell, 1,764 submitted appeals; 198 were granted on grounds of hardship.

45. Men in BAOR and the Mediterranean could take a local release and make their own way home; the services were happy to give them the money it would have cost to send them home. Theoretically men in the Middle and Far East could take a local release, but only if there was a party of 12 including an officer – which makes the possibility that any did highly unlikely. Adrian Walker and Gerry Mortimer made their own way back from Cyprus via the Balkans. 'We were told not to get off the ship in Greece, but of course we did,' Walker says. 'It was only later we realised what a foolish thing it was to do. We were in civilian clothes travelling on civilian passports, but we were still in the army. If we'd got into a fight or been picked up for some other reason, there could have been an almighty row.'

    Discharged on 16 May 1963, Richard Vaughan had the official distinction of being the last national serviceman out but, in fact, there were about 100 others still to be released, either because they were in military prison, detention or hospital. The names of 1,375 deserters, recorded across the national service years, were still unaccounted for.

46. When Britain ended national service, European countries like France, Denmark and the USSR maintained universal obligation, with Switzerland, Sweden and Israel having citizens' militias. After the fall of the Berlin Wall in November 1989, conscription was swiftly abandoned by Belgium (1992), the Netherlands (1996), Spain and France (2001), Germany (2002) and Italy (2003).

11. Paying the price

1. Fatal accidents among male civilians in the national service age group during the 1950s were 586 per 100,000, which would translate into nearly 13,500 among 2.3 million conscripts – many of whom were in situations more dangerous than any in civilian life.
2. *Will This Do?*
3. *TVTimes* Extra
4. The total number of fatal accidents in the RAF during 1946–62 was 1,558, with the loss of 3,402 lives. Some of these accidents were collisions, which wrote off more than one aircraft. Many were multi-crew or transport aircraft, so fatalities vary from 1 to 17 per accident. Total aircraft written off: 5,868. With a few blips on the graph, the accident rate involving fatalities dropped steadily from 226 in 1946 to 26 in 1962.
5. For a fifty-year reunion in May 2001, Myers managed to contact 12 of his course, including three other national servicemen – a businessman, a bank manager and a sculptor. Of the others, four had been subsequently killed in flying accidents.
6. *What's It All About?*
7. Malaria is a parasitic disease spread by the bite of the anopheles mosquito. The disease produces severe fever, usually in three stages: cold, uncontrollable shivering; a temperature that may reach 40.5°C; and a drenching sweat that brings down the temperature. The parasites responsible for malaria are known as plaxmodia, the most virulent being plasmodium falciparum – most likely the cause of Caine's condition. Falciparum affects a greater proportion of the blood cells and can be fatal within a few days. Kidney failure and jaundice are common complications.
8. The BKVA was formed in 1981 through the amalgamation of two earlier associations. It has over 4,000 members in 59 branches in Great Britain and one in Northern Ireland. The association's twice-yearly journal is *The Morning Calm*, of which Reuben Holroyd, who went into the army as a printer and has remained one, is the editor and publisher.

9. Noise is measured in decibels. Continued exposure to noise above 85 decibels (dBA) causes hearing loss over time. A noise level between 110 and 125 can cause 'painless' hearing damage from a single exposure. The average level of noise from artillery fire at 500 feet is 150 dBA. The damage is caused to high frequency hearing, making speech difficult to understand even though it is heard.

10. In March 2001 the government announced the first ever minister for veterans' issues, as well as a task force and forum for tackling issues affecting former armed service personnel. The Veterans' Agency was set up a year later.

11. Not all men who could not cope resorted to taking their own life: some men deliberately wounded or mutilated themselves. Under the heading 'Getting Out', *The Times* on 7 March 1955 reported: Driver Alexander Russell, aged 18, a national serviceman of Old Monkland, Coatbridge, Lanarkshire, who was said to have put his foot on a railway line so that a train ran over it, was sentenced at a district court martial at Chester on Saturday to nine months' detention. He had been found guilty of wilfully maiming himself to render himself unfit for service.

12. Porton Down research laboratory was set up in 1916 at the height of the First World War, in response to the German army's use of chlorine gas. It quickly expanded from a makeshift operation in two huts to a large camp with more than 1,000 staff. Up to the present day, more than 20,000 people – mostly servicemen and all but 3,000 of them before 1945 – have taken part in experiments. Typically, fewer than 100 volunteers a year are now used, mainly to test protective equipment against chemical and biological attacks, as well as anti-gas drugs. Volunteers have not been exposed to poison gases since 1989.

13. Chronic inflammatory disease of the spine leading to stiffening and fixity of the ligaments and bones so that, eventually, almost all movement is lost.

14. Today, the lethal dose of sarin breathed in is estimated to be 25–100mg; on the skin 1,000–1,700mg.

15. The first British atomic bomb was detonated in the hull of an old frigate off the Monte Bello island of Trimoulle, 60 miles from western Australia on 3 October 1952. Two more nuclear bombs were exploded

in May and June 1956. Eight bombs were detonated in the Australian outback. In 1957 the programme moved to Christmas Island for the final series of megaton hydrogen bombs. Three were dropped by Valiant bombers and detonated at about 18,000 feet, some 30 miles south of the island between 15 May and 19 June. In November two further H-bombs were exploded, with the remainder between April and September 1958.

16. In February 1997 the European Commission of Human Rights concluded that Britain had acted illegally and dishonestly to men involved in the tests, yet the claim that went to the European Court of Human Rights in Strasbourg was rejected and in January 2000 the court refused to reopen the case. The MoD has granted pensions to some ex-servicemen and widows without admitting liability. On 6 October 2000 the *Sunday Mirror* published an investigation into a sample of 350 men, which found that 68% had died of cancer, 80% of them before the age of 65. The investigation also found that spina bifida rates among the men's grandchildren were five times the national average, Down's syndrome seven times, leukaemia six times and those born with deformities ten times. The MoD dismissed the sample as being 'self-selected' and 'over-representative' of people with illnesses.

17. During its eighty-year existence, the Ex-Services Mental Welfare Society has helped some 75,000 members and ex-members of the armed forces and the merchant navy who have suffered psychological disability as a result of their service.

18. 'Counselling', by Tony Thorn, The King's Regiment (Liverpool), in *Poetry Of The Korean War*

12. How was it for you?

1. In 1953 the Ministry of Defence tried to assess how conscription affected men's physical well-being. The records of a sample showed that 90% gained weight during their service – an average of ten pounds; the average man leaving at the age of twenty was seven pounds heavier than twenty-year-olds entering. Also in 1953, a big employer, Tube Investments – one of the few to run pre-national service courses

for employees – published a report that judged a third of its 153 returning men had benefited from their time in uniform and only three had deteriorated.

2. Lord Justice Harman
3. *Called Up: The Personal Experiences Of Sixteen National Servicemen*
4. The Manchester Regiment merged with the King's Regiment (Liverpool) in 1958 to become the King's Regiment (Manchester & Liverpool).
5. *Second House*
6. *Daily Mail*, 30 September 1986
7. *Called Up: Impressions Of National Service*
8. *The Peacetime Conscripts*
9. Bellamy was a sub-editor on the *Sun* in the 1970s when his first novel, *The Secret Lemonade Drinker,* became a best-seller and he turned to writing fiction full time. For his third book he drew on an incident that happened four or five years after finishing national service – he ran into the corporal, who had beaten him up in the RAF detention centre in Germany, while walking down the high street in his home town of Farnham. 'He was delivering a tray from a baker's van. We just looked at each other and went on. It was a hell of a shock. As far as I was concerned the account was squared but it did make me wonder what would happen in a situation like that and someone wanted revenge.' The result was *The Sinner's Congregation*.
10. Sydenham played for Southampton until his mid-thirties, then emigrated to Australia where he was player-coach with a club in Perth for another ten years, after which he set up his own insurance consultancy.
11. Corporal Iain Colquhoun, Royal Engineers, quoted in *The Best Years Of Their Lives*
12. *Called Up: The Personal Experience Of Sixteen National Servicemen*
13. Leader in the *New Chronicle*, 18 August 1955
14. Karl Miller in *All Bull*
15. *My Autobiography*
16. 17 December 1960
17. In the spring of 1953 the actor Gabriel Woolf was allowed leave from the RAF to appear on television in Christopher Fry's *The Boy With A Cart*. The next summer he was released for four months to appear (as

Sir Percival) in the film *Knights of the Round Table*. He did have to make up his time subsequently.

18. *Stand By Your Beds!*

19. *All Bull*

20. In the last few years, membership of various veterans' associations has risen rather than fallen and many regimental and other reunions are getting increased attendances. The trend is due to the spread of the Internet on which relevant organisations have set up sites. Another trend, thanks to the ease and cheapness of self-publishing, is a marked increase in memoirs dealing with national service.

21. 'Our Pals' by John Boyd, Royal Signals, King Troop, 28 Brigade, in *Poetry Of The Korean War*

22. ITV's *Lads' Army* put 30 young men through 1950s-style basic with as much, or as little, realism as the BBC in the same year produced another reality-history series, *The Trench*, which simulated fighting conditions in the Great War. Writing about *Lads' Army* in the London *Evening Standard* (18 June 2002), Brian Sewell commented 'one thing worries me. In my day we were in the Army for two years; under conscription, unavoidable and inescapable, we were subject to military law, its sanction harsh, its fairness uncertain, its retribution terrible. None of the young men in *Lads' Army*, however, is under any sanction more severe than a contract to stay with the programme for four weeks or lose his promised payment.'

23. *As Much As I Dare*

24. In February 2003 a wide-ranging study of military training concluded that traditional techniques used in basic training are too much for modern-day youth, who sign up but then quit. Launching the study, Lieutenant-General Anthony Palmer, Deputy Chief of Defence Staff for Personnel, said: 'A lot of them are homesick. A lot come from environments where they have not been used to discipline, either at home or school. They come to us with little deference or respect. If modern-day recruits are shouted at they say, "Stuff you. I'm on my way." They get on the mobile phone and mum comes and picks them up.' As many as three in five recruits fail to make it through basic.

25. *The Private Man, The Public Role*, ITV, 29 June 1994

26. The National Memorial Arboretum at Alrewas in Staffordshire was conceived in 1988 as a living tribute to the wartime generations of the 20th century. An appeal to fund it was launched by Prime Minister John Major in November 1993. The project was supported by a £1.5m grant from the Millennium Commission and matched by private donations, and the Duchess of Kent opened the site in May 2001. The national service memorial, which is 6ft high, consists of four green granite wings supporting a stainless steel crown, between each pair of which is inscribed 1939–1960. A point at issue is that the dedication covers men called up under the National Service Acts during the Second World War and not just the postwar conscripts with whom 'national service' has become synonymous.

    In 2003 the idea for a monument to those who died in Cyprus during the Eoka troubles was raised with President Rauf Denktas of the Turkish Republic of North Cyprus and the local military authorities. Veterans were offered a plot of land and anticipated a favourable response from British MPs but did not get it. Expats in Cyprus or those with holiday homes there refused assistance for fear of raising local antagonisms. The idea has been dropped.

27. Three plinths in Trafalgar Square are occupied by equestrian figures – two 19th-century generals and King George IV. The fourth was reserved for a statue of King William IV but he died without leaving sufficient funds for it. After remaining empty for 160 years, in 1995 the Royal Society of Arts was given permission to fill it and decided on a rotation of contemporary art, which has continued since the project was handed over to the Greater London Council. In 2000 an advisory group under author-playwright Sir John Mortimer was set up to consider the plinth's permanent future; suggestions included a memorial to the women who served in the Second World War (now assigned to Whitehall), the Queen Mother and Diana, Princess of Wales. Sewell gave the group his views. The matter remains unresolved.

28. In 1986 the Imperial War Museum sought items for its first national service exhibition and was engulfed by the response. Over 1,000 items sent in were exhibited – including an entire field kitchen!

29. *Will This Do?*

Acronyms and forces' slang

ADC:	aide-de-camp
AFV:	armoured fighting vehicle
ATC:	Air Training Corps
ATS:	Auxiliary Territorial Service
BAOR:	British Army of the Rhine
BD:	battledress
Beasting:	to give a hard time
BFN:	British Forces Network
CB:	confined to barracks – a punishment
CIGS:	Chief of the Imperial General Staff
CND:	Campaign for Nuclear Disarmament
CO:	commanding officer
CO:	conscientious objector
Compo rations:	mostly tinned foods, meant to 'keep' in the field
COS:	Chiefs of Staff
CSE:	Combined Services Entertainments
CSM:	Company Sergeant-Major
DI:	drill instructor
DP:	displaced person
DSO:	Distinguished Service Order

ENSA:	Entertainments National Service Association
Erk:	a new recruit in the RAF
FARELF:	Far East Land Forces
FFI:	free from infection
Fizzer:	a charge
GD:	general duties
GHQ:	General Headquarters
GSM:	General Service Medal
I Corps:	Intelligence Corps
Jankers:	another term for CB
JSSL:	Joint Services School for Linguists
JTC:	Junior Training Corps
JUO:	Junior Under Officer
KOSB:	King's Own Scottish Borderers
KSLI:	King's Own Shropshire Light Infantry
LAC:	Leading Aircraftman
MASH:	Military Army Service Hospital
MC:	Military Cross
MELF:	Middle East Land Forces
Mill:	to box
MM:	Military Medal
MO:	medical officer
MP:	Military Police
NCO:	non-commissioned officer
NSVA:	National Service Veterans' Association
OC:	officer commanding

OCTU:	officer cadet training unit; sometimes OCTS or OCS – officer cadet training school or just school
OR:	other rank
PAC:	prophylactic aid centre
POM:	potential officer material
PSO:	personal selection officer
PTI:	physical training instructor
QARANC:	Queen Alexandra's Royal Army Nursing Corps
QM:	quartermaster
RA:	Royal Artillery
RAC:	Royal Armoured Corps
RADC:	Royal Army Dental Corps
RAFVR:	Royal Air Force Volunteer Reserve
RAMC:	Royal Army Medical Corps
RASC:	Royal Army Service Corps
REME:	Royal Electrical and Mechanical Engineers
RMP:	Royal Military Police
RNVR:	Royal Naval Volunteer Reserve
RP:	Regimental Police
RSM:	Regimental Sergeant-Major
RTU:	return to unit
SAC:	Senior Aircraftman
SUO:	Senior Under Officer
TA:	Territorial Army
WD:	War Department
WRAC:	Women's Royal Army Corps
WRAF:	Women's Royal Air Force
YCL:	Young Communist League

Call-up dates and addresses at interview

Alan Anderson (1956; Portsmouth)
Neal Ascherson (1950; London N5)
Al Barkley (1954; Ellesmere, Shropshire)
Ron Batchelor (1950; Leatherhead, Surrey)
Peter Batt (1951; London SW19)
Roy Battelle (1957; Spondon, Derby)
Trevor Baylis (1959; Twickenham, Middlesex)
Lawrence Bell (1950; Elie, Fife)
Guy Bellamy (1953; Glastonbury, Somerset)
Acker Bilk (1947; Penford, Somerset)
Derek Bird (1951; Failsworth, Manchester)
John Blair (1952; Perth, Scotland)
Roy Booth (1954; Hoxne, Suffolk)
Billy Boston (1952; Wigan)
Derek Brearley (1956; Halifax)
Terry Brierley (1950; Ossett, near Wakefield, Yorkshire)
Eric Brown (1952; Allestree, Derby)
Don Bullock (1951; Mexborough, Doncaster)
Tom Byng, 8th Earl of Strafford (1957; Winchester)
Peter Carpenter (1950; Haddenham, Bucks)

Ivan Churm (1960; Bishop Auckland, County Durham)

Stanley Colk (1950; Derby)

Smyttan Common (1951; Coldstream, Berwickshire)

Harry Crooks (1952; Whitstable, Kent)

Rodney Dale (1953; Haddenham, Cambs)

Tam Dalyell (Sir Tam Dalyell, Bart) (1950; Linlithgow, West Lothian)

Peter Duffell (1959; Blandford Forum, Dorset)

John Dunn (1953; Croydon, Surrey)

Charlie Eadie (1950; Prestwick, Ayrshire)

Ken Earl (1952; Maidstone, Kent)

Brian Fisher (1951; Darlington)

Michael Frayn (1954; Petersham, Richmond, Surrey)

David Garyford (1955; Wickford, Essex)

Mike Gilman (1957; Egham, Surrey)

Hugh Grant (1957; Inverness)

Tony Hamilton (1954; Lyddington, Uppingham, Rutland)

Nick Harden (1956; London W12)

Nick Harman (1951; County Mayo, Ireland)

Charlie Harris (1950; Kettering, Northants)

Albie Hawkins (1950; Gloucester)

Alan Herbert (1960; Newbold Verdon, Leicester)

Bill Hetherington (1952; Birmingham)

Malcolm Higgins (1955; Up Holland, Wigan)

Cliff Holland (1951; Thornton-Cleveleys, Lancs)

John Hollands (1951; Buckerell, Honiton, Devon)

Mike Hollingworth (1950; London SW8)

Reuben Holroyd (1953; Halifax)

Roger Horton (1953; West Moors, Dorset)

Anthony Howard (1956; London SW3)

Derrick Johns (1957; Whitney, Oxon)

Glyn Jones (1950; Watlington, Oxon)

John Keenan (1960; Wolsingham, County Durham)

Roger Keight (1959; Fulford, Stoke-on-Trent)

James Kelly (1950; Bicester, Oxon)

Norman Kenyon (1949; Osbournby, Sleaford, Lincs)

Lord Lawson of Blaby (Nigel Lawson) (1954; Newnham, Northants)

Charlie Lewis (1948; Haydock, St Helens, Merseyside)

Richard Lindley (1955; Oak Village, London NW5)

John Lyon-Maris (1949; Rickmansworth, Middlesex)

Bryan McDonough (1951; Luton, Bedfordshire)

Hopkin Maddock (1956; Padstow, Cornwall)

Arthur Main (1949; Edinburgh)

John (Jock) Marrs (1952; Stevensville, Ontario, Canada)

Raymond May (1951; Arnside, Cumbria)

Eric Michaels (1951; Currock, Carlisle, Cumbria)

Michael Myers (1949; Westcliff-on-Sea, Essex)

David Oates (1952; Hambrook, Bristol)

Michael Parkinson (1955; Maidenhead, Berks)

David Piercy (1950; Kirkella, near Hull)

Alan Protheroe (1954; Flackwell Heath, Bucks)

Barry Purcell (1956; Ringwood, Hants)

Sir William Purves (1950; London SW1)

Joe Pyper (1950; Irvine, Ayrshire)

Tony Rees (1954; Whitchurch, Bristol)

Brian Sewell (1952; London SW19)

Malcolm Stoakes (1955; Folkstone, Kent)

John Sydenham (1960; Ocean Reef, Western Australia)

Tony Thorn (1949; Oxford)

Alan Tizzard (1950; London SE9)

George Toms (1952; Whitstable, Kent)

Albert Tyas (1950; Wakefield, Yorkshire)

Adrian Walker (1957; London SE4)

Peter Walker (1953; Knebworth, Herts)

Mike Watkins (1955; Ledbury, Herefordshire)

Arnold Wesker (1950; Hay-on-Wye, Powys, Wales)

Barry Whiting (1951; Bridge, Canterbury, Kent)

Phil Wilkinson (1956; Upper Clatford, Andover, Hants)

Gordon Williams (1952; London W6)

Graham Williams (1955; Bishopton, Renfrewshire)

Ian Wormald (1959; Louth, Lincs)

Call-up dates of men quoted from other sources

Joe Ashton 1954; Michael Aspel 1951; Kenneth (Lord) Baker 1953; Alan Bennett 1952; Brian Blessed 1956; Tony Booth 1950; Johnny Briggs 1953; Sir Michael Caine 1950; Ian Carr 1956; Jack Charlton 1953; Colin Clark 1951; Ronnie Corbett 1949; John Drummond 1953; Mike Faunce-Brown 1954; Paul Foot 1956; Peter Gaston 1950; Robert Grettan 1954; Sir Peter Hall 1948; Michael Heseltine 1959; Michael Holroyd 1956; Bruce Kent 1947; David Lodge 1955; E. (Mac) McCullagh 1959; Don McCullin 1953; Karl Miller 1949; Bob Monkhouse 1946; Roger Moore 1946; Jeff Nuttall 1951; Robin Ollington 1948; Peter O'Toole 1950; Eric Pearson 1951; Oliver Reed 1956; Robert Robinson 1946; Ray Selfe 1950; Peter Sharp 1951; Tom Sharpe 1946; Ned Sherrin 1949; Andrew Sinclair 1953; John Spence 1960; Tom Stacey 1948; Leslie Thomas 1949; Tony Thorne 1956; Keith Waterhouse 1947; Auberon Waugh 1957; Denys Whatmore 1949; Les Wiles 1955; Gabriel Woolf 1952

Selected references

Allen, Charles (1990) *The Savage Wars Of Peace*, Michael Joseph

Allen, Paul (2001) *Grinning At The Edge*: *A Biography Of Alan Ayckbourn*, Methuen

Army Quarterly (July 1949, January and July 1950), William Clowes and Sons

Ashton, Joe (2000) *Red Rose Blues*, Macmillan

Baylis, Trevor (1999) *Clock This*, Headline

BBC1, *Second House*, 20 October 1973

BBC1, *Army Of Innocents*, 2 April 1997

BBC Radio 2, *Caught In The Draft*, 10 November 1987

BBC Radio 4, *Called Up: Impressions Of National Service*, 22 November 1983

BBC Radio 4, *Start the Week*, 29 July 1986

BBC Radio 4, *The Peacetime Conscripts*, begun July 2001

Bennett, Alan (1995) *Writing Home*, BCA by arrangement with Faber & Faber

Blair, John (2001) *Centenary History Of The Royal Army Medical Corps*, Iynx Publishing

Blair, John (ed) (2001) *The Conscript Doctors*, The Pentland Press, Bishop Auckland*

* The Pentland Press went out of business shortly after publication. Copies are obtainable from the author at The Brae, 143 Glasgow Road, Perth PH2 0LX

Selected references

Blessed, Brian (1992) *The Dynamite Kid*, BCA by arrangement with Bloomsbury Publishing

Booth, Tony (1989) *Stroll On*, Sidgwick & Jackson

Brassey's Annual – The Armed Forces Year Book (1954, 1956), William Clowes and Sons

Briggs, Johnny (1998) *My Autobiography*, Blake Publishing

Caine, Michael (1992) *What's It All About?*, Random House

Campbell, Major Arthur (1953) *Jungle Green*, Allen and Unwin

Catchpole, Brian (2000) *The Korean War*, Constable

Chambers, P. and Landreth, A. (eds) (1955) *Called Up: The Personal Experiences Of Sixteen National Servicemen*, Allan Wingate

Charlton, Jack (1996) *Jack Charlton*, Partridge Press, Transworld

Clark, Colin (1997) *Younger Brother, Younger Son*, HarperCollins

Clark, David Findlay (2001) *Stand By Your Beds!*, Cualann Press, Dunfermline

Corbett, Ronnie (2000) *High Hopes*, Ebury

Crick, Michael (1997) *Michael Heseltine: A Biography*, Hamish Hamilton

Dale, Rodney (1999) *Halcyon Days*, Fern House Publishing, Haddenham, Cambs

Drummond, John (2000) *Tainted By Experience*, Faber & Faber

Elliott, Geoffrey and Shukman, Harold (2002) *Secret Classrooms*, St Ermin's Press in association with Little, Brown

Forty, George (1980) *Called Up: A National Service Scrapbook*, Ian Allan Ltd

Goodwin, Cliff (2000) *Evil Spirits: The Life Of Oliver Reed*, Virgin

Grant, Hugh (2001) *A Game Of Soldiers*, Beaulieu Books, Inverness; Serendipity, London

Hall, Peter (1993) *Making An Exhibition Of Myself*, Sinclair-Stevenson

Hamilton, Tony (2001) *My Brother Geoff*, Headline

Hastings, Max (1987) *The Korean War*, Michael Joseph

Heseltine, Michael (2000) *Life In The Jungle*, Hodder & Stoughton

Hollands, John (1956) *The Dead, The Dying And The Damned*, Cassell

Hollands, John (1999) *The Exposed*, Edward Gaskell, Bideford, Devon

Holroyd, Reuben (ed) (2003) *Poetry Of The Korean War*, British Korean Veterans' Association

Ions, Edmund (1972) *A Call To Arms: Interlude With The Military*, David and Charles

Jameson, Derek (1988) *Touched By Angels*, Ebury

Johnson, B.S. (ed) (1973) *All Bull*, Allison & Busby simultaneously with Quartet Books

Lodge, David (1984) *Ginger, You're Barmy*, Penguin Books

McCullin, Don (1990) *Unreasonable Behaviour*, Jonathan Cape

Miller, Keith (2003) *730 Days Until Demob!*, National Army Museum

Monkhouse, Bob (1993) *Crying With Laughter*, Random House

O'Toole, Peter (1992) *Loitering With Intent*, Macmillan

Pimlott, John (1993) *The Guinness History Of The British Army*, Guinness Publishing

Robinson, Robert (1997*) Skip All That*, Century

Royle, Trevor (1986) *The Best Years Of Their Lives*, Michael Joseph

Sillitoe, Alan (1995) *Life Without Armour*, HarperCollins

Thomas, Leslie (1966) *The Virgin Soldiers*, Constable

Thorne, Tony (2000) *Brasso, Blanco & Bull*, Constable & Robinson

Walker, Adrian (1993) *Six Campaigns: National Servicemen At War 1948–1960*, Leo Cooper, an imprint of Pen and Sword

Walker, Adrian (1994) *A Barren Place: National Servicemen in Korea 1950–1954*, Leo Cooper, an imprint of Pen and Sword

Waterhouse, Keith (1994) *A Street Life*, Hodder & Stoughton

Waugh, Auberon (1991) *Will This Do?*, Century

Wesker, Arnold (1962) *Chips With Everything*, Jonathan Cape

Wesker, Arnold (1994) *As Much As I Dare*, Century

Whatmore, D.E (1997) *One Road To Imjin*, Dew Line Publications, Cheltenham

Williams, Gordon (1980) *The Camp*, revised edition, Allison and Busby

Index

Note: All references are to national service/men unless otherwise indicated.

Index